The Hockey Handbook

The Hockey Handbook

LLOYD PERCIVAL

Revised by Wayne Major, Larry Sadler,
and Robert Thom

FIREFLY BOOKS

A FIREFLY BOOK

Cataloguing in Publication Data

Percival, Lloyd, 1913–1974
   The hockey handbook

Rev. ed.
Includes index.
ISBN 1-55209-127-9

1. Hockey.   I. Major, Wayne F., 1947- . II. Sadler, Larry.   III. Thom, Bob.
IV. Title.

GV847.P4   1997a   796.962   C97-931178-0

Typesetting: M&S, Toronto
Printed and bound in Canada

Published in 1997 by
Firefly Books (U.S.) Inc.
P.O. Box 1338
Ellicott Station
Buffalo, N.Y.
U.S.A.
14205

1 2 3 4 5 6   02 01 00 99 98 97

Contents

Symbols used in diagrams

F	Forward	**G**	Goaltender
D	Defence	**D**	Opposition Defence
X	Player	**X**	Opposition Player
C	Center	**C**	Opposition Center
LW	Left Wing	**LW**	Opposition Left Wing
RW	Right Wing	**RW**	Opposition Right Wing
LD	Left Defence	**BC**	Backchecker
RD	Right Defence	Ⓒ	Coach
⁑	Puck(s)	⊢─────┤	Bodycheck
▲ ▲ ▲	Pylon(s)	⤶	Tight/180° turn
⟹	Shot	⟲	360° turn
— OR |	Knee Drop	⟜○	Pivot
──────C	Screen/Pick	= OR ‖	Stop
------▶	Pass	⦀⦀⦀⦀⦀	Crossovers
─┤•├─▶	Drop Pass	ᔐᔑᔐᔑ	Cariokas
───────▶	Forward Skating	ᔐᔐᔐ	Backward Skating
∿∿∿▶	Forward Stickhandling	ᔐᔐᔐ	Backward Stickhandling

Preface

When we took on the task of updating *The Hockey Handbook*, we were surprised at the amount of detailed information that was in the book. Trying to update the most technical book ever written about hockey was indeed a difficult project.

While many of the basic principles of play haven't changed a lot, concepts, systems, and terminology have. While parts of the book have been changed and updated, as much of the style and flavour of the original text as possible has been maintained.

Some of the terminology used today was not used when the book was written. Some of these terms not used are read and react, width, depth, space, gap control, etc. While we have not used all the new terminology in the current edition, we felt today's coaches can apply this very easily when using the drills which are described in this book.

While this book is still the most technical single publication available on hockey, it cannot possibly cover all information. We do recommend you purchase all videos, books, and publications available on hockey to supplement your knowledge.

Some of the statistics presented were gathered many years ago. Although some of the statistics may be somewhat outdated, we have included them to show the type of analysis that can be done if you have the time and inclination to do so.

When Lloyd Percival wrote the original book in 1951, hockey was mostly played by males. Accordingly, the pronoun "he" is used throughout the book. Although hockey is now played and coached by men and women, we have used the male gender, for convenience sake. It is our sincere hope that both "females" and "males" should thoroughly enjoy the book.

Our many thanks to the following people who helped with the initial edits or other information in the book.

- **Dave Chambers**, former National Hockey League coach
- **Nancy Clark**, nutritionist, author, Sports Medicine Brookline, Brookline, Massachusetts
- **Jim Matresky**, former Jr. "B" hockey coach, Markham, Ontario
- **E.J. McGuire**, assistant coach, Ottawa Senators, National Hockey League
- **Dr. Thomas M. Sawa**, B.Sc., D.C., F.C.C.S.S.(c), Doctor of Chiropractic
- **Ron Smith**, head coach, Binghampton, American Hockey League
- **Paul Titanic**, head coach, University of Toronto, Toronto, Ontario
- **Marianne Watkins**, power skating instructor for the Peterborough Petes of the Ontario Hockey League
- **Graham Wise**, head coach, York University, Toronto, Ontario
- **Mark Woollard**, power skating instructor, Toronto, Ontario

Our special thanks to Joe Taylor, a close friend of the late Lloyd Percival, for his invaluable knowledge of the original text and his contribution to the updated book. Also, a special thanks to the Percival family for their permission to update the book.

ABOUT THE EDITORS

Wayne Major is an advanced level coach in the National Coaching Certification Program. He has been a coach at the advanced (rep) level, a partner in a Junior "B" hockey team, and has served on many volunteer hockey committees over the years. He was publisher of the *Hockey Coaching Journal* and designer of the hockey Symposiums and Schools.

Larry Sadler, who rewrote the goaltending section, has been a hockey coach (advanced level two), a coaching instructor, and hockey administrator for the past twenty-five years. He lives in Peterborough.

Bob Thom has been a hockey coach at the advanced "AAA" level and an advanced level coach and instructor in the National Coaching Certification Program. He is a writer, lecturer and instructor for many hockey organizations.

Lloyd Percival

by Joe Taylor

Those of us who knew Lloyd Percival were well aware that he was ahead of his time. We didn't realize just how far ahead until the decision was made to reissue and update *The Hockey Handbook*, written more than 40 years ago. It's amazing how much of it is still valid, even innovative, today.

Some things are out of date, of course. Jacques Plante revolutionized goaltending back in the early 1960s. Science and sports medicine have refined conditioning methods. Systems of play have evolved since the free-wheeling Soviets opened our eyes in 1972.

That's ironic, because they used *The Hockey Handbook* as the basis for their development program.

"Your wonderful book which introduced us to the mysteries of Canadian hockey, I have read like a schoolboy," wrote Anatoli Tarasov, the architect of Soviet hockey, on the fly leaf of his own book, *Road To Olympus*, when he sent a copy to Percival in 1969.

Coaches in North America hadn't been quite so complimentary. "The product of a three-year-old mind," snorted Dick Irvin, coach of the then Stanley Cup champion Montreal Canadiens, back in 1950-51.

It's been said that geniuses are often misunderstood or ridiculed because they frighten us. They force us to re-evaluate the way we think about ourselves, and the way we live. Lloyd Percival certainly antagonized many of the best people in hockey, because he implied in *The Hockey Handbook* that they were not adequately exploring the possibilities of the game. Players were not training hard enough or often enough; they were not being taught to skate properly; nor were their skills being adequately developed.

In short, he was a threat because he wanted hockey coaches and players to re-examine the very core of what they thought they did best:

coach and play "the world's fastest game." And it was a fact. The best hockey in the world was to be found in North America.

But Lloyd Percival said the best wasn't good enough. Hockey could be played even faster and better, but only if everyone started applying scientific principles of coaching, training, and performing.

No wonder Irvin and others rejected this book. It wasn't simply that they didn't understand, they didn't want to understand. To have agreed with Lloyd Percival would have meant admitting not only their own inadequacies but those of the game they loved.

That wasn't Lloyd's intention. Here's what he wrote in his preface to the first edition of *The Hockey Handbook*:

"Soon after Sports College (a nation-wide coaching service using radio, booklets, a newspaper, and clinics) was organized, we began a hockey research project. Players and coaches of all ages and reputations were asked thousands of questions, hundreds of games were closely observed and analyzed, countless tests were conducted, and long lists of records and performances were studied.

"In addition, the opinions and findings of coaches in other sports, physical education experts and authorities in medicine and psychology were studied, and where possible they were made a part of this book.

"For nearly six years every possible effort was put forth to compile authentic information that would make possible a really complete instruction guide. I hope that *The Hockey Handbook*, the final result of research, is that book. However, even if the task has been accomplished merely reading this book will not make the reader a skilful player or coach. It does not contain any magic formula that when repeated over a few times in a darkened rink will make every team in the National Hockey League beat a path to your door.

"But if the advice that is given in *The Hockey Handbook* is applied intelligently, I am confident that it will help you with your playing or coaching."

Who was Lloyd Percival, anyway? How did he qualify to write the definitive hockey book without an NHL background or at least minor league credentials?

Lloyd had played the game as a teenager, but soon turned to coaching with the National Sea Flea midgets, leading them to an undefeated season before he was 20. He had a more ambitious future in mind, however. He wanted to help remedy what he saw as a major weakness – not just in hockey but in all sports – a shortage of trained and knowledgeable coaches.

"All during my younger days as a hockey player and later as a coach and referee I was conscious of the need for a handbook on hockey that could be used as a helpful instruction guide by the countless athletes participating in the great game and by the coaches who train them," he wrote in his preface.

"In practically any other major sport, many and varied books were available but in hockey there was none. But even though I had always tried to study the game with the idea of some day being able to teach it intelligently and efficiently, I did not feel I had the background or knowledge necessary to attempt an instruction guide."

He set about remedying his own perceived inadequacies by playing as many sports as he could, and by taking courses and attending seminars in the U.S., England, and Europe. He read widely in such areas as psychology, physiology, coaching techniques, sports medicine, and salesmanship. One of his first tutors was the legendary Knute Rockne of Notre Dame. He also studied at the Sokol Institute in Prague, and Loughborough College in England.

The initial product of all this personal research was called Sports College, a joint venture by Percival, the National Council of YMCAs, and the Canadian Broadcasting Corporation, which was to provide network air time every Saturday for the next 21 years. It was probably the first comprehensive educational program on the airwaves and it attracted some 800,000 members for Sports College from across Canada and parts of the United States.

Lloyd had also been writing hundreds of thousands of words on a wide range of sports, not just hockey but basketball, volleyball, soccer, baseball, and others, and on an array of coaching topics. These became the college's curriculum, and millions of his booklets were sold and distributed over the next 21 years. He also published a regular sports instruction newspaper.

He also found time to coach. His Toronto Red Devils track club became the strongest in the country, producing dozens of national champions in all age groups. Although he retired from active coaching in the mid-50s, he couldn't stay away from it long, returning in the 1960s to found the Don Mills Track Club, which also became a national power.

He was ahead of his time in other areas as well. In the early 1950s he wrote a book on fitness, and another on relaxation. His concern with fitness grew as he discovered that his own cardiovascular health was not strong. Fitness, he decided, would help to keep him going. This area of interest eventually led him to found The Fitness Institute, with the help of two partners: James Gairdner, a Toronto stockbroker, and Murray Koffler, head of the Shoppers Drug Mart chain. In addition to providing fitness assessment and programs for members it became a mecca for all sorts of athletes – from hockey players to golfers, divers, football players, and oarsmen – seeking training advice and injury rehabilitation programs.

He also became a founder of the Coaching Association of Canada, an author of *Game Plan '76* leading up to the Montreal Olympics, and an adviser to the Canadian Olympic Association.

He was named a member of the International Society for Physical Education, Internal Trainers Association, International Federation of Sports and Fitness Medicine, American College of Sports Medicine, and the Canadian Sports Hall of Fame.

In the early 1950s, Lloyd had been asked by Jack Adams, general manager of the Detroit Red Wings, to do a physical evaluation of his players and prescribe a training program. His tests indicated that a young fellow named Gordie Howe was endowed with unbelievable endurance and strength. Not only did he have the potential to become the greatest all-round player in the game, but he could probably handle extra long stints on the ice, given the pace at which hockey was then played.

Overall, he said, Howe was already better than superstar Maurice "The Rocket" Richard. That drew ridicule from coaches and veteran sportswriters alike. Who was this Percival, anyhow? Besides, with the amount of ice time Detroit was giving Howe (up to 40 minutes in some playoff games), he would soon be "burnt out."

As usual, the critics were wrong. Howe went on to eclipse most of Richard's records, and was still able to play in the NHL when his sons entered the league 20 years later. He played professionally into his 50s.

In 1972, Lloyd startled the hockey establishment again by predicting that the NHL's forthcoming series against the Soviet Union would not be the romp most people expected. Using what he called his "Sports Power Index" – in which all the components of the game were given a rating – he decided that Canada was just five points better than the Soviets out of a total rating of 2,388.

He also tested a forward named Paul Henderson, who had an unusually high (for that time) oxygen uptake. Henderson, he said, would have no trouble skating with the seemingly tireless Russians.

The rest, as they say, is history. Canada won the series when Henderson scored a dramatic goal in the final minute of the final game. Percival was hailed as some kind of genius. He knew it was simply the application of the scientific principles he had always advocated – plus a little insider's knowledge of Soviet hockey. Tarasov and others had told him about their programs and he knew they'd have an edge in physical conditioning and skating and passing skills to compensate for their lack of experience in the NHL approach to the game.

Lloyd always wanted to revise and update *The Hockey Handbook* himself. His health let him down before he could get to it. He also wanted to write other books on coaching, utilizing the vast knowledge he had accumulated over the years, and on training and conditioning. It was not to be, and the sports world is the poorer for it.

As a long time associate of Lloyd Percival, I was able to put together a hockey conditioning book based on his notes and with the help of the Canadian Amateur Hockey Association. It is called *Total Conditioning for Hockey* and was published in the late 1970s.

The Hockey Handbook, however, was Lloyd Percival's legacy to the sport he probably loved best of all. It is an enduring one, as this revised edition proves. A paragraph in his preface to the first edition best sums it up:

"To those of you who have been in hockey a long time and feel that some of the ideas, drills and techniques . . . are a little new and different, I would like to suggest that the only sure way of proving anything is to give it a good trial. If you do this, I am certain you will be happy with the results."

Skating

Skating is to hockey what throwing is to baseball, what tackling is to football, or what footwork is to tennis. It is the most important fundamental.

Our research has shown that in an average full length game players skate from two to three miles. When poor line changes are used, players skate as far as four miles per game. Skating is what the player does most. It is the foundation on which everything else is built.

Trying to develop hockey skill without the foundation of skating efficiency is pretty much an impossible job. If you cannot shoot hard, you can perhaps get along by being a good play maker or checker. If you cannot body check you can survive by being a good stick checker. But if your skating is weak there is nothing much you can do. A survey of top level professional hockey executives indicates that more players are prevented from hitting the "big time" by a lack of skating skill than anything else. National Hockey League scouts are always on the lookout for good skaters. But as the scouts will tell you themselves, good skaters are very hard to find. This is hard to explain in a country in which youth are practically brought up on skates. One reason is that, although a lot of skating is done, much of it is done haphazardly. Little attention is given to the development of correct technique. This is unfortunate because there is just as much technical skill and training needed to skate well as there is to run, jump, make a forward pass, or throw a curve ball well. There is no such thing as a "born skater," although some people are born with muscles and co-ordination particularly suited to the art. Skating power, speed, and skill must be developed. Any person can develop top level skating efficiency, provided he works hard and uses the correct methods. In fact, if he works hard enough, he is likely to surpass the "natural skater" simply because the "natural" athlete is usually inclined to take things easy because he has not acquired the work habit.

Many players and coaches, unfortunately, seem to overlook the fact that skating skill can be developed. Seldom do you find players working on skating drills designed to develop specific efficiency. You may see players doing "stops and starts" up and down the ice but this is primarily conditioning. The smart hockey player or coach will continually try to improve skating, and will regularly check style and technique to eliminate bad habits. Suggestions as to how much time should be spent on skating during practice will be given in a later chapter.

It takes a lot of "selling" to shake the average player from his unconscious skating complacency and to get him started on an intelligent and well conducted skating development plan. Even senior amateurs or professional players will be surprised at how much they can improve their skating, something they probably had not considered for years.

In analyzing hockey skating (pleasure, speed, and figure skating are, of course, different propositions), it is found that there are several types of skating. These can be placed in the following categories:

Free skating is straight away, open ice skating, either with or without the puck.

Agility skating. This type of skating is needed to manoeuvre when puck-carrying or checking, trying to shake a checker covering you, or breaking away, stopping quickly, and so on.

Backward skating is most important when checking a puck carrier, trying to cover a man, or manoeuvring to get free during a ganging attack or power play.

A hockey player ought to develop top level efficiency in all three categories. Such ability is rarely seen. Those who are excellent free skaters are quite often not good agility skaters, and vice versa. Too few are good backward skaters, mainly because so little time is spent practising this extremely important type of skating. Athletes, being human, tend to shy away from their weaknesses and concentrate on their strong points. Few who have a weakness in one of these phases of skating get around to doing anything about it.

The first step is to check the various points of technique listed in this chapter against your own style and technique, or against that of your players if you are a coach. Then get to work on the weak points. This analysis of skating efficiency followed up by a determined and well organized effort to improve will make a difference that will surprise you. You can make the biggest improvement in your game by increasing your skating skill.

FREE SKATING SKILL

In developing a skating technique, the prime purpose should be to learn how to skate with a minimum of physical effort. Make every movement pay off in maximum results for the effort used. Few players ever do this. The average player has a skating technique that causes him to expend more physical effort than is needed. As a result he does not skate as powerfully as he should, and tires sooner.

The skating action should be as smooth, as relaxed, and as effortless as possible. Fortunately, the mechanical movements, the posture, and the general controlled relaxation that make graceful and effortless skating possible can all be learned. Here is a technical breakdown of the ordinary free skating action.

Posture. This refers to the general body position of the skater. The stomach should be comfortably drawn in and the chest held high. This position gives the muscles around the lower abdomen and hips plenty of room to move freely and efficiently. The high chest avoids cramping of lungs and heart space and thus enables these important organs to perform their duties efficiently. This posture is important in any form of athletics. On first assuming such a position it may seem a little awkward but sustained effort will soon make it second nature.

However, this position of "stomach in and chest out" should not be over-emphasized. The stomach should merely be drawn in and the chest lifted until you feel a general clean cut and alert feeling. The head should be set in a relaxed and easy position on the neck. There should be no tense straining forward of the head. The shoulders should be loose and relaxed and the knees well bent.

Body lean. When the skater moves forward he should try to keep his upper body a little ahead of his hips. This will give him maximum forward propulsion just as the proper body lean helps the sprinter on the track. This forward body lean should not be overemphasized or considerable body balance and manoeuvrability will be lost. Each body type demands a different degree of lean. Experiment until you find the lean that seems to give you the maximum speed together with a feeling of balance and comfort. Anywhere from a ten to twenty-five degree forward lean of the upper body is sufficient. The forward body lean should be made from the hips, and there should be no forward straining of the head.

Failure to use a forward body lean is one of the common faults of the average hockey player. It is quite common to see players skating down the ice with their body in an erect position. In this position a lot of forward drive is lost when the skate is pressed against the ice, particularly in the pushing off action at the end of each stride. Players who skate with their body erect not only lose forward drive but also run on their skates with a high foot lift. They are easy to knock off their feet.

Knee position. Flexible, relaxed knees are very important in the development of skating efficiency. The only time the knee should be straightened is during the thrust. When the leg begins to go back in the forward action, the knee is straightened out at the last moment, just before the skate leaves the ice to come forward for another stride. When the leg is driven forward to start a new stroke, the knee must be well bent. Then it gradually straightens throughout the stride until it extends completely when pushing in the thrust. As the thrust is made, the knee of the other leg is well bent. This flexible knee action enables the skater to sustain good balance and helps keep the blade of the skate on the ice long enough to get a good glide. The skater should strive always to keep his knee ahead of his foot. Proper bending of the knee always keeps his skates underneath him, and thus gives him power to thrust, and an ability to change direction or manoeuvre quickly.

Balance. The weight should be on the foot on which you are gliding forward. It continues on this foot until the other one is placed on the ice again for a forward glide.

Foot action. After the final thrust has been made at the end of a stride the foot should come forward with the toes facing dead ahead. After a short forward glide, the toe is turned outward. The skate is then pressed backward and well to the side, and a long push motion is made against the ice. On the way back on the thrusting part of the stride the foot gradually turns outward. When the final push is made the toe of the skate is nearly pointing to the side at a right angle.

The moment the final push has been made, the foot is brought forward again as quickly as possible and as close to the ice as is feasible. This recovery for another stride should be led by the knee. It often helps to think of whipping your knee forward again for another stride, instead of the foot. When one foot completes a thrust, it should be brought alongside the other before the next thrust begins.

Stride. There has been in the past a lot of controversy about the importance of the stride in skating, especially in free skating. A simple rule is to take as long a stride as is comfortable. After the final thrust of the skate, try to reach forward a little harder with your knee. Then concentrate on gliding a little longer on your forward skate before you let your foot start moving outward to the side for another stride. The length of your stride depends on the flexibility and length of the muscles you use in the skating action, especially those of your hips and back thighs. How these can be made more flexible and lengthened are dealt with in the chapter on Training.

In free skating, such as back-checking or going up with the puck carrier, you can use a fairly long stride that will save energy. When carrying the puck or covering a zone or a man, it is better to use a shorter stride. Then you will be able to change direction, stop, or turn quickly.

Arm and shoulder action. The arm and shoulder action in skating plays a more important role than is realized by the average hockey player. The arm and shoulder action should be co-ordinated with the leg action in a smooth rhythm. Unlike running, where the arms and shoulders move in rhythm with their opposites (right arm with left leg, etc.), the arm and shoulder work with the leg on the same side (right with right). For example, as you stride with the right foot your right arm and shoulder should go with your foot and leg. This forward motion of the arm and shoulder with the leg on the same side assists the general forward movement of the body by advancing the centre of gravity of the upper trunk.

This type of shoulder and arm action in skating is necessary to keep proper balance and co-ordination. For ordinary glide skating it is not necessary to use the arms and shoulders to any degree once speed has been gained. When greater speed is needed or a fast break is desired, the arm and shoulder action will help a great deal. Remember that success in skating, just as in any athletic activity, is not simply dependent on one thing but a variety of little things which when put together in a smooth, mechanical whole makes for efficiency. By keeping your arms relaxed, especially at the elbow, you can drive the shoulder into the skating action without interfering with the control of your stick. When skating without the puck, as you do when back-checking, you can skate faster if you hold the stick in one hand and concentrate on hard arm and shoulder action.

Hip and body action. The hips are very important in skating. The average player fails to get enough hip action into his skating. Those who seem to lack drive and speed, who seem to work very hard without getting anywhere, are probably failing to utilize the hip sufficiently.

The actual hip movement in skating is difficult to describe. Perhaps the best way is to suggest that each time a forward stride is taken, you try to lead or start the action with your hip, bringing it around and forward in a definite snap. As you do this your upper body co-operates to free your hips by turning slightly sideways. For example, when you take a forward stride with your right leg, you should try to swing your right hip around and into the action, moving it into the direction your foot is taking. As you do this the right shoulder and arm go around and forward in the same way and your upper body twists a little to the left from the waist. When you drive off your right foot at the completion of the stride the same thing is done with your left leg, hip, shoulder and arm, your body of course turning to the right. Since the muscles of the hip are supposed to supply most of the forward propulsion to your skating, co-ordination and flexibility are invaluable in the hip region. Exercises designed to develop hip co-ordination, strength, and flexibility are listed in the chapter on Training.

Remember that the hockey player whose skating is technically sound is in a position to skate fast, will be a hard man to knock down or move off the puck, will tire less rapidly, and will be able to learn many agility skating moves without great difficulty. The player whose skating has even one technical imperfection is seriously handicapped.

There are many common faults in skating which hold back even the best player.

FREE SKATING FAULTS

"Picking them up and laying them down." Some players merely place their skates on the ice and then lift them up again without any emphasis on driving the skate backward and down into the ice in a hard push off action. Above all, make sure you develop the hard pushing off habit. It is this last-moment push that provides propulsion. Because it is not natural and does involve the hard work principle, it is frequently neglected. The odds are that if you check up on your skating, no matter how fast or efficient a skater you happen to be, you will find that you are not pushing off at the end of each stroke as hard as you can. Concentration on this phase of skating will bring much greater speed.

Skating tension. The average skater when trying to move quickly grits his teeth, thrusts his head forward, and tightens every muscle in his body, tiring himself needlessly and spoiling the efficiency of his skating action. Controlled relaxation is very important. Don't let up on your determination to "go hard" but keep it controlled so that your determination and spirit do not work into your muscles and make them stiff and inflexible with tension. Keep your determination firm but your muscles loose. When you tighten a muscle not being used in the skating action, it interferes with the action of the muscle that is supposed to do the work. Then too, it means that more muscles are being used. This throws a greater strain on your heart and lungs, which must force more blood to these muscles.

Lifting feet too high. Many hockey players have a bad habit of lifting the feet well off the ice in an upward backward motion after completing the thrust. This wastes energy and takes away from speed and balance. Make sure that when the thrust has been completed, the foot comes forward again and is not allowed to kick back up. The leg should be fully extended at the end of the thrust, then the knee bent and whipped forward quickly to prevent this wrong foot action. Always try to keep your skates as close to the ice as possible.

Banging the foot. Many hockey players lift their knee too high when the foot is being brought forward for another stride. This faulty movement means that the skates are banged down instead of being placed smoothly on the ice for another forward glide. If you watch a hockey game with this aspect in mind, you will actually hear many players smashing their skates against the ice.

Sitting down. You can very easily detect the player who has this fault because he skates around as if he is sitting in a chair. His knees are always bent, even at the end of the thrust. It means simply that the legs are not being used to their full range of movement on the back thrust. When your skate goes back after the forward thrust movement try to make sure your knee straightens completely.

Railroading. Some skaters look as if they are skating down a railroad track with a skate on either rail. The feet seem to be straddled. Those who are guilty of this technical fault are usually short, husky body types who have short muscles and poor flexibility in their hips and upper legs. However, the main cause of railroading is a failure to perform the recovery from the first thrust of the skate to the start of the next stride properly. The foot is not brought back up to the other one and well under the body again after the thrust. This keeps the legs spread and causes a very short stride with practically no glide on each forward stroke. This style of skating is very hard because it is all effort.

Tight roping. You will recognize this bad habit when you see a player going down the ice with his knees very close together, as if he were skating down a tight rope or a straight line on the ice. He will probably be wavering from side to side as if a good push would upset him (and it would). This habit is caused by not bending the knees sufficiently and not allowing the foot to turn sideways enough after the forward glide. Remember: the skate starts off dead ahead, then gradually moves more and more to the side until it is at a right angle to the direction you are taking at the moment of the final thrust. Then it is brought around forward again during the recovery.

Body sway. Swaying from side to side is also a very common fault that can be seen on practically any rink. It is caused by an incorrect idea of how to get the body, shoulders, and arms into the stride.

The upper body is allowed to twist around from side to side with no forward movement of the hips and legs as they go forward on the stride.

Such skaters also have a sideways fling of the foot after the thrust has been made. Skaters with this fault are staging a continual war between their legs and upper body. The only winner is the opposition.

Skating with arms stretched out in front, parallel to the ice, with a stick laid across the wrists at shoulder height will help correct this.

Toe or heel landing. Many players place either the toe or the heel of their skate on the ice first at the start of each stride. This spoils the movement of the stride and also affects balance and power. It is caused by either too great a forward body lean (front part of the skate touches the ice first) or too erect a position (heel of the skate touches the ice first). Other causes include reaching with the foot instead of the knee as the leg comes forward to take a stride, and keeping the ankle held stiffly when the foot is being brought forward after the thrust. It is important that the ankle be kept loose and relaxed when the foot is coming forward to take another stride. The lower leg should hang loosely from the knee on the recovery.

Muscle weakness. Many players do not skate properly because there is a muscular weakness in some part of the body that prevents the performance of a certain action. When this is the case the player often unconsciously makes some adjustment in style in an attempt to use a stronger muscle. This, of course, creates a faulty, often awkward, style. For example, players with insufficiently developed quadriceps (muscle on front of upper leg) often fail to bend their knees sufficiently. They do this because when the knees are bent, the quadriceps are in continuous hard action. If they are weak, bending the knee will bring on fatigue or cause a sense of insecurity and imbalance, for the muscles quiver under a load they cannot easily handle. The answer, of course, is not to stop bending the knees but to develop the quadriceps through special exercises and persevering in the bent knee action.

Weak ankles. This is another bogey of the person desirous of playing hockey. It is usually caused by a poor development of the supinator foot muscle. Weakness of the muscles up and down the shin bone creates inefficiency and fatigue in skating. However, any muscular weakness can be overcome through special exercises. In fact, every hockey player, no matter how strong he seems to be, should do special exercises designed to strengthen, stretch, and make flexible the muscles used in skating. This is dealt with more fully in the chapter on Training.

Whenever you try to change your technique there will always be a short period of feeling awkward. You should not allow this to bother you, and if you persevere it will soon disappear. There is an old saying that the wrong way is often easier at first, but gets progressively harder, while the right way is often harder at first, but gets progressively easier. Keep this in mind when revamping your skating technique. Perhaps the main move you can make in your attempts to become a good hockey player is never to be content with your skating. Always keep polishing it. If you are a coach, the same thing applies to your efforts in developing skating efficiency with your team.

A good thing to remember when you are working on your skating technique is to work on one thing at a time until you do it well before moving on to another. Do not try to correct everything at once or you will spread your efforts too thinly. When trying to make a change in your technique the best results will be had if you "walk through" the changes first before you try to do them at full speed. Try them while skating slowly and then gradually increase the skating speed during your practice session until you can do them while going full speed. If possible, get someone with a video camera to tape you. This will not only add interest to your work but will show faults very effectively.

Problem of speed. Skating speed and running speed do have certain things in common. Some players have the type of muscles that generate speed. Others have muscles that cannot move quite as fast but which move at a good rate of speed for longer periods of time. The slower, endurance boys, no matter what they do, will never be able to skate as fast as the speed boys. The person with the type of muscle suitable for the mile could never hope to sprint faster than an athlete with muscles built for sprinting.

This is why you will often see a team which was outskated in the first period turn around and outskate the opposition when the last period comes up. Nature has a way of cancelling out natural advantages, and, though you are not one of the speed boys, you will probably find that your greater power and endurance will have you skating as fast as the speed boys during the latter part of the game. However, by paying close attention to your skating technique you can greatly improve your speed. The speed boys should work to increase their endurance and the slow boys should work for every little bit of speed they can. There are special drills and exercises designed to improve reflexes and co-ordination.

Such exercises and drills will be dealt with more fully in the chapter on Training.

Speed is about twenty-five per cent mental. The player who consciously drives himself past the natural tendency to take things easy will skate faster than if he makes no such conscious attempt.

AGILITY SKATING

This important category of skating is to the hockey player what footwork is to the boxer or shifty running is to the ball carrier in football. The player who has developed top level agility in his skating will be a tough puck carrier to check, a hard checker to shake, and a difficult man to get past when on the defence. Efficiency at agility skating makes the hockey player. Though some are naturally more agile than others, all can greatly improve this phase of their skating by observing the general fundamentals of good free skating. Agile skating can only be achieved by working hard at skating drills that are specially designed to develop the co-ordination and patterns.

The following fundamental skating manoeuvres are included under the heading of agility skating. Proficiency in these fundamental moves will make the player better capable of performing the many puck-carrying moves, checking tactics, and scoring plays that are dealt with in the future chapters of this book.

The cross over. Crossing over is the action needed to turn to either left or right (when going around the goal to start up the ice, for example). This action is often referred to as cutting corners.

It is perhaps the most fundamental and most used of all agility skating movements, but strangely not all players can cross over to either side equally well. The left-handed player can usually cross over with maximum efficiency when turning to his left but is very unsure of himself going to his right. The obverse applies to the right-handed player. Even in the NHL, you can see players who go one way much better than the other. Just as some people are right-handed and others left-handed, so some are right- or left-legged. However, through training it is possible to develop two leggedness.

The player lacking this skill will find it very difficult to perform many of the puck-carrying or checking manoeuvres. For example, suppose he is a left-handed player going down the ice with the puck. He sees the defence pair shift over too far to the right side (his left) leaving an opening for him to go around their right side. A quick change of direction to the right and a few fast cross over strides will get him around in the clear and all set up for a possible goal. But, he does not cut very well to the right. As a result he either loses his chance because of his awkwardness and lack of speed when he does try the play, or he does not make the move at all because his mind unconsciously directs him away from his weaker side.

Remember to use this knowledge when checking the opposition. Try to force any player having a weak side to go to his weak side when he is trying to check you or carry the puck past you.

To cross over, the weight should be placed on the inside foot (for example, the left if crossing over to the left). The knee is well bent and then the outside leg (right if crossing over to the left) is brought around and over the inside leg and another stroke is taken. The outside foot is thrust hard in the same direction with a hard push off from the inside edge of the skate. The faster you are going when you make the cross over, the more you must bend the knee of the inside leg and place your weight on this leg and to the inside of the half circle you are making. If you perform the movement properly you can do it at a very high speed.

Common faults include not bending the inside knee enough and not pushing with the outside skate in the direction you want to go. Particular attention should be paid to the proper technique of the cross over when going to your weak side.

Cross over drills. There are several very good drills that if practised on a regular basis will develop a high proficiency in performing this important fundamental manoeuvre. These drills can be used as a part of the regular practice, or can be practised on any available sheet of ice by the individual player. These drills are especially effective in training your players to cross over both ways.

The figure eight. Skate a figure eight as quickly as possible. Start with a large figure eight going, for example, down the ice, around one goal and then back around the other. This will force you to cut across to both sides. When you can do this easily both ways, cut down on the size of the eight you are using. Any type of marker can be used to indicate where the loops of the eight should be finished.

This drill can be used effectively by the coach because he can line up the entire team and send the players through the drill one after another. However, when doing this drill, it is wise for the coach to space the players well apart so that a slow skater will not force nor allow a faster skater to take it easy.

The competitive angle should be worked into this drill frequently. Use a stop watch to time each player or divide the team into two groups. One squad starts at one end of the eight, the other at the opposite loop. Each player completes one eight, returning to touch the next player on his group. This relay feature encourages the players to really work during the drill. Until proficiency in going both ways is well developed, each player should do eights as often as he can on his own.

The threader (Snake drill). The player goes down the ice threading his way in and out of a line of obstacles (other players, pylons, or pucks). As he goes down the ice, he should be cutting across either to one side or the other. No straightaway skating is permitted. The obstacles should be placed about thirty feet apart at first with the distance being cut down as proficiency increases. This drill can be used with the player skating free or carrying a puck on his stick. Competition in this drill will key up interest and proficiency. Time the player over the course or organize teams and use the race method by having two or three lines of obstacles.

Skating the square. Skate around a square, marked off by four corner obstacles (players, pylons, or pucks), as quickly as possible. The player goes to his left around the square once, starting at a point midway between two corners and stops quickly when he completes the square, and turning about, skates the square going to his right.

At first a fifty or sixty foot square should be used with the size being decreased as proficiency is developed. For competition, time the players as they skate the square. Each player should skate the square six to eight times without stopping, half to the left, half to the right. A good drill for the coach to include in practice sessions (several squares can be used at one time), it can also be used anywhere by the individual player. Check the times going to the left and going to the right, and you will see that there is usually quite a difference. This is a good way to demonstrate how much slower a player will manoeuvre around his weak side.

Two foot stop. This manoeuvre hinges on the ability to stop quickly in order to avoid a checker, change position for tactical purposes, or stop and come back down the ice while back checking. This is an important phase of agility skating because the faster you can stop, the sooner you can get back in the play or the easier you can shake an opponent. For example, when you are going down on the wing with a teammate who is carrying the puck and he gets checked, if you can stop quickly, you will be able to come back faster with the opponent who has taken the puck.

Although this is a very fundamental movement, the average hockey player is not able to stop as quickly as he should. This is why you will often see even outstanding players overbalance when they attempt to stop during a particularly fast burst of play. Hockey is a fast, mobile game. Even a split second, taken away from the time it takes you to stop, can make a difference in the successful completion of some play.

To stop efficiently the player should turn his skates quickly to either the right or left, bend his knees well, turn and press down to feel the skate edges (inside and outside) grip the ice. The player's weight should be over the skates. It is also important to stay low upon completion of the stop. The turn for the stop is made by swinging the upper body and hips quickly in a right angle turn, as the skates are turned sideways. As a general rule the player should turn for his stop on the leg on which his weight is placed when he decides to stop. For example, if you have just driven forward on your left leg, you would turn to the left to make your stop.

Common faults in stopping include not turning the upper body and hips quickly and together before the skates are dug in; not transferring the weight in order to get the edges into the ice; failure to push the skates hard into the ice; ankle and lower leg muscle weakness with resultant loss of balance and power to stand the shock of a quick stop and inability to make a strong downward pressure to slow momentum; and failure to turn the skates to a position at full right angles to the line of original direction. Often, a lack of confidence in making a quick turn can be at fault.

If the skates are turned insufficiently, there will be a continued stride in a side-forward angle; if they are turned too much there will be a loss of balance with an inclination to have the feet shoot out behind you. A common bad habit in stopping is to make the stopping turn always in the same direction. The player who always stops after a turn to the same side loses important manoeuvrability. It is interesting to note that a player will probably show a tendency to stop by turning toward the same side to which he likes to cross over. It is another example of right- or left-leggedness. Learn how to stop to both sides.

The single leg stop (one foot stop). This stop is performed in the same general way as the two foot stop with the only difference being that the inside leg (left if stop is prefaced by a left turn) does all the work as the outside foot is lifted off the ice. The advantage of this type of stop is that the outside foot can be brought quickly over and around into a cross over start. However, especially strong ankle and leg muscles are needed to perform the one foot stop. Whenever you are not travelling at all-out speed the one foot stop is perhaps the most efficient.

The knock-kneed stop (snow-plow). The snow-plow stop is performed by turning the toes of the skates in and pressing the inside edges of the skates into the ice. The knees turn in toward each other in a knock-kneed action. The turn is only effective at slow speeds or for beginners.

Line stop. Skate from the goal line to the centre red line at full speed. As the red line is reached, see how close to it a full stop can be accomplished. To make this drill competitive, measure the distance it takes each player to stop. This kind of contest can be used at regular intervals to test the progress of the players.

Players should stop on alternate sides, with a left turn one time and a right the next. Any stop started before the line is reached disqualifies the attempt. This drill can be done on the player's own time on any available ice. Organize it as a contest with your friends as it is a lot of fun.

Obstacle stop. This drill is designed to teach the player to stop quickly by using an obstacle. Experience indicates that many players need such incentive to force them to make a full effort. A good obstacle (safe if the player misjudges his distance) is a hockey stick laid flat on the ice just past the red line. Start with it about five feet past the line and gradually move it up closer as quick stopping skill is developed. If desired both this drill and the line stop can be done in groups of five or six. Organize the groups so that players with approximately the same speed are in each group. However, make sure you check carefully to see that each player skates all out and does not try to stop before the red line is reached.

Quick breaks. The ability to get started quickly is a skill every hockey player should practise. Coaches should emphasize quick breaks as an important part of their practise schedule. Often a team of slower skaters can more than make up for this general lack of speed if they can break quickly. Thus every opportunity is at hand to be in a scoring position after a check has been made or a break-out play has been successfully completed. It irritates a coach to see a member of his team get a break-away chance and spoil it through inability to break quickly. The importance of developing top level ability for the quick break cannot be overemphasized. A coach who makes it a habit to work on quick break development will find it pays real dividends. The player who works to improve his breaking skill will soon be repaid for his efforts.

This important agility skating move is governed by the same principles as a start by a track sprinter. Some have the natural co-ordination and muscle type that make the job easy, but all can do a great deal to improve their breaking skill by close observation of the technique used and frequent practice of specially designed drills.

There are four types of quick break: from a stationary position (front or back), after a quick stop or turn, from a skating position, and from a gliding position.

Stationary quick break (V-start). For example, suppose you are in a starting position (a face-off) and you are facing the way you want to go. First of all make sure you are in a ready start stance. The position from which you can get going in the least amount of time is with one leg slightly ahead of the other, feet comfortably apart, forward skate turned slightly outward at the point (to be ready to thrust), weight mostly on the forward leg, knees slightly bent, stomach in, chest high, and the upper body leaning comfortably forward. The stick should be on the ice so that any quick pass to you will find you ready. This is especially important when in front of the goal. The whole body should be as loose and relaxed as you can make it. Keep your mind alert but your body loose and relaxed. Remember, relaxed muscles move more quickly and efficiently than tensed muscles.

When starting, throw the shoulder, arm and hip on the same side in the same direction as your forward leg and drive off hard with an explosive thrust off the forward skate. At the same time, bring the rear foot forward as quickly as you can. Having kept the weight off the rear foot you will also be able to bring it forward quickly. Get a full, explosive drive off the front foot to get going and then get that rear foot forward and on the ice, giving another hard thrust as quickly as possible. Keep the rear foot close to the ice as it comes forward so no time is wasted getting it on the ice for the second stride. When bringing it forward, be sure to turn the toe outwards so that it will be in a position to thrust hard the moment it makes contact with the ice. The first four to six strides should be as short as you can make them. Then you can gradually lengthen your stride to normal length. Remember, the first few strides must be short with extra emphasis placed on hard push off on the backward thrust, knee bend, and forward body lean.

A common fault is trying to start quickly by just moving the leg without concentrating on short strides and hard push off. Attention should be placed on the importance of a quick break because even a fraction of a second's edge over the player checking you can mean your stick on the puck first, and this may mean the start of a break-out or a clearing play or a goal.

The quick break must also be mastered for those situations in which your back is facing the direction you want to go. This occurs, for example, after a face-off in the offensive zone when opponents have recovered the puck and start a break-out play up your side with a pass to a fast-breaking forward. At such a moment, the ability to get going is extremely important especially if you have been stationed on one of the blue line points and are one of the last men between the puck carrier and your goal. The action of turning and getting started quickly is difficult to perform at peak efficiency because it demands special balance and top level co-ordination.

Your body weight shifts to the side to which you want to turn. Bend your knee and twist the hips and shoulders around as quickly as possible. This will enable you to pivot quickly in a tight circle. Your free leg is swung around and forward with the toe of the skate facing outward so that it is in a sideways position to push hard once it hits the ice. This foot should be placed on the ice as soon as it comes into a position beside the other foot. From this position, the technique of an ordinary start from a starting position should be used (short strides, body lean, etc.). Practise the pivot to each side until you have mastered it.

Line to line drill. The players are lined up just behind the blue line. At a signal the players race for the red line. They then line up on the opposite blue line and at another command race back to the red line. When doing this drill each player should take up the starting stance explained above. The players should be divided into groups with an attempt made to match them evenly regarding speed. This drill can be done with the players free skating or with pucks. When pucks are used in the drill, they should be placed a foot or two in front of the players on the blue line. The players must pick the pucks up and keep them on their sticks throughout the course.

Hold regular contests between the groups for the whole team and between smaller groups such as forward lines, defence pairs, forward line versus forward line, etc. Another good idea is to have the players work alone and check the time it takes to travel from blue to red line. False starts should be watched carefully. The handicap idea can also be used to good effect by placing your fast men a yard or so behind your slower men. Every player must put forth an extra effort. This type of drill is to the hockey player what sprint starts are to the track runner. Used regularly it can help improve quick break ability.

Turn and go drill. This drill should be conducted the same as the line to line drill. However, the players stand with their backs to the starting line and at a signal have to turn and go. When done with a puck, the player should have it on his stick when the start signal is given. Players should alternate pivoting in the break to the left one time and to the right the next. As in the line to line, each player should make at least eight to twelve starts every time the drill is used. Those needing it should be given more work. Always start the players on a signal and never on their own. Mix the signals up so that the players do not know when to expect them.

Start and glide. Station the players on the goal line. Start on a signal but after taking four strides they should glide, remaining perfectly motionless. See how much momentum the players can achieve in those all important first four strides. This drill also gives the players an incentive to drive hard at the start. To be competitive, measure the distance each player is able to glide. The drill can also be done by the player on his own.

The coach should check points of technique carefully during the drill. Between each start he should quickly give each player guidance as to what he needs to work on. However, do not waste too much time talking. It is best to keep the drill running quickly and smoothly. Explain precisely what is to be done before the drill starts so that only simple checking needs to be done between each start. Keeping careful records on everyone's progress and posting results of time trials will reap benefits and add interest to the drills. These drills, as with most skating drills, can also be used as conditioners.

Quick break after quick stop or turn. In making a quick break after you have come to a sharp stop, or after you have made a turn, you merely concentrate on breaking quickly to the new direction using the same general fundamentals as you do in a V-start. There is no need to worry about the initial stance. The main thing is to practise so that you can develop the co-ordination necessary to move quickly into the quick break technique (short hard strides, body well forward, emphasis on thrust). Remember to throw the upper body forward in the direction to which you wish to speed.

Quick start ability is mainly mental because you must remember to force yourself to dig in hard and take those short, hard driving strides. It is natural always to try to take things easy. Also remember that it takes a lot of physical power and good conditioning to continue to break quickly throughout a game. Very often you find that those who do not break fast are either in poor shape or are inclined to be on the lazy side. Nothing will show a player's condition or character better than when he has to tear down the ice at full speed and then break or turn and come back the same way a few times. Practise the movements frequently so that you can make the transition from the quick start skill learned during the stationary phase of the quick break into the continuous action of the stop and start or turn and start.

Go and come back drill. The players are lined up on one of the blue lines as in either line to line or turn and go. At a signal they break for the red line. The moment the red line is hit, they stop and go back to the start position. Have them stop the first time to the left and the second time to right. This should be strictly enforced. Once the players get into good condition they can go up and back two or three times during one section of the drill.

The whole team can work together on this drill or can be divided into groups, line against line, etc., as suggested in line to line. The time check element can also be brought into this drill. Care should be taken to make sure each player does not begin his stopping action before he gets to the red line. This is a particularly good conditioner because it simulates the actual conditions of play and demands frequent acceleration. This is the hardest thing the body can do.

If the average player, particularly the young player, uses the time he spends at the local rink to practise skating moves plus other drills that we have dealt with and the ones we deal with later on, he'll make a huge improvement.

Go, turn, and go drill. In this drill, the players turn instead of coming to a dead stop. The markers (pylons) are set out along the red line, one opposite each of the players lined up along the blue line. The players can do both this and the preceding drill either with or without the puck.

Four and four drill. The players go around the edge of the rink, going outside the nets. They start off by taking four fairly slow strides and then burst all out for four, then they take four more slow ones and then burst again. Each player should count as he goes, making sure he keeps the four slow and four all-out rhythm. The coach can call out the rhythm if the players are slow to catch on to the idea or are not giving everything they have got. The players should go to the left around the rink one time and to the right the next.

This drill is a good conditioner, and can also be done on your own. The thing to watch for is that after the player has gone for a short distance he will be inclined to "swing the lead" because he will find the quick change of pace to be tiring and requiring an aggressive mental attitude. But this drill helps develop the habit and the physical capacity to break fast though tired during a game. If you can do this you will have achieved something very important.

Quick break from gliding. Often during a game the player will assume a gliding position when he is travelling forward on momentum but not skating. This frequently occurs in puck-carrying. Ability to break into full speed quickly from such a position is a great advantage. It is essential, for example, when bursting in to take a pass, to break through an opening when carrying the puck or around defencemen, or when darting in to pick up the loose puck, or break with a teammate who has suddenly recovered the puck and is breaking on a rush. The same technique is used as in any of the quick breaks.

However, remember that when gliding the legs should not be held too far apart. They must be close together to provide a good position to start driving. An ideal spread when gliding (or when battling for the puck) is to have the feet the same distance apart as your hand is from your elbow. Tests have proved this to be the ideal leg spread, giving maximum balance and a basis for any quick action.

In practising to acquire this technique use the four and four drill as described. Instead of going from slow skating to fast skating, go from skating to a glide and then to fast skating again. Take four fast strides, glide for about eight or ten yards around the rink, and then repeat. This can be done both with and without the puck.

Stop and start. This refers to a movement that is a combination of two basic skills. It is one thing to be able to stop quickly. However, it is another thing to be able to start quickly from this stopped position in order to get back into the play. You might, for example, be able to move in front of the goal to receive a pass. In this case, an ability to stop and start gives you a split second advantage.

Instead of making one turning motion in this move as you do to stop, you make two, one to stop and one to start again. For instance, suppose you are going down the ice and you stop with a turn to the left. The moment you come to a standstill the body is whipped around to the right again to get going. Concentrate on whipping the hips around, leaning well forward and driving off the inside foot. If you have turned to the left in your stop, the inside foot will, of course, be your left one. You turn to the left, stop, and swing your body quickly to the right again and at the same time as your body turns you drive hard off the inside foot. Bend the knees well and get that foot on the ice quickly after you have driven off the inside foot. Starting and stopping in this way is primarily a matter of balance. The big secret is to learn to turn the body properly. Make sure you practise stopping and starting, turning your body to the left, and to the right.

Stop and go. In this drill the players travel around the edge of the rink as in the four and four drill, taking four hard strides as in a quick break, stopping, and repeating. The first stop is made to the left, the second to the right, and so on. Care should be taken to make sure the player comes to a complete stop each time. The drill can be done both with and without a puck.

Single leg swing-around (tight turn). This is a manoeuvre that enables the skater to change direction quickly and to come back down the ice or to move to either side without actually stopping. It is the best movement to use to get back into the play in the least amount of time when you or a teammate have been checked on a rush. Many players "go for a skate" after they have been checked or after a teammate has lost possession of the puck. This expression means to take a slow, wide or lazy turn before getting back into the play. This is one of the worst habits a player can acquire. It means the player concerned is out of position and leaves his zone wide open. In a tight game "going for a skate" just once can mean giving up the winning goal. Those who have learned how to tight turn and made a habit of it will rarely be guilty of this cardinal error.

To perform this very important agility skating move you take a stride and then, on a well bent knee, swing your body around in the direction you want to go. As you swing your body about, the free leg (the one on which your weight is not placed) should be brought around quickly in a circular action. However, remember it is the movement of the body, mainly the hips and shoulders, not the leg that does the turning. When you are crossing over, make sure that you keep a good forward body lean. The moment your turn is completed the foot of the free leg which you are swinging around quickly off the ice should be placed on the ice and a hard thrust taken. At this point, all the weight is transferred from the inside leg to the leg you have to swing around. The thrust of this leg will send you straight back in the new direction. To make the move quickly there should be a good co-ordination of any outward turn of the hips and body in the same direction. Then the free leg swings around.

You can make this action into an actual stop by turning the body quickly and exerting pressure on the inside skate into the ice, not bothering to swing the free leg around with the body. The difference between a one foot stop and a quick turn around without any loss of time is governed primarily by the amount of body turn you make and the angle to which you turn your skate. Most players will be able to turn better toward the side they cross over best. Therefore, it is important to practise turning on each leg. In making the turn the body does not turn quickly at right angles as in a full stop, but in a slower, more circular fashion.

Glide and turn. This drill is designed to teach players the technique of a tight turn on one leg. The idea is to skate from the blue line to a point half way between the blue line and the centre red line toward a pylon. When the half-way to the red line point is reached, the player glides with his legs comfortably apart. As he reaches the pylon he moves the leg closest to the pylon ahead of the other leg in a stride, placing all his weight on this leg and making sure the knee is well bent. As this stride is taken, the toe of the skate is turned toward the pylon and at the same time the player does his cross over.

The wavy line shows how the far leg should be crossed over. The circled "X" shows where the foot of this free leg should be placed on the ice for the thrust that completes the cross over and starts the player back in the direction he wishes to go. After the cross over has been completed the player should take four or five quick strides. The drill should be started slowly at first with the speed increased as skill develops. The drill should be alternated with the player going to the left one time, to the right the next.

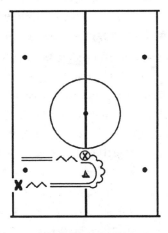

GLIDE and TURN

Remember, a common fault is swinging wide just before the cross over is completed. This can be corrected by leaning the upper body well in toward the obstacle. Do not let that upper body move outward. Keep it well turned in toward the centre of the half circle you are making. By the use of a number of obstacles spread across the ice the whole team can be put through the drill very quickly. If desired, the players can be lined up along the side of the rink about six feet in from the boards. The players on one side skate across the ice, make the turn and return. Then the players on the other side do the drill. As skill increases have the players, around whom the turn will be made, stand closer and closer to the side boards.

This is an excellent drill if you want your team to come back quickly on their backchecking assignments. Although it requires an effort to convince players to practise it, the time is well spent.

Skate and turn. This is the same drill as glide and turn, but instead of gliding toward the pylon the skaters should skate. It should be started slowly but the players ought to practise the drill while skating at full speed as soon as they are capable. The drill can be done with or without the puck.

Power turn (swing around both legs). This is yet another way of turning quickly. It can be used both to make a turn in order to get back into the play or as a skating move during puck-carrying. It is not quite as efficient for a quick turn as is the single leg tight turn, but it has the advantage of enabling you to keep better balance.

The two leg swing around is performed in much the same way as the one leg tight turn. The main difference is that there is no free leg. Instead of swinging the leg around, the skate is kept on the ice and the point of it is turned in the same direction as the inside skate. It follows the front skate around. Weight is kept down the centre of the body equally on both feet. Both knees are equally bent. When the swing-around is nearly completed the weight is transferred to the forward foot and the rear foot is brought around quickly with the toe facing well out and then placed on the ice quickly for a thrust.

To improve technique use the same type of drill as used in glide and turn and skate and turn, but employ the two leg action instead of the single leg action.

The secret of both the single and double leg swing-around is the technique of getting that outside foot onto the ice and thrusting as soon as possible after the cross over has been made. The figure eight is also an excellent drill for the swing-around. The player skates the lines and swings around the ends.

PIVOTING

This means reversing your forward skating to backward skating (and vice versa) while continuing in the same direction without actually stopping. It is an advantage both for the offensive and defensive players to be able to change quickly from forward to backward skating. It is a very important skill for defencemen.

The secret of being able to pivot from forward to backward skating is in developing the ability to shift your weight quickly and with good balance. Frequent practice and frequent practice alone will enable you to develop such skill. Those with a more natural sense of balance and especially good co-ordination will be able to get the technique more quickly than the average player but anyone can develop the needed skill with work.

Pivot turn. This type of pivot is made off one leg. The idea is to take a stride and then as the stride starts, turn your body quickly in a complete turn. As you turn your body the free leg (right leg if you have taken the last stride on to the left) is swung around in front of you from your right side to your left side. As your body and leg swing around, you pivot in the same direction on your skate. When turning your body, make sure you snap those hips around as this action is the key to a quick turn. Make sure your knees are well bent, especially the knee of the leg you swing around. The first of the two diagrams shows a pivot off the left foot. The slanted marks indicate the strides you make with your leading foot. The pivot on the left foot is shown by "A"; the manner in which the leg is swung quickly around to complete the turn is shown by "B." The backward skating action starts the moment the leg completes its swing into position. In reversing the direction from backward to forward skating, the same principles are used. The weight is placed on one foot

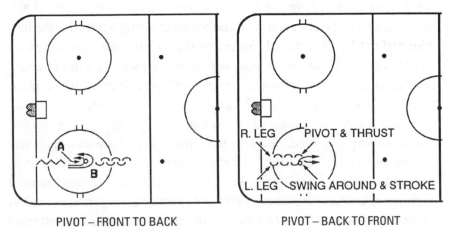

PIVOT – FRONT TO BACK   PIVOT – BACK TO FRONT

(the one farthest behind you), the body is turned quickly and the other leg is swung around. As the foot on which the pivot is made completes the turn it pushes off hard on a thrust forward. The free leg, as it completes its swing around, goes forward on a stroke. It is important that the knees be kept well bent.

Pivot race. In this drill the players are lined up at the goal line, back facing the other end of the rink. At a signal they start skating backwards. At another signal the players pivot and skate forward. Every few yards another signal is given and on each signal the players pivot. The last signal should he given when the players are skating backward about six or seven yards from the end boards. This means that when they reach the end of the rink they will be skating forward. They then touch the boards, pivot, and come back down the ice doing pivots on the signal. Do the drill as a race, dividing the team into groups or line against line, etc. Seven to nine pivots can be worked in on the average size rink. The players should be watched carefully to see that they are all pivoting correctly. The first turn should be to the right, the next to the left and so on. If it is done with the players trying to carry the puck, it is also a good puck control drill.

Glide pivot race. This is conducted along the same line as the pivot race. But the players take six strides to start and then glide, making as many pivots (first to right, then to left) as they can before losing momentum. The player cannot take a skating stride after the first six. The player who can go the farthest, with the most pivots, is the winner. Any contest element worked in can also be conducted on a team basis (line vs. line, etc.). Besides developing the ability to pivot when skating, this drill is also a great general balance and co-ordination developer.

Glide turn. When a new skill is practised at full speed without understanding its principle, injuries can result. This drill teaches the pivot turn quickly and helps avoid sprained ankles, sore hips, etc.

Skate from the goal line halfway to the blue line then glide with feet comfortably apart. On reaching the blue line, place all the weight on one foot, move it ahead in a stroke and then quickly whip the body around, pivot on the skate and bring the free leg around quickly, getting it on the ice as quickly as possible. Then skate backward for a few yards, glide, and turn forward again. This can be done up and down the ice as often as desired. The team can do it in groups, or in lines, defence pairs, etc. It can also be done solo. If you have difficulty learning to pivot, try it from a stationary position (facing forward and then backward) until you have the basic idea. Then do it moving slowly.

Skate and pivot. In this drill the players travel up and down the ice at full speed, pivoting on signals from the coach. A race can also be made out of the drill. An excellent plan is to form three or four groups and do them as relay races. This can be done with practically any of the skating drills. Down the ice and back again is an ideal distance for a race. The distance can be increased for a race if conditioning is a factor. Make sure you signal for a turn every few yards but also mix up the length of time between signals so the players will not be set for a pivot. Trying to do this drill while carrying a puck is the next challenge to the player.

Pivot and stop. This drill is an especially good one to develop agility and pivoting ability. Start from the blue line skating forward. When the centre red line is reached, the player pivots and comes to a complete stop. He then breaks back to the blue line, pivots when he reaches it and repeats, going back and forth as often as desired. Four to six times is usually sufficient in one run. It can become a competitive exercise by making a race between squads or by timing the players over the course (going back and forth from line to line four to six times). Close attention should be paid to see that the players do not pivot until they reach the line. The drill can be done with the player starting with forward skating during one section, backward the next. To stop quickly when skating backwards, turn the toes of the skates outward, press the feet hard on the ice, bend the knees well, and then bring them toward each other in a slightly knock-kneed position. The upper body should lean well forward.

SCOOTING

This move is perhaps the most overlooked of all agility skating moves. It is an offensive move that can be used to great advantage when carrying the puck. It is a glide or a turn to either side prolonged by a series of quick short bursts on the back foot. Scooting is accomplished by taking a stride on the left leg, for example, and then giving a series of quick, hard thrusts with the right foot. This moves the skater quickly forward.

It is most effective when used as part of a cross over or a quick change of direction. It is also effectively used to speed up the skating action when shifting or moving around a checker or defenceman. It is useful, too, to break away from a group of players quickly and into the open to take a pass out or retrieve a loose puck. In such cases there is often only a small opening. By taking a stride toward the opening, turning sideways, and scooting for a few feet, one can often break through when ordinary skating would mean a collision. Scooting can also be used to move in on goal sharply after taking a pass when on the wing. The illustrated drills will not only develop an ability to use this type of agility scooting manoeuvre but will also act as good leg conditioners and developers. The scooting action off the one foot throws quite a strain on the muscles of this foot and leg and as a result will develop added foot, ankle, and leg strength and power.

Angle scooting. The player scoots down a line of obstacles such as pylons. The pylons should be placed either between the various lines, or at thirty-foot intervals. The closer they are, the more difficult the drill. The player stands on the starting line and takes a stride at an angle toward the outside of the obstacle. He only takes the one stride and keeps moving by a series of scooting strides from the other foot. When he gets to the pylon, he brings his rear foot forward and turns it at an angle, well in toward the pylon and starts scooting toward the next pylon, off the other foot. This is repeated as he angles down the ice turning sharply as he reaches each obstacle. For competition, have several lines of obstacles and have races, making sure all the players scoot at all times without sneaking in any skating. Time trials can also be used or the shuttle relay principle with one player going down and touching another player who then goes the other way. This drill can be used also without obstacles. The players can change their angle of direction on signals from the coach. However, the use of pylons will give you the best results.

Scooting the square. This drill teaches the player to make quick sharp-angled turns while scooting. He starts at the centre of one side of the square (which should be a thirty to thirty-five foot square, the smaller the more difficult the drill) and takes one stride with the leg closest to the square. Then he scoots as quickly as he can around the

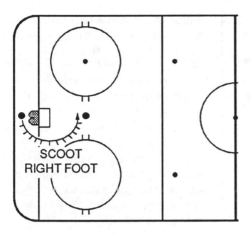

SCOOTING FOR THE GOAL
Start a turn with the foot closest to the goal. The other foot then begins the scoot, driving the player out and around as the front foot turns. Lean the upper body well in toward the goal.

square. If desired, he can go left around the square, and stop quickly. When the starting point is reached, he turns and goes around the other way. The competitive element can be utilized by timing the player.

Scooting the goal. The player stands stationary behind the net. He then skates until he gets to the far post. He turns the inside skate in the direction he wants to go and skates hard with the outside foot until he makes the turn and scoots across the goal mouth. The scooting finishes when he reaches the point from which he started. Care should be taken to make sure the player learns to scoot in both the left and right turn. The competitive angle can be utilized by timing the players.

Scooting the line. This is the quick stop and right-angle scoot which gets a player clear for a shot on goal, or which can be used in the cut

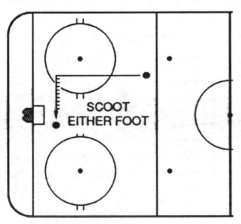

SCOOTING WHEN BLOCKED
Stop suddenly and turn to the side, shooting the inside leg (closest to the goal) out in a right-angled turn on a stroke. The other foot gives momentum by taking a series of hard push-offs. The same move can be used when you get a passout in front of the net but can't shoot as you are blocked by an opposing player or group.

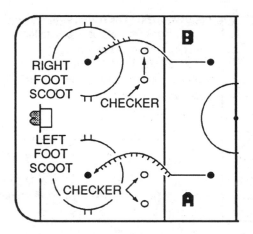

SCOOTING TO BEAT A CHECKER
A. Shift into the centre to draw the checker after you. Then shift back, thrusting hard on the foot closest to the checker. Take a series of short hard thrusts which allows the other foot a long swerving stride. Guiding is done by the front foot going out, around, and then back again quickly.
B. Use a sudden scoot on the foot farthest from the defenceman who has you well covered. It will give needed momentum either to break around him or force you by him.

across play to beat a goalkeeper. The player skates from the centre red line to the blue line, about seven yards from the side boards. As he hits the blue line, he stops quickly and tries to scoot along it to a point directly in front of the goal. This drill can be conducted from both the left and right side. The point in using the line is to give the player a definite guide, which is an important factor. In doing this drill, the player uses the two foot stop technique previously described in this chapter. As he comes to a stop, he drives off at a new angle. You will be surprised how fast you will be able to skate to the line, stop, and scoot. After you have practised the drill for a while, you can start your scooting without a moment's hesitation.

Adding one or two moves can add variety. For example, a player skates from the goal to the blue line, scoots along the line for twenty feet,

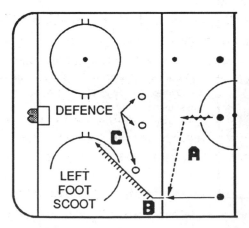

SCOOTING AFTER A PASS
Suppose you want to cut in on goal after a pass at the side of the rink. Line "A" shows the pass, line "B" shows how the player should burst into full speed after he has taken the pass to get by the defence. Line "C" shows how the player cuts in on goal using the scoot. In this case, being on the left side, he takes a stride with his right foot, turns the skate toward the goal, bends his knee well, leans into the centre area and takes a series of short, hard skating thrusts with his left foot.

stops, breaks fast to the next line, scoots to the right for twenty feet, then on to the other blue line.

All the skating drills can be done with or without the puck. If there is difficulty in learning the technique, practise it slowly at first. "Walking through" a new drill manoeuvre should be a standard practice.

ZIG-ZAG

This is also an offensive move, and is a variation of the cross over. It is an excellent move to use in order to get by a checker or to thread one's way through a scramble. It demands quite a lot of agility and balance but it can be learned through regular practice. The zig-zag, often called a double cross over, is one of the most difficult skating agility manoeuvres. Skate in a straight line. Suddenly bring one foot over in front of the other as if you were going to start a cross over on that side but just as the foot that you bring across hits the ice whip the other foot back in a cross over step in the opposite direction. For example, if you go to the left the first time you bring your right leg over in front of your left leg. Then to put the zag after the zig, bring the left leg back across the right one and continue to skate ahead.

One of the secrets of being able to move efficiently is to keep the knees well bent and flexible and to shift the weight of your upper body quickly. When you take the cross over with the first leg, for example the right one, lean the body well over to the left. Just as your skate hits the ice, move your weight quickly back to the right so that you can push hard off your right skate in the new direction.

Used properly, the zig-zag will give you a skating move that will make your puck-carrying much more effective. It can be used to beat a checker who is facing you, or to thread your way through a group of players. It is a wonderful means of faking a checker out of position (which you do with the first cross over). Learning this move will not only give you a very important addition to your agility skating moves but also will do a great job in developing your all-around balance and co-ordination. When you are first trying to learn this move, move very slowly.

Zigging the puck. Place four pucks on either side of the red and blue lines about six feet apart (the distance can be varied). Zig-zag down the line of pucks. At first, skate to a spot about four or five feet from the first puck. Then glide into your first zig-zag. When skill increases, eliminate the glide. When more skill is developed, the pucks should be closer together and more added to the obstacle course. The drill can be run as a race or on a time basis.

Skate and zig. The player starts at the goal line, takes two skating strides, zig-zags, takes three skating strides, zig-zags, and so on to the far end. This can be alternated with the double zig-zag in which he crosses over four times instead of twice.

A variation of this drill is to start the player free skating and then have him zigzag on a whistle. Two quick whistles could indicate a call for a double zig-zag, three for a triple, and so on. Do zig-zag walks with the players walking through the manoeuvre up and down the ice with their skates on. This helps the players to get used to the drill, and trains muscles for co-ordination. Try it slowly without skates if you do not get the knack of it at first.

Side jumps. This is another agility skating move that increases the skater's manoeuvrability. It is a quick two foot stop with a jump to the side. The jump is usually followed by a second burst of speed. It is a prime necessity to avoid a charging defenceman. Used against the head-long type of checker it can be effective.

The side jump is an important skating move. It provides you with the ability to avoid body checks and collisions. It is also a valuable asset for getting into the clear during scrambles, during a fight for the puck in a corner, and in blocking out opponents when playing defensively. To perform it and its variations requires a great deal of ankle and lower leg strength. Practising these drills will help develop the needed strength as will the special exercises in the chapter on Training. There are a number of side jump variations.

Stop and jump. Come to a quick stop. Then jump sideways in the same direction as you turned to make your stop. The idea is to stop quickly then jump sideways driving hard off the foot furthest from the direction in which you wish to jump. For example, if you wish to jump to the left you drive off the right foot. The left foot is lifted off the ice and flung in the direction in which you want to jump. Just before you jump, the knee should be well bent to give you spring. When you land, most of the weight is on the right leg. Accordingly the right knee should be well bent on the landing so as to absorb the shock and give you good balance. When you land the weight is quickly transferred onto the left leg from which you start any new skating action you want. If jumping from left to right, it is your left leg from which you drive and on which you land.

Stationary jump. When side jumping from a stationary position for example, to the left, place the weight on the right foot and drive sideways, throwing out the other foot in the direction in which you want to go. It is the same action as the stop and jump, after the stop has been made.

Stop, jump, and go. This drill teaches you the stop and jump and, at the same time, develops the technique of breaking quickly forward again after the side jump. The player skates from the goal line to the blue line and then stops before he reaches a puck or any suitable obstacle placed on the ice a few feet past the line. Then, as quickly as possible after stopping, he jumps sideways to the left past another puck placed a few feet to the side of the first puck. As he lands, he breaks quickly ahead again until he reaches the third obstacle placed halfway between the blue line and the red line. At this point, he stops and jumps to the right past another puck. He continues like this down the ice.

Pucks can also be placed at twenty- to thirty-foot intervals instead of on and between the lines. The pucks placed beside each other should be about three feet apart. When the side jump is developed, the distance can be increased. Use pylons as they give the player a definite assignment. Competition can be worked into the drill by doing races or having regular time trials. The drill can also be done with the players going up and down the ice, stopping and side jumping on the coach's signal.

Stationary side jump. The players are lined up down one side of the blue lines. (Use two blue lines if you wish to work all the players at once.) The players spread the feet comfortably, one foot on the line (not over it). At a signal, the players jump sideways and stay in the landing position. At another signal, they try to return to their original position with another jump. The players can do it as long as required.

Work the competitive angle into this drill by having check-ups on how far each player is jumping. Creating a team side jump standard and trying to break it every now and then develops interest in this drill. If a more loosely organized drill is desired, the players can be lined up, spacing each player well and using lines of four or five. Then put them through a series of side jumps (to the left and then back) as you would any calisthenics drill.

The Draw-away. This is another agility move that is an excellent way to avoid body checking or collision. Used correctly, it will often enable a player to sneak through with the puck when apparently well blocked out. It refers to the action of drawing the leg, hip, and upper body back from the square dead on position so that the player is travelling side-ways. By doing this, the player avoids contact that would have otherwise been made on this side of his body.

To perform this manoeuvre, place all the weight on the foot farthest from the obstacle you wish to avoid (perhaps a fast moving defence-man's hip or the goal post), and turn your upper body and hips sideways toward the obstacle. As the body and hips are turned, swing the leg closest to the obstacle back and away from the obstacle in the same direction you turn the body. For example, if you are trying to avoid a hip check by a defenceman on your left side, place your weight on your right foot and turn your body and hip to the left, moving the left leg to the left and behind you. The skate of the right foot continues to go dead ahead or slightly to the right. When the obstacle is cleared, the upper body, hips, and the inside leg are whipped around again and the foot placed on the ice for a new stroke. If weight is on the foot closest to the checker, as would be the case if you had just taken a stride toward him, you must quickly shift it to the other leg by pushing off on a new stride, and then make your draw-away.

Anyone can acquire this skill by practising it. The situation in which you use a draw-away develops so quickly that there is no time to think, "Ah, I'll use the draw-away to beat him." You must first use the move as a drill until it is set in your mind then you will find yourself using it auto-matically when the right situation comes up. This is the case with many skating agility moves.

It is quite possible to use a double draw-away, swinging the upper body around so that you are going sideways with, for example, your right leg forward. As you recover, and stride with your left leg, the body and right leg are crossed over. This can be used in snaking through a defence pair especially when one is slightly ahead of the other instead of parallel. It can also be used when threading yourself through a group of players during a session of scrambled play, or when you place the puck between the checker's legs and move around him to retrieve it.

Glide draw-away. This is the most effective way to get the idea of the draw-away in your mind. The player skates toward another obstacle. When he is about twenty feet away, he starts to glide with his legs spread comfortably, knees well bent. He aims his left leg at the other player's left leg, or the inside of the obstacle. Then, just before he collides with the obstacle, he turns his body sideways, and goes into the draw-away action. As he completes it, he takes several more strides.

The big secret is to get the hips turned quickly so that they are facing the side of the obstacle. After the player goes past the obstacle, he takes a few strides, stops, and comes back doing the draw-away around the same side of the obstacle so that he draws away with the other leg. The whole team can do this drill together if you divide them into two groups with one group acting as obstacles and the other doing the drill. Change the positions after one group has had six to eight attempts. Repeat as often as time allows.

The skate draw-away. This drill is similar to the glide draw-away, except that the player skates up to the obstacles instead of gliding. He should try to arrange his striding so that just as he gets to the obstacle he is taking a stride forward with the leg closest to it. The player should skate slowly at first until he gets the technique of arranging his strides. A variation is to have the players skate right at the obstacle and let him draw-away according to the position of his feet when he gets to it. This should not be attempted until the player understands it.

The snake through. This is a good way to make the player draw-away. Place two pylons or players in a parallel position, about two or three feet apart (depending upon the size of the players). The player then skates up to the obstacle, turns sideways, draws one leg away and snakes through sideways. The obstacles must be placed close enough together so that the player has to turn sideways to get through. Three or four pairs of obstacles can be used, spread about three feet from each other. He then skates toward the next pair of obstacles and repeats, going through by doing the draw-away to a different side. Both ends of the ice can be used. If the coach prefers he can use his defence pair as obstacles, stationing them on the blue line and his players can line up and take turns going between them, turning left one time, right the next.

360° pivot or escape. This "spin-a-rama" type move is very effective to get free from a checker who is guarding you in front of the net. It is also an excellent puck-carrying move. It demands a high degree of timing, balance, and agility but can be learned from frequent practice.

The manoeuvre is accomplished by the player placing all his weight on one foot, and then turning his hips and upper body around in a tight circle. The other leg swings around off the ice in the same direction the body is turned. The knees, especially the knee on which the weight is placed, must be well bent and a good forward body lean must be kept. The speed of the pivot is governed by the quickness of the body turn especially the action of the hips. You must turn the hips around with a quick motion. The upper body must be leaned to the inside during the pivot. If it is allowed to move outward, the player may lose his balance.

Pivot and go. The player stands on the blue line and faces the opposite blue line. On a signal he pivots completely around (to the left) and breaks up the ice in the same direction he was facing originally. At another signal he comes to a full stop. At a further signal he then pivots (this time to his right) and so on down the ice. The coach can work in as many signals as he desires. A variation is to do the drill without the players coming to a dead stop before the pivot. The drill can be done with or without a puck.

Skate, stop, and go. A line of pylons is placed down the ice about twenty-five feet apart in a jagged line. The player then skates as hard as he can to the outside of the obstacle and a little beyond it. Then he stops suddenly, pivots to the outside and breaks at an angle across ice for the next obstacle where he pivots again and so on.

The pivot must always be made to the outside. For example, if the player is going to his left, he would place his weight on his left leg and swing to the outside, bringing his right leg around and then forward toward the next obstacle. If he was going to the right, the pivot would be on the right leg with the left swinging around and toward the next obstacle. When he completes the course he goes around the goal and then back down the course again.

The drill can be done without obstacles, the players changing direction, and pivoting at signals. However, tests show that when obstacles are used, greater efficiency is developed. The drill can be done as a race or on a time trial basis if desired.

Pivot, skate, pivot. This drill helps to develop the straight ahead pivot with the player skating up to the obstacle, stopping just enough to make the pivot (the quicker, the better), and then going on again to the next obstacle (pylon). Obstacles (pylons) lined up down the ice about twenty to thirty feet apart are suitable. This is also a useful, competitive drill. It can also be done without obstacles, the players skating and pivoting on signals. This pivot move will add a lot of strength to your puck-carrying skill.

Stride, pivot, stride. Take a long stride and glide on the forward foot with the other foot held off the ice. After you have just about run out of momentum, pivot and take a long stride on the other foot. Glide as long as possible and then pivot again and so on down the ice. As the player comes out of each pivot he should thrust hard off the foot on which he has pivoted and drive the other foot forward on the new stride. The knees should be kept well bent at all times. The upper body, as on any pivot, should lean well to the inside at all times. Keep the stride as much forward as possible. As you step out in each new stride, try to keep skating straight ahead.

Lunge striding. This is the most simple of all agility skating manoeuvres but, in spite of its simplicity, few have bothered to learn the skill.

The only skill needed to acquire this move is to develop strong foot, ankle, and leg muscles so that you can take an especially hard thrust off the back foot. By practising it, you will develop the co-ordination needed. Actually, all a lunge stride consists of is a sudden hard, long stride in the midst of an ordinary skating action. You can follow this with another one if there is any need. It is, in a way, a type of quick break.

Stride variation. Skate around the ice surface alternating the speed of your skating, taking two lunge strides (as hard and long as you can) at the end of each type of skating. Start off behind the goal, skate slowly for twenty or thirty feet, then lunge stride, then skate for a while at medium speed, and lunge stride again. By skating in this fashion, it will give you practice in lunge striding at different speeds.

One variation is taking a single lunge stride, gliding a few feet, and then taking another, and so on around the rink. You can also take six short strides, then two lunge strides, alternating around the rink. The reason the lunge stride will get you free is that your opponent cannot expect it and by the time he sees you, there is plenty of ice between you and him.

The secret of using this move effectively is to drive off very hard on the back foot and at the same time move your front hip and shoulder into the forward action of the front leg. This is when the lunge comes in, as it is practically a lunge ahead onto the forward leg helped by the hard thrust off the back foot. But reading about it will not make you able to execute the move; you must practise it.

Turn gliding: This is the same as the two-legged swing around. However, you do not swing right around, but only glide with one foot in front of the other at an angle to either side. It can be used as a skating manoeuvre to beat a checker or to zig-zag through a group of players.

Skate hard and then glide for just a moment with feet parallel. Just as your glide starts, you move one foot in front of the other at an angle and then turn in the direction you want to go. At the same time you lean well to the same side. The knees, as in most skating moves, should be well bent. Then, when you wish to, straighten out or turn glide in the other direction you turn your skates, and lean that way. The sharper you want to turn and glide in a new direction the more you must lean.

The position of your feet can be shifted as you change direction if you wish, or you can leave them as they were. It is preferable to learn how to do both. To change foot position, bring the rear foot up ahead of the foot that has been in the lead as you shift your body weight to a different direction. Turn glides can be made as gradually or as sharply as you wish by the amount of lean and skate turn.

Double turn glide. Two pylons are placed on the ice. The pylons should be placed ten or fifteen feet apart (closer as the skill increases and the players are more confident going through drill). The player skates hard until he is about six feet away from the pylon. Then he turn glides perhaps to the left. As he rounds the pylon, he leans back the other way, turns his skates in the new direction, and rounds the other pylon. After he passes the last one he straightens out (still gliding), and then turns, and skates back to the line for another turn.

Players should alternate the way they round the first obstacle, going to the left one time, to the right the next. The drill should be done slowly until the players have enough skill and confidence to skate hard at the first obstacle. It is suggested that the drill be done without pucks until some skill has been developed.

Single turn glide. This drill is an ordinary single turn glide that ends with a straightening out. Three pucks are placed parallel on the ice about six feet apart. The player skates hard at one of the end pucks. Then, when he is about six feet away, he turn glides until he is just past the middle puck. He then straightens out, goes between the middle puck and the far puck, turns, and skates back to the line-up.

The players should alternate the way they turn glide. First head at the puck on the right end of the obstacle, then at the puck on the left end. To guide the player as to when he should start his turn glide, a puck can be placed at the required spot. As the skill level increases, the player should start closer and closer to the line of pucks.

Parallel zig-zag glide. This is a very effective skating manoeuvre when carrying the puck. It is a move that every player should learn. It is easy to learn and will enable you to keep excellent balance.

In performing this agility skating manoeuvre, the player bursts into full speed, and then glides with his feet comfortably spread and parallel. Following a very short glide he leans for example, to the left, bends his knees, turns his shoulders to the left, and turns his skates to the same side with the left skate slightly ahead of the right skate. This turns him to that side. He then leans back to the other side, shifts his shoulders around, turning his skates again in the same direction as he turns his body. As he turns, the right foot goes slightly ahead of the left foot. The more body lean used, the sharper the turns will be. As the player completes the zag (the second turn,) he bursts into full stride again, using the quick break technique.

This skating move is an excellent one for all puck carriers because it gives a variation from the ordinary side to side fake. It is very similar to the turn glide only the feet are kept very close in a parallel position throughout. The main advantage of the parallel zig-zag is that it enables the player to keep an excellent balance. Done after a full burst of speed, it can get the player past many a puck carrier or defence. Some call it a swerve.

Parallel zig-zag drills. Use the same drill as the double turn glide, substituting the parallel zig-zag for the turn glide. An alternative is to use the single turn glide. However, substitute the parallel zig-zag for the turn glide. Straighten out to go between pucks as in the basic drill.

For a more loosely organized drill not requiring obstacles, the players can be lined up and sent up and down the ice, doing the manoeuvre on signals.

Allen slide glide. This move can be learned by anyone willing to take the time to practise it. It is a very disconcerting manoeuvre because the player comes right at you one minute and disappears the next. This move is a real challenge to anyone who takes pride in his skating ability. Let us take as an example a slide glide to the left. The player skates at full speed. Then, as his right foot and leg go forward in a stroke, he suddenly turns the point of his skate inward, skids a little, pushes hard against the ice, turns to his left, and strides out with his left leg at a right angle to the direction he was going. The stride on the left foot is a long one, a sort of glide. The right foot must push into the ice twice in order to effect a stop, and to thrust hard enough to send the body sideways into a new stride.

The weight is thrown upon the right foot (the one that is turned in) as the stop and thrust sideways is made, and then it is quickly transferred to the left foot as the long stride is taken. Make sure that the right hip is turned quickly inward as the skate is turned in to start the manoeuvre. The player must shift his weight quickly so that the manoeuvre is performed well.

As the side glide is completed, the body is leaned quickly to the right, and the skate on the left foot turned sideways to the right so that the player is going straight again. As the skate is turned, the left foot digs in with a hard thrust so as to complete the second right angle turn and provide momentum for the forward movement. Actually, the manoeuvre consists of a one foot stop, only on the outside foot instead of the inside foot, a slide to the side, another one-foot stop and skate straight ahead. To aid the second sharp turn, the rear skate can be dropped to the ice and dragged sideways to help bring the body around. Make the stop with the forward foot and thrust the body off to the side in the same action. This same drag can be used by the rear foot during the first move when the stop and turn is made in the middle of a forward stride.

When done well, it gives you a change of direction that is tops in manoeuvrability. However, difficult as it is, it can be learned very quickly too. Do it slowly at first, and as you get the technique, add speed. Be sure you learn to do it off both the right foot as well as the left.

Slide glide drill. This drill is the best way to learn the slide glide. Three obstacles (pylons) are placed in a line on the blue line. One should be placed six feet from the centre one, the other one about three feet. The player approaches the obstacle that is six feet from the middle one, and then as he gets to a spot a few feet away from it, he takes a stride as if to go around the outside of it. Halfway through this stride he goes into the slide glide. He comes back across the line of pylons and then, as he gets to the middle one, he goes into the final turn, and goes between the middle pylon, and the one close beside it. Then he skates back and takes his place in the line for another try.

The drag. This skating manoeuvre is an effective one to learn because it can be worked in as a part of many puck-carrying moves. It is another way for changing direction quickly. You'll find that it lends itself to manoeuvring at close quarters.

Take a stride with the right leg, then halfway through the stride place the left foot suddenly on the ice and drag hard in a sideways position on the inside edge. As the skate begins the drag, the player turns his hips and forward foot hard to the left. This body turn plus the drag whips the body around quickly to effect a quick left turn. To do it to the right, merely drag the right foot and turn to the right. It is done after a stroke forward with the left leg. Keep the knees well bent during the move.

The best way to develop skill in this manoeuvre is to skate up and down the ice using the drag to turn you around in a quarter turn every few strides.

Change of pace. As in football or basketball, the ability to change pace is a valuable skill. By using pace changes, it is possible to get free from a checker or fool him while carrying the puck. Done well it makes the player very difficult to check. The player with no change of pace is easier to body check, or stay with when checking. This is a "must for players."

To change pace, decrease or increase the push off on the back foot. As the amount of push off on the backward thrust of the skate at the end of each stride governs the speed of the player, it naturally follows that pace is controlled by the amount of push off given by the player.

The best way to develop change of pace is to skate around or up and down the rink changing pace every few strides. However, you should not always follow the same pattern. For example, go from slow to medium to fast to faster one time, and the next time go from fast to slow to full speed to slow to medium. When practising, try to make your pace changes smoothly and without a lot of body action. Vary your push off. The more successfully you can hide your intention to change pace, the more effective it will be.

Hurdling. Hurdling is jumping into the air when travelling forward. Though there are times when it is dangerous and ineffective to use it, it can be a great aid to the hockey player. For example, it is perhaps the only way to avoid a checker's stick that has been held flat on the ice or the legs of a fallen player. Properly learned and regularly practised, it can be an important part of your skating.

To get the body up and in the air when skating, thrust hard in an upward action off the back foot and at the same time drive the knee of the forward leg up. The arms should be lifted at the same time, coming up fast as you jump or hurdle. They should be lifted as the knee of the forward leg comes up. Most trips and falls occur when the rear leg is dragged after it pushes off to start the jump. Therefore, as you push off on the jump concentrate on lifting the rear foot up off the ice by raising the knee of the rear leg. Try to get the rear knee as high as the knee of the front leg. The upper body comes erect for the jump action and then leans forward again as the landing is made.

When you land, make sure the leg on which you land (usually the leg that was forward when the jump was made) is well bent at the knee. This is the secret of keeping your balance. Though you usually land on the leg that was forward when the jump was made, there are times when you land on the same leg from which you jumped, or with both legs together. Remember to keep those knees well bent. The technique of being able to hurdle or jump over an obstacle quickly and safely is something players should learn and all coaches should teach. Those knowing the technique will avoid many injuries (to themselves, opponents, or teammates) and have another addition to manoeuvrability.

The use of drills to develop this technique is especially recommended because the average player does not hurdle or jump enough during regular play to develop high level skill. Besides this, hurdle drills will develop all-round agility, balance, co-ordination, and leg and foot strength.

The hurdle. The best way to build a hurdle is to have pairs of pylons of different heights. With pairs the same height, place a stick on top of the pylons.

Hurdle racing. For hurdle racing set the first hurdle forty-five feet from the starting line, and the rest thirty feet apart. Use as many as you can work in on your ice surface so that there is at least forty-five feet from the last hurdle to the end boards. The players start at a signal, go down the hurdle course, touch the end boards and come back down, finishing on the spot from which they started. Emphasize the competitive angle in this drill by using lanes of hurdles or time trials over one lane.

The type of hurdling should be varied between the three styles (take off and land on opposite legs; take off and land same leg; take off and land both legs). It is important that this variation is emphasized because, during scrimmage or a game, it is frequently impossible to get set for any particular type of jump. Therefore, be adept at all variations.

The drill can be done with or without a puck. If a puck is used the player pushes it under the hurdle, takes the jump, and then picks up the puck on the other side. But start the drill at the lowest height and work it up as skill increases. In any contests make it a rule that only one hurdle can be knocked over during a race. More than one down disqualifies the player.

Stationary high jumping. This drill is designed to develop the foot and leg strength necessary to hurdle or jump effectively while skating. The player stands with his feet comfortably apart. Then, he bends his knees deeply and jumps straight up as high as he can, trying to lift his knees up to his chest, actually making contact. When he lands, he does so with well bent knees. A variation is to do the jump off one leg, landing on the same leg and also landing on the other leg. Half a dozen all-out jumps with each style (eighteen in all) will provide a good workout.

These drills are a real challenge to the player's strength, balance, and skating ability. Done with enthusiasm they can do a very effective job of developing leg strength, general agility and co-ordination.

Agility skating survey. To further test the efficiency of the drills listed in this book and in order to discover and tabulate the factors involved in agility skating, research has shown us a number of things. A large group of players, including all body type classifications, different ages and degrees of experience were used in our testing. This group included many selected athletes in controlled conditions while others were gathered through general observation and by thorough reports sent in from coaches and players all over Canada who tried many tests of the same type used in the survey.

In recruiting for the tests, special attention was paid to selecting both star players and those very low in efficiency. This was done to find out how ability in agility skating correlated with all-round ability. We also wanted to find out just how much value special drills could be in developing players not blessed with natural co-ordination or who had not had proper opportunity or association with skilful players.

After all the group had been thoroughly tested it was found that the star players had the highest rating, even though most of them had never done any of the drills before. As the drills were practised, an even higher level of efficiency was quickly developed. As efficiency at the drills was increased, a further increase in actual playing ability was apparent. The players report a greater confidence (which enabled them to try many new manoeuvres, turn at sharper angles, etc.), a feeling of greater power and balance in their skating, and an instinctive inclination to use the manoeuvres they had been practising.

After several weeks of practice, many of the star players had improved their times over 50 yards by as much as .4 seconds – actually a very significant increase. The greatest improvement was noted in quick break ability. Players who had taken 1.9 seconds to travel the first 10 yards were able to cut their times to 1.7 seconds. Several succeeded in cutting their times to 1.6 seconds. Players who had formerly had difficulty in shifting to one or other side developed the technique as their skill at crossing over or swinging around to that side improved. Marked improvements were also shown in the times for skating 50 yards to a stop and return, sometimes as much as .6 seconds.

When a one-legged swing around was used instead of a stop and return, there was an improvement in time of as much as 1.1 seconds. Players who could skate the course .6 seconds faster when either stopping or swinging around to a particular side were able to cut this difference by .4 seconds after emphasis had been placed on practising to the weak side. Players who could skate a half-circle (crossing over) .8 seconds faster to one side than to the other reduced the difference by as much as .7 seconds. (Some of these star players were actually showing a time loss of 1.2 seconds when not skating to their favourite side.) Players who previously took 7.8 seconds to cover a 50 yard course with pivots every 10 yards showed an improvement of as much as 1.1 seconds after practising. Puck-carrying during drills at first increased times by up to .3 seconds over 50 yards, but this differential was also greatly reduced by practising.

The manoeuvres found most difficult by the star players were, in order, crossing over to weak side; swing around to weak side; skate, pivot, skate; zig-zag; hurdling; pivoting; and the slide glide.

The ability to learn the slide glide was surprising to those conducting the tests. The reason, it was decided was that this was one of the tests given later in the survey after a lot of agility and confidence had been developed. Though some of the recruited players started off viewing the idea rather dismally (they saw no value to it, and thought that just playing was the best way to improve) everyone ended up completely "sold."

Those with especially well developed lower leg and ankle muscles, knee and hip flexibility, and the inclination to be long muscled earned high ratings. Lack of ankle strength and knee flexibility were the prime causes of many of the failures, especially in the difficult manoeuvres such as the zig-zag.

With the other groups (inexperienced, experienced but poor player ratings, fair to good player ratings) the same general results were demonstrated. However, greater degrees of improvement in actual playing ratings after practising were noticed especially in the "experienced but poor" group. Every single player, even those who showed very poor athletic ability, showed playing improvement after doing drills. Of those who did the tests just as well as the star players (there were quite a few of these in the inexperienced and good player groups) some showed an important rise in the playing efficiency ratings. The young groups (twelve, thirteen, fourteen, and fifteen) learned more quickly than any of the others.

Of those who came up with the best ratings, nearly all reported a lot of extra skating when they were kids (tag, figure skating, etc.). The inexperienced players used a greater number of manoeuvres in their actual play than did any other group. This, of course, was due to the fact that they had not developed any favourite manoeuvre. Those who had plenty of experience had more difficulty making the transition from the drills to their actual play. The habits formed by the experienced players were hard to break down and they kept reverting to their old ways.

However, as practices continued, more and more transitions were made. It was apparent, however, that the younger a player starts the drills, the easier it is for him to learn them and use them in actual play. Another interesting fact uncovered was that many of the players showed an improvement in stickhandling, shooting, checking, and especially body checking and guarding opponents. This was apparently due to the general increase in balance and co-ordination due to the drills. It is reasonable to assume that when a player's skating balance and agility improves he is better "set" to perform other movements from a skating stance. Still another interesting point was that difficulty in doing any of the manoeuvres at first seemed to show no indication of what skill level could finally he reached. Many who had a very difficult time doing a certain drill ended up with greater skill than some who took to the idea at first like a coach takes to a hard back-checker. The slow learners often ended up better than the fast learner. This, of course, is a common experience in any skill endeavour.

BACKWARD SKATING

The skill level reached by many backward skaters is far from the level that could be achieved if more time were spent on it. This is why so many coaches find it difficult to find good backward skating defencemen. Skating backward should be practised by all players of a team but especially defencemen. A good backward skater who has good agility and mobility will be able to defend against most puck carriers. Most professional defencemen can start backward skating from the opposition blue line without pivoting to skate forward then pivoting to skate backward again to defend against an attacker. This is because they have developed the ability to start their backward skating very quickly.

In its simplest form, skating backward is a series of backward semi-circle cuts in the ice. If you practise this on freshly flooded ice, you will see that the skate cut in the ice is arc shaped and is referred to as a backward "C" cut or "C" push.

Balance. Balance and posture are the first requirements for a sound foundation to develop backward skating. You should start from a stationary position and build from there. Keep the knees well bent with your shoulders held back while maintaining a forward, upright position from the waist up and with a straight back.

Many players lean too far forward, putting their weight on their toes thus causing an imbalance and a tendency to fall flat on their face. While the weight should be on the front of the blade, the entire blade of the skate should be on the ice. If you are rocking forward on your toes, your weight will shift too much to the front of the skate blade forcing the back of the blade off the ice and subsequently losing your balance.

Another weakness for backward skating is movement of the hips from side to side in a "wiggling" motion, rather than keeping the hips square and using strong leg action to develop speed and direction.

Backward stride. The backward stride is a series of backward "C" pushes by alternating legs to build up speed.

To start the backward stride, your weight must be evenly balanced with your skates hip width apart. Your gliding leg must glide straight backward since the gliding foot will determine which direction you will be travelling. Your thrusting foot is used to push the inside edge into the ice while creating the "C" cut. Turn the heel of your thrusting skate outward to a 45 degree angle, and, using your inside edge, push the skate into a "C" formation in the ice by using a powerful snap action of the leg. After completing the "C" cut, your thrusting leg should come back to its original position. Practise with the left (or right) foot making a number of "C" cuts with the same leg. Then practise the other leg. Once a comfort level is established, practise the "C" cut with each leg in sequence. Remember to keep your glide skate straight for direction purposes.

To achieve maximum power and speed, try to develop the thrusting leg extension with each stride. Speed will improve with strong leg action and the recovery time from finishing your extension to get it back to the start of the next "C" push.

Backward cross over. From a starting position, push off the inside edge of the right skate, using full extension, while forming a "C" cut in the ice. After finishing the "C" cut with the right skate, bring the skate back across and in front of the left skate. As the right skate comes back in front, drive the outside edge of the left skate underneath and across, behind the heel of the right skate. It is important to push the left skate under to full extension, using the outside edge. At completion of the left skate extension, push out with the right skate using the inside edge, as previously done, and bring the left skate back to its original position. The power is developed by the pushing under of the inside leg driving off the outside edge of the skate. Pushing on the inside edge of the outside leg provides backward thrust; outside edge thrusts provide backward and lateral acceleration.

Remember to keep the shoulders level and maintain a good balance by not leaning forward too much.

A good way to work on backward cross overs is to skate a figure eight around the face-off circles. This will force you to use all four edges in both directions.

In summary, backward cross overs are accomplished by a series of "C" pushes with the inside skate edge and "pull-widers" with the outside edge.

Agility backward skating. Ordinary backward skating is important, but to be a good hockey player (especially a defenceman) you must be able to manoeuvre while skating backwards. The following drills will develop manoeuvrability as well as backward skating. You can develop as much agility as you give time to the drills. These drills will assist your general agility, balance, shift, and co-ordination which in turn will aid your skating in general.

To practise quick breaking in skating backwards, use the same drills as listed for forward skating quick break development. However, do these drills skating backwards. To start from a stationary position place feet comfortably apart and parallel. Backward quick break drills are tough to do and provide lots of fun. Also use the same drills given for forward skating stop and start practice. However, a different technique is used in stopping.

Backward stops. There are two ways to stop when skating backwards. You can use the backward snow-plow and the backward side stop.

The backward snow-plow. To perform this stop, the toes of the skates are turned outwards, the heels turned in, and insides of the knees are brought toward each other in a knock-kneed action. This brings the centre of gravity to the inside edges of your skates which are pushed hard into the ice. Lean the body forward as you press down on the balls of your feet.

Side stop. Turn your skates and body quickly to either side. Lean well in and press the skates sideways into the ice. The knees should be well bent at the start of the action.

You can also use a one foot stop by placing all the weight on one leg, turning the toe of the skate sideways, pointing it out to the side, and pushing hard into the ice. Then, as you stop, you can push off quickly for a forward stride.

Skill at stopping while skating backwards and then starting again, still going backwards, is a very important factor in backward skating manoeuvrability and should be practised frequently. Stopping and then breaking forward should also be given lots of work. Also emphasize the competitive angle in backward skating drills just as suggested for the forward skating section.

Stop and side glide. This is a very important manoeuvre which, when well learned, will help your defence play tremendously. It consists of a quick stop (preferably a snow-plow or a one foot stop) followed by a turn of the body to either side, and a quick long stride. For example, if you stop on your right leg in a one foot stop, you would drive off the right foot to the left and take a long stride with your left leg at a right angle to the direction you were skating. As you stop, drive off, and stroke to the side, your body is turned in the same direction by a quick twist of the hips. As you stride to the side, the knee of the leg going out in the stride should be well bent. This manoeuvre will enable you to move across to check or go with a puck carrier trying to fake or skate past you. Emphasis should be placed on trying to do the drill equally well to either side, something few players can do.

Blue line glide. In this, the players are lined up halfway between the centre red line and the blue line. At a signal they skate backwards as quickly as possible to the blue line. When they reach the blue line they stop and drive off in a glide along the blue line toward the side of the rink. The whole ice surface can be used in this drill with the team divided into two or three groups. The objective should be to make the side turn and stride as close to a right angle as possible. The players should go to the left one time, and to the right the next. It should be done slowly at first, increasing the speed as skill develops.

The stop, glide alternate. In this drill the players start, for example, at the goal line, and at a signal begin skating backwards down the ice. At another signal they stop and side glide. Then at another signal they stop and skate backwards again. They continue until a further signal when they stop and side glide to the other side. The whole team, divided into three or four groups of lines and defencemen can do this drill together. If preferred, it can be done as a race or on a time trial basis.

The distance glide. In this drill the player skates backwards across the ice from one side of the rink to the other. Then, just before he reaches the side, he stops and glides, seeing how far he can go to the side on the one stride. For example, if he pushes off to the left side by a thrust off the right foot, left foot going out in the side glide, he stays on his left foot, right foot off the ice, until he loses momentum. This teaches the player really to push off on the driving foot at the start of the stride. To be competitive, measure the distance covered by each man.

Stop and skate. This refers to the manoeuvre in which the player stops quickly, turns, and then skates quickly to either side. It is used, for example, when the defenceman has to stop and move quickly some distance to cover an opposing player who has come down the ice close to the boards and has taken a long wide pass from the puck carrier, whom the defenceman had been lining up. It is also used when the puck carrier (especially if a fast skater) suddenly tries to burst out and go wide around the defence. The idea is to stop, turn, and then quick-break with a series of short, quick, hard, driving strides to the side. The principle of the forward quick-break should be used after the stop has been made. The secret of doing this move well is to stop quickly and then, getting lots of push-off from the foot furthest from the direction you turn to (the right foot if going to the left). Concentrate on getting a strong drive in that first push-off.

Variations. Use the same type of drill as explained in the stop and slide glide and the stop, glide alternate. Instead of stopping and going off in one long glide, stop and skate. A variation is to skate backwards, stop, turn, and skate along the line to the opposite side of the rink. Stop, skate backwards to the next line, stop, and go across the rink to the other side, alternating as you hit each blue line. The drill can be made a competition by timing the players or by starting one player at one goal line, another at the opposite end, and seeing who gets down the ice first. A mass drill can also be organized by lining up the players on one side of the rink and sending them off at one-second intervals.

Stop and side glide. This refers to the action when the defenceman goes to the side in a slide glide to check a man, only to see his opponent stop and shift back to the inside again. Learning to do the stop and side glide will help you to make this recovery manoeuvre but the actual two-way move must be practised for top level efficiency to be developed. A player who learns this manoeuvre will be a tough one for any puck carrier to beat.

Stop, side glide, and return. This is the same as the stop and slide glide drill, but the players, after going a few feet in the first side glide, stop, and glide back to the spot they started from. To make a quick recovery stop and return glide, the skate going out in the first side glide is quickly turned sideways and a hard thrust made into the ice. If the thrust is made hard and long enough, it will not only stop you but drive you back on the return glide. As the foot is turned and driven into the ice, the body is twisted quickly with a hard twist at the hips (keeping the knee of the leg that makes the sideways stroke well bent is important). Ankle, foot, and knee strength and flexibility are prime needs. Practising this will help develop them. See Training chapter for special exercises.

Variation for stop, glide, alternate. This is a variation in which the player skates backwards, stops, slide glides, and then stops and comes back before he continues with his backward skating.

Back pivot. Pivoting from a backward skating position is at first more difficult than from the front position but when practised, comes easily. The technique, as far as principle is concerned, is the same as for the front pivot previously described. The player takes a stride backwards, and then, placing the weight on the rear foot, swings his body around with a quick twist of the hips as he pivots on his skate. The other leg is swung around quickly with the knee held high, in the same direction as the body is turned. You keep your balance by leaning the upper body well into the centre of the pivot. For example, if you pivot on the left foot, you lean the upper body well in to the left.

Starting pivot. This drill will teach even the most timid skater the technique and will give him confidence to try it while actually moving.

The player stands with his feet comfortably apart, knees bent. Then he may move his left foot back about twelve inches. As he moves it back, he turns his body quickly to the left with a snap of the hips, swings his right leg around, knee high and well bent, in a complete circle so that when he completes the pivot his feet are in the same position they were at the start, only a little further back from where he stood originally. Then, the player pivots to the right. This drill can be done by the whole team on whistle signals.

Glide pivot. This is the next progression to learn the move. The player skates backward a few feet and then glides. After he has glided a few more feet, he goes into the pivot. He then skates again, glides, and does another pivot, this time the opposite way. The coach signals to start the skating for the glide, the pivot, etc.

Skate and pivot. This is the same drill as the glide pivot only the player skates and pivots. This should be started slowly with the speed gradually increased as the skill and confidence of the player also increases. The competition angle can easily be brought in with the drill done as a race, the coach signalling for the pivot at suitable intervals.

Back cross over. The action here is the same as crossing over in forward skating, but instead of bringing over the outside foot (the right if crossing over to the left) as you would in a forward skating cross over, bring the inside leg over in front of the outside leg. For example, if you were crossing over backwards to the left, you would keep bringing the right foot over in front of the left, pushing off in a twisting action toward the direction you are turning, the knees well bent, and the upper body well into the inside (left if going toward the left).

To work on technique, use the same drills as given for forward cross-over skating, but do it backwards. The figure eight is a real test of backward skating skill.

Hip thrust check. This manoeuvre is one of the fundamentals of good hip checking and should be given lots of attention by those anxious to develop high level defensive skill of the rugged type. The manoeuvre is fundamentally the same as the side glide, but done backwards.

The player places all his weight on the leg farthest from the direction he wishes to go (the left if going to the right), and pushes off hard at right angles to the right side. As he pushes off, he swings his hips to the right and places his right foot on the ice in a long backward and sideways glide. The best time to do it is when the weight goes on the left foot, after a push off by the right foot during the backward skating action. Practise this to both sides.

In many respects the action is first a strong, fast backward stride with the usual hip sway. However, you keep going into a sharp turn by not swinging the hips back again as in ordinary backward skating. It is a sharp-angled turn with a very hard thrust off the foot farthest from the direction you wish to go and a long backward stride.

After pushing off, the pushing foot is brought up to the other foot. This moves your buttocks and hips into any player trying to go around you or through the centre between you and a defence partner.

Use the same type of drills as given for the stop and side glide but go backward to either side instead of gliding forward. If you have difficulty doing it when skating quickly backwards, practise doing it from a backward glide. Also practise it from a stationary position, twisting and driving off backwards to the side in an explosive action. When doing this, see how far you can go after one hard turn and push off. Your distance depends on your push-off.

Back cross over and go. This is another backward skating agility move that every player should learn. It is used to turn and catch, or to keep on the inside of an opponent who is going past on the outside, or when chasing the puck into the corner. The player, if skating backwards at the time, shifts his weight quickly to the foot closest to the direction he wants to go, swings his hips around quickly in the same direction, leans well forward from the waist, and brings one leg well over in front of the other leg. The distance the leg is brought across depends upon the angle the player wishes to make. The farther back the player wants to go, perhaps toward the corner from the blue line, the farther the leg comes over. As the leg comes across, it moves out in a stride with the knee well bent and the other foot, on which your weight is placed, thrusts hard to get you going. Though a simple move, few players do it with good balance and speed. Most are slow in making the cross over and quick break. Watch a game and see how many players fall when trying it.

Glide, cross over, and go. In this drill the defence pairs (or any two players) start by the centre red line. At a signal, they skate hard backwards, keeping parallel. When they are about halfway to the blue line they glide. As they get to the blue line, they cross over and skate to the side and rear. The changes from skating to glide and to cross over can be controlled by the coach with signals. Players should skate to definite points at different angles.

Variation on glide, cross over, and go. This is the same as the preceding drill except the player does not glide. To develop quick break skill from this position, do it from a stationary stance. Start with feet comfortably apart, facing down the ice. At a signal, you then whip around and go back at an angle, using the spin and thrust on the outside leg, and the cross over with the other. As you turn, see how many short, hard strides you can take.

Back turn glide. This move is the backward version of a forward turn glide.

GENERAL SKATING SUMMARY

Hockey is a game of special drills and practices. However, there is no reason why hockey cannot learn from the techniques used by coaches involved in other sports to improve the game.

There are probably many other moves dependent on some special technique or body build that players develop unconsciously. However, the player who learns all of the agility skating manoeuvres contained in this book will make his presence felt in any class of hockey. He will have skills that will make it possible for him to excel either on offence or defence. He will also develop an all-round balance, agility, and coordination that will enable him to react effectively in numerous situations. Some players will find certain moves easy but being content with two or three is a mistake.

In conclusion, it seems wise to re-emphasize the great importance of skating. The main danger to the average player or coach is that because skating is the number one fundamental, it is taken for granted, and nothing much done about it. Everyone knows how important it is but few actually do anything about emphasizing it. Skating makes the hockey player. With it, there are many possibilities. Without it, there are limited possibilities.

Puck Control

If a player is to score goals or set up scoring plays for his teammates he must be skilful at getting the puck out of his own end, down the ice, and into the scoring zone. The shift from defensive to offensive play demands expert puck control skills, and players who have them are worth their weight in gold. However, as in skating, goal scoring, or any other phase of the game, few players have developed puckhandling skills to the degree of which they are capable.

In the average game, players do not have very many chances to perform a particular puckhandling move. Moreover, the average player during an actual game hesitates to try a new move that he has not got down-pat in case he messes up an opportunity. He is under too much pressure to use anything but moves he already knows. Unless he learns new moves through special practice he goes on from game to game, from season to season, using the same techniques, never developing additional skills.

The technique of puck-carrying lends itself to detailed analysis just as do skating and goal scoring. Such an analysis can provide players and coaches with a guide whereby the moves and manoeuvres can be taught and practised. The player, of course, will always give each play his own particular style and variations, and will probably develop new ones.

In compiling the list of moves given in this chapter, hundreds of hockey players were carefully observed over long periods of time, questions were asked regarding how particular manoeuvres should be performed (most could not explain their own technique), tapes were recorded and analyzed, and tests were made to see if the moves that were filmed could be taught. None was found that could not be taught.

Puck manipulation. This particular skill, often referred to as stick-handling, was at one time a skill quite a few players had developed to a high level. However, in recent years the stickhandling expert is not seen so frequently, although there still are many who can manipulate the puck in bewildering patterns.

There are several reasons why stickhandling has become less common. In today's game, the forward pass allows greater freedom and enables the player to by-pass checkers with a pass to a teammate in situations that once would have forced him to stickhandle out of trouble. For example, when a player is checked as he is coming out of his defence zone, perhaps close to his own goal, he can pass to a teammate, and then accept a return pass as he breaks past the checker (give and go). This would not have been possible before the forward pass was permitted.

With the forward pass providing such an extremely fast way to get the puck down the ice the emphasis has been on fast skating breaks with the puck carrier always passing up to the man in front. In the 1930s, the only way to get the puck into the goal scoring zone was to carry it in or pass laterally. Now the trend is to shoot it in, and then follow up, regain possession, and pass the puck around until a man gets into the clear.

Now that minor hockey is more organized with thousands of teams playing in hundreds of leagues, the old game of shinny with perhaps as many as twenty or thirty players on each team, and perhaps two games going at once, has practically disappeared. Maybe this is a step in the right direction. But the fact remains that the modern youngster, playing in organized six-player-to-a-side games, does not learn the stickhandling skills he used in the old "shinny" games. In many of these games, it was a stickhandling feat to get the puck past your own players and those playing in another game, to say nothing of carrying it past the opposition.

Even though there are not as many wizard stickhandlers around as there used to be, and even though there may not be as great a demand for stickhandling prowess in today's game, observers have noticed that the players with stickhandling skill are usually stand-outs. No matter how the rules are changed, it will still more than pay the player or the coach to emphasize the development of stickhandling skill. If this is combined with the other puck-carrying moves, good passing, and skating, the player will soon find professional scouts noticing his skills.

In the stickhandling action there are three basic patterns: the side to side, the diagonal, and the back to front. The side to side pattern is the most commonly used. There are many times when the puck must be manipulated diagonally, and occasionally it is necessary to move the puck back to front. A player should practise all of these patterns while stationary and moving. A basic repertoire of stickhandling skills will give the dexterity to control the puck in any pattern required to carry it past an opponent.

Side to side. The player moves the puck from side to side in front of him in a path that varies in width from three to four inches to as wide as he can reach with his stick and arms. The puck is moved to one side, then the stick is lifted over and in front of the puck, and then smoothly moved back again. When lifting the stick at the end of the sweep, let the puck move a little ahead of the blade so that it is not flipped by the stick as it is lifted. Often, a player needs only to move the puck a few inches to avoid a check, sometimes he must move it as wide as possible.

The player who moves it only as far as is needed to avoid a stick or some other obstacle has an advantage because any unnecessary movement slows up his forward speed and makes it more likely that he will lose control of the puck. The puck should be feathered back and forth with a light, smooth touch in a series of short or long sweeps. Do not bang or bat the puck because this will cause it to roll and jump around. This is the most common of all stickhandling faults.

Another common fault is letting the blade of the stick get into a position that will cause the puck to roll off. Such incorrect positions are: letting the under edge slant toward the puck; letting the top edge move too much over the puck; letting the toe of the blade point out a little to the side instead of straight ahead or slightly inward. If the bottom edge is slanting toward the puck the result will be a jumping or rolling puck. If the upper part of the blade is turned over toward the puck too much, the pressure on the top edge of the puck will also cause it to roll. When the toe of the blade does not face dead forward or slightly in toward the puck it may slide off the toe in front instead of coming right back across to the other side. To avoid these stickhandling errors the player should keep his elbows well out from his sides, his arms and shoulders should be as relaxed as possible (letting the wrists do the work), and he should always move his hands with the puck so that they are directly above and behind it. If his elbows are in close to his body, and his arms and shoulders are stiff, especially at the elbows, he will not be able to move his hands (and thus the shaft of the stick) from side to side with the puck. Moving the hands this way is more important as the width of the side to side path is increased. When this width becomes great, the player will help keep his hands in position behind the puck by moving his upper body to the side with the action of the stick.

The hands and wrists should be kept as loose and easy on the stick as possible with only as much strength used as needed to hold the stick. This will give you a soft "touch" and a greater control. Always keep in mind that relaxed muscles can move more quickly and will respond to your mental commands with more efficiency. The hands should be as high on the stick as possible with the hands as close together as the player finds comfortable. The more comfortable the hands, the greater is the control of the stick.

The puck should be cradled in a spot halfway between the heel and toe of the blade. The blade of the stick must always be kept at right angles to the direction in which the puck is being moved. In very wide patterns the toe of the blade should be turned in a little toward the puck so that it will not roll off the end of the blade. Keeping the elbows well out to the sides, especially the one on the side to which the puck is being moved, and avoiding any turning of the hands on the stick shaft will keep the blade in proper position.

To get the widest possible side to side path, the player can increase the distance he can move the puck sideways by releasing the lower hand (left if moving to the right) and using only the top hand on the stick. Quite a few players can do this to one side (the right if right-handed) but few can do it equally well to both sides. As soon as the puck is started back the lower hand is placed on the stick again. Moving the puck to one side, releasing the lower hand, bringing the stick back, and then doing the same to the other side, will give the player the widest possible path.

Anyone who has trouble controlling the puck when stickhandling quickly or in a wide path should check the above points carefully. A failure to observe any one of these fundamentals can cause loss of control. There is no need to guess why you cannot control the puck at certain times. You find out by checking your technique.

Diagonal. Many of the rules listed for the side to side pattern apply also in the performance of this pattern. However, there are a few differences.

The shoulders turn so that they are as square as possible to the path of the puck while it is moved back and forth. For example, if the puck is being moved from a spot just outside the left foot to a spot well out in front and to the side of the right foot by a left-handed player, the shoulders will have to be twist around to the left.

The grip of the lower hand changes to a finger grip with the shaft being held mainly by the thumb and index finger. The top arm is carried well out with the elbow pointing in the direction of the far end of the path in which the puck is being moved back and forth. By loosening the hard grip of the lower hand to a finger grip, it is possible to bring the stick in close and to the side, for example, to the left foot if the player is left-handed. By taking the lower hand off the shaft of the stick and controlling the stick with just the top hand, you can move the puck farther out in front in a diagonal path.

Back to front. This is the most difficult path on which to move the puck back and forth, but regular practice will enable the player to develop a surprising amount of control. The grip by the low hand must only be a thumb and index finger grip and the arm must be close to the front of the body. The other arm is held well out in front of the body with the elbow high. The stick is turned so that the blade faces from side to side (toe of blade to the left, heel to the right of a left-handed player). A very wide path on which to move the puck back and forth is not possible because of the cramped arm position. However, it can be increased by letting the lower hand go on the forward movement with the stick controlled by the top hand until the shaft is brought back close enough again for the low hand to resume the grip. The higher lie the stick has, the easier it is for the player to stickhandle back and forth.

Although the side to side, diagonal, and back and forth are the basic patterns, there are several others that should be practised.

Circular. This involves bringing the puck from one side to the other in a half circle in front of you. It should be practised with the top hand only on the stick and with both hands. The danger point during the path of the puck is midway in the half circle, when the puck is directly out in front of the player. If the right technique is not followed, the puck can very easily slide off the toe of the blade. As the puck is brought around in the half circle, the hands should turn over in the direction the puck is being moved. This will turn the toe of the blade faster than the puck and will slant the blade over the puck to keep it under control.

Back and forth at the side. This pattern is performed by bringing the puck to one side of the body, turning the shoulders well to that side, and then moving the puck back and forth. The lower hand and arm should be close to the side, elbow well bent, pointing behind, and the other arm should be well away from the body with the elbow up and pointing ahead.

Protected diagonal. In doing this pattern the player moves the blade to one side and as far back as possible, turns his upper body around in the same direction, and moves the puck back and forth in a diagonal path (if left-handed, from a position close to the heels to a spot as far from the left side of the leg as possible). The player often uses such a pattern when trying to keep his body between the puck and a checker.

STICKHANDLING DRILLS

To develop skill at moving the puck back and forth in the various patterns and paths the player must do them over and over again until his control becomes perfect. Once he can move the puck through all the various patterns suggested, at full speed and with full control, he will find his skill at manipulating the puck during games will have improved tremendously.

Shadow stickhandling (stationary). This drill is based on the same principle as shadow boxing during which the boxer moves around the ring going through all the many punches and combinations, slips, and footwork manoeuvres in his repertoire, as he punches an imaginary opponent. The shadow stickhandling bout consists of a given number of each pattern to be done in correct sequence as quickly as possible. However, until the player gets the knack and develops some skill, it should be done slowly. The player stands with his feet comfortably apart, knees well bent, and his head up. Then, at a signal, he goes through the drill as follows.

The player begins with a side to side, making two short movements, two medium, and two as wide as possible with only one hand controlling the stick on either side. Then he executes a diagonal with four moves on one side and then four moves on the other. It is then followed by a back and forth, four moves in all, and four moves of a back and forth at the side. He then does a protected diagonal, making four moves to either side. Finally, he finishes with a circular, four with two hands, and four with one hand. The drill is then repeated.

The sequence can be changed around as desired from day to day as can the number of moves made with each pattern. It is wise to change around the sequence and number of moves regularly so that the assignment never gets too easy. This drill is a real challenge to the player who enjoys his puck control and it offers him fun and interesting variety as well as invaluable training.

In using the competitive angle, the players should compete against time standards, seeing who can finish the drill first without a mistake, or a group of players should start at the same time to see who finishes first. Any player losing control of the puck, or using a pattern in the wrong sequence, is disqualified immediately. The individual can do the drill on any suitable sheet of ice by himself against time or in competition with one or two others. It can be done inside on any highly polished floor or on a plastic practice sheet.

Once the drill can be done fairly well with the player watching the puck he should do it with his head up, eyes always straight ahead. Doing it blindfold is a tough assignment, but it can be done!

Shadow stickhandling (moving). This is the same drill as the stationary exercise, only done with the player skating back and forth within an assigned area, for example, from the blue line to the red line. The player must continue to skate at all times either backwards or forwards. As soon as skill has been developed, he should do the drills with his eyes off the puck.

Individual pattern drill. This drill is actually a series of drills during which the players concentrate on just one pattern. These should be performed in a stationary position, while skating slowly, then while skating at full speed. When the stationary position is used, the player should be given a time limit, for example, thirty seconds. The idea is to see how many moves can be made within this time. The same principle should be used when the drill is done with a player skating slowly.

When the drill is done with the player skating at full speed, the player should skate a given distance (for example, from blue line to blue line) as quickly as he can, and at the same time work in a definite number of moves in an assigned pattern. For example, if the short path side to side pattern was assigned he would have to make about fifty moves of the puck from side to side between the blue lines.

Skating drills with puck. Any suitable drill given in the section on agility skating can be used, for example, the figure eight. Such a drill can be done in two ways, carrying the puck with as little motion as possible, or using any of the patterns listed (such as the side to side) as the skating drill is done. These drills teach the player to co-ordinate his puck control with his skating manoeuvres.

When doing any of these drills, the player should keep his head up, eyes in front so that he develops skill at controlling the puck by feel instead of by sight. At first this will be difficult but, as the player perseveres, it will get easier.

One hand. Puckhandling in this drill, the player goes through the various patterns previously described. However, he does them with only one hand on the stick. Besides developing dexterity and puck control, these drills will also develop hand, wrist, and forearm strength. An excellent variation is one hand scrimmage, during which all puck-carrying must be done with one hand. In all drills the player uses one hand for a while and then uses the other for an equal length of time.

Obstacle course. This drill is one of the very best ways to develop top level puck control in a player. It also provides an interesting contest angle and will be very popular with the players. The equipment can be made quite easily by anyone and used on any available sheet of ice, or on an indoor practice area.

The equipment needed for the control course is a thirty-foot long obstacle made of ten-foot lengths of wood. This obstacle can be made by following the diagram below. The width should be three to four inches and each guard part and general space should be six inches. The vertical height should be between three and four inches. The obstacle is easily made by getting three pieces of four by six (each ten feet long), sawing and chiselling out the open spaces needed. Or you can get the blocks of

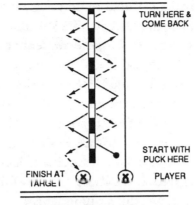

TURN HERE &
COME BACK

START WITH
PUCK HERE

FINISH AT
TARGET

PLAYER

CONTROL COURSE DIAGRAM OF OBSTACLE

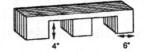

4"   6"

CONTROL COURSE OBSTACLE

wood needed for the guards and nail them to a ten-foot piece of lumber four to six inches wide. The obstacle should then be placed at the edge of the red line (or any line or mark on the ice).

The puck is placed twelve inches out to the right side of the first open space, and the player stands behind it with his stick beside the puck ready to start. At a signal, start skating down beside the obstacle stick-handling the puck in and out of the open spaces as shown by the lines on the diagram. After the last hole, bring the puck to the red line in front of the obstacle, turn around, and come back through the obstacle. After the last hole on the way back, move the puck at the finish target (as shown on the diagram). The finish target can be any object the size of a small tin can. If the target is missed, retrieve the puck and hit the target before being considered officially through. Check the time it takes each player to go up and down the course. The winner is the player who records the fastest time. The player must get the puck through each hole on his way up and down the course. If he misses, he keeps trying until he succeeds.

An excellent variation is to have the player skate or glide down and up the obstacle, straddling it, one leg on one side and the other leg on the opposite side.

Small area shinny. This drill is based on the theory discussed at the start of the chapter. Playing hockey on a small ice surface with a large number of players taking part, will, as a matter of course, develop puck-handling and puck-carrying skills.

Divide the team into two squads (ten to a side is not too many) and then have a game of shinny inside a small area, for example, between the blue line and the centre red line. The goal should be in the centre of the area against the sideboards with the teams trying to manoeuvre the puck across the ice. The puck must be stickhandled into the goal; shooting is not allowed. This drill can also be a lot of fun and therefore provides a way to add variety to the training schedule.

Blindfold test. This drill is designed to develop the player's skill in handling the puck by feel. The player is blindfolded and then told to keep skating, stickhandling the puck in any way he desires, as long as he keeps it moving. The idea is to see which player can keep control of the puck for the longest period of time.

Keep it going. This is an ideal drill that will do a good job developing puck control and muscles used in the stickhandling action. The idea is, while standing stationary, to start a pattern and to see how long it can be kept going at high speed without a loss of puck control. For example, you start off with the widest possible side to side pattern and keep moving the puck back and forth as quickly as possible until either there is a loss of control or the hands and arms become too tired to continue. It should be done with the eyes looking straight ahead. It can also be done blindfolded. The competitive angle can be used by timing the players.

Turn and pattern. The player stands with his feet fairly close together and slowly turns, staying on the one spot, stickhandling a pattern as he turns. The player should turn completely around two or three times in one direction and then reverse the procedure. It should be done faster as skill is developed. This is a good co-ordination test and developer.

Keep away. This drill is based on the principle of shinny and is fun as well as being an efficient developer of a player's puckhandling skills.

The ice is separated into four areas: from the goal line to the blue line, from the blue line to the centre red line, and so on. Six players are stationed in each area. One player in each area is given the puck to start off. He tries to keep the puck as long as he can before it is taken away from him by one of the other players. The player who gets the puck then tries to keep it as long as he can. In other words, there are five players against one all trying to check the puck-handler. If there are not sufficient players to have four games, divide the players into two or three groups with perhaps seven on one, eight on the other.

The competitive angle can be worked in by calling a halt each time a player has been checked. Then give it to another man, with the time each man is able to hold it being recorded. In trying to avoid being checked by his five opponents, the puck carrier will find himself using every manoeuvre possible. As he does the drill regularly, he will find himself developing an agility in puck control and manoeuvrability that will surprise him.

The amount of control and dexterity developed in these drills will, of course, depend upon the interest, intelligence, and effort the player uses in his practising. Though many of the drills can and should be included by the coach as part of regular practice sessions, the player should augment this with individual practice sessions of his own. He will develop a basic puck control that will enable him to manipulate the puck to make any play.

Any deke or move usually involves the combined use of puckhandling, body deception, and skating agility. To develop this top level agility that will enable him to perform the many moves it is possible to use, the player must concentrate on practising the various manoeuvres and drills listed in the section on skating agility. Once he has done this, he will find it possible to use these manoeuvres to get past a checker. The agility skating moves as described in the first chapter, are most used in puck-carrying: scooting; zig-zag; the draw-away; pivot; lunge striding; turn glide; parallel zig-zag; Allen slide glide; change of pace; and hurdling.

BODY DECEPTION

Body deception refers to those body movements the puck carrier can make to deceive the checker into making the wrong move or getting the wrong impression regarding what move the puck carrier is going to use or in what direction he has decided to go. Included are such manoeuvres as shifting, body weaving, head faking, and shoulder dipping. The player who develops a good variety of convincing body deception moves and combines this with top level puck control and skating agility cannot help but become a puck-handler who will be a real problem to the best of checkers or defence pairs.

Body deception does not depend on any special talent inherited by the player. It can be developed by any player willing to work on it. There are some who will take to it and learn it easier than others because they have better co-ordination and flexibility. However, normal players can become skilful regardless of body type. Each player, after he learns the fundamentals of hockey deception will, of course, develop certain personal variations and style that will make his shift or weave a little different from those of any other player, though it will be fundamentally the same. The secret is to train the muscles of the body (primarily the upper body) so that they will answer to any direction from the mind. For example, if the player is skating down the ice, comes to a checker, and then thinks "I will shift to the left and go to the right," his body will react smoothly and efficiently if his muscles have been trained in the type of movement involved. If he has never performed the movement before, the response to his mental thought will not be very efficient. This is one reason why top level results can never be gained when a player just tries new moves in a game without first practising them.

Body deception drills. Here are a few drills that will develop the players' muscles and co-ordination to perform the basic movements involved in many of the body deception moves. Doing them will give a player the body control required.

Stationary shifting. The player stands with his feet fairly close together (about six inches apart), bends at the knees, and places his stick in front of him, blade on the ice beside the puck. Then he places all his weight on one leg (for example, on the right). Taking a short step to the left, he bends his body from the waist well over to the same side. As he steps and bends to the side, he slides the puck with him. Then, after a moment's hesitation in this position, he moves back to the original position. Then he makes the same move to the other side. He does this four times to either side. This is the single shift. Then he changes to the following double shift action.

He takes the short step to the side and leans his body in the same direction as he did in the first part of the drill. But after he hesitates there for a moment, he takes a step to the right and bends his upper body in the same direction. Then, after a momentary hesitation in this position, he moves back to the original position. This is done four times and then the player starts over with the single shift movement. Each section should be done at least four or five times. The drill must be done slowly at first and then as quickly as possible once the players gets the idea. The individual player can practise this drill, or it can be run as a team drill by the coach.

Once a high skill level has been developed, variations should be included. For example, the player should mix up the pattern, going to the right and back to the original position, then back to the right again instead of to the left. The sequence and speed should be scrambled in every conceivable way. Another variation is to add a twist of the body to the sideways bend. In other words, if going to the left, the player would take a step, bend, and twist to the left from the waist. When only the bend is used, the shoulders stay square to the front. When a twist is added, the shoulders turn (to the left, the right shoulder is brought around to the front).

Stationary body weaving. In this drill the player stands with his feet comfortably apart and then, without moving his feet, weaves his body from side to side from the waist. The upper body should go to each side as far as possible each time. The player should alternate, moving the puck with the upper body one time, and leaving it out in front with the blade of the stick beside it the next. At first, this drill should be done slowly and then the speed increased. The same variations as suggested for stationary shifting should be used.

Shoulder drop. The same starting position as given for the other drills is to be assumed. Then, the player begins the following side to side pattern. Keeping the rest of his body still, also the puck and stick, he leans his head to the left and at the same time drops his left shoulder down. He then returns to a straight ahead position. The action is repeated to the right. This is done four or five times. Then the head is moved from one side to the other with no return to the straight ahead position. The speed and sequence should be mixed as suggested for the other drills.

Stationary head turns. The same starting position is assumed as in the previous drills. Then the player turns his head as if he suddenly looked to that side to see someone calling him. At the same time he moves the puck over to the left. Then, after a brief hesitation, he moves his head and the puck back to the original position. The move is repeated to the other side. The drill should be done slowly at first with the speed being gradually increased as the player gets the idea.

These four drills should also be done with the player gliding and then skating. In this way he can progressively develop the technique of co-ordinating his body deception moves with his skating and puck control. Do them to both sides.

PUCK CONTROL MOVES

The following are the actual moves a puck carrier can use by combining his puck control, skating, and body deception skills. The moves listed are given definite names and can be used in many situations. The player, by his actions, develops the situation needed to perform the move successfully. Variations of these moves will be developed by the player according to the situation. Every player should learn each of these basic moves because he will then avoid being in the unenviable position of being checked time and time again because his opponents have him tabbed as only going one way in a fake or as always trying a change of pace.

Fake. The basic fake gets its name from the fact that the body is moved in one direction in order to convince the checker that the puck carrier is going that way, and is then shifted back to go a different way. The basic move is a fake to the left with a final move to the right or vice versa. However, there are many variations of this, such as faking to the left, starting back to the right, and then going left again. The more a player experiments and practises with the various possibilities, the more ways he will find to use them. The thing to do is to learn the basic fake to either side and then go to work on developing variations. The fake is one of the most effective of all puck-carrying tricks and is something every player should set out to learn and develop to the highest possible level.

The most common fault is faking only one way, for example, faking left and going right. The fake can be used from a gliding position or from a skating position. If it is used from the gliding position, it should be prefaced with a hard burst of speed and finished off with a strong quick break after the fake has developed an opening for the puck carrier.

A classic example of this fake would be as follows. The puck carrier approaches the checker straight on. As he gets close to the checker, the puck carrier takes a stride to the left side, bends his body well over in the same direction and moves the puck over at the same time. Then, from this direction, the puck carrier quickly moves back to the right side, going around the checker who has covered the first move by the puck carrier. To be most effective a puck carrier must go right through with his first move occasionally so that he will not develop a definite pattern to which the checkers will soon catch on.

The secrets of successful faking are timing the move properly, so as not to be either too soon or too late, making the fake convincingly, and perhaps most important, taking advantage of the fake by putting on added speed at the end of the move.

If the fake is started too soon, the checker will have time to recover and cover the final movement. If it is started too late, the puck carrier will be so close to the checker that, when he moves back, he may well collide with him or run into a body check. The exact time to fake is difficult to determine as it depends upon the speed the puck carrier is travelling and whether or not the checker is stationary, moving toward the puck carrier, or backing up. Research shows however, that, as a general rule, the fake should start about four to five feet away from the checker. This is a point, however, that the puck carrier should figure out for himself by experimenting. If he analyses his play intelligently, he will soon find out for himself when he should fake a little later or a little sooner against certain types of players. The hardest type of man to beat with a fake is a checker backing up in front of the puck carrier. Let us examine some of the basic variations of the fake.

Fake to one side, then start back, but at the half way mark, fake back again to the same side. Such a fake should be started early in order to let the checker see you start back so that he will be convinced that this is your final move.

Fake to one side, fake right back to the other, and then go to the original side again. This fake should also start early.

Skate right at the player until a collision seems likely. Then fake to one side just before contact is about to take place. This is actually a half fake.

In performing these variations, the player must be sure to shift wide.

Other variations are "narrow and wide" fakes in which the width of the fake is varied according to the situation. For example, if you find that a checker is easily fooled, there is no need to make a very wide fake. Some coaches feel that all puck carrying plays should be made while travelling at top speed and there is no doubt that the player should learn to make them as well as possible under such conditions. However, there is much to be said for the fake made from a glide position or at three quarter skating speed. When a fake is made from either of these positions, it is usually more effective because the skater has better balance and manoeuvrability. Then, too, it brings in the change of pace factor when the player bursts into full speed at the completion of the fake, thus taking full advantage of the opening created. The fake is most effective against the over-eager checker or the checker who rushes at the puck carrier.

The weave. The weave is actually a fake without any stride or movement of the leg in the same direction the body takes. It is a most effective move to use when there isn't much room to manoeuvre or when you are trying to beat a checker who is easily faked. The player, when he is four or five feet away from a checker, bends his upper body to one side and then goes quickly in the opposite direction. Alternatively, he can use the same variations as suggested for the fake, such as moving the upper body to the left, coming part way back, and then going to the left. Another variation is to weave all the way in. In other words, as the puck carrier gets nine or ten feet from the checker, he starts his upper body weaving back and forth to try and unsettle the checker and perhaps force him into making a move too soon.

Shoulder drop. The shoulder drop is another variation of upper body deception and can quite often be used to fake a checker out of position. Just as the puck carrier gets to within checking distance of the checker, he leans his head over to one side and drops the shoulder on the same side. This can be done in the same variations as the other types of body deception. As with all body deception moves, the puck carrier should often try the shoulder drop but then occasionally go in that direction in order to keep the checkers unsettled as to how the manoeuvre is going to end up. A puck carrier should also make sure that his fakes do not become predictable.

Shoulder turn. This is another type of upper body deception that will often fake the checker out of position. It is an excellent variation to the weave. The player, instead of bending to the side as he does in the shift or weave, turns his shoulders (for example he brings his right shoulder forward and his left shoulder back) as if he were going to head in that direction. Then he quickly whips his shoulders around in the opposite direction and goes around that side. The same variations that are possible for the previous fake type moves can also be used in the shoulder turn.

Fake pass. This can be a very effective fake which will frequently draw the checker out of position. It is most effective, of course, when there is a teammate going up the ice with you but it can be used even when you are alone, because the checker will often act involuntarily to cover the pass, even though he knows there is no one there. As the puck carrier gets to a spot four or five feet away from the checker (or the distance found to be ideal through experiment by the player), he turns his head to either side as if looking at a teammate in order to aim the pass, and, at the same time, actually starts a pass. However, as the puck gets well to that side, he stops it, and then moves the puck quickly back to the other side and goes past the checker. This move is most effective against a checker who is good at intercepting passes. Such a player is always looking for a chance to intercept the pass and will thus be easier to fool. The player should make sure as in all moves, that he can fake equally well to either side.

The zig-zag. This move, which is often referred to as the double cross over, is a fairly difficult one to learn but it is worth all the time spent on it because it is a very effective move. When the puck carrier gets to a spot just before the checker can reach him, he crosses one leg over in front of the other and moves the puck to that side as if he is going to skate out and around the checker. Then he quickly brings the other leg back over and in front of the leg he started the manoeuvre with, bringing the puck with him. For example, the puck carrier can cross his right leg over his left leg and move the puck back to the right. Such a manoeuvre can often be used to thread your way through a group of opposing players.

Parallel zig-zag. In performing this move the player skates hard, and then when about six or seven feet away from the checker, he starts to glide, feet parallel. He turns the toes of his skates to one side and leans in the same direction. Then he quickly reverses the procedure and turns the other way, bursting into full speed again as he completes the final move.

Change of pace. This is always an excellent manoeuvre because it helps to unsettle the checker. The idea is to approach the checker at about three quarter speed. When you are close to him, suddenly burst into full speed. The checker will probably try to time his move according to your speed of approach. Then, when you suddenly change your pace, it will throw him off and, before he can recover, you can get by. There are endless variations to this move. For example, the player can come in fast, slow down a little, then burst again.

Slip through. This refers to the move in which the puck carrier slips the puck through the checker's legs and then goes quickly around him to pick it up again. Though a simple trick, this is one of the most effective when properly timed. The main thing is not to use it too often. It can be used against the single checker or against one of the defence-man. The puck carrier, after he has slipped the puck through his legs, can shift or use the draw away by turning sideways and slipping by the checker. The move is most effective when prefaced by a couple of fakes to lead the checker to believe that you are going to carry the puck around him. The player should make sure he does not always go around the same side to follow the puck.

Against the boards. This is a placement type of move, the same as the slip through, and is used when the play is at the side of the rink. Approach the player as if you were going to try to beat him with an ordinary puck-carrying move. Then, just before you get within checking distance, shoot the puck against the boards at a forward angle, shift around the checker and then pick the puck up again. The angle and speed with which you shoot the puck against the boards depends on the type of rink on which you are playing. A little experimenting will soon tell you the best speed and angle to use. It is most effective when the puck carrier fakes to the same side as the boards and then lets the puck go against them as he fakes back the other way to go around the checker. By using the fake, the puck carrier can often get the checker to move in toward the boards, giving the puck carrier room to get around him quickly. Properly used, this can do a very effective job. It is not used nearly as much as it could be.

Fake shot. Of all the moves this is perhaps the one that will bring the most consistent results if properly performed. Not only is it a good fake, but it also brings into action the factor of possible hurt to the checker. As he is naturally anxious to protect himself from any hard shot the puck carrier might make, he will be much more inclined to go for the fake. The secret is to make the fake convincing by actually starting the shot. The player who has a hard shot will find this move will be especially effective because the checker will be even more anxious to get out of the way or protect himself from the shot.

The fake is made by actually starting the shot. The player assumes a shooting position and indeed starts the puck forward, emphasizing his shoulder movement as if it is going to be a very hard shot. The secret lies in the way the stick is handled. It should move the puck forward fairly quickly until the moment when the shot would ordinarily be made. Then it is lifted quickly and placed in front of the puck to stop it in its forward action and then is moved well out to the side as the player moves to go around the checker. A great deal of deception can be added to the move if the player actually whips his stick with a hard snap of the wrist while he is lifting it from behind the puck to in front of it. This takes a little practice but can be learned if the player perseveres. Frequent practice of the back and forth stickhandling pattern previously described is a big help in developing the dexterity needed to perform this move well. The player should learn to fake both with his backhand and forehand shot as there are many opportunities to use it when the puck is on the backhand side. Very few players can fake a shot off their backhand.

Stop and start. This move, in a way, is a variation of the change of pace. It is particularly effective when used by the player who has worked hard on his start and stop drills and, as a result, has developed high level skill. This is an excellent play to use when a checker is coming at you from the side trying to cut you off.

Skate as hard as you can. Then just as he gets within checking distance, stop quickly, and start up again, cutting inside as he goes past. If the move is timed properly, the checker will rarely be able to recover in time to stop you.

The move can be used when rounding the defence if the defenceman comes over quickly and fails to protect the cut back angle properly. It can

also be used when you have taken a pass that has been made too soon
and thus given the defenceman a chance to move over to cover you. If
the stop is made just as he gets to you, he will find it difficult to stop and
prevent you from cutting inside of him as you start up again. By utilizing this play, many goal scoring opportunities that are seemingly lost
because of a premature pass can be saved. It is also a good move to use
when a defenceman rushes out in an attempt to check or body check,
especially when he is coming out on an angle.

There are many variations of this move but the main one is a fake stop
and start. In using this, the player makes his stop when the checker is
nine or ten feet away. Then, when he sees the checker stop to cover him,
he starts up again and goes in the original direction. Make sure players
can perform this while skating to either side.

Side step. This is for use primarily during scrambles or when a
checker rushes at you. The play is made by the puck carrier coming to a
quick stop and then stepping sideways, moving the puck with him.
Properly timed it can be used to avoid many hard body checks and collisions during scrambled play. The player who can come to a stop
quickly, step well to one side, and then start up again quickly will find
that this skill helps him out in many a tough spot.

Flip through. This play is primarily for use against the defence pair,
particularly a pair who are ardent body checkers and like to hit the puck
carrier as he skates in.

The idea is to fake as if you are going to try to slip through the centre.
Then when the defence pair comes together to bodycheck you, flip the
puck in between them and shift wide around them to pick the puck up on
the other side. Timed just right, this move is very effective, especially if you
have a wide shift and the defence pair are on the big, rough, but slow side.

This play is often spoiled because the puck carrier flips the puck too
fast causing it to slide too close to the goalkeeper. Another common
fault is flipping the puck too soon and thus giving away the intention. It
must be made close to the defence and it requires a hard, quick, angled
shift. An agile player can often stop dead, flipping the puck through at
the same time, side jump, and then move around. Once the player has
done this a few times, the defence pair will be set up for a fake off this
play with the player faking as if to go around and then cutting in
between the defence after the puck.

Outside carry. This is a very effective move to use in beating one checker or rounding the defence pair.

Approach a checker with the puck carried straight out in front of you. Then just before you reach him, use a body weave, fake, shoulder turn, or any other body deception move to make him think you are going to the inside. Then you quickly move the puck as far as you can to the outside, holding your stick with one hand. As you do this, cut out and round the checker with the free hand held out in front of you to ward him off. Your body should be turned so that your back is practically facing him. You must keep your body between the checker and the puck as you round the checker. Then, cut back quickly behind him bringing the puck into a position in front of you again. The free hand can also be used to ward off any attempts by the checker to get at the puck with his stick. The checker's stick must not, of course, be grabbed but it can be warded off. As the player brings the puck around in the half circle sweep, the blade of the stick must be turned over and in so that the puck is kept under control. The circular pattern drill given in the section on stick-handling will develop skill at doing this.

It is often possible to round a checker who has you well covered. The main thing is to get a little outside him so that you can lean into him as you bring the puck around. If you skate hard and lean well into the checker, you can often get by. The player should learn to perform the outside carry using either hand. The majority of players can only do the outside carry on one side. For example, players who shoot right would carry best to their left, left-handed players to their right. This might appear strange, but follows naturally from the fact that right-handers usually shoot left and vice versa.

Cut in. This refers to the action of cutting in to a spot in front of the net after rounding the defence or taking a pass when on the wing. It is not actually a puck-carrying move but an all important fundamental manoeuvre. The average player misses many opportunities because he has not developed the habit of cutting in. The player should remember that the moment he has rounded the defence or has taken the pass that sets him up to cut in behind the defence, the first and most important move is to get to that ideal scoring position or as close to it as possible. To cut in, the player can use either the cross over, leaning his body well to the inside to make his approach, or he can use the turn glide if it is needed. The skating skill developed by the player, if he does the skating agility drills listed in the chapter on skating, will give him the ability to cut in sharply and with good balance. Most players can only cut in from one side. Players should practise cutting in from their weak side until they can do it equally well to both sides.

Give and take. This move is one that takes a good deal of dexterity but it can be learned through frequent practice. It is done by moving the puck toward the checker as you get to him as if to say "Here, Joe, you can have it." Then, as he makes a move at the puck, pull it back quickly toward your feet, then out to one side, and go past him with a strong burst of speed. The move is very effective because by the action of moving the puck toward him, the player can force the checker to make the first move, which is always a great advantage.

Practise bringing it back and out to either side. The easiest way is to move it out, bring it back, and then move the puck to the backhand side. For example, a left-handed player should move it out in front of his left foot, bring it back quickly, and then out to his right. The player should learn to do this move to either side.

Fake slip through. In doing this move the player moves the puck forward as if he is going to slip it through the checker's legs. As the checker moves with his stick or as he frequently does, closes his feet, the player moves the puck to one side and goes around. This is effective because it is a natural instinct for the checker to close his feet to stop the expected slip through. The moving together of his feet will put the checker in a position from which he cannot recover quickly to move with the puck carrier who is going around him.

Stationary carry. The principle of this is very simple. The puck carrier carries the puck in toward the checker in a set position, for example, out in front of him on his forehand side. He continues to carry the puck in this position until the checker makes a move toward it with his stick. Then the puck carrier moves the puck away from the check. Actually, the move invites the checker to make a check.

Flip out. This play is particularly effective when used by a puck carrier who can break quickly. It is mainly for use when the puck is recovered in a scramble or with a lot of players milling around, or if a checker has the puck carrier cut off. For example, it occurs if he is in front of the puck carrier when the puck carrier is in a corner. The idea is to flip the puck quickly into open ice and then break after it immediately. When the puck carrier flips the puck, the checker will move and go after it, even though his best play is to block you with his body. The puck carrier has the advantage because he knows what he is going to do and thus will probably beat the checker to the puck because he starts sooner. Then too, the puck carrier will be facing the direction in which he will go after the puck, whereas the checker will have to make at least a half turn, probably a full turn, before he can go after the puck. The average player, when he gets the puck in a scramble or when he is cut off, tries to stick-handle out of trouble and is frequently checked. The best plan is usually to flip the puck into open ice and break after it.

Change of direction. This trick consists of either one or more changes of direction. Properly used by an agile skater, it is a good way to get the puck down the ice or to open up the defence.

The fundamental principle is to make the checker move in a certain direction to cover you, then just before he gets to you, suddenly change direction. A good example is when you are going down centre ice. You head at an angle toward the right wing. Then, when the checker moves over to cover you, change direction quickly and head toward the left, putting on an extra burst of speed. The move is effective because the puck carrier knows he is going to change direction and thus will gain an edge when he makes the move; the checker cannot make a move until after he sees the puck carrier take the new direction. Whereas the puck carrier will make his change in a forward action, the checker may have to stop dead and then go back to the new direction which, of course, gives the puck carrier time to outskate him.

Just as a football player running back a kick sometimes manoeuvres through the whole team with some well planned changes of direction, so too can a hockey player manoeuvre down the ice through the opposition. The great advantage of moving in one definite direction and then quickly changing is that the player forces the checker to commit himself to a move which sets him up for the puck carrier. The player should realize that by planning his moves as he goes down the ice, he can set up a situation to his own liking. The puck carrier who merely carries the puck down the ice, meeting each situation as it happens may very well be forced into making a play or manoeuvre at which he is not particularly skilful, or he may find himself stopped. But the puck carrier who, by his own manoeuvring, sets up the situation the way he wants it can then use the move or manoeuvre at which he is most efficient.

The protected push through. This move is not used frequently but is a good one to add to your bag of hockey moves.

Move the puck ahead to either side of the checker or between two checkers and hold your stick over it, staving off any attempts to get the puck by using the stick to ward off the checker's stick. By pushing the puck out in front of you to either side of the checker, the player entices the checker to move his stick at the puck, thus committing himself. Then, when his stick is quickly guarded off or knocked aside, the puck carrier has a moment to get by.

Summary. By learning the various puck-carrying moves the player will develop techniques that will enable him to plan and carry out definite pattern plays. The number of strategic possibilities will be increased as he learns more moves. These puck-carrying moves are actually the fundamentals that make it possible to use many different types of pattern plays with teammates.

If the player is to develop top level skill at performing these various moves, he must do them over and over again. Just trying them in games is not enough. He must concentrate on trying them at every opportunity during practice. However, top level skill can only be developed if he concentrates on learning each move as a drill he does over and over again.

See the chapter on Offensive Strategy and Tactics for information on tactics to use if you are slow or fast, if the ice is poor, and if the play is open or close, etc.

PUCK-CARRYING DRILLS

Shadow rush. In this drill the player starts at one end of the ice and skates down the ice and back again, trying a different move every few feet. The idea is to use your imagination as a boxer does when he is shadow boxing and beat imaginary checkers with a different move every time. One time take four or five moves and work on them. The next time work on a few others until you develop the habit of using them.

Situation drill. In this drill the situation needed for each move is set up and the player practises doing the move concerned. For example, the puck carrier goes to a corner with the puck and tries the flip out play to beat a teammate stationed in front of him. The coach can easily give the individual players a chance to practise the various moves.

Obstacle course. In this drill five or six of the players are lined up down the ice about fifteen feet apart. The puck carrier then goes in and around these stationary players practising a certain move. The stationary players do not try to check the puck carrier but merely make the puck carrier's move necessary. For example, if the puck carrier is practising the fake slip through, the stationary player should close his feet as if to stop it. The whole team can be set to work at such a drill with two or three lines of stationary players spread across the ice and everybody taking turns carrying the puck. Such practice will give the players a method of developing a degree of skill at doing the various moves that cannot be developed in any other way.

The coach should make sure he gives each player a chance to practise the various puck-carrying moves because it is the only way the player will develop skill at using them. It will be time well spent. The more puck-carrying moves each player can do, the easier it will be to develop systems of strategy. There is no point in the coach developing tactics and strategy that he knows will win if the players are not capable of making the various moves that make the strategy possible. A similar situation would be the basketball or football coach who plans a wonderful system of play or a particular play pattern without first developing in his players the ability to perform the fakes, blocks, or ballhandling plays necessary to make the strategy work.

Mental planning (visualization). This is a mental drill that will help players establish a series of mental visual pictures of how to use each of the different moves. By using mental pictures, the player will find himself instinctively making the right plays at the right time. Usually this is something that can only be learned through experience. By visualizing the moves or plays over and over, they become established in the mind. When the situation arises, the players will instinctively make the play or move that they had previously visualized. After each game or scrimmage, the players should take a minute to sit and think about the plays that they made and decide if it is the play that they should have made or will make the next time.

Players should use their imagination for all its worth and do rush after rush against all types of checkers solving each situation as they come to it. The coach, of course, can help in this way through the organization of discussions on what is the right thing to do under certain situations and through having chalk talks. This is the principle of the chalk talk or the "mind" session. The coach illustrates certain situations and points out what should be done. The player recognizes these subconsciously when the situation develops in a game, and reacts in the right way.

Trick scrimmage. This is an ordinary scrimmage in which the coach instructs his players that, when carrying the puck, they must use only a certain number of moves. For example, during one scrimmage the players could be confined to the slip through, stop and start, and the zigzag. By making the players concentrate on three or four specific moves, each player will develop a better all-round puck-carrying skill than would be possible if he were left on his own each time.

Summary. In practising the various moves the player should first skate through them slowly, gradually increasing the speed with which they are done as he gets the feel. The principle of "walking through" a move or manoeuvre first is very important. The player, who first tries to perform the move at full speed will often end up not learning it at all because it will be too difficult. Get the feel of it first and then add speed.

Above all, the player should remember that he is not to stickhandle or move his body around unnecessarily unless there is a checker to beat. If in the clear, the player concentrates on merely skating with the puck under control in front of him. As our research indicated, unnecessary stickhandling, manoeuvring, and body movement slow the player down and thus spoil many opportunities to take advantage of a break. There are many players who, every time they get the puck, start stickhandling madly back and forth and dipsy-doodling all over the place. Save it until it counts!

PASSING AND PASS RECEIVING

Passing and receiving are included in this chapter since they are part of puck-carrying. These are two of the most important parts of the game and a lot of time and effort should be spent on learning how to make and take the various types of passes. There is nothing more irritating to a coach or the player himself than to see a pass go wide or slip off the end of the stick.

Sweep pass. In making a sweep pass, the player moves the puck toward the direction he wishes it to go with a smooth, sweeping motion, avoiding any quick, jerky action. The blade of the stick should follow through along the ice so that the pass will not be lifted. Many good play possibilities are spoiled because the puck is lifted unintentionally. The player should make sure to check his follow through at all times. If the blade of the stick follows through along the ice after the puck, the puck cannot lift off the ice. This is an easy thing to forget in the excitement of the play when an opportunity to pass suddenly comes up. The player is inclined to just make the pass and not think of technique.

The sweep pass is used when deception is not an important factor or when the puck carrier has time to set up a pass. The blade of the stick should always follow through in the direction of the intended pass. This is an important point to remember if the pass is to be accurate. Aim your follow through at the target to which you are passing. The same gentle touch should be used as advocated for stickhandling.

Snap pass. If there is little time in which to make the pass or if the puck carrier wants to make a quick, unexpected pass in the midst of a stickhandling pattern, he should use the snap pass. To make this type of pass the puck is sent on its way by a quick snap of the wrists. There is no sweep. It is very easy to loft this type of pass if the puck carrier does not remember to let the blade of his stick follow through along the ice. The player, who can snap a pass accurately will find it a big advantage because he will be able to make the pass without giving away his intention.

Just as with the sweep pass, the blade of the stick should follow through in the direction the puck carrier wishes the puck to take. The player must first take the puck to a good starting position. The time saved by whipping the puck away without first getting it into a good position is more than offset by the resulting lack of accuracy. If making a forward snap pass, the players uses the same principle as in taking a snap shot. However, he makes sure of that low follow through to prevent any loft.

Flip pass. This is the pass that is used when the puck carrier wishes to raise the puck over an opponent's stick, a player or prostrate goaltender on the ice or, perhaps, between the defence, or from out of a scramble. It is made with a forward and upward flip of the wrists with a high follow through. The forward and upward flip of the wrists and the high follow through will bring the bottom edge of the blade up underneath the puck and give it the loft needed. There is usually no sweep to it but merely a quick flick of the wrists. The blade of the stick is placed right behind the puck and then the wrists are flipped. A good way to make sure the puck is lofted is to move it quickly for a couple of inches in the opposite direction from which you wish to make the pass. Then place the blade of the stick behind it and flip it in the desired direction.

Actually, you perform a very narrow stickhandling pattern ending up with the quick flip pass. Moving the puck in this way will bring it hard against the blade of the stick just before the pass is made. This will cause it to climb up the blade a little enabling you to get the blade under the puck to flip it. The flip pass is used primarily when the receiver is fairly close, or merely to flip the puck to a point where it will remain stationary or move slowly so that a teammate can move to get it. Examples of this are when the puck is flipped out of a scramble into open ice, to a teammate up ahead, or when it is flipped between the defence for a teammate cutting in behind them.

Lift pass. To make a lift pass you merely let the blade of the stick follow through to the height required. The lift pass is used when the puck is to be sent some distance and has to pass over a stick, or a player on the ice on the way. Direction is controlled by letting the blade of the stick follow through toward the target.

Touch pass. This pass is used mainly when the puck carrier wishes to make a quick pass to a teammate when the puck comes to him after a pass up or during a scramble. Another time it is used is on a return pass when the man receiving the first pass wishes to get the puck back to a teammate without first stopping it.

The blade of the stick, as in any other type of pass, should follow through in the direction the pass is going. This is one of the secrets of accuracy.

General principles. Many passes are messed up because the passer gets excited. To make a good pass the player must keep cool, calm, and relaxed. If a player is excited, it will be very difficult for him to pass accurately. When passing, make sure the player's arms and shoulders are loose and relaxed because it will give him better control of his muscles. Also, most players can only pass to one side, Make sure they can pass equally well to either side.

Never pass blindly. Many good scoring opportunities are lost because the player does not take a look first to line up the pass. Wild passing, especially in your own blue line zone, often results in scoring opportunities being given to your opponents.

Unless the play demands a slow pass, for example when a pass receiver is coming up from behind or using a flip pass or back pass on a trailer player, the pass should be made quickly. The quicker the pass, the more effective the play as it will give the defending players less time to cover the receiver.

Perhaps the most common mistake is holding the pass until the passer gets too close to the checker. This means the pass is frequently intercepted and hits a stick or skate, or is out of the receiver's reach, or blocked altogether. It is better to make the pass a little too soon than too late because, even though making the pass too soon gives the opponents time to see the play shape up, you will still have possession of the puck. It is very hard to say just when a pass should be made because there are so many situations, all a little different. However, a good general rule to use when the pass is designed to beat a checker is to pass the puck just before you get within actual checking distance. This is usually somewhere about five or six feet away from the checker.

The passer should remember that when he is being covered by a checker he can often get a pass away through the spot between the checker's stick and his feet.

Many players spoil their passes because they telegraph their intention by looking at the receiver and lining up the play without any deception. A good idea is to take a good look to see the situation, then follow with a quick fake as if you were going to carry the puck yourself, or pass in a different direction, and then let the actual pass go. Good play makers usually have excellent peripheral vision, good vision to the side even when looking ahead. This enables them to line up a pass without giving away their intention by looking to the side.

Though this type of vision is to a large degree inherited, it can be developed to an important degree through practice. Once the player realizes that he actually can see quite a lot without turning his head, he will begin using it and, as he uses it, his side vision will develop. Coaches can use split vision drills to develop this sense. There are two very simple drills. Line up the players across the ice about fifteen to twenty feet apart and have them pass the puck back and forth to each other while keeping their eyes dead ahead. Form a square with four players and have them pass the puck to each other in a variety of patterns while keeping their eyes on the man directly opposite them.

Such drills will develop in the player a consciousness that he can see a lot without turning his head as well as develop the faculty itself. They will help the players to make accurate passes without giving away their intention by turning their head, a useful skill during scrambles.

Pass receiving. The player who has developed top pass receiving skill and can accordingly not only handle all types of passes but also snaffle off many poorly directed passes, at his feet, for example, will always be a welcome addition to any team. His name usually will be found near the top of the point getters. However, there are comparatively few who can take a pass smoothly and safely, especially if it is a little on the fast side or does not come across in an ideal receiving position. To demonstrate this point, all you need is an analysis of the average game in which the observer will see pass after pass missing its target. The technique is actually quite simple because there are only a few rules to be observed.

Always nurse the puck as it comes to the stick. Never stab or poke at it or try to receive it with a hard stick. A hard stick refers to a stick held in a tight grip and which, as a result, does not give and go with the puck a little when contact is made. If the stick is held hard, the puck will rebound from it or slide off the end of the blade. Keep the hands and arms loose and relaxed so that the stick will be soft. The principle is exactly the same as with catching a football pass or a fast travelling baseball – there must be a slight give when contact is made.

Do not reach out for the puck, let it come to you. The common fault of reaching out to get the pass before it comes right in is caused mainly by over-eagerness and tension. Keep cool and let it come; do not fight it.

Always lay the blade of the stick slightly over the puck as contact is made. The blade of the stick can be laid over the puck by turning the hands a little on the shaft of the stick toward the direction from which the puck has come. This turning over of the blade will help you nurse the puck and will prevent it from sliding off the end of the blade, as so often happens when the pass is fast and a little too far ahead for easy handling. The player, when trying to reach for one of these "too far ahead" passes, will grab off a lot more if he will only remember to turn his hands on the shaft of the stick toward the puck. This will move the blade over and bring the end of the blade a little toward the player, thus forming a pocket that will hold the puck and prevent it from sliding off.

The blade of the stick must be squarely facing the direction from which the puck is coming. This is something the average player fails to check up on very often. Any time the blade of the stick is not facing the direction from which the puck is coming, the puck will be likely to slide off the blade as it makes contact. The average player fails to take into consideration the angle at which the blade of his stick is facing when it makes contact with the puck because he never thought of it. As a result, he nearly always has the toe of the blade of the stick facing dead ahead of him. This is all right if the pass comes directly from the side, but the puck will be inclined to slide off the blade if it comes from an angle, as it would, if passed up to the receiver in a forward pass. Keeping the angle of the blade so that it takes the puck squarely is one of the main secrets of top level pass receiving.

One of the chief reasons so few hockey players can handle a pass directed at their feet is that they use a stick that has too low a lie. For example, a player using a lie any lower than four will find it practically impossible to get the blade of the stick to the puck when it comes to the feet. This is still another argument in favour of using a high lie stick. Another way to handle a pass directed at the feet is to bend the knees and take a low grip on the stick. This brings the heel of the stick closer to the ice. A player, expert with his feet, can often kick the puck up ahead of him when he cannot get his stick on it. Holding the stick with a low grip, and only in the hand on the side to which the puck is coming, also helps you get your stick on the puck and move it into position.

When taking a pass directed a little too far ahead, the player should keep his elbows high when reaching for it and slip his hands up together right at the end of the shaft in order to give him maximum reach. By raising the elbows, it will be possible to hold the end of the shaft higher and thus keep the blade of the stick flat on the ice. If the elbows are not raised, the toe of the blade will come up and thus give the puck a chance to slide under.

If the pass is well ahead the player can often snare it by bending the forward knee and reaching out with the stick flat on the ice, the toe of the blade facing the direction from which the pass is coming so as to form a hook, as in a hook check. The stick should be held in one hand with the grip right at the end of the shaft. By using this technique the player can get many passes that would otherwise go free or slide off the end of the stick because he cannot reach far enough forward with two hands on the stick and the body upright. By bending the knee the player adds the amount of bend to his reach and avoids over-balancing.

In trying to get a pass directed to a spot behind him, the receiver is, of course, in a tight spot as he will leave himself wide open to a body check from an opposition player. However, the player who is willing to work at his agility skating and special drills can learn to take such a pass by quickly shifting from forward to backward skating. This will enable him to get the blade of his stick on the puck so that he can bring it under control and return to forward skating. This move, however, is not as hard as it sounds. All that is needed is a little practice. The only other way to handle such a pass is to turn the upper body well around in the direction of the puck and reach back with the stick, hoping to get the blade on it long enough to flip the puck up closer so that it can be brought under control. A left-handed player, taking a pass coming from his right, would reach back and take the puck with a backhanded stick position.

Pass study. The need for an emphasis on development of passing technique is indicated in the results of the pass study made in our research. In the average National Hockey League game four hundred and eighty passes were attempted. Fifty-five per cent of these passes were completed. Of the forty-five per cent that were incomplete, twenty-five per cent were missed because of inaccurate passing or poor receiving technique, and twenty per cent were intercepted by the opposition. Sixty-five per cent of the inaccurate passes were made too far in front of the receiver, and thirty-five per cent were behind him. Most of the passes messed up by the receiver were spoiled because his stick blade was not at right angles to the direction of the pass.

Passing efficiency dropped considerably when the pressure was on the offensive team such as when trying to break out of their own end or when trying to score while having a man advantage. Most interceptions were made when the puck was passed from one side to the other across the centre lane. The same general picture is seen in other levels of hockey although fewer passes are attempted.

Emphasis on passing during practice scrimmage will help develop these skills. However, if the highest type of skill is to be developed, special drills should be used, at least until the players have developed a fundamental technique, understand the principles involved, and have established a correct pattern.

PASSING DRILLS

Passing the square. Players, in groups of four form squares. Enough squares can be formed to include all the players. The size of the square can be varied to provide both long and short pass practice. The puck is given to one of the players. At a signal, he passes to his left, and the puck is then received and passed around the square. The puck goes from left to right until it has been passed around the square five times. Then, at a signal, the puck is passed from right to left. Then, when it has been around the square five times, another signal indicates that the puck must be passed to the left again. However, this time as each man gets a pass he returns it to the man who passes it to him. He then passes it back again. This time the receiver passes it to the player on his left. This back and forth and then pass to the left pattern is continued around the square five times, and at a signal it is done to the right.

A good way to bring in the contest idea is to see how many times each squad can get the puck around the square in thirty seconds. If the puck gets loose, it must be regained as quickly as possible and the pass sent on to the man who was to have received the next pass.

Variations. You can use a "free for all" system of passing, too, with the players passing to any side or across the square, in any way they wish. Then, two, three, or four pucks can be used in what is called "juggle drill." Each man has a puck and at a signal they all pass to the left and try to keep each puck going around the square in the correct order. This "juggle" type of "passing the square" with two or more pucks, demands great skill and timing – just try it and see! Another variation is "keep it moving" with the players keeping the puck in motion by sweeping the puck to the next man without stopping it first. Another excellent variation is the "position exchange" in which the players change positions after each pass is made. The first player passes to the player on his left and then follows the puck while he passes to the third player and then follows the puck, etc. If you like, you can use a triangle set up and have each forward line as a unit. You can also use a five-man box. One man stands in the centre with four other players grouped in a rectangular position about him. The puck starts from the man in the centre and is returned to him after each pass. Each man takes a turn as the player in the centre.

Give and take (go). The give and take is designed to develop the player's accuracy in passing and receiving when on the move. However, this drill also aids the standing player in taking and giving passes from a stationary position. It is also excellent for training the players to make breakout plays from their own blue line zone.

Seven players are stationed up the boards. These players all face toward the spot where the puck carrier starts. These stationary players should be placed on spots halfway between the goal line and the blue line, on the blue line, halfway between blue and red lines, and so on all the way down the ice. At a signal, the puck carrier breaks fast, takes two or three strides, and then makes a pass to the first man in the line. He takes the pass then returns it to the original puck carrier with a lateral pass. The puck carrier must keep going all-out all the way down the line, trying to break a little faster after each pass he makes to a stationary player. He must not slow down to take the return lateral pass. After he takes the first return pass, he takes a stride or two and repeats the play with the next man. This is continued all the way down the ice. When he gets the puck from the last man he carries it down to the goal line, turns as quickly as possible, and comes back down the ice, this time passing from the opposite side (a left-handed player goes down the ice passing from his natural side and comes back passing backhand). The stationary players must turn around to face the puck carrier as he comes back down the ice. The drill is completed when the puck carrier gets back to the spot from which he started.

The passes should be made at medium speed except when a fast or slow pass is needed to keep the timing right. The players must be alert for this and must not pass the puck aimlessly. When the drill has been completed by one player, he goes to the end of the line of stationary players and the first man in the line becomes the puck carrier. Courses can be set up on both sides of the rink so as to include all players in the drill. If desired more than seven players can be used in the stationary positions. This will create a demand for faster and more frequent passing and an even greater degree of timing. However, this should not be done until skill has been developed with a seven-man line up.

This drill can be organized as a contest with the time it takes each player to negotiate the drill being checked, the winner being the player with the best time. Each player should have at least three to five trials during each session. Any missed pass or loss of puck control is a foul and the player must regain it, come back into line, and start over. Another way to organize this drill is to have races between two groups, one on either side of the ice. The squad that gets every man through the course first is the winner. This is an excellent contest as it brings into play the factors of team work.

Relay racer. This drill is designed to develop skill at passing and receiving the puck while on the move, and going at full speed. In today's game it is very important that the player learns the technique of giving and taking passes in all conceivable positions, especially in getting the puck up to the man ahead, or receiving it in the man ahead position. This drill gives excellent training in developing those skills. Relay racer is also a very effective all around "conditioner."

In the inner circle (marked "A" on the diagram) the relay idea is of the shuttle type. Your group is divided into six, eight, or ten-man groups. These groups are then divided into teams that line up on the blue lines, one team at one blue line, the other groups on the opposite blue line. They line up behind each other with the first players in the line standing on the blue line. The other groups are lined up the same way. The first player of each group is given a puck. Then, at a signal, the first man breaks down the ice toward the second man. Just as he gets about four to five feet away the second man starts to skate up the ice toward the spot from which the first man started. As he passes the first man coming down, he is given a pass. Then he heads for the far blue line and exchanges it in the same way with the third man. The team continues shuttling back and forth in this way until all have had a turn and the last man gets to the blue line for which he is headed. The group getting the last man to the objective first is the winner. When each man has made his leg of the relay, he gets back into line in last place. If preferred, the

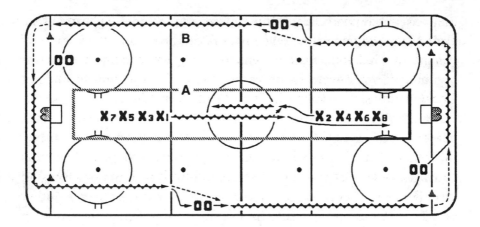

race can consist of three or four legs by each player. The time check plan can be used, too, with each group trying to make the best possible time. You can establish team records for two, four, six, eight, and ten-man groups over various distances. This is an excellent plan because it gives added incentive each time the drill is used.

If you like, you can use a three-man shuttle and have your various forward lines work as units. If this is done, there is one man at one blue line and two at the other. The relay is started at the end where there are two players and the man who starts must quickly stop and take his place at the blue line after he has made his first exchange. In the outer circle (marked "B" on the diagram) the man ahead type of relay race is explained.

Man ahead. The team is divided into four-man units. The first man is given the puck and takes up a position directly behind the goal. At a signal he starts to skate as fast as he can around the rink and up to the blue line. A pylon should be placed in the corner, and he must go around the pylon. As he gets to the blue line, the second man on his team starts to skate ahead toward the red line. Then the first man passes the puck up ahead to the second man who continues around the rink until he reaches the next exchange area where he passes ahead to the third man in the same way as before. This continues with the third man either finishing the race behind the goal where the first man started or giving it to the first man again for another turn around the rink. If this plan is used, the players must return quickly to their original positions after they have made an exchange. If preferred, you can have eight men to a team instead of having four who exchange twice.

When an exchange is made the incoming player must be behind the outgoing player. The exchange must be started and completed somewhere in the exchange area. The objective should be to make the exchange with both players skating at top speed. The contests organized can be against time or with two or three groups all racing around the course. Records for various distances (one lap, two laps, etc.) should be established, as attempting to set new records will establish greater incentive. Then, too, it is interesting to see how the records improve as skill is developed.

Break-away pass. This drill is designed to develop the player's timing at making and taking forward passes at full speed as is often the case when a player breaks free. Two of the players start on the goal line. The other player stands on the far blue line. The first man has the puck and skates slowly. The second man breaks up the side as quickly as possible. As he reaches the blue line, he passes up to the first man who should get the pass just as he reaches the centre red line. He then breaks for the far blue line. Just as he reaches it, the third man breaks in toward the goal and takes the forward pass from the second man and then shoots. The drill can be done with groups of three going up the ice one after the other. The position of each player should be changed so everyone gets a chance at each position.

Flip pass. This drill will do an excellent job of teaching the player to both take and make the difficult flip pass. A long box is placed just past the blue line and parallel to it, and a player stationed just in front of it. At a signal he flips the puck over the box. One of the players travels up from the blue line, cuts back behind the box, and gets the pass. He then shoots on goal and returns to the end of the line on the other side. The next time a player from the opposite side cuts across to take the pass. The drill can be also be conducted with the players divided into lines of three. The line skates in line up to the box and the puck carrier stops dead and flips the puck over the box as one of the players on the side cuts in to get it. The coach can call out "left" or "right" as the puck carrier gets to the box with the player on the side designated going in for the pass. All players should get equal opportunity to go in from each side and to make the pass.

Alternatively, place the box at right angles to the blue line. The players are lined up in two lines with each player in line "A" having a puck. At a signal, the first two players in each line break fast. As the puck carrier gets to the box he flips a side pass over the box which is picked up by the player on the other side. He then either cuts over and shoots on goal or carries the puck back and takes his place in the line of receivers. The drill should be done to both right and left.

Pass scrimmage. In this drill, the players must keep the puck for only three seconds before passing. Any time a player fails to pass within three seconds after getting possession, the whistle is blown for a face-off. The value of the drill is that it places a definite emphasis on passing and makes the players "think" passing. It will also make the players pass conscious and will demonstrate to all concerned the way passing can be used both on defence and offence to get the puck out of danger, or down into the scoring zone safely and quickly, with an economical use of energy.

Two puck passing. In this drill the players work in two-man groups, with each man having a puck. The pair skate up and down the ice passing the puck back and forth, trying to make as many exchanges as possible. A real challenge to the player's dexterity and control, this drill emphasizes the fun element.

Back and forth. In performing this drill the players are separated into teams of three players. One line faces down the ice, the other line has its back to the far end. The lines are about ten feet apart. One puck is used. Then, at a signal, the lines move down the ice, one line skating backwards, the other forwards. The line skating backwards sets the pace, going back as quickly as possible. The puck is passed back and forth from one side to the other going from a front man to a backward skating man and so on. They come back down the ice with positions reversed. As variations, two or more pucks can be used, or different exchange patterns.

Timing drill. This drill is designed to teach both the passer and the receiver how to time either the pass or the pick-up. Markers are placed two feet on either side of the blue line about six to eight feet out from the boards on both sides of the rink. The passers stand in the centre of the ice between the two sets of markers. The receivers line up behind each other at the centre red line. At a signal the first ten break and pick up the pass made by the passer servicing their group. The pass must be made so that it is picked up somewhere between the two markers. After each group has received a pass, a new passer is used with the first passer taking his place in the line of receivers. One day fast sweep passes should be used, the next, slow ones, and so on with emphasis placed on a different type and speed of pass being used each time. If desired the receiver can take the pass and go in to shoot on goal from a specific spot.

Passing tests. To test the passing accuracy of the players and to bring in variety and the competitive element definite targets can be set up. These targets can be placed on the ice with the players trying to hit them with a pass made from specific locations. The passes can be made from a stationary position, while skating slowly, at full speed, or from any desired position. The moving target element can be included by using any large ball, such as a soccer or volley ball. Test the players first, then give them a few weeks of practice and then test again.

General suggestions. Virtually any of these drills can be organized by any group of players, even if they only have limited facilities. As often as possible, as many types of passes and different speeds should be used. As the coach discovers the particular needs of his players, he can select the type of drill he requires in order for them to improve. See the chapter on Offensive Play for further hints on passing strategy and tactics, where and when not to pass, and passing possibilities.

Scoring Goals

Scoring a goal is the pay-off play, the ultimate objective of every player, the big thrill. No game can be won unless the puck is put in the net. There are some who believe that the knack of goal scoring is something that some players have and some lack. The late Coleman Griffith of the University of Illinois, who has become known as the "Father of Sport Psychology," said, "It is not possible to be born with a skill such as a football or baseball skill; this must be developed. Skill at anything is only a group of correct habits formed through practice of the correct technical principles." Whoever works hard to develop a good scoring technique can improve his goal scoring average. Any hockey player can develop his goal scoring skill by doing practise drills designed to give him the technical skill to do what he wants to do when he wants to do it. To see an opening is one thing, but to take advantage of it is another.

To help us efficiently analyze the technique of goal scoring, to develop it, and identify the points to emphasize in any practice plan, let's take a look at some of the facts uncovered by our research.

NHL SCORING SURVEY

Scoring percentages. The results of this survey refer to the goals scored per good opportunity. The best percentage was one in four. The average percentage was one in ten. Some players showed a record of scoring only once in every fifteen clear opportunities.

Failure facts. In compiling the facts and figures listed, the researchers analyzed over five hundred failures to score on clear opportunities by seventy players, most of the players studied being members from the Toronto Maple Leafs.

- Twenty-five per cent of the shots were made from too close to the goaltender. This habit makes it impossible for the players to get the puck into the net.
- Twenty-four per cent of the shots missed the net. Twenty per cent of the tries went to either side while four per cent went over the net. Right-handed shooters missed more often to the left of the goal. Left-handed shooters missed more often to the right of the goal.
- Four per cent were missed through loss of puck control. This occurs when trying to stickhandle past the goaltender or letting the puck get away from the stick before the shot is made.
- Twenty per cent shot so that the goaltender had no difficulty getting in front of them.
- Twelve per cent of the tries were well placed but weak shots. This enabled the goaltender to cover the shot even though it was to his weak spot or open area.
- Saves made by goaltenders were fifteen per cent, and these were shots that were hard and well directed or on well performed dekes.
- In an analysis of one hundred goals scored by individuals with clean chances, seventy-four per cent were made on shots while twenty-six per cent were made on dekes.

How Goals Were Scored. Goal scorers maximize the opportunities they get, as the survey also showed.

- Sixty-two per cent of goals were scored from in front of the net, ten to twenty-five feet out. Seventy per cent of this sixty-two per cent were from twelve to fifteen feet out. Twenty-nine per cent were made from slightly angled shots while six per cent were scored from well angled shots. Three per cent were sharp angled shots.
- Sixty-nine per cent were shots below the knees. Eighty per cent of these successful shots were ankle high or lower. Twenty-one per cent of the shots were shoulder high. Of those, ten per cent were from knee to shoulder high. Eighty-two per cent were scored on forehands and eighteen on backhands.
- Seventy-three per cent were scored to the goaltender's stick side (right side of a goaltender who held his stick in his right hand). Eighteen per cent were scored on the glove side, and nine per cent made between the goaltender's legs, or were deflected in by the goalie.

- Eighty-eight per cent of the successful shots were to the far side of the net (to the goaltender's left hand by left-handed shooters, to his right hand by right-handed shooters). Seventy-nine per cent of the shots made were over knee high. Seventy per cent of this group were made between the knees and shoulders. Ten per cent were shoulder high and twelve per cent were below the knees.

Shooting habits. Nearly all players had a definite pattern in their shooting. They would shoot almost always to the same height and spot. Many of them had "hot spots" to which they frequently tried to manoeuvre before shooting. A "hot spot" is a position from which the player best likes to take a shot on goal. This is usually unconscious and the player is frequently surprised when he is told by his coach that he shoots from a "hot spot."

Few players, when in a bad shooting position (i.e., at a sharp angle to the sides), tried to improve their position before shooting. A high percentage of these "shoot and hope" attempts were noted.

The same habits were noted when the players tried to deke the goaltender and slip the puck past him. They nearly all tried the same move time after time. The most popular move was a fake shot to one side followed by a puck shift to the other with a flip shot to finish off. The most successful dekes ended up with the final scoring attempt made to the goaltender's stick side. Most unsuccessful dekes were missed because the puck carrier waited too long to start his play, and this enabled the goaltender to smother the puck because there was not sufficient room for the puck carrier to manipulate it.

Another pattern was noticed in regard to the speed and power of the shots used. Rarely did a player shoot as hard as he could when he had a chance to shoot on goal. Indeed, few shot as hard as in the pre-game warm-up. Most players seemed to have a shooting groove involving the same amount of effort each time. Only a very few appeared to try to shoot with a definite attempt to use all the power at their disposal.

In the modern game, it is quickness rather than pinpoint accuracy which spells the most success for today's best shooters.

Survey of other levels of hockey (senior, intermediate, junior, juvenile, midget, etc.). Practically the same results were compiled in these levels. However, the NHL players got into position to shoot on goal more frequently. This was particulary noticeable when the puck was taken on a pass at the defence. The NHL players cut in on goal more quickly and to better position than did the players in other groups. The younger the level of players studied, the poorer record the players had in this respect. The only other major difference was that the younger the age group was, the better was the goal scoring per attempt. This is probably due to the fact that as the age limit gets higher the calibre of goaltending improves faster than does the calibre of shooting and general goal scoring technique.

Goaltending demands a high level of muscular co-ordination and this increases as the athlete matures. It is, therefore, natural to expect an increase in the agility and speed of movement that is the basis of good netminding. Then, too, the young goaltender rarely gets enough organized practice. This results in the goaltenders being the latest to mature for play in the NHL. In fact, the average age of NHL goalies is significantly higher than the rest of the players in the league.

A young goaltender does not get the opportunity to develop skill as does the player who does not play goal. The skater is always playing shinny and thus develops skill beyond that developed in comparison by the young goaltender. While the average NHL hockey player seems to play the same type of hockey with the same patterns as he did when a youngster, he plays it much better.

All these facts and figures are significant with regard to the most effective ways to develop goal scoring technique. From the survey's report, we can now deal with the proper technique of goal scoring.

SCORING TECHNIQUE

Position. The survey indicates very strongly that the best spot from which to shoot on goal is between ten and twenty-five feet out and directly in front of the net. With a younger player, the ideal distance decreases. The principle seems to be that the ideal time to shoot is when you are far enough away from the goaltender to prevent him from cutting off your target area by moving in to the puck but close enough to give him the minimum amount of time to make his move once you shoot. The ideal distance changes according to how far the goal tender plays out in front of his net, his size, and his amount of forward glide into your shot. Some netminders, for example, stand just in front of the

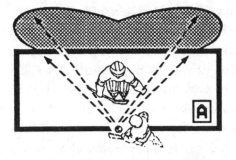

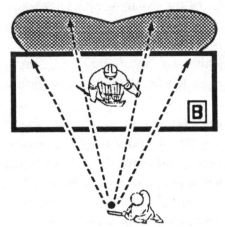

EXPOSED NET AREAS
The exposed area of the net is much smaller when the puck carrier skates too far in before shooting, as a comparison of (A) and (B) indicates. The same loss of scoring area occurs on angle shots from too close in on the goaltender. The general principle is that for each foot you get closer to the goaltender, the shooting area is cut down by one foot.

goal line and stay there. Others stand at the edge of the goal crease and then move forward as the shot is made. This means you can move in closer on the goaltender who keeps close to his goal.

Remember that as you get closer to the goaltender the goal areas you have to shoot at get smaller and smaller. The reason it is best to shoot from directly in front of the goal is that, from this position, you can shoot to either side of the goaltender. When you come in from the side, you usually only have one side to shoot at. This gives the goaltender an advantage as he can be ready to move, knowing where the shot is going. When the shot comes from directly in front of him, he has to wait to see to which side it is going.

The harder a player shoots, the farther away he can shoot with effect because the goaltender has less time to move to block the shot. So many hockey players move in too close before they shoot because they want to get as close as possible because they know their shot is not very hard. Our survey showed that twenty-five per cent of all missed chances were caused by the player shooting from a spot too close to the goaltender. This habit is the number one fault. Correcting it by staying out of this "Low Percentage Area" alone can raise your goal scoring average a great deal. Tests indicate that if you are closer than seven feet, it is best to take the puck right in and try to deke the goaltender. Do not spoil a good chance by taking a shot that has almost no chance of going in.

In order to confirm the findings of the survey of play in the NHL, a further study was made in which twenty-five players (under twenty years of age) tried one hundred shots from different positions. This was repeated several times and each time the results confirmed the figures compiled in the NHL survey. These tests also indicated that the younger the player, the closer the shooter can go. However, six feet seemed to be the closest any player could go without cutting down the goal area at which he could shoot.

To improve your goal scoring average and that of your team, get into the ideal position before you shoot. If you are not able to get into a good position, look around for a teammate who may be open in such a position. If you cannot see anyone, and cannot manoeuvre into position, shoot low at the goaltender's feet, and go in for the rebound. The average player does not fight hard enough to get into good scoring position. He is too easily forced into shooting from a bad angle. Any energy used in getting into position will be well spent. This is why it is important to work on your agility skating because the more manoeuvrability you have the easier it will be for you to get into position. The moment a player gets the puck and has a chance to score, his first thought should be to get into position. Once done, the odds start to swing to his side and against the goaltender.

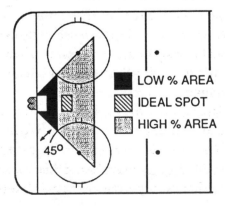

LOW % AREA
IDEAL SPOT
HIGH % AREA

45°

The average unimpeded puck carrier should score more often than indicated in the survey inasmuch as he knows what he is going to do and the goaltender must wait until he does it before he can make his move. If the average puck carrier planned his goal scoring plays coolly, making sure to keep the odds on his side by taking up a good position and using the other information available to him, he'd have a much better score than once every ten tries. Skill at cutting into a spot directly in front of the goal helps you to get good position before you shoot.

The same principle of position holds when you go right in and try to stick-handle or fake the goaltender into making a move so that you can slip the puck past him. The average puck carrier goes in too close, giving the goaltender a chance to smother the play. Remember, the closer the player gets, the less room he has to manoeuvre. Repeated tests indicate that the deke should be made about four or five feet away from the goaltender. The principle is to make him move first. Then you should be home free. By staying away from him you will be more able to force him into making a move. At such times a goaltender is really tense and on edge. This is why the player must not get too close and give him a chance to get you covered. Get close enough that the goaltender must follow a fake but far enough away to give you room to manoeuvre.

Once you, the player, have decided to deke rather than shoot, your best results will be had if you slow down a little. This makes the goaltender even more nervous. It also gives you a chance to manoeuvre in a way that would be impossible if you moved in at full speed. Failure to get set for a deke is one reason why you see so many players miss when the opportunity arises. They fly in at top speed and, unless everything clicks just right, their chance is gone before they know it, and they are lying against the endboards or untangling their skates from the net. There are times, of course, when a player cannot get set (for example, when being checked) but if there is a chance the player should slow a little and move with cool purpose.

SCORING STRATEGY

As previously mentioned, quickness scores. Indecision on a player's part regarding exactly when to shoot is one of the chief reasons so many goal scoring opportunities are missed. By the time he makes up his mind, he is frequently too close. If he is over-anxious, as is often the case, he will probably shoot too soon and give the goaltender a break. The answer to the problem is given in the section on position. However, there is one other problem, that of knowing when you are from ten to twenty-five feet out. The development of this "distance sense" is well worth a special drill in practice.

Place a mark on the ice ten feet out from the edge of the goal crease. Coaches can actually paint the mark onto the ice as it will come off when scrapped by a player's skates. Then practise skating up to this mark and shooting. Put a mark directly in front of the net (ideal spot) and marks at various angles. After the players have practised in this way for a while, they will develop a sense of just where the spot is ten feet out. The coach can conduct this drill using both ends of the ice.

In deciding whether to shoot or go in and deke, there are several factors to consider. First, what is your strong point: a shot or a deke? Have you time to go in for a deke or is there an opponent coming to check you? How is it easiest to beat the goaltender against whom you are playing? Does the goaltender stay back in the net or come out and challenge? Is your shooting right on or are you having an off night? Are you in control of your game? What did you do on any previous chances? How far has the game progressed?

The answers to these questions should decide your strategy. If you are a better shooter than a deker, shoot. Do not deke until you have developed high level skill by working on it at practice or in unimportant games. If you have the time to try a deke, the answers to the third and fourth questions should be the deciding factor. If you know the goaltender is easier to beat with a deke, by all means go in and try to pull him out. If your shooting has been off, go in. If you are experiencing trouble stickhandling, lay off the deke and shoot. If you shot the last few times you were in on goal, try a deke to keep the goaltender from getting set. If you tried to deke him, try a shot because he may be expecting you to come right in again.

Needless to say, there will be no time during actual play to weigh these alternatives, much less to look them up in this book! But if they have been carefully worked on in practice situations your reaction will be instinctive, instantaneous, and – most important of all – right!

At the start of the game, mix up your plays to give you a chance to find the goaltender's weak spots. When the game is tight, use your strong point. If your club has a good lead, experiment a little. However, it is wise to remember that more goals are scored on shots than on dekes. Therefore, if you can shoot or deke exceptionally well, always shoot when the chips are down unless the situation is such that a deke is the best play (for example, if you know from past experience you can often fool him from close in). Usually it works out that the better the goaltender the harder he is to beat on a deke.

Once the player decides to shoot, he must then decide what kind of shot to use. Should it be high, low, or in between? According to the results of the survey made of goal scoring in the NHL and many carefully staged practice tests, the player should make his selection as follows:

First choice. Shoot below the knee, preferably about ankle high or even right along the ice. The only time this is not the best type of shot to use is when the goaltender is on the ice or is especially good at handling low shots. You will find this especially true with butterfly goaltenders. The player should decide against shooting low, too, when he knows the goaltender cannot handle a different type of shot; perhaps he has a special weakness for shoulder high shots. However, nine times out of ten, the low shot will be the best. Low shots are harder to stop, give better rebounds, and are easier to place. Most goaltenders say that they are by far the hardest shots to handle.

Second choice. The shoulder high type of shot is a good one to use against goaltenders who crouch very low when getting set for the shot, butterfly goaltenders, goaltenders who show timidity in handling high shots, or who are slow with their hands. It is also the best shot to use, of course, if the goaltender is down on the ice. Another factor to consider is that to stop a shoulder high shot the goaltender must move his hand the longest distance in order to stop the shot. Usually the goaltender keeps his free hand at his side, which means he must raise it about three feet to stop a shoulder high shot. This is why a waist or knee high shot is not as effective; the hand has less distance to go to reach the shot. One of the things that makes a shoulder high shot take second place to the low shot is that there is less margin for error. If the shot is just a little too high, it will go over the net; if it is just a little too low, it will be in the easy-to-stop waist to chest area. Then too, the goaltender can use his hands to stop a shoulder high shot. As his gloves are a goaltender's best line of defence (he can move them much quicker than his feet), you are giving him the edge instead of keeping the odds on your side. One of the main uses of a shoulder high shot is as a means of keeping the goaltender on edge. If you always shoot low, he may well be able to get set for your shot and thus improve his chances of making the stop. However, when the chips are down, shoot low. Controlling the height of a shot is dealt with under shooting skill.

From our results, tests, and experience, we find there are two types of target areas.

Best. This is a shot to either corner of the net (if in perfect shooting position). It may be a low shot to the far corner if coming in from an angle. If possible, shoot low to the goaltender's stick side.

Good. This is a high shot to either top corner (if in ideal scoring area), or high to far top corner if coming in from the side.

Make goaltender move first. The prime objective of a shooter is to make the goaltender move first. Once the goalie has made the first move, he's much easier to beat. The player who develops this skill increases his scoring chances a great deal.

Here are some methods the player can use to make the goaltender move first.

Fake shot. This is self-explanatory and consists of a faked shot aimed in one direction quickly followed by the real shot aimed in another. For example, the player could fake a shot to the right side and end up shooting to the left. However, even if the fake shot is not pointed in any special direction, it is still valuable because it frequently causes the goaltender to tighten up and often spoils his balance and stance. This move can be used from any distance or in the form of a deke if in close. As it is a simple move, it is surprising more players don't use it. It is not only a good way to make the goaltender move first but also a good one to use to get by a checker.

Moving the puck. The puck is moved back and forth in a side to side action (dribbling) just before a shot is made. This is a very effective move to use because, though it may not make the goaltender actually move his body, it will make him move his eyes. Now the reader may ask, "So what?" Here is the explanation.

The eyes, when they focus on an object, such as a puck on a puck carrier's stick, move on to a perch (level). When they are on the perch, they are most efficient. If they have to move to a new perch (level) to re-focus, there is a short period of blackout and adjustment between the time they move from one perch (level) position to the new one. This is why in baseball a curve or fork ball is harder to hit than a straight ball.

The shot should be made as soon as possible after the stickhandling motion has been done. By practising this, the player will soon be able to make the preliminary motion and the fast shot very quickly and easily. Avoid the serious mistake of carrying the puck at the side or in ready-to-shoot position as you move in to shoot. This gives the goaltender a chance to focus his eyes and line up the angle of the shot. The best way to carry in on goal is with the puck directly in front of you. From this position, you can stickhandle the puck back and forth before shooting or you can move it to either side and shoot. This front carry is best whether you are planning a shot or intending to go in for a deke. There are times, of course, when this is not possible, for example, when you have to cut in quickly from the side.

Some will say, "This moving the puck around before shooting may sound O.K., but will it not spoil the accuracy and power of the shot? After all, doesn't a player have to get the puck lined up on his stick before he shoots?" This is an understandable question with this technique. However, tests found that goalies admitted it was harder to line up and stop a shot prefaced by a puck movement. Practised regularly and at game conditions, this move will soon become automatic.

Manoeuvring. This refers to quick changes of position by skating manoeuvres or moving the puck around. These force the goaltender to move in order to stay in front of the puck. If he does not move, he will allow you to get opposite an open net area. Such manoeuvres are listed in the section on deking.

Analyzing the goaltender. Every player should study all opposing goaltenders at every opportunity in order to determine weak and strong points. The coach, of course, should also make a point of collecting data of this type and passing it on to his players, either doing it himself or assigning it to an assistant. This has become one of the expected duties of the assistant coach of NHL teams. The videotaping of opponents' tendencies from their previous games has made this aspect of "pre-scouting" both an art and a science. This is a simple assignment when your team plays in a regular league with perhaps three or four games or more against the same club. However, it is a much more difficult problem when you are playing new teams all the time without an opportunity to scout them.

In the latter case, the goaltender should be watched carefully during the pre-game warm-up and as play progresses. When on the bench, the player can learn a lot about the opposing goaltender if he watches him carefully. Too many players just watch the game and fail to look for information they can use to their advantage the next time they are on the ice.

Check the following details: Is the goalie slower moving to one side than to the other? Does he go down to the ice often and what gets him down there? Is he good with his hands? Which hand is best? How and when does he clear? Does he let low shots come out again by deflection off his stick, skates, or pads? Is he over-anxious and jittery? Does he stay in his goal or come out to cut off the angle? Does he keep his legs together or let them drift apart? Does he cover the short side or leave it open on shots for the long side?

Once you have the answers to these questions you will have information that can mean more goals. There is no need for the player to stage a mental check-up of the goaltender's weak and strong points as he goes in on goal because the information he has will be in his mind and will automatically come into action. A mental review before the game, when on the bench resting, and between periods will get your mind ready to click when the time comes. Just as every big league catcher knows the hitting habits of every batter in his league, so should the hockey player do a job on the opposing goaltenders.

SHOOTING

Shooting skill is, of course, the main factor in scoring. It doesn't matter how good your position or your strategy may be. If you can't shoot with a quick release, accurately and with sheer speed, you're not going to score very often.

Accuracy and control. Just as control is the vital fundamental of great baseball pitching, so is it with shooting in hockey. However, this is a skill that only a comparatively few players develop to high level. The main reason, it appears, is that the average player has so little chance to develop his accuracy and control. To prove this point try to recall how often you have practised shooting in a scientific, organized way. Then, figure out how many shots on goal you have during an average practice or game. For example, in the average NHL game, there may be up to a total of sixty to seventy shots on goal. Divide this up among approximately thirty players and you will see how little opportunity the average player gets to develop accuracy and control in game conditions.

Being able to shoot a puck hard and accurately at a small target while skating at full speed, or while changing direction quickly, is a high level skill that cannot be developed to any important level of efficiency without considerable time and intelligent, well organized effort. The only answer is – get more practice. The individual player can do this by working on his own, using the drills given under shooting accuracy drills. The coach can develop the accuracy and control of his team's shooting by using a major portion of his practice sessions to do similar drills.

Many players do not have a shooting technique that is mechanically perfect. It is the same problem that exists in baseball or football. Many players can throw or forward pass, but how many do so correctly? The fact that a player can shoot is usually satisfying enough for him. He is not aware that his shooting is mechanically incorrect, and that if corrected, both his speed and accuracy would improve. The smart player will check his shooting technique and try to make it perfect. He realizes that the better he shoots, the more goals he scores.

There are five types of shots possible to use: the sweep/wrist, slap, flip, snap, and drag.

Sweep/wrist. This is the name given to the most common type of shot in hockey. It is so named because it is performed with a smooth, sweeping action of the stick, from either the forehand side or the backhand side.

Bring the puck well back behind you. Then, with a forward sweeping motion of the stick, bring it quickly forward. At the same time, keep your weight on the stick by leaning your upper body over the puck, and by keeping your head low. At the start of the sweep, keep your wrists cocked back. Then, just before the puck begins to go out in front of you, snap the wrists viciously, putting every ounce of forearm and wrist strength you have into it. Whip that puck forward as if you were angry at it. As you snap the puck forward, make very sure you do not pull away from the shot by letting your head and shoulders come up and away. Instead, keep over the puck until it has gone well on its way. This is the same principle as in hitting a golf ball, a baseball, or a tennis ball. Don't pull your head away as the action is made.

When the sweeping action starts the weight is on the rear leg (left if a left-handed shot) and then is placed on to the forward leg as the puck is snapped forward with that all-important explosive effort. After the puck has gone, make sure you allow your stick to follow through smoothly. Do not stop it with a jerk. Let the blade of the stick follow through until it is pointing at the target you aimed for. The puck should be about halfway between the heel and end of the blade. The hands should be as close together on the shaft of the stick as possible, because the closer they are, the more whip you can get. However, the best plan is to experiment with the spread of your hand grip until you find the best one for you. The back of the lower hand should face back, with the back of the upper hand facing toward the direction in which you are going to shoot. To cock the wrists at the start of the shot, move the hands back from the wrists. To get the wrist snap, whip them forward again. Keeping the wrists stiff all through the shooting action is a common fault that makes it impossible for the player to get maximum speed and accuracy.

To keep this shot low, lean your body well over the stick, keep the shaft of the stick well ahead of the blade, let the puck go with the wrist snap a little sooner and follow through after the shot with your stick on the ice or just a little above it. It is your follow through that will be most important. If you follow through low, the puck cannot go any higher. To help you make a low follow through, keep the forward shoulder (right if a left-handed shot) well down and forward, ahead of the shaft of your stick.

To lift the puck, let the blade of the stick come through until it is ahead of the shaft and then snap with wrists and let the puck go. To control the height of your shot, let your stick follow through to the height required. If, for example, you want to shoot shoulder high, follow through to a shoulder high position. Above all, avoid the common mistake of trying to scoop the puck up with an upward scooping action of the blade. Remember to let your follow through do the work.

In developing the correct shooting technique for the sweep shot (or any type of shot), or to correct any fault you detect after a check-up, go through the shooting action slowly for a while until you are able to achieve the feel of the correct action. Then, gradually repeat the action faster and faster until you are at game-like speed. The same general principles apply both to the forehand and backhand shots.

Relaxation is also an important factor in the correct shooting technique. Try to avoid tensing the muscles of your arms and shoulders as you go through the shooting action. Keep your hands as loose as possible until the time to use the hard, explosive wrist snap. Another thing to avoid is clenching the jaw hard when the shot is made. This usually accompanies an extra effort. However, it does not help a bit. In fact, if you tighten your jaw you are more likely to tense up all over. One good way to relax is to take a deep breath just before you shoot and then exhale in a heavy sighing action as you shoot.

Slap shot. The body is parallel to the direction which you want the puck to travel and the puck is positioned in line with approximately the heel of the front skate. The lower hand is moved down the shaft of the stick until it is fully extended. Take your stick back behind you to shoulder height. You will see that the lower arm is fully extended. Keep your eyes focused on the puck. As you swing down on the puck, your weight transfers from the back leg to the front leg. The stick should hit the ice first, approximately one to two inches behind the puck. (Hitting the ice first will cause the stick to bend in the middle.) At the point the wrist moves from extension to flexion and, as the puck is struck in the middle of the blade, the force unleashed by the straightening of the shaft propels the puck. Tighten the hand grip just before contact is made with the ice so that there is no give on the part of the stick when it hits the ice.

All the other principles of controlling the shot, as listed for the wrist shot, such as follow through, keeping over the puck, and not pulling away also apply to the slap shot. Hand, wrist, forearm strength and weight, and also the weight of the stick are important factors.

The advantages of the slap shot over the wrist shot are very few. As far as its usefulness, our research has shown that the slap shot is at least forty per cent less accurate than the wrist shot. A lot of players can get more speed with a slap shot and, when used occasionally, it prevents the goaltender from getting used to your wrist shot action.

The slap shot is valuable as the puck can be shot at greater velocity and from further out, such as shooting from the blue line. A good low slap shot from the blue line will give your forwards good scoring opportunities from tip-ins and rebounds.

If speed is important in getting the puck away, the wrist and snap shots are quicker to release than the slap shot. Because the slap shot tends not to be as accurate and takes longer to get away, it should be developed after the other shots have been learned. More goals will be scored with the other shots rather than the slap shot.

Flip shot. This shot is used when the player is close to the goal and is most effective when the goaltender is on the ice in front of the puck carrier. It is one of the hardest of all shots to learn. This fact is well demonstrated over and over again during the season when you see player after player fail to flip the puck over a goaltender who is flat on the ice.

The shot is performed by using a very short shooting action. The blade of the stick is placed just behind the puck with the top edge of the blade well forward. Then the wrists are flipped forward and upward, bringing the bottom edge of the blade forward. The blade follows through to the height the player wishes to lift the puck. It is the action of the wrists that flips the blade of the stick under the puck, providing the quick lift needed. Every player should learn to use this shot off both the backhand and forehand.

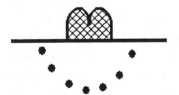

A great practice drill to become accustomed to is to line up ten pucks along the circular crease and discipline yourself to "hit the roof" or flat part of the top netting. Just as in school, fifty per cent (five of ten pucks) is barely passing. One hundred per cent is an "A" performance!

Snap shot. This is a short edition of the slap shot and is used when the player wants to get the puck away quickly, for example, after taking a pass in front of the goal. When carrying the puck in front of you, this shot can also be used effectively to take the goaltender by surprise. Quickly move the puck to the side, place the cupped blade of the stick behind it, draw the stick back six to eight inches and shoot. The wrists are extended and flexed when the stick blade hits the puck.

Although this shot may not be as accurate as the wrist shot, a player with strong, flexible wrists and forearms can get remarkable speed into a snap shot and thus reduce some of the disadvantage of it not being as accurate.

Drag shot. This is performed exactly in the same manner as the wrist shot with one major difference. There is no hard snap of the wrists as the puck is shot. The wrists are stiffened and held back as the puck leaves the blade. Then, as soon as the puck has gone, the stick is whipped forward in a fast follow through. The start and end of the shooting action are fast, but at the time the puck is let go, the action of the stick is slowed momentarily by a stiffening of the wrists together with a slight holding up of the forward action of the blade. The player moves his shoulders down and into the shot and generally acts as if he is trying to blast it with all his power. The fast follow through after the puck has started on its way adds to the illusion that the shot is a fast one. When the wrists are not snapped, the forward action of the blade is held up momentarily. As the puck leaves the stick, the shot is much slower than it looks and it is sometimes mis-timed by the goaltender.

The drag shot should only be used occasionally for variety. It is worthwhile to learn in that it helps you develop puck control. It can be effective against goaltenders who are over-anxious. The drag shot can be compared to a change of pace pitch in baseball because it operates on the principle that it spoils the timing of the goalie just as a change of pace spoils the timing of a batter.

Taking aim. To control the direction the puck will take, the player must depend on only one thing – his eyes. It is through the eyes that anyone aims anything – an arrow shot from a bow, a bullet from a rifle, a bowling ball at the pins, a baseball at the strike area, or a puck at the goal area. If, during the action of throwing a baseball, a bowling ball, or shooting a puck, the eyes are taken off the target, the sense of balance and control is lost. For all intents and purposes, the player is blind. Therefore, when the player is approaching the net for a shot on goal, he should keep his eyes on the net, first of all, to find the opening; second, to make sure his muscles are directed through his eyes so that the puck is propelled toward the target.

Strangely enough, however, this basic principle of aiming and direction control is disregarded by many coaches and players in the NHL. They follow the theory that the player should take a quick look at the net, pick his spot, and then focus his eyes on the puck. The reasons given are that if the player keeps his eyes on the spot at which he is aiming, the goaltender will be given warning and will be set for it.

In analyzing this theory, it is important to remember that many goaltenders keep their eyes on the puck at all times, and therefore can't see where the puck carrier is looking. For this reason, a player should learn to manipulate the puck by feel. If a player can stickhandle by feel, he can learn to shoot the same way. There is no reason why watching the puck as the shot is made will improve either the shooting action or the direction. A baseball pitcher or a bowler doesn't watch the ball during the first part of the delivery. The delivery of the puck should be just as subconscious.

In our research, we have made many experimental comparisons between concentrating on the target area and concentrating on the puck and stick. The results turned in when watching the target area have been as much as seventy per cent better than when the eyes have been on the puck at the moment of the shot. These tests were made from different distances, different angles, at standing and moving targets. Tests were also conducted under simulated game conditions.

When deking the goaltender, the best results will be achieved when the puck carrier keeps his eyes on the goaltender and again manipulates the puck by feel. As soon as the goaltender is drawn out of position, the eyes should focus on the area where the player wants to put the puck.

In the survey, a check was made to see how many hockey players kept their eyes on the target area. It was startling to discover that only one player in twenty actually used his eyes to control the direction of his shot! On being asked, six out of ten said that they had never thought about it and did not really know what they did.

Shooting speed. The speed with which the player propels the puck at the target area is naturally a very important factor in scoring goals. The faster it goes, the less time the goaltender has to make his play. Therefore, emphasis should be placed on the development of as much speed as possible because the more speed, the better the odds are that the shot will end up hitting the twine inside the goal area. Only a few players, even in the NHL, are noted for their fast shooting.

However, it seems safe to say that very few players have a really hard shot. The reason was made very apparent when our researchers began to ask the question "Have you ever consciously tried to develop a hard shot?" The answer ninety per cent of the time was – no! Some, on further thought, said that, at one time or another, they had consciously tried to shoot hard but had not done any special work to develop a hard shot. Of the other ten per cent the answers indicated only a casual effort, such as doing a few exercises to build wrist or forearm strength, or time spent trying to shoot hard. Only one reported any attempt to study the technique of shooting. Of the coaches asked, only a few said that they worked on teaching shooting skill in an organized fashion.

The factors that go to make up shooting speed are good mechanics, physical effort, strength and flexibility, controlled relaxation, and equipment. The mechanics have been dealt with, so let us start with the factor of physical effort.

Shooting hard necessitates a burst of energy, an explosive effort in which the player tries to shoot hard. This involves a real mental effort.

First of all, remember to *try*: second, make yourself use all the power and energy available. Unfortunately, this is not done enough. When this situation exists the athlete is lazy. Psychologists tell us we are all inclined to take things easy – we must learn to drive ourselves to make extra effort. This is why players develop a lazy pattern in their shooting. To break it they must concentrate on making the effort at practice and by working on special drills until the lazy habit is replaced with the all-out effort pattern. You can shoot hard if you do shoot hard!

The next step is to develop strength and flexibility in the muscles used to whip the puck forward. The muscles concerned are those of the hands, wrists, and forearms. Doing lots of all-out effort shooting and playing hockey itself will help develop them but they can be increased to tremendous strength and flexibility through special exercises and drills. In this way added power will be transmitted into your shot.

Then, the player must make sure he learns the technique of controlled relaxation when he moves into the shooting action. If, when shooting, you tense your upper arm and shoulder muscles, you will take away from the power of your shot because the hands, wrists, and forearm muscles will be interfered with. To demonstrate this point, hold your hockey stick in the shooting position. Then, stiffen your arm and shoulder muscles and shoot. Then, try the same thing keeping them loose and easy, letting the hands and wrists do the work. Notice the difference?

Finally, the player must consider what kind of stick he is going to use. The stronger and more whippy the stick is the greater the speed it will be possible to put into the shot. A stick with the grain running in a straight line along the length of the blade and horizontally up the shaft is usually the best. The narrower the grains the stronger the stick. Many players today use a stick with an aluminum shaft. Introduced in the late 1980s, it has added a whole new dimension to stick selection. Not only does it reduce the cost via fewer broken sticks, but it is lighter in weight for quicker shooting, and the shafts are more uniform.

After a player considers the "feel" of the stick, he must consider the lie of it. According to tests, the flatter the lie of the stick the less power it is possible to get behind the shot. This is due to the fact that when using a lie from one to three, the player has to hold his stick well away from the body. While using a five to seven lie, the player has to hold his stick closer to the body and thus the stick can be more powerfully whipped. Furthermore, you have better puck control when the puck is closer to your feet and the stick is closer to the body, a definite advantage during scrambled play.

One must also consider the curvature of the stick blade. A stick with a straight blade is best because the puck is easier to control. With the advent of the curved blade, backhand passing and shooting have become less and less of an option for many players. The more curvature you have on the blade of the stick the less you are able to control the puck.

Shooting and passing accuracy tests made with different lie sticks indicated strongly that the close lie stick was the most effective. Since then, we have found that a straight blade is more effective than a curved one. A small thing like a tape job can hinder puck control and shooting accuracy to some degree. It affects the way the puck leaves the stick in a pass.

Deking skill. Most of the moves the player can use to beat the goal-tender are included in the puck-carrying moves which get the puck past any checker. The player who develops high level puck control skills, body fakes, and skating moves will do a good job deking the goaltender.

Get as much practice using them on a goaltender as possible. Remember that it is not necessary to get your body past the goaltender, just the puck. In games or practice scrimmage the player gets only a few chances to go in on goal. Accordingly, he will not be able to develop a great deal of skill and confidence unless such opportunities are greatly augmented by special practice at carrying in on the goal and trying to deke the goaltender. An excellent plan is to give each player a certain number of breakaways, putting the drill on a compet-itive level by keeping a progressive check on the number of goals scored during each drill. This will also give the coach information regarding how the player is improving. Trying your deke out on your own goaltender and then checking with him to see how it can be improved is an excellent plan as he will be able to tell you things that you would never notice.

Analyzing what happened on certain dekes that failed is something that will help the player score more goals. Often, giving some thought to "why," will teach you how to make a move start working for you. Check on all details. Is your fake convincing? Do you start your play too soon or late? Have you any habits that are "giveaways" for the move you are going to try? Get the goaltender on your team to try to stop you in different ways, sliding out one time, and standing up the next. This will give you a chance to see what moves are most effective against the different types of goaltending styles.

Deking the goaltender. Many of the ordinary puck-carrying moves can be used on the goaltender when you carry in close. However, there are several special dekes that are for use on goaltenders only.

Cut across. This effective move forces the goaltender to move first. The puck carrier heads for a spot just outside one of the goal posts, as if he were going to shoot the puck in that side of the goal. This brings the goaltender over to that side of the goal. Then, when he is about seven to eight feet away from the goaltender, the puck carrier suddenly cuts at a

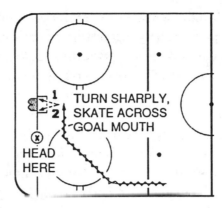

right angle across the goal toward the other goal post. This forces the goaltender to move again since he must go across with the puck carrier in case he shoots it quickly into the far side of the net.

As the puck carrier moves across the goal, he watches the goaltender carefully. If he starts across quickly with the puck carrier, the puck carrier should shoot low and hard at the side of the goal the goaltender has just left (2). If the goaltender is slow in getting across, the puck carrier shoots at the open net on the side of the goal to which he is heading (1). Often the goaltender will slide across to cover the shot. If he does this, the puck carrier can either shoot high over the goaltender or can let a low shot go under his upper body since this part of his body usually takes a while to get to the ice.

Just how close the puck carrier should go before he cuts across depends a lot on the speed at which he is travelling and the position and skill of the goaltender. The best thing is to experiment until you find the ideal distance for you. It will probably be somewhere between six and eight feet out. This play is also well adapted for use when you are coming in from the side, cutting in quickly after having taken a pass or having rounded the defence. If can be done to either side.

Fake shot. This is also an effective deke because it is frequently successful in getting the goaltender to move first. The player skates at the goaltender. Then, when he is about five or six feet away, he slows right up or stops dead, and fakes a shot to either side of the goaltender. If the goaltender is sliding out to block the shot, the puck carrier will have several plays open to him.

He can step back and fire the puck over the goaltender who has gone down, or slide the puck under the goaltender as he is on his way down, or move to either side and flip the puck into the net as the goaltender comes sliding out. If the goaltender stays on his feet but moves to cover the fake, the puck carrier shoots to the other side or any spot the goaltender leaves open by his move. If the goaltender glides out on his feet, trying to block the shot by cutting off the angles, the puck carrier shifts around him and slips the puck in behind in the open net.

The success of this move, of course, depends upon the effect of the fake. To keep the goaltender on edge and unsettled as to how to play, you stop to shoot, and fake alternately. The time spent in learning a convincing fake shot will be a worthwhile investment because it can be used in so many puck-carrying situations.

If you use a fake shot when in close to the goaltender, it is best to actually start the shot, and then stop it by moving the blade of the stick quickly in front of the puck. By repeated practice, any player can learn to perform this move with real conviction. The fake should also be learned on the backhand side because there will be many occasions when the player has the puck in this position with no time to shift to his forehand side. Fake shots can be used successfully when the player has broken away and has lots of time to make his move on the goaltender.

Side to side. To perform this skill the player carries the puck ahead of him in front of the middle of his body. Then, when he gets about four feet away from the goalie, he shifts the puck wide to one side, as though he were going to try to slip it past the goaltender into the net on that side. Then, if the goaltender moves, the puck carrier brings it back across in front of him again in a side to side stickhandling action, and slips the puck in on the opposite side. This trick can be done with a body shift or with merely the side to side movement of the puck.

Backhand to forehand shift. In doing this move, the puck carrier carries in with the puck in front of him. About six feet away from the goaltender, he shifts the puck to his backhand as if he is going to shoot for the far corner (to the right of the goaltender if a left-hand shot). He starts the shot but instead of letting the puck go, he slips it quickly to his forehand side and shoots for the other side of the net. The move can be done backhand to forehand or vice versa.

One way shift. This is a somewhat similar play to the cut across, but it is done later. The player heads for one side of the net, and then, as soon as he sees the goaltender move to cover him, he shifts the puck far to the opposite side and shoots to that side of the net. Done quickly and at the right time (the moment the goaltender moves to cover the side of the net the player is heading for), it can be very effective. It should be practised to either side. Otherwise, the player will be tabbed by the goaltender as one who always tries it to the same side.

The short sider. This is a play for use when cutting in from the side. As he cuts in, the player begins to shoot for the far side of the net. But just before he releases the puck he brings his front shoulder (right shoulder if a left-handed player) around to the left, moves his front elbow well out in front, and brings the other elbow in close to his side. This will slide the puck to the short side instead of across the goal at an angle to the far corner, where the goaltender is expecting it.

It is best to shoot fairly high in this case as it is likely that the goaltender's feet will still be in the way when his upper body falls across the goal to cover the expected angle shot. Even if the goaltender glides across instead of falling, one of his feet will probably still be in the way. If the goaltender is in the habit of doing splits on such a play, or slides across with one leg bent in a long stride, there is often an open spot between the legs. To direct the puck at this spot, the front shoulder and elbow are not moved across to the side so much. This deke is sometimes called a drag shot.

Summary. The player who works hard to develop general puck-carrying skill, body deception, and skating agility will find that many variations of the moves listed here will be developed as he practises going in on the goaltender.

No matter which you do, shoot or deke, you must not spoil a scoring chance by getting flustered and excited. This is what often happens when a player suddenly realizes he has a chance to score, perhaps to win the game. When the player realizes it, he thinks more about if he is going to score instead of how he is going to get the puck in the net. The idea is to go in with abandon, concentrating on what you are doing. A good move is to say to yourself as you move in, "Take it easy, take it easy" or any other expression designed to remind you to keep loose and relaxed.

Too many players can pull off sensational scoring plays at practice but nearly always mess up a scoring opportunity in a game. This is caused by tension induced by the excitement of the situation. The practice of relaxation methods and mental control will soon make the "practice wonder" able to do equally well in a game.

GENERAL SCORING HINTS

Backhand shooting. The average player tends to neglect his backhand shooting, preferring to shoot from his forehand when possible, even during practice scrimmage or shooting practice drills. This is a great mistake because a lot of goal scoring punch will be added if speed and accuracy are added to the backhand. If the backhand is weak, the player will unconsciously try to avoid using it by switching the puck to the other side before shooting. This can be the cause of many missed goals since the puck often comes to your backhand side on a quick pass out or during a scramble. If you try to shift to the forehand, the goalie may have time to get into position, or a checker may have time to take you out of the play.

Screen shots. During the average game there are many opportunities to shoot on goal from a screen created by either one or more players (opponents or teammates). This situation often just happens. It can also be created by the puck carrier who manoeuvres until he sets up a screen or a teammate sets up a screen in front. The player should always be alert for this situation to develop, firing the puck carefully through an open spot. When there are players in front of the shooter, it is best to shoot low since there is a better chance of the puck getting through.

An ideal opportunity to use a screen shot occurs when the defence pair or a single defenceman backs up too close to the goal. Many defencemen have this fault. When playing against such opponents the puck carrier should slow a little, let the defence back up as far as possible, and then snap a shot through their legs, or between them. Such a shot often gets by a goalie without him even seeing it. Be alert for such opportunities.

Follow your shot. Another way to pick up more goals is to get the habit of following up on your shot as quickly as you can. The average goaltender is slow to clear and allows many rebounds to come out, especially from low shots. If you follow up quickly, many of these rebounds can be turned into goals. Studying the goaltender to see how he clears and how the average rebound comes out from his pads, stick, or skates will often give you an important clue regarding just where to follow up. When shooting from the blue line during a ganging play, keep your shots low so that teammates around the goal can get any rebounds. High shots will probably be caught and easily cleared. Avoid at all times the bad habit of shooting and then watching to see what happens. Follow that shot right in as hard as you can. Also be alert to follow in shots by teammates.

Another worthwhile play is to study the way the puck comes off the backboards. Each rink is a little different and if you study how the puck rebounds off the backboards, you will often be able to rush in and pick up the puck for a shot or a pass to a free teammate because you will know where it is going to rebound. This is one reason why NHL teams utilize the "morning skate" on game days. It allows the players to refamiliarize themselves with the characteristics of each playing surface.

A good play, when you have the puck beside the goal but are at a bad angle or blocked off, is to flip the puck so that it will land at the goaltender's feet and then follow it in quickly. Your quick follow up may result in your picking up a rebound or may unsettle the goaltender and cause him to mess up the original shot. Flipping the puck instead of shooting hard will give you time to follow it in.

Scrambles. Scoring from scrambles involves being able to shoot loose pucks, pass outs, and rebounds into the net during the wild scrambled play that often occurs around the goal during ganging or power plays. To develop skill at this type of play, observe the following points carefully.

When waiting for a pass out, make sure your feet are well spread, knees well bent, and the upper body leans forward. This position will give you balance and make you hard to block out of the play or shove off the puck just as you get it.

The stick should be on the ice with your weight on it. If the stick is on the ice, you will be ready to shoot in a pass out. If the stick is in the air, the pass out can go by you before you have a chance to shoot it. In a game, see how many pass outs and loose pucks are missed because the player did not have his stick on the ice.

Many a player has the bad habit of frequently turning his back on the puck during ganging plays or on any offensive thrust if he loses the puck, or if the puck seems to have been recovered by an opponent. Often, just as he turns his back, the puck comes to him or is recovered by a teammate. By the time he notices this, the chance is gone. Make it a rule to keep your eye on the puck at all times.

When a player is being watched by an opponent out in front of the net, he can often break free to take a pass out or a loose puck. He first fakes a move to the spot opposite the one he actually wants to move to or to which the pass out is coming. Such a fake can be very effective because the opponent guarding is usually watching you and not the puck. Therefore, if you fake to go a certain way, how does he know that you are not moving to get a pass out coming in that direction?

The strong player has a big advantage during scrambles because through his strength he can often out scuffle his opponent, shove him away, lift his stick and perform the many other manoeuvres that are common to such play. Therefore, the development of muscular strength should be a must with all players.

By using skates to stop passes or kick the puck free, the player can often get the puck out of spots where it is impossible to use his stick. A good drill to develop skill at controlling the puck with skates is to get a puck and skate up and down the ice with it, using only your skates to control it. Another good idea is to stand in front of the goal and take passes with your skates. Stop the puck with your skates, slip it onto your stick and then shoot.

Another important skill involved in scoring goals during pressure plays or scrambles is being able to sweep a pass coming at you at the net with accuracy and speed and to deflect it toward an open spot in the goal area. In the average game, you will see players fanning on such plays or shooting wildly. Or you will see the player stop the puck and then try to shoot only to be knocked off the puck or checked because he took the time to stop the puck before shooting. Being able to intercept or deflect a fast moving puck in this way demands a high level of skill that does not just come to the player. It must be practised. The amount of practice the player gets during games or in the usual practice scrimmage is not sufficient.

The most common fault in making this type of shot is lifting the head and taking the eyes off the approaching puck before contact has been made. Sweeping the stick at the puck across its line of flight takes fine timing in which the eyes play a vital role. Do not look at where you hope the puck has gone before contact has been made. It is usually impossible to aim such a shot. Contact must be made and the puck sent on its way without hesitation.

When a checker has you covered do not stand there and stay covered. Instead, move around, fake a move, try every move in the book to get free. Keeping still and inactive for a moment and then breaking away quickly is a good plan as the period of keeping still may lull your checker into a moment's inattention that will enable you to get free with your quick break. Too many players, when covered, just stand there confining their action to perhaps a few shoves with the stick or the odd push.

Faking by goaltender. The player should keep in mind that a good goaltender often purposely leaves openings or fakes a movement in order to draw shots for which he is prepared. Study him carefully so he won't be able to fool you.

The swerve and shoot. This is a form of shooting strategy ideal for use when there is a defenceman or checker backing up in front of you toward the goal. As you get close to the goal, suddenly swerve toward either side. Then just as the checker moves over with you, shoot hard and low to the far corner of the net. This manoeuvre may well unsettle the goaltender. The best way to use the move is to swerve to the left and then shoot at an angle past the checker's left leg to the left side of the goaltender. If right-handed, swerve to the right, and shoot at an angle across to the right side of the goal.

When the defenceman goes down. Going down to block shots is a technique that many defencemen developed. Today, it is a skill which is seldom mastered by inexperienced defencemen at any particular level of play. As a result, it should be coached and encouraged with cautious limitations. A defenceman who goes to his knees in front of a puck carrier trying to shoot on goal can block many dangerous shots. The best possible way to outwit a defenceman using this move is to use the fake shot. Once the defenceman goes down to block a shot he believes is coming, you can easily shift around him. If a defenceman is close to you and goes down, there is not much sense in shooting as the odds are heavily on his side.

Position. The average forward is inclined to be lazy and misses many opportunities to score or to set up a score. If he is a little out of position and left behind his teammates who are breaking up the ice, he will often follow up quite slowly thinking that he is out of the play. Because he follows up slowly, he often misses a scoring opportunity. Perhaps there is a rebound or perhaps the puck carrier gets trapped and starts to manoeuvre around looking for a teammate to whom he can pass. Make a point of getting up there on the play.

The Richard trick. This trick is so named because the great Maurice Richard used it very successfully during his career. To perform it, the player skates up to the defence on one side and then suddenly starts across the defence. Just as he starts across, he snaps a shot on goal between the defencemen. If this trick is well timed, it will often catch a goaltender not ready for the shot and a goal will result. It is a move to use whenever the defence is backed up fairly close to the goal. There is not much point in using it if the defence pair is out at the blue line as the goaltender will have time to see the shot. Left-handers should try the trick by heading toward the right defenceman.

Never be content with just one or two goal-scoring tricks even if they work well for you a large part of the time. Always keep hard at work trying to add new tricks. The player who gets lazy about developing additional tricks, will suddenly find his goal scoring average dropping off as the opposition gets on to him.

The scoring slump. Just as a hitter in baseball will suddenly go into a hitting slump for no apparent reason, so will the hockey player find himself in a scoring slump. No matter what he does, he seems to be unable to get the puck into the net. Something always seems to happen to spoil his shot. He hits the post, the puck hits somebody's skate and is deflected, or the goaltenders seem to go into a "hot" streak and stop everything shot their way. Such a slump will often discourage a player and thus spoil his determination and spirit. In other cases it will make him try even harder until he is pressing too hard. Many people claim that a slump is just one of those things and there is nothing much you can do about it except wait for it to run out. However, this is a fallacy. If you analyze the play of someone in a scoring slump you'll probably find that he has developed some bad habits in his shooting technique or strategy. He may be pressing too hard and too tense to perform at peak efficiency.

When a slump hits a player, he should check to see if his fundamentals are sound. He should concentrate on keeping loose and relaxed around the goal and check to see if he is stale. The problem of staleness is dealt with in the chapter on Training. The player should do all he can to make sure his technique is not at fault and then assume an "I'll do my best and the heck with it" attitude so he will not start to press and worry to a point of poor efficiency.

A determined, cheerful, and optimistic attitude is very important. Above all, the player should not put his slump down to bad breaks and leave it at that. Bad breaks are usually the result of some technical error or fault. For example, if you hit the post, your accuracy is at fault. It does not mean that the gods of hockey have decided to turn sour on you.

Keep a book. "Keeping a book" is another expression used to describe the practice of keeping careful notes of all worthwhile hits and misses. By studying the results and facts compiled in this way, you can avoid making the same mistake again. You will run across many interesting things that can help improve all round scoring punch. It is fairly hard to do this on your own. A good plan is to get an interested friend to help. The coach should assign some member of his staff to do it for the team. Too many players are unable to tell you what they did or did not do after the game. Once again, the use of videotape is an effective tool for this purpose.

DEVELOPING SHOOTING ACCURACY

In developing shooting accuracy, two methods can be practised. Shots may be made from different distances and angles in order to place the puck in different areas of the net past a goaltender. Alternatively, the definite target system may be used without a goalie in the net.

Those who feel the first method is best are of the opinion that to be useful, practice must be conducted under game-like conditions with the goaltender blocking the way. Their claim is that these are the conditions under which the player has to shoot in a game. Consequently any practice under different conditions could not develop the skill actually needed.

The advantages of a shooting practice and using definite targets placed in the goal are based on the learning principle that shooting at definite targets will develop much greater levels of control and accuracy than haphazard practice. Those who support this system also claim that any accuracy and control gained by shooting at definite targets can quickly be transferred into game-like shooting conditions. The sense of control and accuracy gained stays with the players. Those who support this system say that the clearer the target is (targets with bull's-eyes painted on them) the better the results. During our survey the settling of this discussion was one of the major projects. Careful tests were conducted and results analyzed in detail. The following are the findings of this study.

Shooting accuracy practice survey. The players participating in the tests were separated into groups according to their general proficiency so that there were three groups in all, good shooters, fair shooters, and poor shooters. Each of these groups were divided into two further groups, one to practise shooting accuracy drills with the goaltender in the net, and another to practise with some targets placed in the net.

To start, each group was given one hundred shots with the goaltender in the net. Each shot was called with the players shooting at selected targets. Twenty-five shots were from a stationary position, twenty-five while skating slowly, twenty-five while at full speed, and twenty-five while cutting across in front of the net.

The results were carefully listed. Then each player took one hundred shots at targets placed-in the goal. These results were also tabulated. Then for two weeks each group practised according to the system assigned to their group. Then the players were put through the same shooting accuracy tests with which the study was started and the improvement rates carefully noted. The players were also put through several other shooting accuracy tests that they had never tried before, such as trying to knock a tin can off a box. In ninety per cent of the cases, the players who had been practising under the target system showed greater improvement with better results in the special tests.

Following these tests, frequent scrimmages were held and the shooting accuracy of the players once again carefully checked. Those who had been practising under the target system again showed the best results. On an average, the players trained by target practice were sixty per cent better than those who had practised against a goaltender. This is a big difference but, in following check-up tests with selected individuals, it was proved again. The greatest comparative rates of improvement of the players trained under the target system over the others were noted in the poor shooters group. Many of those rated as poor shooters at the start of the study showed better accuracy in the final tests than did many of those rated as good shooters who had been practising against the goaltender in the net system.

A further test was made in which one group practised with the target system alone and another group used the target system for three-quarters of the time, finishing the last quarter of the workout with shooting drills against the goaltender. The results obtained by the group using the combination were best when tested under simulated game conditions. The conclusion reached from our tests was that the ideal type of shooting accuracy practice is when the target system is used with a short period of shooting on the goaltender to finish off the workout.

Players who practised under the target system reported more fun and interest in the practice work than the other group. All of the players who had been shooting at definite targets reported that, when they played an actual game or scrimmage, they noticed that they thought a lot more about where they should shoot and therefore selected a target more often than previously. They had developed the target selection habit and rarely shot haphazardly. Still another advantage is that it is easy to bring in the competitive angle under the target system. This is an important point because when drills are competitive, they are greatly enhanced in value.

SHOOTING ACCURACY TARGETS

The portable insert goal. The idea of the accuracy target is to use it as an insert that can be placed in any goal, such as is found on any rink. It is easy to store and quick to put up. The idea is merely to make a strong wooden insert as illustrated in the diagram. This insert is exactly the same as the front of the goal. This wood should be strong and the target area should be of the same dimensions. The insert is attached to the goal with soft wire or clamps attached to the cross bar and the standards. Measure the insert carefully so that it fits snugly. Use a good

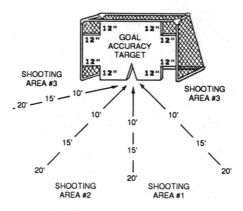

number of strong attachments so the insert does not rattle around when hit straight on.

To make these two targets even more effective, metal or wooden discs can be attached so that they hang in the centre of each target area. These should be painted with bull's-eyes. Attach them with a long hinge so when hit, they will bend back.

Measure the distance from the goal line, as shown below, and have the players practice shooting different types of shots from all of the distances and angles.

(Editor's note: Recently, the Shooter Tutor has come onto the market. This is the same as the portable insert goal except it is made of heavy duty vinyl which will stand up to shots from novice to pro. The Shooter Tutor is light, can be rolled up and transported very easily.)

Moving target. This type of target provides the player with an opportunity to develop accuracy while shooting at moving targets. The skill developed trying to hit this target will improve the players' capacity to hit the ordinary stationary target. Then too, this target can provide a lot of fun and much interesting competition.

To build a moving target you need a strong flat sled, a two by eight piece of wood, a support for the upright three by four feet long, three pieces of metal sheeting, paint, nails, and screws. The two by eight is firmly attached to the sled and three metal sheeting discs are attached to the faces of it as shown in the diagram. A long rope is then attached to the sled. You can use wider pieces of wood for the upright from which you have cut circular pieces eight inches in diameter. If these are backed with chicken wire, you will have a pocket into which the player can shoot

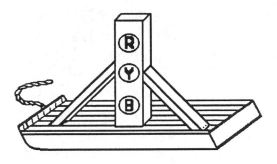

MOVING TARGET

the puck instead of trying to hit the metal sheeting target discs. Anyone can make a very suitable target using the general principles outlined here. The target can be drawn back and forth across the ice by someone who will be out of danger through the use of a rope. The speed and direction can be controlled easily.

Ball target. An excellent moving target for accuracy is a large rubber beach ball. It is thrown high in the air and allowed to bounce. The player stationed at a particular spot must try to hit it, either on a given bounce, or at will. He must hit it, however, before it stops bouncing.

Painted targets. The goal insert, used in the accuracy goal and portable insert goal target, can easily be painted on the side of a back fence, a barn, a wall, etc. if it is not convenient to make an actual portable goal because of a lack of space.

Tin can target. The old battered tin can can be used to good effect. Place it on a platform at different heights or hang it up at a desired spot in the goal. To be most effective, paint the can a bright red.

Shooting platform. To practise shooting during the off season, use a shooting platform. All you need is a square of wood or a long plank. This, if waxed, will make an ideal piece of equipment.

Dress up your equipment. When making your equipment, remember that the better made it is, and the smarter it looks, the better results you will have. A good idea is to paint your equipment with the school or team colours.

Stationary shooting. Markers are placed on the ice at different distances and at different angles from the centre of the goals. There should be five of them, one in the centre, and two at either side for the angles.

Twelve pucks are used with the player shooting two at each target area. He can start at the lower right hand marker and go around the target taking each target area as he comes to it.

Each player takes his twelve shots from the ten foot shooting distances. The group then starts from the fifteen foot distance and finally the twenty foot distance. The drill can progress until each player has had a crack at shooting from each distance and from each angle. The length of the drill can be decided by the coach according to the time available. If several of these goal targets are used, the players can be divided into small groups and a lot of drilling accomplished. In keeping score, one point should be given to the player if he hits one of the corner target areas, two points if he hits the small target area and the bottom of the target, and five points if the small target area in the centre of the target is hit. Care should be taken to determine the most difficult positions.

Extra practice should be emphasized in shooting at these areas. It is important that a definite record be kept. The drills should be done with the players shooting from both the forehand and the backhand. The players and coaches will be surprised to find that after a certain amount of practice, better scores will be turned from the backhand side. At first shooting should be done at a medium speed. Then, when skill has been developed, have the players shoot as hard as they can. One day the drill can be done with the players using sweep shots, the next snap, slap, or flip shots, or any combination of these. The individual player can have a lot of fun at such practice by trying to improve his score or by organizing competitions with his friends.

Glide shooting. The same system is used in this drill as in stationary shooting. However, the players skate until they are about six feet from the shooting marker. They then glide and shoot at the marker.

Slow skating shooting. The same principle is followed as for stationary shooting and glide shooting, but the player skates slowly up to the marker and shoots.

Fast skating shooting. The same as the previous three drills, only the player skates to the marker at full speed and then shoots.

Target goal scrimmage. In many ways this is an ideal drill because it simulates game conditions. However, it should be used merely as a drill variation, not instead of the previously listed drill. The idea is simple. Goal accuracy targets are set up in the goals and the players scrimmage.

To score, the player must shoot. It can be played with the players choosing their own targets as they shoot, or with the coach selecting specific targets and calling the target as the player gets ready to shoot.

The drill provides a very effective method of teaching the player how to pick definite targets instead of just shooting at random. This is a good idea for public rink hockey, or for play in your back yard, because it provides the one thing that is so often missing in this type of hockey, a goaltender. This drill also gives the coach an excellent chance to study the shooting weaknesses of this players.

Cut across shooting. In this drill, the player comes down the ice and cuts across the front of the goal, shooting at any assigned target as he moves across. This should be done with the players cutting across and shooting from the backhand and the forehand side.

Pass out shooting. To conduct this drill the players should stand in front and to the side of the goal on specific spots. They practise shooting the puck at assigned areas on the target as the puck is passed out to them. It is an excellent way for the player to practise the interception and deflection shots mentioned previously for scramble play. For example, long passes can be made to a player stationed at either side of the goal which he must deflect into one of the low corner targets.

Flip shooting. To develop flip shooting accuracy, station the player about four feet in front of the net. From there he must try to put the puck into one of the high target areas or into the upper third of the target, indicated by a red line drawn along the width of the target.

With a little ingenuity, drills involving all the different types of scoring plays can used. For example, the player can try to hit the target after making a fake shot or after swerving to one side as he would do in the swerve and shoot trick previously dealt with. Screen shots can be practised by placing a defence pair or a checker in front of the player to simulate actual conditions. When using these drills the player and coach should keep in mind that low shots are most effective, and that it would be wise to practice shooting at these targets.

Used with intelligence in a well organized fashion these drills can do a wonderful job developing added shooting accuracy. They also add fun and variety to practice schedules. They can be used as a regular part of the practice session or at intervals. To make each shooting drill session most effective, the coach should remind each player briefly what points to watch in his shooting technique. These drills give the coach and the individual player an ideal way to combine work on the mechanics of shooting and actual accuracy practice. Made into contests these drills provide very interesting and worthwhile events for organized hockey field days as previously suggested.

Ordinary shooting practice. If, for any reason, the player or coach feels that the target system is not for him, the next best thing is to make sure that whatever method used is well organized and varied, including as much of the competitive angle as possible. Avoid haphazard shooting practice during which the player merely shoots on goal without any definite assignments. Such practice will not develop the player's full scoring potential.

DEVELOPING SHOOTING POWER

Added shooting power will be developed also as a matter of course if the player, when shooting, makes an all-out effort to shoot hard. However, a lot more power can be developed if the following suggestions are used.

Heavy stick. In order to increase the muscular load involved in shooting and thus develop more muscular power, spend a certain amount of the time using "heavy" sticks (sticks with lead weights on the shaft). These "heavy" sticks create greater hand, wrist, and forearm strength. For special exercises and stick drills especially designed to develop the hand, wrist, and forearm for powerful shooting, see the chapter on Training.

Shooting power test. An excellent way to test the actual shooting power and, at the same time, get the habit of putting full effort into the shooting action is to use what our researchers have named the power test block. This is a block of wood eighteen inches square (twelve inches for younger players). A bull's eye is painted on one side of the block. This block is placed on a line (perhaps one of the blue lines). The player then takes up a position at a marker six feet from the block. He shoots at the block trying to knock it as far back from the line as possible. The further back it goes, the more power is indicated. This should be done with both forehand and backhand shots.

At first the player will not move the block very much with his backhand but as more time is given to this drill, power will increase remarkably. The competitive angle can be worked into this test very easily by measuring the distance each player sends the block back. Each club should have four or five of these blocks available so that small groups of players can take the test or do the drill at one time. The young player, wishing to practise on his own, can work at constantly improving his best distance record.

If the proper type of wood block is hard to find, a strong wooden box can be used. It could be weighted with sand or stones. The total weight should be between five and ten pounds. The younger the player, the lighter the box should be. In using this power target for drilling or testing, the players should shoot from stationary, slow skating, gliding, and fast skating positions, in each drill letting the puck go from the same distance. In this drill or test increase the competitive angle by forming the players into groups and measuring the total distance made by each.

Shooting records and standards. In order to establish standards for players and coaches, we conducted a series of special tests following completion of their survey.

It is interesting to note that shooting accuracy was sometimes greater on backhand than on forehand shots, e.g., when shooting for high corner areas.

The results showed an average improvement of forty-eight per cent over those achieved on the same tests prior to the two-week practice period. In some instances, the improvement was as high as eighty per cent.

It will be noted that better records were made when shooting at low corner areas. Here is further proof that a low shot is usually the best!

In the target-on-stand test, a quart-size can (painted red) was employed on stands measuring two, three, and six inches in height. The shots against this target were delivered from fifteen feet, and from stationary, skating, and cutting across positions. The tabulation shows that as the amount of motion by the player increases, his accuracy decreases. It is obviously desirable, therefore, that shots should be made from positions approximating the stationary as closely as possible, although the opportunity for true stationary shots may not appear in game-like conditions.

The bouncing ball test was done at fifteen feet distance. Shots were permitted at any time before the ball stopped bouncing. Forehand deliveries showed a highest score of six in twenty shots, with an average of two in twenty. Backhand deliveries showed a top of two in twenty and an average of one in twenty.

It is hard to say to what levels of accuracy a hockey player can develop his shooting skill by applying the principles of scientific training. However, according to the information now available, there, is every reason to believe that standards now accepted as top notch would be far excelled. Baseball experts have found that the use of strike area targets develop control more efficiently than just pitching to batters; football coaches have had the same experience in developing forward passing skill. Therefore, there is no reason why practice methods in which the same target principle is used will not bring improved results to the hockey player. To many, the use of such practice methods are new and because they are new, will be viewed with suspicion and scepticism. We suggest that the player or coach need not accept the results of the tests or the opinion of any expert; all they need to do is give them a try and see for themselves.

Offensive Strategy
and Tactics

In hockey, as in any game, there are two general types of players. Perhaps the most common is the headlong type who rushes around like mad, trying very hard but not doing too much thinking or planning. The other type is the cool-mannered player who is always thinking, always trying to work out the smart move. He sometimes tries to use too much brain, substituting it for hard effort when the use of such effort is the only smart move to make. A combination of the two is, of course, the ideal type. Teams, too, can be divided into the same two groups. There is the team that goes out and gives everything it has without too much attention to thinking and planning. There is also the team that plays to a system and emphasizes the use of the thinking process.

The most effective type seems to be a squad that combines both. The players skate hard, never shirking an opportunity to "turn it on"; yet they play smart, "heads up" hockey, never using brawn when brains could do the trick.

The degree to which tactics and strategy are used by the player or the team will, of course, depend on the knowledge the player or team may have of the various tactics and forms of strategy possible. Therefore, the player who does not learn to plan his movements will probably remain a headlong player who, though he may do well in the lower categories of hockey because of his work ethic and determination, will probably find that the going gets tougher and tougher as the level of hockey in which he is playing improves. The same remarks apply to the coach who believes in teaching nothing but "get in there and fight." However, he will find it hard to win when up against teams coached to play smart, systems-oriented hockey.

The development of the tactical and strategic elements of hockey is progressing to more sophisticated levels. This is similar to such games as baseball, football, and basketball. The subject of strategy and tactics in offensive play must be considered in relation to the individual player as well as in relation to the team, and is dealt with below.

The first section deals with the various forms of tactics and strategy open to the player himself as he performs the many individual plays he must do strictly on his own. The team section deals with the tactics and strategy open to the team as a whole or groups within the team, such as forward lines, defence pairs, and so on.

The individual's general attitude toward the game will influence his playing style. If he sees hockey as a game in which the important elements are muscles, aggressive body contact, and effort, he will play accordingly. If he pictures it as a game of skill in which the payoff is for intelligence and cool-headed smartness, he will probably play that way. The wise player, however, will see the whole picture and give each phase of the game the attention it deserves, choosing a style that will best take advantage of his strong points.

Though you cannot help but admire the player who, in spite of his lack of size and weight, plays a rugged body contact style of game, you cannot hold the same admiration for his intelligence. Therefore, the first move the player should make is to adapt tactics and strategy to his own physique. He will then get the best results for the energy expended and perhaps avoid many disappointments and unnecessary injuries during games.

The young player should keep this point in mind when he tries to pattern his play after a big league hero because he may not have the same type of physique. As many youngsters find out, it is one thing to play a tough, aggressive game when you have a strong, well developed physique and a tough mental attitude toward hard bumps. But it is a much different proposition to use such tactics with lighter physiques and minds that hesitate to expose the body to the bone-shaking results of repeated body contact. Above all, play the kind of game that suits you.

INDIVIDUAL TACTICS

Beating the checker. In deciding what method to use to beat the checker, the puck carrier must take into consideration several factors. What are his opponent's defensive weak spots? What are his opponent's defensive strong points? Is he a charger? Is he faster than I am? Does he back up? Is he a good checker? Does he play the body or the puck?

The puck carrier does not have time to stage such a mental check-up before every play but if he develops the habit of analyzing the opposing players when on the bench and at every other conceivable opportunity, he will soon have a remarkable store of knowledge that will enable him to react instinctively whenever he approaches a player. By developing such an attitude, the player will avoid the all too common habits of shifting into a checker's strong side, or carrying the puck into his opponent's favourite type of check, or trying to outskate someone who is much faster. Here are some rules to follow.

- Use skating moves such as change of pace and direction, moving to open ice, etc., to beat slow opponents. Make the faster player come to you and use fakes to avoid him. Invite action by a headlong checker or a charger, and then use shifts and agility moves to turn his aggressiveness against him.
- If he plays the puck, invite a check and then deke him.
- If he plays the body, open things up, making him move, and use such moves as change of direction and change of pace to spoil his timing. Stickhandling moves and other dekes in which you get close to the checker are less effective against one who plays your body and allows the puck to take care of itself. In such cases, agility skating moves such as the zig-zag and pivot should be used.
- If he is strong on one side (for example, if he has a good hook check), fake to that side. He will probably be only too willing to use his best weapon.
- If he is big and tough but on the awkward or slow side, make him skate fast and then make your play. The more you make him move and manoeuvre, the better your chances are. Do not try plays that bring you too close to him.
- If he likes to use his body, fake as if you are going right at him. When he gets set to body check, or as he starts to move to do so, deke him. Stops and starts, cut backs, and fakes can be introduced effectively here.
- If he backs up, slow down and let him back up. Try to force him into making a play, and then make your move and break fast. If he is close to the goal, let him back up as far as he wants within the time at your disposal.

- If he goes with you, instead of coming to a check, use change of pace and stops and starts to throw him off. If you are faster than he is, slow down and then burst and keep going.
- If he likes to come at you from the side, keep your body between him and the puck. Use the outside carry, or fake as if to skate away from him, stopping to go inside as he comes over.
- If you are really fast, get the puck into open ice and skate, skate, skate. Stay away from the checker, and use the rebound off the boards and other placement moves.
- If your dekes and moves are not working, figure out why. Are you moving too soon? Too late? Are you using the same move too often?
- Play the weak checker. When rushing, try to head for the checker you are most confident of beating. If a checker has your number, find out why, and in the meantime pass the puck.
- Do not always follow the same pattern as you go up the ice. Go straight up one time, and move from side to side the next. However, if you get a break, go straight and hard.
- If you are being closely checked by an opponent who clings to you, keep changing your pace, make him work, and keep him unsettled with fakes. The player on the offensive should always be able to get at least a little free ice on his check because he knows what he is going to do, and the checker must wait until the move is made. An edge in conditioning always pays off in this situation. The player keeps making his check work. Then, when the checker begins to tire, his determination to stay with you will start to subside. If you have such an edge, make him work, work, and work. If he has the conditioning edge, keep it as easy as you can and only try to break away when there is a good chance to make it pay off. To find out the situation, watch his breathing as compared to yours. This will tell the story. If you are heavier, use your weight, and lean into him. Another excellent tactic is to act as if you are not planning to take part in the play and then suddenly burst out. Keep thinking. Experiment until you find a way to get free from your check.

Watch the puck. Many offensive opportunities are lost when the player fails to keep his eye on the puck. Since the puck can move so quickly from one place to another, unless the player has his eye on it he may well lose a golden opportunity. As long as the player is watching the puck, he is in a position to make the right move when it changes possession.

The puck carrier makes the situation. The puck carrier should realize that he can set up the situation any way he wants it. Because he has the puck, he can take it anywhere he wants to and thus force the defensive players or individual checker to take up a certain position. If he likes open play, he can set this up by the way he manoeuvres. If the attack is against the defence, and the attacker's manoeuvrability is high, and he likes to make his plays with lots of room, he can head for a spot half way between one defenceman and the side boards, thus forcing the defence to move. If he likes close play, he can head for the defence. This is why it is important for the puck carrier to take a look ahead of him the moment he gets possession. He can then see the defensive pattern in front of him (read the play) and make his approach accordingly. Some players instinctively make their move down the ice in a way that will spread the defensive players as much as possible but many others will head down the ice to a spot where the defensive players are thickest. By taking a look and using his head, the puck carrier can take full advantage of any poor positional play of the opposing team or his own particular check.

Talk it over. Many smart offensive moves can be implemented if the puck carrier brings an analytical attitude to his play and finds out why he is checked, who checks him, and what kind of moves are most effective. He should, at every opportunity, discuss this with his line mates so that every one can take advantage of the information. For example, if he finds he is being checked by an opponent swooping at him from any position, he should check with his line mate who is supposedly being watched by this opponent so that a play can be made to him. Some players just cannot resist taking a crack at the puck carrier and are always leaving their position to do this, thus leaving the man they are supposed to be watching free. This works both ways. If the players on either side of the puck carrier are not in position to take part in any passing play or are uninterested because they think they are well checked, the checker assigned to guard them will be free to go after the puck carrier.

The individual player must remember that it is an offensive obligation to be in position at all times. The slightest deviation from proper position will mean the man against man set up will be destroyed, thus enabling the defensive squad to have perhaps two men against the puck carrier. This is why keeping up on the play is such an important obligation for the individual player. Opportunity after opportunity is lost when some player destroys the balance of power by being lazy, or being caught out of position behind the play and not moving up with the play.

Get up on the play. No matter how far he has been left behind, or for what reason, the individual player has this offensive obligation. Scoring records indicate that the player coming up from behind scores many goals. The reason is that as he comes up from behind he is usually free and can often move in to take a pass because the defensive players will be engrossed in their task of taking care of the players who were first up on the rush. You are never too far out of the play to make an effort to catch up.

Another positional factor. One of the most important individual obligations when your team is on the offensive is to make sure you do not spoil scoring opportunities by going off-side. Our research has shown an average 21 scoring plays per game in professional hockey were spoiled by a player going across the blue line too soon, thus creating an off-side. In youth hockey, the number is even higher. Many times the cause of such a play is that the player making the off-side fails to view the whole situation and thinks only of himself. He believes that he has a chance to score and just tears in hoping for a pass. What he does not realize is that the puck carrier might not plan the situation in the same way, or perhaps is not in a good position from which to make a pass.

The best plan is for the players going down the ice with the puck carrier to take their cue from this player. They should, of course, try to manoeuvre themselves into a scoring position but they should base the moves they make on the play of the puck carrier. This is why a forward line should get a lot of practice at trying all sorts of pattern plays against different situations with plenty of discussion of what they will do under various circumstances. If such things are not discussed, offensive opportunities will definitely be lost by frequent off-sides. The player should try to keep in mind the whole pattern of the play and not just his own individual desire to score. When the individual player thinks in this way, he will be less inclined to spoil scoring chances. This is one vital reason why the player should concentrate on learning to stop and start quickly. He then will have the necessary skill to react quickly when a play is made or he sees an opportunity.

Be aggressive. The individual player should always try to think aggressively. He should avoid at all costs the kind of mental attitude that causes him to wait for opportunities to develop. The aggressive player who is always working to get into position will be able to set up many play opportunities. The player who just skates up and down, waiting for an opportunity to come his way, will often wait a long time. Many of the so-called breaks of a game are merely situations that developed because an individual player was being aggressive. For example, when the player is skating up beside a puck carrier, he should be working hard to get in position to take a pass and not just going along for the ride. By doing this, he will not only create scoring opportunities but will, at the very least, lighten the load of the puck carrier by making the defence keep alert for any passing play. If the players coming up with the puck carrier are passive, the defence can then concentrate on the puck carrier. Even though the players coming up the ice with the puck carrier do not succeed in building up an opportunity, if they are seriously trying to keep active and act aggressively, they will force the opposing defencemen to take them into consideration. Thus the puck carrier will have the ability to make more convincing fakes or set up individual plays.

If you are not clicking. Sometimes a player will find that he just cannot seem to get untracked. Every move he tries is messed up. When this happens, the player should change his pattern of play, trying new moves. The old adage, "never change a winning game, always change a losing game," is a good one to keep in mind.

Giving credit. One of the greatest individual contributions the player can make is to give credit and avoid all complaining. When the player scores a goal, he should make sure he gives credit to anyone who took even the smallest part in setting up the play. Such an attitude creates a play making spirit which means the various players will probably be looking for opportunities to pass the puck around. If no credit is given, the player who set up the play cannot help but feel resentful and may be inclined, at least subconsciously, not to do the same thing in the future. When an individual does not give credit it can spoil the whole offensive strategy of the team.

Complaining when a pass does not come your way is a fault to avoid. By all means point out to your teammate that you were free, but do this in a friendly, uncritical way. While watching the average hockey game you will see many instances in which this rule is broken. Probably the most frequent is when a player, who was in a good position to score, did not get a pass or got a badly directed one. You will often see him shake his head in disgust, glare at the player at fault, or show some other sign of irritation and displeasure. This should be avoided. The coach should not tolerate such habits.

When to pass. Though it is true that the average player does not pass the puck enough, there are many who pass too often or at the wrong time. A good general rule is to pass only when such a move will better the team's offensive situation. If a teammate is in a better position than you are, you should always pass to him. This rule is most frequently broken when the puck carrier chooses to carry the puck past a checker, when there is a teammate up ahead. The only time a pass is not the best play is when the checker gives away his intention of trying to intercept the pass or if the puck carrier is too close to the checker to get a pass away. If the pass is made at the right time, it is always the best play. The player should always remember that passing is the fastest and safest method to advance the puck.

When you pass, break! One of the most common individual offensive faults of the average player is failing to stay in the play after he makes a pass to a free teammate. In other words, the player makes the pass and then watches to see what happens without taking any further offensive action himself. A good example would be a play at the blue line. The puck carrier brings it up to his own blue line then, when reaching the checker, passes over or across in front to a free, fast skating teammate. He fails to stay in the play by continuing slowly up the ice watching the play. This is always a mark of laziness, lack of aggressiveness, or stupidity. The moment the player makes the pass he should endeavour to get into position for a return pass. By breaking fast after the pass has been made the player can often leave the checker he beat by making the pass far behind, thus opening up a better offensive threat. In practice, you should work on plays with game-like conditions, i.e., you support the puck carrier.

If the ice is slow. When the ice is slow, many puck-carrying moves are ineffective. The player should realize this and adjust his individual play accordingly. Using the boards and all the other placement tactics, such as flipping the puck into open ice and going after it, offer the best opportunities. Plays demanding a lot of puck movement should not be avoided but you are definitely going to have to pass the puck harder. The player should also remember that when receiving a pass, the puck will slow considerably before it gets to him.

Get off if tired. If the player becomes tired or is slowed down by a hard body check or collision, he should not try to hide the situation just to stay on the ice. His obligation is to the team and, if he is tired or hurt, he should get off the ice because, when in such a condition, he represents a weakness in the team. Some athletes feel that such a strategy indicates a weakness of character and puts them in the "sissy" class. Unless there is a definite reason that forces the player to keep going under such circumstances, he should get off the ice. The players should keep in mind that courage is only useful when it is used intelligently.

Receiving (taking) a body check. Whenever you see that a body check or collision is coming your way, you can lessen its effect by lunging into your opponent first, before he starts his drive into you. By doing this you gain more forward body momentum, and hit him harder than he hits you. As you lunge, lean your upper body forward, hit him with your shoulder, and drive off your back leg, straightening it out, and bending your forward leg as you go into the checker. In this way, your balance is improved and you will be in a position to absorb the shock of contact a great deal easier.

Beating the defence. Because hockey is a mobile game, the individual player will often find himself in possession of the puck with no opponents ahead except the defence pair and no teammates near enough to him to help. When this situation arises the player can do one of three things. He can try to set up a scoring opportunity by carrying the puck in on his own. He may work the puck in as far as possible without endangering his possession, take a shot, and fall back. He may manoeuvre until a teammate can catch up on the play.

Which of the above choices the player should make will depend on the state of the game, his own individual skill, and the position of his teammates. If his team is ahead by perhaps a goal or two and he is not a particularly clever puck carrier, he should either shoot and fall back or he should manoeuvre around, keeping possession of the puck until a teammate can get up on the play. This is the wise thing to do because, if he tries to carry the puck past the defence, he may well get checked and give the defence pair a chance to break down the ice with an odd man advantage. If his team is behind and needs goals or is well ahead by three or four goals, the puck carrier can try to set up a scoring play. If there is any possibility of a teammate getting up fairly quickly, he should try to manoeuvre into a position from which he can make a play to his approaching teammate. If he is on his own, he should try to work the puck in as close as possible and try to score. The fundamental principle that should govern his choice of plays is that a defence pair is always easier to beat when they have to move. If they can stay in position, they are tough to beat because they can operate as one effective unit, covering a lot of territory. However, in spite of this fact being very apparent, many players head straight for the defence, taking the roughest and toughest possible road to the goal. If the puck carrier can manoeuvre so that he can take the defence pair one by one, the situation becomes ideal. The following are a few of many plays open to a puck carrier.

If the defence pair is comprised of players who like to body check, it is usually wise to resort to a move that appears to promise them such an opportunity. For example, the player can skate hard at a point between the two defencemen as if he is going to try to split them. Then, as he sees them move together to check him, he can either slide the puck between them and shift around, or fake as if to go through after the puck and then shift around. The idea of this play is to get the defence pair moving together so that when the play to go around them is made they will have to stop, recover, and then try to go with the play. Only attempt this if you have a lot of agility and can execute a wide fake.

Another good play is to skate as if to go fairly wide around one side and then, as the defence opens up, cut back quickly between them. When the puck carrier heads around one side he will often find the defenceman farthest from him will be a little lazy. He may think that the defenceman nearest the puck carrier will take care of the play. This will give the puck carrier a chance to cut back between the defence. If the puck carrier knows one defenceman is faster than the other, he should aim his first move around the side of the fast man. There will probably be a wider gap for him because the other defenceman will be a little slow in following. This play is sometimes referred to as the cut back. Sometimes the puck carrier will find both defencemen moving over together with, perhaps, the one farthest away coming over behind the other man. In this case, he should make his cut back wider so that both men can be taken out of the play. This situation often arises when the far defenceman is the faster and more agile.

Another good piece of strategy is to head directly at one defenceman. Then, shift to the inside in order to fake the other defenceman into getting set for you. At this point shift back quickly to the outside. Accordingly the puck carrier has only to beat one man. Another good play is for the puck carrier to fake a shot between the defencemen or between the legs of one particular defenceman. Then shift out and around. The fake shot may well cause the defence pair to stiffen momentarily in order to protect themselves or to block the shot, which will give the puck carrier that all important fraction of a second to move around them. A fake shot is often successful when aimed at one defenceman because it can neutralize both men. The defenceman at whom the shot is aimed is likely to tense in protective reaction, and the other is likely to go in toward the goal to clear a possible rebound.

Another good play is to flip a slow shot that bounces at the feet of the goalie and then follow after it quickly. If the defence pair are playing their positions properly they will body block the puck carrier, but their natural instinct will be to follow the puck. This move will often force them into an error. The slow flip shot will give the puck carrier time to go in for a rebound.

Yet another good play is a fake shot followed by an actual shot. Use it if the defence pair are fairly close to the goal. The goalie will tense for the first move. When it does not come, he may be inattentive at the moment the real shot is taken. If blocked, the player can shift quickly to the side to get clear for the actual shot.

If the player is agile and can pivot well, he can often use the following play with real success. For example, the player heads wide around the defence. Then, as he sees both of the defence pair coming over to stop him, he suddenly stops, pivots around, and cuts behind them. In performing this trick the puck carrier should start around the defence as quickly as possible, slowing just a little to allow the defence pair to get as much in front of him as possible so that the road to the goal will be clear when he makes his pivot. In setting up this play, it is often a good move for the puck carrier to head for a spot directly between one defenceman and the boards.

A combination change of pace and change of direction can often make a defence look bad. In doing this trick the puck carrier, while still well away from the defence, heads toward one side as if he is going to try to skate around him. He should skate just under full speed, perhaps as slow as three quarter speed. Then, as the defence pair move over and come close to him, he should suddenly scoot in at an angle to the other side and burst into full speed. A quick change of pace and change of direction may well give him the leeway he needs to get around the defence.

The slow motion makes the defencemen move, which immediately gives the advantage to the puck carrier when he makes his faster move. Since he knows what he'll do, he'll be able to move more quickly as he'll not have to stop, recover, and make a new move, as do the defence.

Aiming his play down along the boards is another way the puck carrier can force the defence to commit itself, and open up. You will often find that, as the puck carrier moves down the boards, only one defenceman will come to cover him. The other defenceman will often stay in centre ice to cover a possible pass to a teammate coming up, even though he is too far away to take part in the play at the moment. Then too, he may lag behind feeling that his partner, who is closer to the puck carrier, will take care of the situation. This will give the puck carrier an opportunity to beat the defencemen one by one.

There are, of course, many variations of these fundamental manoeuvres. However, if the player learns to do each of the basic plays, he will then have a pattern from which each of these variations can be made. The main thing is that the puck carrier bases the play he makes on some sort of principle, such as forcing the defence to move first or getting them spread. The average puck carrier tends to head for the defence and then improvise at the last moment, hoping to get through. He will be more successful if he practises the various plays as he will likely react with a definite plan that he will select instinctively.

The wise coach will give his players plenty of practice at beating the defence pair on their own. During such practice, however, the coach should make sure the player is trying definite plays and not just ad libbing as he goes in. Though hockey is a game in which the player must do a lot of improvising because of the ever changing play patterns, he will be able to select the right move more often if he has learned as many basic manoeuvres as it is possible to teach him. After all, there are only so many play situations that are possible, even in hockey. The coach who charts these plays and teaches his players the proper manoeuvres for each situation will find that his efforts pay off in games.

When the puck carrier has either one or two teammates along with him, whether they are well guarded or not, the situation is a great deal different. He can then use his teammates as decoys or start a manoeuvre designed to set up an actual play, which one of his teammates can finish off. In such a case it is much easier to beat the defence. See the next section, Team Tactics, or group play pattern.

TEAM TACTICS

A coach, by the clever use of strategy and tactics, can defeat a team superior in individual playing skill. As mentioned earlier, there is a great opportunity in this phase of the game for the coach who is willing to spend a lot of time and energy studying the many possibilities.

Though many of the strategic and tactical factors are dealt with below, there is still a lot of research to be done. Therefore, it is suggested that the coach who has a scientific, well organized approach and the necessary facilities can make a real contribution to the game if he uses them for a further study of such projects as the charting of the many play situations that can develop in hockey. The basic play situations are covered in this section but there are many others that can be charted by the research-minded coach.

Selecting the system. Hockey has evolved into a game that uses a large variety of systems. These depend usually upon the philosophy of the coach. In some cases this philosophy is formed by the way he played as an individual or by the way the team, of which he was a member, played. In others, it is through study and hard work that a coach develops his philosophies.

The system phase of hockey can be divided into two areas. There is the basic system which is the way the team plays generally, and special systems used at certain times according to the play of the opponents or situation of the game.

To select the basic system the coach must remember that it must be adapted to the player personnel available. This is very important because many coaches are inclined to force the players at their disposal to adapt themselves to a certain system of play, regardless of their suitability for it. If, as in the case of a professional club, the coach can select and buy his players, he can then stick to a basic system because he can get the right kind of personnel. In the case of the average coach, though, he must wait to see what player talent is available before he will be in a position to decide on a general system of play.

The problem of the overall strategy to be used can be complex. Quite often a football coach must figure out the best system to use on each of ten or twelve succeeding Saturdays against teams that use different systems. In hockey, a team will probably play three or four games against the same opposition. Accordingly, the same principle of adapting the system of strategy should be followed. The style of game played by the opposition is always an important contributing factor when a coach is trying to decide what general system of strategy to use. For example, it might be possible to play a pressing, aggressive game with success against one type of team but impossible against another type of opponent who is perhaps more adept at this type of game and has better basic personnel.

First of all, let us deal with the various basic systems possible, and then with the various specialized systems of strategy and tactics to be used under special circumstances.

Pressure play. The basic idea of this system is to play a very aggressive game, which will overwhelm the opposition by disorganizing them and tiring them out through constant application of offensive pressure. The fundamental weapons used are aggressive forechecking, fighting continually for position in all parts of the rink but especially in the opponents' defensive zone, continuous fast, hard skating (both ways), aggressive use of the body, getting the puck into the opposing end with five men up, forcing the game, and generally keeping the pace of the play high. Though passing plays an important role in such a type of game, it is most important to get the puck inside the opposing defensive zone and keep it there. This means that the puck will be shot rather than carried in and then followed. Its success depends on superior conditioning, fast, hard skating players, determined to fight for the puck at all times and to fly back down the ice when possession of the puck is lost.

The headlong type of player fits into such a system very well whereas the heady type of player, who likes to take his time and build his scoring opportunities through strategy and manoeuvrability, will probably find himself a little lost. If he tries to play this type of game, he will probably lose a great deal of his effectiveness. Actually it is a matter of player temperament and mental make-up. There are, of course, variations of this system, such as the use of a great deal of continuous, ever increasing pressure together with emphasis on definite play patterns.

While using this system will not make you a better conditioned athlete, you must be in better physical condition to use it. The application of pressure will soon develop an advantage for the team applying it as they will be able to stand it better than their opponents. It is a very hard system to play against because the constant pressure can upset even a well organized, smart thinking team. It is an irritating type of strategy that can often force the opponents into displays of temper. The main secret is superior conditioning.

However, the aggressive pattern of such an offensive strategy can be a weakness, since it is not tight defensively. Featuring mass attack, it gives the opposing team more opportunities to break away. This is why speed and determined back-checking are such important factors. It works best against teams who do not have a good system for getting the puck out of their own end, who are short on conditioning, and who do not feature team play. It is particularly effective against big, heavy teams, whose players will not take kindly to the continuous manoeuvring they will have to do. Providing the coach has the necessary player material and uses every method at his disposal to develop the physical conditioning, it can often produce top results. However, unless the coach has player personnel willing to accept the hard work and continual "try" elements, it can easily backfire.

The tight game. This system of play is a conservative one. Aggressive offence is not emphasized except when there is a definite advantage.

The main principle is to play very tight defensively, sending only two men up on a rush. The third man always trails, on the look-out for loss of possession. The defence only moves up to join in the attack if there is a clear opportunity or an advantage through penalties. The puck is not carried very deep inside the opposing blue line zone unless an excellent opportunity arises. There is no attempt to force scoring opportunities by aggressive play. The general idea is to capitalize on any loose play by opponents. There is a lot of shooting done from outside the defence, because the idea is to avoid getting caught deep inside the offensive zone, giving the opponents an opportunity to break away with a man or two advantage. This is an excellent system to use when the player personnel does not include many fast skating puck carriers but a lot of good checkers. Positional play is very important because the system depends upon close checking. Skill at breaking fast is important if full advantage is to be taken of any loose play by the opposition. It is also important that every player conform to the system all the time and not look for goals unless there is a definite opportunity.

This type of game is most effective against the smart passing squad who may become disorganized when their plays are repeatedly broken up through the close checking. It is also an ideal system to use against the team using pressure play. Conducted coolly, it can often break up a pressure attack through quick breaks. The coach should emphasize the development of passing plays because this will form the basis of the general attack. As there is usually a trailer, use of the various types of trailer plays is also indicated.

A definite pattern must be determined regarding whose responsibility it is to rush when possession is gained. For example, the man in possession may regularly go forward with the teammate closest at the time. The team playing this system will likely have a lot fewer scoring opportunities but they will probably be good ones when they come because many of them will be on breakaways. As the number of opportunities will be smaller, it is particularly important that every player have an accurate shot and be well versed in the different goal scoring plays. This is a good system to use in the early stages of a game when not too much is known about the opponent.

Pattern plays. This system is based on the use of pattern plays with the emphasis on passing. The fundamental principle of this system is that passing the puck will create the greatest number of scoring opportunities. This system does not depend so much on fast skating and aggressive attempts to keep position as it does on clever passing and planned manoeuvres. In many ways it is a great leveller of playing skill because, through its emphasis on passing, it can often defeat a system based primarily on individual puck-carrying skill. It is more of a team game with every player playing an equally important role.

Pattern play is far more effective when the player personnel includes a large proportion of heavy players who are very keen. There is no place in it for the lone wolf, no matter how talented he may be. The whole idea is pass, and pass. Such a system is not usually geared at a very high pace and concentrates on setting up passing plays. Actually there are two speeds to it; easy pace concentrating on the calm, cool application of the passing patterns and then the quick speed up when an opportunity opens up because of the passing. Short passing plays and never carrying the puck past the checker are keys to any pattern play.

As the use of passing cannot help but open up a defensive set up, and as it is the least wearing on the player, any team concentrating on such an attack may well prove that such a system is the most effective of all.

Pattern playing is certainly the answer to the coach's problem when he finds himself without any particularly outstanding player or if his team lacks group speed. It is most effective when used against the headlong type of team that emphasizes aggressive play and does a lot of unplanned tearing around with the accent on effort and continual action. By stressing the passing attack, wonders can be worked with ordinary players.

In our research, fans were asked what type of hockey they preferred to watch. Some seventy per cent of them called for smart, clever hockey with a lot of passing. Actually such a system represents the best type of hockey, because it emphasizes skill. The professional hockey executive may take issue with this argument and point to the gate receipts to prove that people like to watch rugged, scrambly hockey. However, according to the results of our survey, it is quite possible that the gate receipts would climb even higher if the emphasis were shifted to a smooth, smart, passing game.

Percentage play. In this system, the idea is to play according to the score and existing conditions, and to let the situation govern the style of play used. For example, the team may start off by putting on the pressure and continue as long as it seems to be effective. However, the moment it does not seem to be working, a switch is made to one of the other styles of play that seem to be indicated. The basic idea of this system is to take chances only if the odds are well on your side, for example, when the opponents have their weakest men on the ice, when there is a man advantage or a two man advantage, when the opponent's conditioning seems to be going, or when they show any signs of disorganization. The idea is to play very tightly until such a situation arises and then turn on the pressure full blast, falling back to the tight game the moment the odds even up again. This type of percentage play can be effective providing the player material includes a good number of players who can adapt themselves to different styles of play. It is a difficult system to use unless the players are successful at changing their styles of play and do not take very long to make the change. Its weakness lies in the fact that the players must change their styles of play perhaps four or five times, which spoils their general effectiveness.

However, the odds are on your side.

By teaching the team to play different styles of hockey, it is always possible to change strategy when the opposing team shows signs of being able to handle one particular type of play. If such a system is used, the coach must be very clever at noticing trends in the play and signs of disorganization or weakness in the opposing team. However it is not a particularly good system to use for young players because it throws a very heavy load on their learning capacity. Just as a wise football coach does not try to teach a young team too many plays, so should the hockey coach avoid throwing too much of a load on his players' learning skills.

Counter (transition) play. This system is based on the same principle as the counter punch in boxing. Let the opponent start the play and then concentrate on breaking it up, taking advantage of the disorganization of the defence that follows after the attack has failed. The fundamental elements of this system are tight, close checking and fast breaking, which take advantage of an opening created by breaking up an attack. Counter with a quick return to the defensive pattern as soon as the counter has either failed or succeeded. Use this system when the team is stronger defensively than offensively and does not have the offensive strength of the opponents. It is also very important to have players who do not get flustered when under pressure. In using this system, the opponents are always allowed to bring the puck down and are not rushed or forechecked. To make this work effectively, the fast break system (so popular in basketball) is used with emphasis on flipping the puck out into the neutral ice zone whenever possession is gained inside a defensive area, the players breaking fast after it. Definite fast break plays of this type should be carefully organized and practised with each player knowing his particular assignment or responsibilities for all situations.

Summary. To make a system work, practise it regularly during scrimmages. It is not enough just to tell the players how they should play when their game comes up. Organized practice is essential to develop technique. Football and basketball coaches frequently set their teams against a practice squad that is using the system of the team's next opponents. This is a training technique that hockey coaches might well utilize. Usually there is little preparation of this type when the team is practising for a particular game. If the coach is expecting to run up against a close checking defence, he should make sure his players scrimmage against such a style as often as possible so that they are adjusted to this play pattern. If this is not done, the possibility of disorganization in the early parts of the game is very great.

OPERATIONAL TACTICS

Changing players. The problem of just when to substitute forward lines, defence pairs, or whole units is the concern of every coach. If he is wise in his strategy the coach can often gain real advantages, perhaps turn an apparent defeat into a victory, or even defeat a team with superior skill by evening things up through clever substitution, thus enabling his team to keep up more pressure or take advantage of opportunities effectively.

Questioning of the players indicated that the average one dislikes being taken off when he is hot or immediately after a poor play. He does not mind being taken off if he cannot get going, but he feels that taking him off right after a bad play makes him look bad. As his mental attitude affects his endurance, this factor should always be considered. Happy athletes will show better endurance than unhappy, disgruntled ones. Further investigation shows that players demonstrate a falling off in endurance, energy, and skill after a session of arguing, complaining, displays of temper, or fights. Any incident which involves emotions seems to have a detrimental result as far as endurance is concerned.

Tests showed that if three forward lines are used, there is no reason for a hockey player to lose effectiveness through fatigue no matter on what schedule he is played, providing he is in good physical condition. See the chapter on Training for more details concerning the endurance factor and ideal conditioning methods.

To change the players in fives, in defence pairs, in forward lines. Should the coach change the defence pair every time he changes the forward line, or change them at definite timed intervals? The one time that forward line changes should signal a defence pair change as well is when the team has been playing a very hard pressure play system during which the defencemen have had to do a lot of hard skating. If this is the case, the defencemen should not be allowed out for any longer than a forward, or, at the most, just a little longer, perhaps for a forward line change and a half.

The other time you look at changing all five players at approximately the same time is when the coach is playing five man units and wants to keep the units together.

Under ordinary circumstances, most defencemen should be able to play a little longer than a forward without interfering with their ability to continue. However, if you are not using a five man unit system, then the defence should change independent of the forwards. The changes should be based on a forty second to one minute workload but sometimes this practice can be affected by the tempo of the play. For example, if the defence or forwards have a shift where they have to go very hard, then you might shorten their respective shifts. If the shift hasn't been active, then you might lengthen it a little.

The factor of strategy must also be considered. If the coach has defence pairs, who are also excellent on the offence, he should use this pair with his strongest offensive line, working the other pair with his defensive forwards. The system of using two definite player squads, one for offence, and one for defence, can probably be used to good effect by a hockey coach. He should play each group according to the situation in the game.

The great advantage of such a system is that the players can concentrate on one particular thing and thus develop a higher level of efficiency.

To leave a hot line on or not. There are some coaches who stick to the principle of so much time for each line regardless of how they are playing. It is hard to agree with this idea because it fails to take into consideration both the state of the game and how each line is performing.

Both from the psychological and physical viewpoint it seems to be best to leave a line or group on the ice as long as is practical whenever they are hot. They should never, of course, be left on long enough to impair their conditioning seriously, but they should be given as much work as they can do up to that point. For example, when a goal is scored, some coaches immediately change the line. This is hard to understand unless it may be that such coaches believe that there will be a let down. It is simply untrue that the flush of goal scoring will in itself cause a line to lose interest! The only possible exception to this rule should be if the goal was scored after a particulary sustained offensive effort which has tired the players. The coach can decide on his strategy by looking at the players carefully for signs of fatigue. If there is any doubt, take them off.

Who to put on for special teams. If short-handed, the obvious strategy is to use the players who the coach knows are the best checkers and skaters, and whose reaction to a tight spot is to put forth the extra effort necessary. To decide who to use when there is a player advantage or when a goal is needed, the best plan is to keep a book on players that perform well in such situations and adjust your personnel accordingly.

When to replace a player or group who is not doing well. A good strategy is to get the players concerned off the ice quickly, giving them a chance to get reorganized and use the time on the bench to point out mistakes. However, it is usually not a wise thing to pull players off the ice immediately following a poor play, especially if it has been a really bad one. This only makes the player stand out for his mistake and will not do his morale or mental attitude any good. A player or group should never be pulled off the ice because of bad play unless some attempt is made to point out what they were doing wrong and ways to correct it.

What units to use against opposing units. In deciding what combination of players to use against opposing lines, the best bet is to use the book system explained previously. If playing against a team you have never played against before, then the proper strategy is to try various combinations until the pattern of who is best against whom becomes apparent. The coach should always shift his players around in the early part of a game until he finds the information he is after. Then he should use every effort to play his combinations upon the opposing groups against which they seem most effective.

The same principle applies for other special situations such as important face-offs. This problem and others are best worked out through keeping a book and continually testing the players in the various situations in practice scrimmages.

Who to start the game. A good start, even more than that first goal, can do a lot to set the pattern for the rest of the game. This will help the team morale, shake that of your opponents, and get everyone into a smooth, working groove. Keep the first shift for each line very short so all of the players are into the game early.

However, even though there is not a definite system of measurement to use, the coach can find out a lot by watching his players closely when they are dressing and warming up for the game. Players who are ready will usually be in an aggressive state of mind. Very often they are a little on the noisy side and full of life. During the warm up they usually show plenty of pep and drive. The player who is not ready is quite often quiet and moody and does not show too much bounce during the pre-game warm up. There are, of course, exceptions to this rule but the coach, who makes a point of watching the mental and physical actions of his players before the game, will usually get a pretty good idea of who is up and who is down. The same procedure applies if there is any selection of players needed before the game. The habit of keeping a book is also of help in this problem. Facts and figures will show what players did the best job of starting off against what teams.

Taking out the goalkeeper. This is usually done in the last minute of the game when your team is behind. However, a daring coach could well use it at other times. For example, such a play could pay off any time there is a face-off in the offensive zone when your opponent is one or more men short.

When using it at the end of the game, the substitution should be made when there is a face-off in the offensive zone or on the fly when you are in possession of the puck. It is dangerous because your goal is wide open for a long shot. However, surprisingly enough, there are comparatively few goals scored in this way. The fundamental strategy is to make full use of the extra offensive man gained by the substitution of the goalkeeper. There should be a definite pattern play attempted instead of haphazard scrambles hoping the extra man will pay off. If there is just disorganized pressure with no definite pattern to the play, it is likely the man advantage will be nullified as one defence player will be in a position to cover two offensive men. This often happens if the players are not organized.

The success of such a play depends, as do so many ganging or power plays, on winning the draw at the face-offs. This can be left up to a man specially trained at face-offs or by a two on one play in which the player facing off takes out the opposing player and a teammate, stationed close by, moves in to get the puck. Such plays must be organized and performed carefully so that the interference rule is not broken. When positioning the players for the face-off and play, if possession is gained, make sure your extra man is free in open ice and keep the puck going to him. If a defence player moves to cover him, the player he leaves should move into open ice. All the offensive players excepting the free man should manoeuvre in such a way as to draw their checkers away from the free man who should try to get a good spot in the scoring zone. If he is followed by a checker who sees the free man in a dangerous spot, the man he leaves should follow so that the offensive team will have at least a two on one in the scoring zone.

As in any power play, the offensive team should try to bring the defence team to the outer areas of the zone leaving the centre goal scoring area free. Rapid and accurate passing is the secret of success, with each player keeping cool and well organized mentally. A coach, having studied his players and the opposing players, can set up any number of play patterns for the various circumstances that may arise. At the very least, he should have practised his whole squad as special units of six players in this play until they have thoroughly grasped the pattern for their attack. Many a game seemingly lost can be recalled from the darkness of defeat with a well executed six-man attack. If possession of the puck is lost, the players must react very aggressively, checking furiously, and try to regain possession. The odd man, or the man closest to the vacant goal, should retreat a little the moment the puck is lost and try to keep directly in front of it. He then will be in a position to stop a long shot or get the puck if it is flipped out in an attempted break-away or a clearing play. The "point" player on the team is very logically the man for this job.

The goalkeeper substitution play can also be used when there is a man or two advantage through penalties.

By substituting an offensive man for the goalkeeper, tremendous offensive power can be generated because at least a two man advantage (three, if two men are off) can be gained. Any team with well organized plays should score a goal or two. If a goal is scored or a face-off forced outside the opposition blue line, or if possession is definitely lost, the goalkeeper should be returned, on the fly if necessary. However, he should be returned to the ice a few seconds before the penalized player or players are due to return. This play, though daring, is not as dangerous as it seems and can often be used to get a couple of goals that will sew up the game very tightly. It is a very good play to use if badly behind during the last half of the game, or if the opposition is so strong that some kind of daring or different strategy offers the only chance for a victory.

Playing the points. The points are the two positions back on the blue line usually taken up by the two offensive defencemen during a power play or for a face-off inside the defending blue line zone. One point is by the boards on the blue line, the other about half way between the sides of the rink. The players playing the points shift back and forth along the blue line depending on where the puck is. For the purpose of deciding when to shift position, the blue line zone is cut into two equal halves with an imaginary line drawn from the centre of the goal out to the blue line. The point players should always position themselves on the points of whatever half the puck is in. One secret of the successful performance of any power play is to have point men who are aggressive and fast so that they can and will keep in proper position. A lazy or slow thinking point man can ruin pressure play time after time.

The players assigned to these all important positions should be specially trained and given regular doses of organized practice during which they practise stopping the puck from coming out, manoeuvring from side to side, shooting or passing the puck back in, and learning when they should retreat or hold their position. Point men should be considered as two offensive goalkeepers because their most important job is to stop the puck from being shot or flipped out of the blue line zone. Accordingly, they should be trained to use their hands to stop the puck (without closing their hand on the puck.) Point men should also be taught to move quickly in a bent knee glide from side to side so that they can get to the puck quickly. How the puck comes off the sideboards is another thing they should study and practise. This is important because many clearing shots are made at an angle against the boards. Other factors of good point play that are very important are: a hard low shot that is accurate (a low shot has a better chance of penetrating a packed defence and sets up better rebounds), a well developed passing sense, a cool attitude to select the right play, skill at turning quickly to either side, breaking fast in case of a break-away, a good fake shot to set up plays and to fool a checker who goes down in front of a shoot-in. Also know how the puck acts when shot against the boards at different angles. With such knowledge, a point man can often get the puck back in very effectively.

The point man should carry the puck in from the blue line if he is given a clear opportunity to work the puck in close for a shot or to set up a play. He should never attempt this, however, if he is likely to be checked without a teammate backing him up. If the point man does carry in, the player closest to him should fall back and cover for him. In today's game, in which power plays and various other five- or six-man patterns are used, the development of good point player should he given a top priority in the practice schedule. Playing the points is a definite but rare skill. Therefore, every measure should be taken to develop it. Point men can be selected from any position. They do not necessarily have to be defencemen.

Should defencemen rush? This depends on their ability to carry the puck or make plays; the state of the game; the circumstances under which the rush is made; and the defensive ability of the forwards on the ice, one of whom might take his place depending on your play pattern. Observe the following general rules:

- Poor puck carriers/playmakers should not rush unless they are the only players in position to take advantage of a break.
- Those with excellent puck-carrying or passing skill should rush any time they get a clear chance to break-away.

- They should not rush, for example, if they get the puck deep in their own zone with checkers ahead.
- If the game is tight, the defencemen should rush only on a first class opportunity.
- More rushing can be done if the forwards cannot get going.
- If the forwards on the ice at the time are poor defensively, then the defencemen should rarely rush.

If the defencemen do a lot of rushing, it tends to make them too anxious to move up the ice and therefore causes a loss of attention to their defensive duties.

From the offensive viewpoint the defenceman should be a cool, skilful playmaker so that he can get his forwards away on a rush when he gains possession of the puck. He should be carefully trained at making passes out into the neutral zone to fast moving forwards, making passes at angles off the sideboards, and making fast accurate long passes, straight up the ice or across the ice at a forward angle. Such a defence-man is worth his weight in goals! If a defenceman rushes, his place should always be taken by the forward farthest out of the play. The only exception is if he leads a power play that sees every man going up. Careful attention to this rule will save a lot of goals scored by the oppos-ing team who break-away with only one man back. The forwards should be instructed on this rule of responsibility for the cover.

Starting the play. In getting an offensive move started, remember that fast passing is the safest and quickest way to get moving, perhaps leaving an opponent or two behind. Puck-carrying out of your own defence zone should be kept to a minimum unless, of course, there is a clean break-away situation. Immediately on gaining possession of the puck, all the players strive to break clear into a good offensive position. Too many players at such a time coast and watch to see what is going to happen. This is a mistake. Each man should act aggressively and try to set up a play of some kind as soon as possible. This is why the coach who spends a great deal of time practising break-out plays will always have high scoring teams. The objective should be a break-out play for every situation. This takes time and thought but it is well worthwhile.

The secret of strong offence is organization. There will, of course, be many situations when the player must ad lib but if he has practised a number of basic pattern plays, he will have developed a play sense and will probably come up with a variation of one of the plays he has been practising. This is why time spent practising pattern plays is always worthwhile.

Skill at breaking fast is perhaps the most important factor in getting the play started and making it pay off. Therefore, the coach should never cease emphasizing the development of this skill during practice. It will bring more scoring chances than any other single factor.

A key to good offence. One of the most important factors in the offence is the player's attitude. If he does go on the offensive with a carefree aggression, fighting hard until the play is either successful or definitely broken up, he will make many a play work that at one time may seem to have petered out. The average player is too quick to give up, to concede that he has no possibilities. Such players will not force the pattern on the defending team, will not keep trying to make it work.

One of the reasons so many players do not fight for a play is that they tend to be criticized if they are caught out of position or fail to back-check. This makes them timid about their offensive play and they often fail to keep boring in or trying to set up position because they stay in a spot from which they can cover their man or back-check. The coach should take this into consideration and explain specifically his philosophy. If an offence is to work, the players must be told to fight for it, emphasizing offence until possession has been definitely lost.

Thinking offensively and defensively at the same time is a difficult job that takes the punch out of the offence. The coach should demand a full back-checking chore, but should not spoil the offensive attitude of the players by saying such things as "I want you to bore in, to fight to sustain a scoring situation but, for heaven's sake, don't get caught so that you fail to come back!" Clearly define when the defensive obligation begins.

Following in. Many scoring opportunities are lost because the player making the shot on goal, as well as his teammates who are in a position to do so, fail to follow the shot in. The tendency is to shoot and then see what happens. The defence players are inclined to do the same thing. This is why a fast follow-in can often lead to a scoring opportunity. The defending players will be left flat-footed. Even if they turn to follow in to cover the offensive players, they are at a disadvantage because they must turn and go, whereas the offensive players do not have to turn and are already in motion.

A team that has been trained to follow in quickly will often get two or three men, who will be free from any checkers for a moment or two, into the goal scoring zone, or right in on the goalkeeper. This is why an organized follow-in play will often work very well. The puck is shot or flipped in slowly and the forwards break in after it quickly. If the offensive player is at approximately three-quarter speed before the puck is shot in, he can then burst into full speed as it is shot into the offensive zone. The play could even be more successful with this technique.

If the coach is offence-minded, he can instruct any player who is in a position that makes it possible for him to follow in, to do so. If he is cautious he can assign only the man closest to the play, as well, of course, as the shooter. The clearing habits of the goalkeeper should also be carefully checked so that the players following in will know for what spot to head. This is a valuable thing that will help set up many scoring plays following a shot on goal. By knowing where to go to get the cleared puck, the player following in can often get to it sufficiently ahead of a defenceman to set up a play.

Such plays should be practised over and over again because they involve skills that can only be learned by doing. Mere verbal instructions before games and during games will not enable the player to develop such skill to the utmost. Following in is a top priority offensive manoeuvres that every coach should emphasize.

The play approach. Many coaches insist that all their players fly in at full speed on the defence when they have possession. Some coaches even lose interest in a player who slows up at a defence, thinking he lacks courage. What should be considered is that, in the first place, the player who flies at the defence at full speed eliminates many play possibilities since there are many manoeuvres that cannot be performed at full speed. In the second place, the habit amounts to an approach pattern that will help the defence players time their moves and set up their checks. Finally, such a philosophy fails to take into consideration the mental and emotional make-up of the player and his natural stance. Some players are quick moving, quick thinking, and have a fiery, brisk emotional stance. Others like to get set for their actions.

The best policy is to teach the value of variety in approach and let the player use as his fundamental approach the way that best suits him. Wild abandon when going in on the defence may be something to admire or it may indicate a lack of common sense or imagination. The player who seeks to avoid being knocked into the bleachers is not necessarily lacking in courage. He may be just too smart or normal. The player who avoids body contact at all costs, is, of course, a difficult problem. Such a player however, should not be cast off without an attempt to find the cause for his fear and work on the cure. Most cases of timidity can be traced to a source and cured. Often a family background in which the player was always being exhorted to take care of himself is the cause. A coach should be a careful student of psychology and if possible, have access to an expert as a team consultant. If this is done, the whole difficulty of the problem player can often be quietly solved to the team's advantage.

The first goal. According to the facts and figures compiled by Sports College researchers, there is no doubt that scoring the first goal is a great advantage. Of some five hundred games studied, the team scoring the first goal won seventy-one per cent of the time.

How a game begins seems frequently to set the pattern for the whole game. Because of the great importance of the first goal, the coach would be well advised to organize and practise special opening pressure plays that will set a pattern in his team to start off fast and furious. A terrific burst of pressure right from the opening face-off will often disorganize the opposition for the whole game. Sell your players the idea of driving hard at the start. Such factors as the pre-game warm-up and talk should be organized and conducted carefully. See the chapter on Training for suggestions on the warm-up.

An offensive fundamental. Always have a definite plan. There are some who feel a game of hockey cannot be planned in the same manner as a football game. This may be true up to a point but there is no reason why a team cannot base its offensive tactics on certain principles and pre-arranged strategies. This planning will provide a much more effective offence than one depending on the haphazard play of a team that is just playing. After all, when there is a plan, the players will play better. It will also give them a sense of organization and team spirit. The famous Field Marshall Montgomery, noted as a tactician, always insisted on all his noncombatants knowing the basic plan of battle. He knew it provided a co-ordinating factor. The coach who trains his players to keep trying to set up an organized plan, to keep setting definite objectives, forcing the pattern on the opposition by working at it, will find his team developing an ever-improving offensive strength.

The missed goal let down. Experience shows that on many occasions the players of the team (especially those most concerned) who have just missed a goal will let down for a short time immediately following a missed opportunity. This is a very natural reaction. Take advantage of it with a sudden burst of pressure.

Exerting pressure. In the average game there are many times when a little extra offensive pressure will bring good results. These occur when opponents seem to be tiring; when an opposing line or unit seems to be off form or disorganized; when the opposing team's morale is low due to a bad break or complaining between the players; after a scrap or brawl of any kind, or after the opposition has been arguing in vain with an official; after you have scored a goal; after you have successfully fought off the opponents when a man short; when there is a new line or defence unit brought into the game by the opponents; right after any bad play by the opposing team; after any period of inactivity; at the start of each period; whenever play has been stopped for any appreciable time, such as a player injury, or there has been an argument, or the fans have thrown debris on the ice.

If sudden, well organized pressure is used at such times, it is often possible to take advantage of the natural let up or emotional state of the opposition and ram home a goal or two, or at least further their disorganization. The coach, therefore, should be constantly alert to take advantage of such situations. An excellent plan is to have an assistant assigned to watch for such situations arising. The coach with his many responsibilities may well overlook a situation that an assistant concentrating on nothing else will be able to tab. Special plays to use for such situations should be practised so that the attempt to apply pressure will be well organized.

The centre the playmaker? In the past the centre was always considered to be the playmaker and most offensive attacks were aimed down the middle of the ice. However, the situation has changed. Although many plays are still directed up the middle and though the centre often carries the puck, the playmaking responsibility does not rest on one man. All the members of a forward line carry the puck and are expected to set up plays.

By having only one playmaker per line and aiming the play up the middle, the theory is that it sets too much of a pattern to the play and makes it easier to break up. In today's game, every player on the team has to be a playmaker.

As far as the lane from which the play is aimed at the defence is concerned, the offence should be varied so that the attack isn't predictable. However, many teams carry the puck up the middle because there are more play patterns possible. The puck carrier can, for example, make a play to either side, whereas, if he was on a wing, he could only make his play to one side. This emphasis on direction attack should be governed by the weakness of the opposing defencemen. This can be learned by varying the attack. If there is time to get the attack organized as far as the position of the players are concerned, the best puck carrier and playmaker should carry the puck into the zone.

Emphasize the flip out. Teaching every player how to use the flip out pass or clearing shot is an important fundamental of building a good offence. When the other team is putting on the pressure or forechecking aggressively, it is difficult to get a counter attack organized. One of the best ways is to flip the puck out into the centre area and break after it. If the puck is shot out hard, it may travel too far. This is why the flip out pass is so effective. As it is lifted quite slowly, it rarely goes too far down the ice to cause an offside or an "icing" infraction. Few players make this play well. Therefore, it should be emphasized at practice sessions until all have developed top level skill.

If ahead. The coach is often faced with the problem of whether or not to sustain offensive pressure after a lead has been created. It is a difficult problem to solve because there are so many factors involved. However, the best plan is to remember that as long as an offence is working well and keeping the opposition busy, it is also the best form of defence. If your team has the puck, the opposing team cannot score a goal. Switching a team from an offensive system to a defensive one is dangerous because it gives the opposition a chance to get organized and also may disorganize the team making the switch for awhile. Just what strategy should be used actually depends upon the general system the team is using. For example, if the pressure play system is being used, a switch to a defensive pattern may well be fatal. But if the team has been trained to play percentage hockey and is used to switching from offence to defence, a changeover may be made without any disruption. In protecting a lead, it is well to remember that just as a boxer is safest when he has his opponent off balance and thinking of defence, so too is a team with a lead. It only seems wise to go into a completely defensive pattern when there is just a minute or two left in a game.

Scouting. Building a successful offensive strategy against a certain team will be a lot easier if a study is made of the defensive habits, weaknesses, and strong points of the other team. This can be done by scouting them every time they play. This is an easy matter if you are playing perhaps in a city league where those doing the scouting do not have to travel. However, it is rarely possible to organize much of a scouting system if a lot of travel is necessary and the budget is low. If practical, of course, every bit of scouting possible should be done, especially if you are playing different teams each week.

Spotting. In hockey the coach is very close to the play and as a result will miss many things that would be apparent to him if he was farther away and had a panoramic view of the play. Accordingly, it is a great help to place spotters in the crowd who can then relay information to the coach. Many a game has been won because of the things a spotter has noticed. Good locations are high behind either goal, in a corner or high in the centre of the rink. From such positions it is possible to see the various plays take form and notice many phases of the play that are hard to see from close up. By being in the stands, you can see the whole rink better and you can see many of the pattern plays of the teams more clearly than from the bench. The odd trip into the bleachers by the coach will give him many clues regarding what his team is doing wrong or why certain plays are not clicking. This can be done during a game or during practice scrimmage. Spotters can also be used very effectively to help the coach develop a book on the general play of each player, line, or defence pair. Properly used, they can be invaluable.

Selecting the line. As far as the offence is concerned, just how a line should be made up will, of course, depend upon the general system of play being used by the coach. Whether or not he puts all his top offensive men together and combines his defensive players is a problem that can be solved only be deciding what strategy would be best to fit into the overall picture. However, the following general principles can be used with good effect.

The players on a line should be mentally and physically compatible. In other words, the coach should study the players carefully both in regard to their attitude and physical qualifications and try to form his groups so that the players will complement each other. If this is not done, you will often find a player on a line with two teammates who interferes with the co-ordination and cohesion of the line.

There seems to be no reason why three players who are compatible should not be placed on one line regardless of whether or not they all shoot from the same side. It has been proved that a right-handed player, for example, loses nothing of his effectiveness when playing on left wing. If a coach wants a certain line or group to be an offensive threat, he must think offensively when making up the line.

The players must be taught an understandable definition of when the offensive obligation shifts to a defensive one. To make an offence work to peak efficiency, the players must be able to concentrate on it without a haunting feeling that they are neglecting their defensive play. Trying to bring the defensive picture into the offensive has the same result as if a track coach told his miler, "I want you to get out there and run a terrific three-quarters, be aggressive, turn on the pace, disorganize the race, but for heaven's sake don't get tired, and save something in case somebody stays with you." The defensive instructions probably ruin the effectiveness of the offensive pattern that the coach requested. It seems that in any game the offence that works best is the one that is organized and carried out with great intensity.

The break-away trailer. A good form of offensive strategy is always to have a player moving around your defensive blue line whenever the puck is inside this zone. He will then be in a position to take a pass the moment possession of the puck is gained. Using a man in this way not only opens up many offensive possibilities, but also weakens the attack because the opposing team will be forced to watch him.

To take advantage of such strategy the man appointed to the break-away position should be a quick skater with high goal scoring skill. It is always wise to have a planned pattern once he gets an opportunity to break away. The rule requiring that the two men closest to him should go up with him works quite well. The break-away player's actions should be governed by the state of the defensive play. Though he should be concerned with manoeuvring, in order to take a pass and get going, he should stay alert in case the defensive picture becomes very dangerous. He then should make the move that will do the best job of helping it.

The big advantage of using such a system is that the defensive players have a definite play set up for them. Whenever they get the puck, they know what move they should make. There is the basis for an organized attack already set up. The main disadvantage is, of course, that there is one less man actively checking. Whether to use the system or not is something that will be decided by the coach's philosophy of the game. If he is offence-minded, he will probably use it or some variation of it. If he is defence-minded, he will likely regard it with much perturbation.

ORGANIZED PLAYS

Even though hockey is a game in which the situations are always changing, it offers great opportunities for the use of organized plays. Any team that has practised such plays until they can be set up and performed with real skill will have a great advantage over the team that plays ad lib hockey, trying to work out a play at the last minute with no preconceived plan. It is possible to work out some set plays and use them.

In building up a repertoire of plays, the coach must study the various play situations that can arise and then teach his players to recognize them and use the play that will work best. The following are some basic play situations together with some suggested organized play patterns. The well organized, scientifically minded coach can figure out further plays and variations on the ones suggested. The coach who delves into this phase of the game may well make an important contribution to the hockey of the future.

Two on one. In this situation, the offensive players should win out every time, provided that they make the right move at the right moment. Even if the defenceman covers perfectly within the possibilities open to him, the offensive players should at least end up with a shot on goal. One of the chief reasons why such a play situation is so frequently not taken full advantage of is that the offensive players do not have a plan and thus fail to conduct their actions to best effect. Another reason for failure in such a promising situation is that timing of the play is faulty because a pass is made too soon or too late. Still another fault is poor position in which the offensive players approach in a way that gives the defenceman a chance to cover both of them, or at least to stay with the play.

Always approach this play in such a way as to force the checker into making a move that will place the player accompanying the puck carrier in a free position from which he can quickly go in on goal. The puck carrier, by his manoeuvres, should force the checker to move away from the accompanying man. Many plays are made to the free man in which, after he gets the puck, he is still in a poor scoring position and can perhaps even be covered again by the checker. The diagram gives one example of how to beat the checker.

Play No. 1

(X1) makes a pass to (X2) just as he goes over the centre line. The latter then carries the puck down the side of the rink to a spot just over the blue line. A good plan is for (X2) to put on a burst of speed just before he crosses the blue line so that the lone defenceman will think he is going to try and take the puck in himself. Consequently, if the defenceman (D) moves back and over to check him then he should make a return pass to (X1) who has followed up the centre of the ice. However, if (D) does not move back and over to check (X2), then he can continue in for a shot on goal. He should be careful that he does not hang on to the puck too long if he is going to make a return pass. If he does it will simplify the defence-man's job of intercepting the pass, thus breaking up an excellent scoring

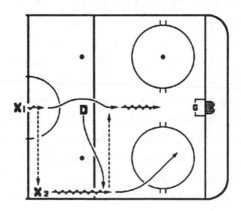

opportunity. If (D) should move back and over to cover (X2) and lay his stick on the ice to stop a pass, then (X2) should use a flip pass that is not too high. The puck is flipped just high enough so that it clears the defenceman's stick, which is on the ice.

Remember, (X1) should be careful after passing that he doesn't skate over the blue line ahead of (X2), causing an off-side. Many scoring chances are spoiled because of an over-anxious player going over the blue line ahead of the puck carrier.

If the defenceman moves back, trying to keep in front of the play and to slow it down, as he should, the offensive players should keep the puck far enough away from him that he cannot make a stick check. Instead, he should be allowed to go back until he blocks the goal-keeper's view. Then a screen shot should be used. If there is not time for such a play, for example, if back-checkers are hurrying to the rescue, the best way to beat a retreating checker is with a pass following a fake shot. The fake shot will probably cause him to come to a stop or stiffen in self-protection, if it is aimed at him, and it will be possible to pass around him.

Two on two. In many ways this is the same situation as one on one and the puck carrier can act accordingly, trying to carry past the check on his own, with one of the tricks suggested in the first part of this chapter. The other attacker, however, can help out by acting aggressively as if trying to get free. However, he must be sure he does not cut down on the area in which the puck carrier can manoeuvre with any of his actions. He must also avoid going off-side. In many ways the best thing for the other forward to do is to manoeuvre so that he takes his cover away from the play. By doing this, he precludes the possibility of his cover breaking in to check the puck carrier if he has the defence beaten. Therefore, it is often good tactics for the wing to slow up and keep his cover out of the play.

With a two on two, we are not getting into play situations that have endless variations. However, they are all based either on the principle that both checkers are forced to cover one man, leaving the other one free, or on the principle that the pattern succeeds in putting the two offensive men against one checker. Some of the basic possibilities are shown in the illustrated play situations.

Play No. 2

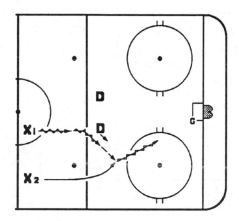

This play is based on the two on one principle. The puck carrier (X1) in the centre heads straight for the defence. The wing (X2) stays fairly close. Then, at the last moment, the puck carrier swerves and starts to go around the defenceman closest to the winger. He must carry the puck wide to the side. As he starts this manoeuvre, the other forward breaks ahead and takes a forward pass. This play is most successful when the puck carrier fakes a shift into the centre of the defence pair or toward the opposite side from which he plans to make the pass. This will at least partially immobilize that checker thus enabling the two on one principle to work. If the far defenceman moves over too soon as if to cover the play, or to take the other forward, the puck carrier can move through the spot he leaves. This often happens when the pass play has been worked a few times. The puck carrier, as he passes, should try to burst hard enough to keep between the checker and wing.

Play No. 3

In this play, the puck carrier heads right at the defence pair as if he is going to try to go through them. They are forced to stay set in case he does. Just before he reaches them, he lateral passes to the wing and then bursts between the defence. If the wing is free after getting the pass, which is often the case, the original puck carrier follows in for any rebound and to act as a "pick" or "block" on at least one of the defence-men. If the defenceman closest to the wing does a good job of moving

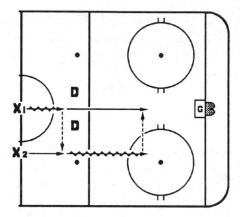

over to cover the wing, he passes back to the original puck carrier who, even though covered by the other defenceman, is still inside him and able to take a pass. However, if both offence players break fast as the play is made, at least one of them should get free. If the defence pair back in too far on their goaltender, the puck is held for a screen shot.

Play No. 4

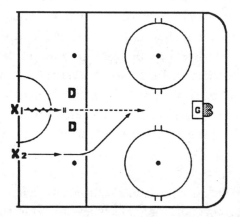

This play is based on the principle of a defence pair closing the gap too quickly at the blue line. The puck carrier carries the puck hard at a spot between the defence, then bursts as if to go through. However, he quickly stops dead and flips the puck through so that the wing can cut behind and pick it up. This is a good play against an over-eager body checking defence pair that are anxious to give the puck carrier a going over and thus be more inclined to go for the puck carrier when he starts his burst between them.

Play No. 5

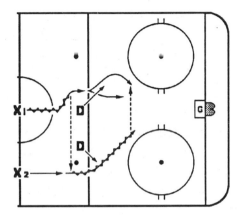

In this play the puck carrier heads for the defence and then when twenty-five or thirty feet away, he starts going wide at top speed, as if he is going to try to skate around the defence. Just as he gets to a spot a little out of reach of the defence he lateral passes to the wing. Then, if the defenceman closest to him has come well over to cover him, he cuts inside and goes for the goal. By cutting inside he is in a position to take a pass because he will be between the puck and the checker. If the defenceman on his side goes for the wing when the pass is made or goes back to the centre of the ice, the original puck carrier continues around and goes in on goal at full speed so as to get the pass, he should take a look to see what has happened to his teammate and pass accordingly.

Play No. 6
This is another effective play, based on the two on two principle. The puck carrier heads for a spot outside one defenceman. Then, when fifteen to twenty feet away, he suddenly cuts into centre and, as he sees the defence get set for him, probably stopping their sideways movement

to cover the play, he lateral passes to the wing who is then free. If the defenceman on that side doesn't stop to cover the original puck carrier as he cuts in, but moves quickly to cover the wing, the original puck carrier drives hard between the two defencemen. This means that even if the far defenceman tries to cover him, he'll be in a spot to take a return pass because he will be closer to the wing than the defenceman.

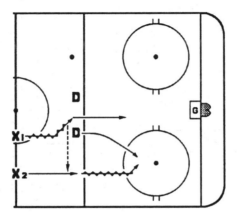

Play No. 7

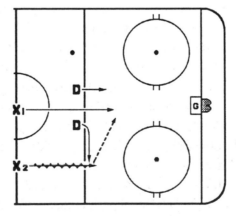

This play is based on an approach from the wing that forces one of the defence to move, and thus create a spread. The wing carries the puck between one defenceman and the sideboards, trying to outskate him on that side and then cut in for the goal. If he does get around the defenceman but is covered by the other checker who cuts back at an angle, he back passes to the man in centre. If he is covered by the defenceman on his side, he passes forward to the man in centre who should keep on the inside of the other defenceman or try to burst into the clear.

Play No. 8

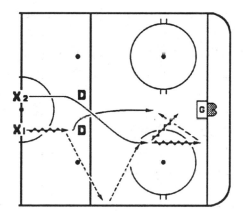

The original puck carrier (X1), coming up a little to the right of centre ice, heads straight for the near defenceman. On his left, skating close to him, follows (X2). As (X1) approaches the near defenceman, he suddenly shoots a medium fast pass against the boards on his side and then breaks fast between the two defencemen, heading toward the goal. The moment that (X2) sees the board shot being made, he bursts quickly forward ahead of the puck carrier between the defence to pick up the puck off the boards as shown in the accompanying diagram. In other words, (X1) and (X2) cross, with (X1) following and (X2) picking up the pass as it rebounds from the boards. There will be no off-side in this play if the pass is correctly timed, as the puck will have crossed the blue line first.

After (X2) has picked up the puck, he can do either of two things. He may head straight for the goal if his path is clear, or he may continue on the side if being checked and make a quick return pass to (X1), who by this time should be parked in front of the goal.

If this play is to have any chance of succeeding, (X2) must break through the defence pair quickly to beat other defending players to the puck. It is a good plan to shoot the puck against the boards a few times during the warm-up (or in practice if you play at the same arena in which you practise) in order to become accustomed to the rebound of that particular rink.

It is also important that (X1) should draw the near defenceman toward the boards before making the original shot to the boards. By doing so, he opens up the defencemen for himself and his teammate, making the double break through possible. To be most effective, both (X1) and (X2) should come up a little below full speed and then break fast as the play is begun.

Summary. The offensive men should stay active no matter how well a play seems to have worked. After making a pass, the passer should follow up in a position for a possible return pass. He must not coast and watch as many goals are missed in this way.

The offensive men should always analyze the result of each play, checking how the defencemen reacted. By doing this, future plays can be selected to take advantage of habits indicated by the defencemen. For example, one defenceman may be a little slower or less agile than the other, or perhaps he is over-eager and moves too soon. Such habits should be noted and kept in mind for future use. A large number of play patterns for the two on two situation have been given as it is the situation that occurs most frequently.

Two on two (with back checker). The key here in this case is for the wing to act aggressively and thus attract the attention of the defence-men. This will make the puck carrier's job that much easier. If the wing is covered well, the puck carrier should act as if it was a straight one on two situation. However, take advantage of the fact that the defence pair will figure the puck carrier is set up for rough treatment and be ready to give him the works if he attempts to beat them, especially if he plans to go between the two of them.

Play No. 9
The puck carrier should head for the defence as if he is going to go through them, and then stop and flip a pass between them. The wing breaks fast to pick it up. If properly timed, the play will often work well because, with a quick burst, the wing can usually get at least a foot or two on his cover.

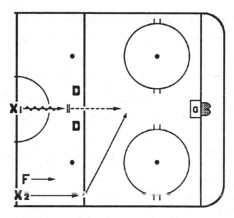

Another possibility is for the puck carrier to swerve toward the wing. This brings the defence pair over. As he sees the puck carrier swerve toward him, the wing bursts quickly behind him going laterally across the ice toward the far boards. The puck carrier then passes (laterally) quickly in the same direction. The original puck carrier must be careful not to cross the blue line before the wing who took the pass.

If the wing starts his play before the puck carrier swerves, it will open up two possibilities. If he gets free with his sudden burst, he can take a pass. If he does not, he will at least cause the defence to hesitate, especially the defenceman on the side to which he is moving, and thus make it easier for the puck carrier to get through or around the other side. Such a play often draws the defence pair to the side and, on many occasions, the defenceman on the side to which the wing makes his move will instantly move to cover him thus opening up the defence. If the defence pair is behind the blue line, the wing can help by cutting behind the puck carrier as he swerves, yelling "trailer." This may make the defenceman farthest from the puck carrier hesitate, looking for a possible trailer pass. This can open up the defence pair and give the puck carrier a chance to cut back between them. It is always smart to remember that the threat of a pass is often as effective as a pass.

Three on two (wings covered). In many respects this is similar to the two on two (wings covered) set up and the main duty of the wings is to act aggressively and to try to set up a pass possibility. The following are a few of the basic play patterns that aggressive wing men who do not passively accept cover can set up, and which should be practised regularly.

Play No. 10

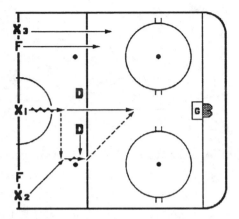

This is a very simple one to execute and is very effective. Do not let its
simplicity blind you to its effectiveness.

The puck carrier (X1) carries the puck up the centre ice to a spot nine
or ten feet from the defence, where he makes a pass to (X2) who has cut
hard inside his check to receive this pass. The defending left defenceman
will naturally move over to take him out. When the left defenceman moves
over to cover him, (X2) dumps a flip pass, not too hard, that ends up
behind the defence about halfway between the goal and the defenceman.

As (X2) receives the pass from (X1), (X3) yells as loud as he can for a
pass from (X2) which will probably cause the right defenceman to pause
and consider such a possibility. This may well allow (X1) to put on a
quick burst of speed in between the two defencemen allowing him to
pick up the loose puck behind the defence. It is important that (X2) not
cross the blue line ahead of the puck causing an off-side. The best plan is
for him to swerve along the blue line, to prevent an off-side, until the
puck has crossed the line, then he can act as a trailer on the play and
either go in for a possible rebound, or be ready to take a man if the play
is broken up and the defending team breaks out.

However, for this play to be a success, the timing on the part of (X2)
has to be very accurate. He should slow down after receiving the pass

from (X1). Then, just as soon as (X2) sees (X1) start to put on his quick burst of speed to dart between the defencemen, he should make his dump pass behind the defence. Remember, too, that (X1) must be on the lookout to avoid any possible body check thrown at him by the right defenceman. As with all planned plays, this one must be practised repeatedly before it will work. Do not try it a few times and then give up because it does not click. It often takes more time to get some plays to click smoothly as with all planned plays, but the time invested will pay off for you in more clear scoring chances, especially against close checking teams.

Play No. 11

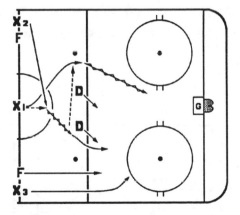

This play must be started well away from the defence, preferably fifteen or twenty feet. The puck carrier (X1) goes down centre. Then when he is about fifteen or twenty feet away from the defence, one of wings (X2) suddenly cuts over *in front* of the puck carrier, takes the puck, and heads for the far side of the defence. The puck carrier, as soon as he sees the wing is close to him, moves the puck a little ahead of him so that it is in the path of the wing coming across, and then cuts behind the wing, skating over to take the position the wing has just vacated.

If the wing who picked up the puck sees that he has a good chance to go around the defencemen, he should do so. However, if the defence moves over quickly to block him, he should pass the puck back to the original puck carrier who, by now, will be over on the wing. Such a pass is very effective because the defence will be well out of position as they must move over in the opposite direction to which the pass is made to cover the puck carrier.

This play should be practised until the two wings and the centre men are all skilful at making both the cut across from the wing and the original puck-carrying play. The original puck carrier skates over toward the wing a little as if he were going to round the defence before he moves the puck ahead for the wing to take as he cuts across in front of the puck carrier. This will often draw the defence over with him and thus get them out of position so that the wing cutting over will be able to round the defence before they can recover. The odd man (X3) should drive to the net once the puck crosses the blue line but should always be careful not to spoil the play by going off-side. This play often confuses the backcheckers who are not sure whether to follow their man or stay in their zone. The momentary confusion it causes is the basis for its success.

Play No. 12

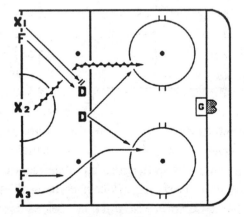

This is an excellent play through which to get a puck carrier past the defence and in for a clean shot on goal.

The puck carrier (X2) heads up the centre of the ice with the wings going up parallel. About twenty feet from the defence, one of the wingers (X1) cuts across at an angle toward the defenceman closest to him. Just as the wing gets close to the defence, the puck carrier suddenly bursts into full speed and goes behind the winger, going out and around him over the blue line. This wing continues on and stops dead in front of the defencemen so that he is between the defencemen and the puck carrier. If, after the puck carrier goes around behind his winger and over the blue line, he is covered by the other defenceman, he can flip a pass over to his other wing (X3), who should break quickly into a scoring position as soon as the puck carrier is over the blue line.

This play is very effective when the defence is standing in front of the blue line because the wing need not worry so much about off-sides as he heads over toward the defence. This play should be practiced to either side so all line-mates get an opportunity to learn all its phases. If the play is to be effective, full speed should be turned on at the moment the defence players are hesitating or blocked out of the play. The other man (X3) should be careful not to go off-side.

Another good play to use in the three on two situation (with back checkers) is the flip through, similar to the play given in the two on two (with back checker) section. You can make this more effective by using the extra man to advantage. The wing, who will not cut in to pick up the flip pass behind the defence, should act aggressively as if he was going to build up a lateral pass to him. This will force the defenceman on his side to give him some attention, especially if he breaks free for a moment from his back checker. The man cutting in should be the wing with the best quick break.

Summary. When play pattern possibilities are studied, the importance of the quick break is again re-emphasized. It is one of the great skills of hockey that is felt in practically any situation whether it be offensive or defensive play patterns.

Plays 10, 11, and 12 can be used, of course, in any three on two situation (wings covered, one wing covered, both wings free). However, they are particularly good for the three on two (wings covered) situation because they offer a chance to disorganize the cover and set up the free man. Forward lines who use them in the three on two (wings covered) situation cannot help but keep the defensive set-up a good deal looser. This will increase the puck carrier's chance of carrying through alone. Coaches and players should remember that even trying them loosens the defence. How often they work in a game will depend upon the amount of time spent practising them.

Play No. 13

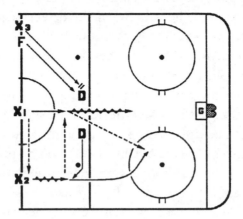

(X1) passes to (X2) while still away from the defence. (X2) skates forward as if to go around the defenceman closest to him. As the defenceman comes over to cover (X2) he then passes back to (X1) who goes straight through the opened defence. Alternatively, (X1) returns a flip pass forward at an angle to (X2) who should burst around the defenceman after (X2) had made the pass back to (X1). The other defenceman, covering (X3), can then be immobilized if (X3) acts aggressively, cutting in quickly and getting free to receive a pass. The winger that is covered should be very careful not to go off-side and spoil the play.

Three on two (one wing covered). This is a very good goal scoring situation which should end up in, at least, a shot on goal from a good position. If such an ending doesn't occur, it usually means one or more of the offensive players have messed things up. Many such chances are lost when the offensive men end up figuring this play differently as there is no set plan that will work if not properly performed.

The play used should be selected according to the type of defence pair to beat and how they react to the situation. If they play it well and back up slowly, trying to slow the play up to give back-checkers a chance to come to the rescue, the only way to take full advantage of the situation is to hold the puck in good position until they have backed in far enough to set up a screen shot between them. This should be followed up quickly by the offensive men.

The player with the puck should pick his spot carefully and not spoil his chance by shooting into the defencemen's legs. The shot should be made from the centre of the defence and should be low to either side of the net. If one of the defencemen makes it a habit to go down in front of a shot in an effort to block it, a fake shot can be used with a quick pass to the side when the defenceman commits himself. This play should be made before the defence pair gets too far back so that there will be room for the pass receiver to get into good scoring position.

If the defence pair gives the offensive men a chance to set up a play that will get one of them in the clear, there are many possible play patterns to use. For example, any of the three on two (wings covered) patterns can be used.

Play No. 14

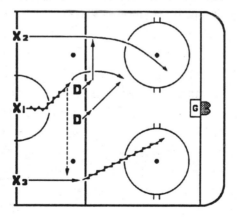

The puck carrier (X1) heads straight for the defence. Then, when he is about twenty feet out from the defence, he starts cutting toward one side of the defence as if he is going to combine with the man (X3) on that side in a short passing play. Then, the moment he sees the defence move over to cover him, he slips a long pass back to the other wing (X2) who has a good chance to go completely into the clear because the defence has been pulled over. If the defence does not move over, but waits watchfully, the puck carrier can turn back and head for the defenceman closest to the play. When he gets to the defenceman, he passes the puck back to the side where it is picked up by the wing (X3) on the short side. Watch that the long rink-wide pass that is made if the defence does move over is not intercepted by the far defenceman. In order to assure this, the final play should be made far enough out so that the defenceman cannot reach the puck to intercept it.

The diagram shows the defence backing in front of the play. However, if you notice the defence does not back in, you must take this into consideration and act accordingly. If the defence pair rush the puck carrier, a single lateral pass should be sufficient. If one defenceman rushes the puck carrier, he should swerve toward the inside, making a pass behind the rushing defenceman to the free wing (X2).

Variations of this play can be used with two on two or two on one plays. In this situation, the same play goes more or less with the puck carrier cutting to one side in an attempt to draw the player or players over to that side before he makes a pass.

It is best if the wings trail behind the puck carrier just a little on this play, especially the man who is on the long side (X2) so as to avoid unnecessary off-sides.

A good way to make the defence pair move to cover, fooling them into forgetting to first move back and protect the ideal scoring zone, is to use one of the many variations of the trailer play. The following is a basic such play. Variations of this can be designed on the blackboard.

Play No. 15

The puck carrier (X1) takes the puck over the blue line to one side of the defence as if he is going to go around the defence. Then, just as he begins

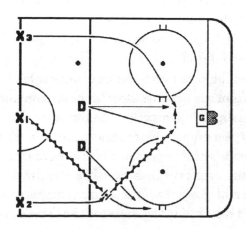

his spurt, he leaves a drop pass. The defenceman will start to move with him to stop him from going around the defence and in on goal and this will leave an open path for the puck carrier's teammate (X2) who goes in as close as possible and then shoots. The original puck carrier (X1) continues on toward the side of the goal from which position he will be able to bang in a rebound or take a goal-mouth pass. The player who picks up the puck on the trailer should not cut behind the puck carrier until the last moment. By timing this move correctly, the player assigned to pick up the trailer pass adds deception and prevents the defence from reading the play before it actually starts.

Perhaps the best way to set up the play is to have the centre man carry the puck in and go around the defence, leaving the puck as soon as he sees the defenceman come over. The wing on that side of the ice then cuts in from his position and picks up the puck. This puck carrier should be careful as he makes his move around the defence and should continue to carry the puck if it looks as if the defenceman is hanging back to stop the trailer play. This will sometimes happen after you have worked the trailer play a few times. In such a situation, of course, the puck carrier has a chance to take the puck around himself. Be very careful, when using the trailer play, not to leave the puck behind unless you know a teammate is in position to pick it up. If the third man is covered when he gets in close to the goal, a pass to the other attacker may be a good play.

This play, as well as the others listed for the three on two (wings free) situation, can also be used in other situations, for example the three on two (wings or one wing covered). Used when wings are covered, the play depends on quick bursts of speed by the covered wings who must make the play through their skill at getting free.

Play No. 16
Another excellent play pattern is the triangle. It often forces the defence pair to depart from the effective slow backing up manoeuvre that protects the scoring area.

In this play, the puck carrier (X1) heads for a spot halfway between the boards and one of the defencemen. The other two offensive players trail behind him, one directly behind, one about ten or twelve feet closer to centre and in line with the other trailing player. Suddenly (X1) breaks hard as if he is going to go around the defence and cut in. As the defenceman on his side comes over to cover, he back passes to the player (X2) directly behind him. As the pass is made, the other trailer (X3) breaks in toward the goal to take up a position in the ideal scoring area. If the other defenceman goes with (X3) to cover him, (X2) goes in on goal and shoots or passes up to (X3) if his own cover comes out to cover him. If the second defenceman leaves (X1) and tries to cover (X2) as he goes in, then (X2) can pass to (X1). If the defence pair back in straight down the centre, (X1) should carry the puck down the side to bring the defence pair well back. Then he (X1) back passes to one of the trailing men to shoot, using the defence as a screen.

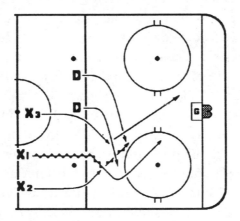

Three on one (one wing covered). This is the same situation as two on one (wing free) and the plays for the latter can be used. The covered man should, of course, act aggressively to help set up the play and loosen up the defence.

Three on one (both wings covered). This is the same as the one on one, and the puck carrier can use any of the plays described earlier for beating one man. The covered wings should act aggressively so as to be threats that will unsettle the defencemen and keep the covering wings too busy to go after the puck carrier, especially if he beats the defenceman.

Three on one (both wings free). This, of course, is a difficult position for the lone checker. His only hope is to slow the play down a little, trying to keep in front of the play. The basic purpose behind any play pattern in this situation is to force the checker to move out of the centre lane, from where he can force the offensive players to shoot from an angle. What must be avoided is carrying the puck close enough to him or passing it close enough to him to give him a chance to break up the play. This occurs more often than you would imagine. The main reason such a good scoring situation as this is often messed up is because the attackers come in without a definite play in mind. Someone misunderstands what the puck carrier has in mind and the play blows up. Here are several basic play patterns that can be used. Variations can be worked out easily.

Play No. 17

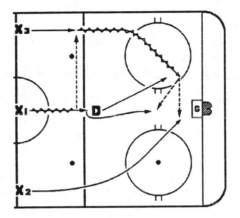

The puck carrier (X1) heads for the defenceman, and when he is just out of checking distance (making sure he is far enough away), he passes laterally to (X3) who bursts and tries to go around the checker and in on goal. If he is certain he can do so, he continues in, but the moment he sees that the checker is going to get close, he passes back to either (X1) or (X2) who have followed up, (X1) in the centre lane a little behind (X2) who should be a little to one side and in front of (X1).

Play No. 18

The puck carrier (X2) heads as fast as he can for a spot between the checker and the boards. If the checker fails to come over, he goes right in. If he comes over to cover him (X2) passes back to (X1) who should trail behind (X2), but in a spot a little closer to the centre. If the checker recovers quickly and moves to check (X1), he passes to (X3), who has skated up to a spot just a little to the left of (X1).

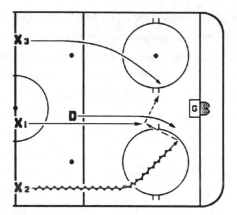

If the checker just goes back slowly down the centre lane, the puck carrier should hold the shot until be backs up far enough for a screen shot to be used. Sometimes a fake shot will freeze him and set up a play to either side.

Ganging plays (opponents one man short). Theoretically the team with the extra man should have a great advantage and be able to set up many goal scoring plays. However, you will often see the team with the advantage fail to get a good shot on the goal. Many more goals will be scored if the coach sees to it that his team has a number of organized plays that have been well practised. Here are a few samples; others can be worked out with a little thought and testing.

Play No. 19

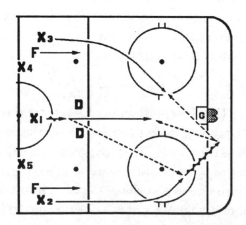

The puck carrier (X1) heads toward one defenceman. Then, when six or eight feet away, he heads in toward the centre of the defence so as to bring them together. Just as he heads in between them, he (X1) shoots (actually flips) the puck into the defence zone at an angle toward the corner of the rink. The wing (X2) on that side then breaks fast to get the puck before it can be covered or before it reaches the corner. That is why the shoot-in or flip must be slow. After the wing picks up the puck, he heads for a spot behind and to the side of the goal from where he can pass it to one of his line mates who has followed up to a spot in front of the goal. However, if he is not covered (which often happens if the play is timed perfectly), he can cut in to a spot in front of the goal and try to score himself.

Practised regularly, with emphasis placed on the fast break in for the puck by the wingers and a cool and accurate shoot-in (after a good fake by the puck carrier), this play can score many clean-cut goals, especially when playing against a poorly managed team or a big, slow defence pair. The follow-up to the front of the goal by (X1) and (X3) should always be made to approximately the same spots so that (X2) will know where to pass without having to take too long to look around – something that often messes up an opportunity to score. Practise this play for both sides.

The wing breaking in after the puck, whether on the inside or outside of his check, should make sure he breaks in ahead of his check as the flip pass is made. This will make sure he reaches the puck first. Then, too, the puck carrier will have to be very careful that he makes the pass at the right time so that he does not put his wing off-side. A good plan is for the wing to lag a couple of feet behind his check and, at the moment the pass is to be made, suddenly put on a quick burst of speed, breaking in front of the man checking him.

Play No. 20

The puck carrier (X2) carries the puck directly at one of the defencemen. Just as he gets about twenty feet away from the defencemen, one of the wings (X1) cuts across directly at the defenceman for whom the puck carrier is heading, as if he is going to get a forward pass from the puck carrier, as in the criss-cross play. He stops just in front of the puck carrier (X2), who swerves to the centre of the defence and, as he does so, lays a

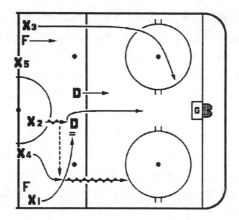

slow pass over to his right. Thereupon (X4), who has been trailing about fifteen or twenty feet behind the puck carrier, breaks fast, picks up the pass, and goes through the vacant space created by (X1) blocking out or distracting the defenceman. Just as (X1) comes over at the defence, (X4) should start to break up for the pass. The pass by (X2) is a slow one in case (X4) is a little slow getting to a spot opposite him. It is better for him to be a little behind time than ahead of schedule. The left wing (X3) skates in hard and takes up a spot suitable for a shot on goal if a pass is made to him or if the puck goes loose. At the same time, (X5) follows up and stops at the blue line. The other man stationed at the blue line then becomes (X1). Thus (X2) breaks past the defence and goes in on goal, watching for a pass from (X4) or for a rebound if (X4) himself goes in on goal.

This play should be practised to both sides of the defence, as should any play that can go to either side of the defence. If the back-checker is on the inside and slightly ahead of (X1), he can still cut across and stop in front of the defenceman by going across *behind the back-checker*. (X1) should not try to *cut in front* of the back-checker as he may be forced off side, which is something everyone should be very careful of – unless, of course, the back-checker is a little behind him when the moment arrives for the cut across.

Play No. 21
The puck should be carried down centre ice by your best puck-carrying defenceman. The two wings go down parallel with him and they should

both be as close as possible to the boards. The centre player (or the fastest and best forward) trails along about fifteen or sixteen feet directly behind the puck carrier. The remaining player trails about twenty-five feet behind. As the puck carrier approaches the defence, he heads as if he were going to shoot in between them. But just as he gets to a spot about eight or nine feet away from them, the centre ice player bursts in at top speed, cutting over to a spot directly between the puck carrier and the wing. The puck carrier then passes laterally to the centre player and he takes it and goes in. The original puck carrier, after he makes the pass, speeds ahead, and either crashes into or through the defence and goes on in for any rebound. The wing on the side to which the pass was made trails a little, waiting at a spot about halfway between the blue line and the goal and between centre ice and the boards. The other wing, as soon as he sees the pass go to the opposite side, takes up a position on the blue line by the boards. Then the other defenceman takes up a blue line position in the middle of the ice – directly out in front of the goal.

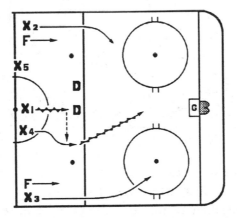

If the play is to be most effective, the centre man must get away quickly, take the pass, and go in on goal at top speed. If, when he takes the pass, he finds that the defenceman on his side comes over very quickly to cover him, he should flip the puck into centre and slightly ahead so that the original puck carrier can pick it up as he dashes through. Frequent practice will soon teach your players the technique of timing the play properly. Give them lots of opportunity to practise it.

The reason this play is so effective is that you get a man advantage just as you hit the defence.

Finally, remember this. If the original puck carrier finds that the defence starts to back in as he approaches, he should hold the puck and slow up a little, letting the defence back in as far as they will go. Then, when they are close to the goal, the puck carrier can shoot between their legs.

Practise this play to both sides. The third and fourth players (those on the wing) should be careful not to go off-side and spoil the play. Also do not worry if the back-checkers are on the outside of the wing men, because if that is the case they will really be out of the play.

All the ganging plays listed can also be used on any three on two (wings covered) situation when the teams are even.

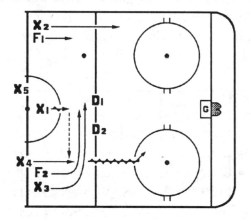

Criss-cross ganging play

This is another good play when there is a man advantage. As the puck carrier approaches the defence, yet well in front of them, the wing suddenly cuts in front of the puck carrier as if to take a pass and go around the far side. His check will likely go with him. A trailer suddenly bursts up the side, and takes a pass. This play, if well timed, often gets the trailer home free as the defence may be immobilized by the trailer's sudden cross over. The puck carrier can make the play even more effective with a fake pass to the trailer as he crosses.

Shoot-in plays. The following list of organized shoot-in plays is designed for use when putting on a pressure or power play with either a man extra or when on even terms. Most teams use a very haphazard system of shooting the puck inside the opposing blue line. Usually whoever has the puck shoots it in without any definite plan. Then everyone chases in after it. As a result, the odds are that the defending team will recover the puck. Our survey uncovered some interesting facts. Out of 300 shoot-in plays, the defending team recovered the puck over 214 times! On nearly half of these occasions, the offensive team following up the shoot-in, failed to get within yards of the puck before it was recovered. In other words, two-thirds of the time it was a waste of effort to shoot it in – the play was really a time-saver for the opposing team. Such aimless giving away of possession of the puck is to be avoided at all costs, especially by the team that has a man advantage. All shoot-in plays should have a plan behind them and be made in such a way as to put the odds on recovering the puck on your side. The accompanying diagrams illustrate the following shoot-in plays.

Play No. 22

The original puck carrier (X1) brings the puck up the right side of the rink. Just before he reaches the defending team's blue line he shoots the puck quickly down the side of the boards so that it continues down and around behind the net. On seeing this, (X3) puts on a quick burst of speed straight toward a spot in the opposite corner of the rink where he knows the puck will end up. If (X3) beats his opposing check to the puck (which he should try to make sure he does by timing his quick burst of speed correctly), then he can make a pass over to (X2), who has skated

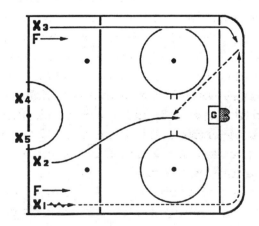

in to a spot in front of the net. Should the pass come out, and (X3) have possession of the puck, then all members of the attacking team can take up their regular attack positions with (X4) and (X5) on the points. This play can be worked just as well from the opposite wing, with (X3) carrying the puck. This play does not work well in all rinks due to the construction of the end boards. However, try it before each game in a new rink by shooting the puck down the boards a few times to see how the puck bounces. With frequent practice you will discover just how hard the shot must be made for the best results and to work in with the speed of the players concerned.

Play No. 23

The original puck carrier (X1) heads for a spot directly at the defending team's left defenceman. The puck carrier in this case should be one of the point players. The reason for this is because it gives your three attacking forwards an opportunity to tear in after that puck, taking advantage of the extra man. As (X1) approaches the left defenceman, he shoots a medium-paced pass forward and against the boards to the spot indicated on the accompanying diagram. He must be careful not just to shoot the puck in the corner. As the pass starts, (X2) and (X3) burst in as quickly as they can to the spot where they know the puck will end up. One of them should be able to gain possession, and have a good opportunity for either a clear break in on goal or a chance to pass to (X4), who has burst in to a position in front of the goal. On this play, (X5) hangs back a few yards ready to back up the play should the pass be intercepted and the play broken up. In other words, (X5) is the safety man. However,

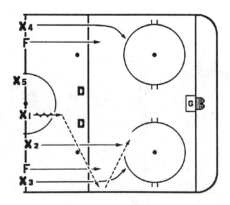

should his team gain possession of the puck, he then takes up a point position inside the blue line. This play can of course be worked just as effectively on the opposite side of the rink.

Play No. 24

This play can be a very dangerous one unless it is done properly. The things to remember are that the puck must be flipped and the entire attacking team must be on guard to back-check quickly should the pass be intercepted.

The original puck carrier (X1) comes up ice. As he reaches a spot about five or six feet from the defence, he flips the puck in between the opposing defencemen. The pass should not be so hard that the goalkeeper can reach it and clear the puck to a corner, but should end up approximately fifteen feet from the goal. As the pass is made, (X2), (X3), and (X4) should break in fast to pick up the puck. If the pass is intercepted, these three men will be caught out of the play. However, even though they will be travelling in at full speed, if they turn sharply and get back as fast as possible, one or two of them should be able to get back in time to help (X5), who is already backing up the play, should the opposing team break away. Then too, the opposing team cannot take the chance of breaking away, unless their break is a clear one, because they are a man short and would be leaving their defence wide open. In this play, the original puck carrier is one of the point players and he should be very adept at making flip passes, since this is the key to the whole play. The flip has to be well timed, well executed, and accurate if the play is to be successful.

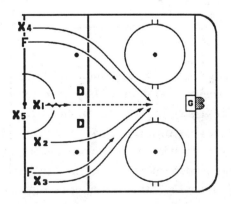

Play No. 25

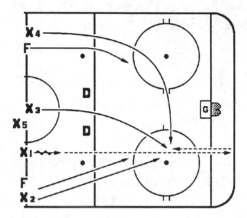

In this play, the original puck carrier (X1) skates up the ice between centre and the right side. As he reaches a spot about fifteen or twenty feet away from the defence, he shoots a hard shot along the ice to a spot on the end boards between the goal and the corner of the rink. If the shot is made correctly, the puck rebounds off the end boards and comes back out fifteen or twenty feet to a spot in front and to the right of the opposing goal. As the puck is shot in to the opposing zone, (X1) and (X5) take up positions on the points just inside the blue line, with (X1) on the right side of the rink and (X5) in the centre. If the shot is by any chance intercepted, (X5) will be backing up the play ready to get back to protect his own end of the rink. This play can be worked equally well to the left side of the rink by simply reversing the procedure. In some rinks the puck will not rebound in this manner off the boards. Before a game, test the boards beside each goal end by taking a few hard shots along the ice during the warm-up.

Play No. 26

The original puck carrier (X4) approaches the opposing defence up centre ice. As he reaches a spot about fifteen to twenty feet away from them he passes to (X1), who comes up quickly between (X4) and (X2). Thereupon (X1) takes two or three strides and dumps a flip pass behind the defence and toward the left to (X3), who has burst very quickly away from his check and headed for a spot behind the defence and in front of the goal to pick up the pass. If the pass goes behind the defence without

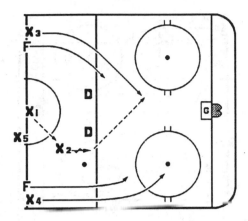

interception, then (X2) can go into the opposing zone and take up his ganging attack position, as also can (X4) and (X5) on the points just inside the blue line. Of course, if the second man sees that he has a clear road to the goal before he makes his flip pass, then he should continue. You should practise this on both sides of the rink so the opposition is not always prepared for the same thing.

Two man advantage patterns. When there is a two man advantage, the main thing is to get possession of the puck and then get the attack organized. Such a situation should produce goals; if it fails, the coach should check the organization of his attack. There is no point in using the shoot-in system in this situation. With a two man advantage, there is a wonderful opportunity to carry the puck in for clear-cut scoring plays. Therefore, it seems to be a wise thing to take the puck back and get the attack organized. Shooting it in only gives the defenders a chance to gain possession of the puck. Practically any of the plays listed for the three on two (one wing covered) situation can be used, with the point men following up to set up an organized pattern if the first play fails to click on the way in. However, there are several other plays that can be used successfully. The following is a basic pattern.

Play No. 27

The main purpose of carrying the puck in wide on the wing is to set up the pattern inside the blue line. Once the puck is well in the zone and in good position, then the two man advantage can be utilized to its fullest possibilities. If the puck was carried in at the defence, they can hold the

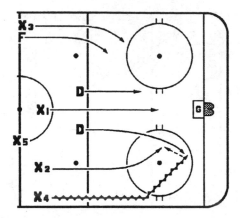

play up longer, keep good position together as they go back, and perhaps even break up the play with a check or pass interception.

In this play, (X4) carries the puck into the zone. He is followed by (X2), who is a little closer to the centre and about ten feet back. (X1) keeps a little behind (X4), making sure he is not off-side, and then as (X4) crosses the blue line, he skates hard to a spot in front and to the left of the goal. The defenceman on his side has to go with him, or he would be open to receive a pass from (X4). (X5) follows up between (X1) and (X2) and stops at the blue line to act as a safety man. When the left defenceman moves over to cover (X4) as he goes in, (X4) passes back to (X2), who can then head for the ideal shooting area. If the pass is made a little too soon and either defenceman has a chance to cover (X2) as he goes in, (X2) can pass to either (X1) or (X4), whichever player is left open. (X3) goes in on the side, trying to keep his cover too busy to take part in the play. He should act aggressively as if he is trying to get in on the play; he must not be lackadaisical. If his cover leaves him, he should immediately get into a good position so as to be free to take a pass. The play, of course, can be worked on either side. All ganging plays with the two man advantage situation existing should generally follow the trailer principle because the defence pair will probably back in and thus set up the trailer chance. The opportunity must not be lost due to over-anxious play; the cool, calm, and well organized approach will pay off.

General strategy suggestions. Carrying the puck in will provide better scoring situations than shooting it in, provided that the plays are well practised, and the puck carrier able. If sufficiently good puck carriers are not available or the carry-in plays do not seem to be working, the shoot-in strategy should be tried. Use the shoot-in plan when your team is faster and has first class quick breakers. These plays should be the basis on which the pressure play system is organized. They are not just suitable when you have a man advantage but also provide a method of organized pressure when the teams are even.

It is often a good plan to have a special power-play line to use whenever you have a man advantage. These players should be selected after careful testing at practice and given plenty of practice performing the actual plays. If some of them are on the ice at the time the man advantage comes up and are tired, take them off for a minute's rest and then put them back on again with the rest of the special squad. Sometimes five forwards are used, sometimes a mix of forwards and defencemen. The main thing is to find the five best. All lines and units of five should, of course, get lots of practice trying the various shoot-in plays for use as a general pattern of pressure attack.

If the actual break-in play fails to click for a goal, or for a shot on goal, due to good covering by the defensive team, but you still have possession of the puck, the best plan is for the offensive team to go into an organized manoeuvre in an attempt to set up a free man in a good scoring position. If there is a set plan for such a situation, better results will be had than if the players merely mill around in haphazard fashion, all ad libbing without any group plan. The man who is in possession of the puck must fight to keep possession until the pattern can get organized. If he cannot keep the puck, he should, of course, pass to a teammate if there is one in position. If there is not a good possibility of a play being completed and possession kept, the puck carrier should force a face-off, jamming the puck against the boards, for example, and warding off the checker until a whistle stops the play. Then, if possession can be gained from the face-off, the pattern can be set up.

One pattern play is the "square." The attacking players form a wide square, two on the blue line points, two deep in the zone, for example one near the corner, and the other at the side of the goal near the end boards. The fifth man acts as a floater, trying to keep in a free position so that he can take a pass to keep the play moving. Then, as soon as the passing around the square brings the defenders out of position, the free man breaks in to the centre of the ice to an ideal scoring position. The puck is passed to him as quickly as possible.

There are many variations of this play. By trying to follow a set pattern, designed to get a man free, the attack will have purpose and organization. If, for example, the defensive players concentrate their strength on the players deep inside the zone, this will leave the men on the points free. The puck should then be passed to them so that they can bring it in and force the defenders to rush to cover them or let them come right in for a close shot. If the defenders come out, the point player with the puck can pass to one of the free players deep in the zone. The attack should be conducted coolly, without a scoring play being attempted until a good situation develops. Trying to force a scoring play too soon, before a good situation develops, usually winds up with the attacking players losing possession of the puck. Too hectic a rush to take advantage of the man advantage rarely pays off. Such a situation calls for cool play and a well organized pattern.

When possession of the puck is lost during a man advantage situation, the team with the advantage should check very closely and hard, forcing face-offs deep in the opposing zone when possible. There should be no hanging back.

If the puck is recovered inside the opposing blue line, the players should immediately try to get an organized pattern going, unless, of course, there is a good chance to shoot on goal or make a play immediately. To help set up a pattern, the point men should be moving into the play quickly so that they can be ready to take up their position in the pattern. By dragging behind the play, the point men will often spoil an opportunity to set up a pattern. The puck will be lost again before a pattern can be set up because the defenders will outnumber the attackers inside the blue line. When possession is gained in centre ice or farther back, the attacking team should get organized quickly and put a definite play into action. Often the player who recovers the puck will break up the ice without waiting or taking a look to get the whole team in the play. This is a serious mistake. The team with the man advantage should always be alert to get organized as a unit whenever possession is gained. Positional play is all important to take advantage of the situation.

Break-out plays. One of the things that ruins the offence of a team, especially when the pressure is on and time is important, is the inability to get a play going from inside one's own blue line. There is nothing more irritating to the players, the coach, and the team's supporters than to see the team's effort to get an attack organized being continually frustrated inside their own blue line, especially when a goal is needed to tie the score near the end of the game. This unfortunately is a situation frequently seen, mainly because so few teams have a well organized set of breakout plays and are, therefore, easily contained by a good forechecking attack. As it is basic strategy in today's game to forecheck fiercely, the team that has not got a good system for getting the puck out of its own zone will always be in trouble. In the opinion of many experts there is no more important phase of offensive play on which to concentrate time an effort. This is true at all levels of hockey. The following are a few basic plays that will give the team a chance to get an attack organized.

Play No. 28

This is perhaps the fundamental breakout play, and can be used whenever the puck is recovered deep in your own end of the rink. It is actually a post play. Whoever becomes the puck carrier (X_1) carries the puck behind his own net. As he comes out from behind his net, he looks to see if a forechecker is coming toward him. If one is, he waits until the forechecker is just out of checking reach and then passes quickly to (X_2), who is in a position close to the boards at the hash marks. (X_2) will be

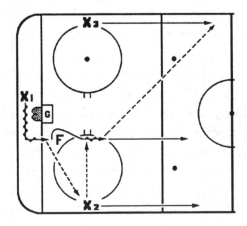

whatever line mate of the puck carrier was closest to the position when the puck was recovered.

As soon as he passes, (X1) side steps past the forechecker and breaks as quickly as possible up the centre of the ice. As (X1) comes opposite or a little ahead, (X2) returns the pass to him, making sure it is accurate and not at his feet or behind him. After taking two or three more hard strides, (X1) passes across the blue line to the breaking (X3). It is necessary that (X3) should have begun to move quickly up the boards just as soon as he saw (X1) start around the net, in order to take the long pass well before he hits the red line at centre ice. As soon as (X2) passes back to (X1), he should break quickly up his wing, and (X1) should do likewise up centre ice after his pass to (X3). If the players perform properly, all three should be in on the play at the opposing defence with several opponents left behind the play. The defencemen, (X4) and (X5), should be ready to act quickly if it goes wrong.

Play No. 29

This is most effective to get the puck out of your zone quickly. As the puck is dropped on the face-off, the centre tries to get his stick between the opponent's stick and the puck. The idea is to hold off the opposing centre's stick until the player closest to the face-off (X2) can move in and get the puck. If the play works (X2) steps in quickly, picks up the loose puck, and fires it across the rink to (X3), who streaks up the opposite side of the rink as soon as the puck is dropped on the face-off. This play should be done to both sides and all lines should learn and practise it

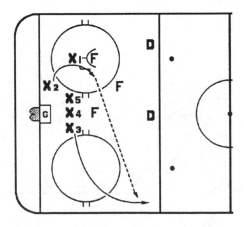

often. After the pass across has been made, the centre and the wing who took the loose puck and made the pass across should break up the ice after the wing who received the pass. The main danger is a bad pass by (X2) or the pass being intercepted by an opposing player. (X2) has to be sure to make a good pass to (X3). The shooter (X2) should be cool and relaxed.

Play No. 30

This play is used to get the puck out of your own end when your team is being attacked by three, four, or five men. In the diagram, a defenceman (X4) has recovered the puck deep in his own end. He then takes a quick look to see if his teammate is open and shoots a long, hard pass up the middle to the centre (X2), who is stationed in the middle of the ice anywhere between the blue line and the red line. (X2) has to face the man with the puck. He should be skating, waiting for the quick pass. When he receives the pass, he watches for (X3) to break up the right wing for a quick pass which can be taken at full speed and thus give him a good break-away chance.

The pass from (X4) does not have to come from the exact spot marked on the diagram. It can come from any area where the puck carrier happens to be, as long as his pass goes hard and accurately to (X2), who should already be in his position. Just as soon as (X3) sees his own teammate recover the puck, he should break very quickly up his side of the rink anticipating the pass from (X2). As soon as (X2) has made his pass to (X3), he should turn quickly and get up on the play as

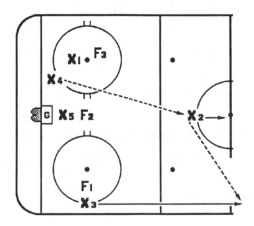

fast as possible. This also applies to the other wing (X1). However, (X1) should not follow up the ice until he is sure that (X2) has possession of the puck; otherwise he will be leaving his check (F3) unguarded if the long pass up the centre is intercepted.

This play can be risky, particularly if five opponents are forcing, because an intercepted pass can mean a dangerous attack on your goal. However, a smart player, when gaining possession of the puck in his own end, will take a look and size up the situation, judging his chances of getting a fast pass up to the centre, and then act accordingly. He should always keep in mind that when he does recover the puck he has to think quickly, because a long delay will spoil the play. At all costs he should not just give the puck away to his opponents by making a weak pass or allow himself to be checked. Instead, he should cause a face-off by icing the puck or allowing himself to be pinned against the boards. Remember, the pass up the centre must be fast! One great advantage of this play is that it is fast and, when properly worked, gives you a clean break-away, often without a man back to stop a play on goal.

Play No. 31

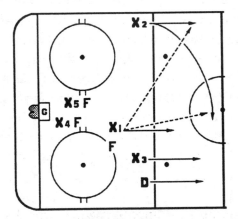

In the diagram, (X1) has recovered the puck fairly deep in his own end of the rink. He then takes a quick look to see in which direction (X2) is going to travel. If (X2) heads straight up the left side of the rink to his second position in the accompanying diagram, the pass by (X1)

should be made ahead of (X2) so that he can receive the pass at the point shown (just inside the centre red line) without losing any speed. However, if (X1) sees that (X2) is going to cut across the ice to the alternative position, then, his pass should go up the centre between the opposing defence.

For this play to succeed, watch for the following points. When the puck is in his own end, (X2) should be hovering around just inside his own blue line and, as soon as his teammate recovers the puck, he should lose no time deciding to which of the two points illustrated he is going to go. His choice depends on how the opposition is spread and how well he takes a pass.

The pass from (X1) should in most cases be a fast pass along the ice, because it is less likely that a fast pass will be intercepted. Then, too, such a pass helps the forward breaking away to get away quickly, which is all important for the play's success. Of course, if (X1) sees that (X2) is slow starting and that he will be slow getting to the receiving point, a slow flip pass will be an effective one to use. A slow pass, which is easily intercepted, should be flipped to make this possibility more difficult for your opponent. After (X2) has received the break-away pass, it is the all-important duty of (X3) and (X1) to follow up after (X2) as quickly as possible, either to receive a pass, or to put in a rebound. The fastest breakers and best pass receivers should be given the break-away assignment when your team is being forced. The player assigned should be instructed to float around the blue line ready to break as soon as someone on your team receives the puck. The threat of such plays will make the ganging attack by your opponents less effective. The break-away man should be a sleeper who seems to be loafing at the blue line. Nothing should be done to attract the opposition's attention.

Play No. 32

If possession of the puck is gained by (X2), (X3), or (X5) anywhere in the shaded area marked on this diagram, (X1) should break as fast as he can into open ice, making sure he starts his break just as soon as he sees his own teammate recover the puck. The person recovering the puck, whether (X2), (X3), or (X5), should take a quick look and slide a pass to him, aiming it so that it ends up at a spot no further than ten or fifteen

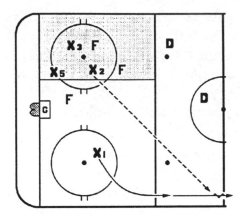

feet inside the centre red line so that (X1) can pick the puck up on the inside of the red line while travelling at full speed. The person in possession of the puck should be very careful to aim his pass ahead of (X1). He can thus pick it up without slowing down.

The success of this play depends on several things. Most important, (X1) must break fast! The pass must be accurate. The person recovering the puck must not telegraph his play. (It is often a good idea to fake a rush or a pass up his side, before he sends the pass across to the breaker. However, he must not spoil the break by holding up the play too long.)

In organizing this as one of your planned plays, the idea is to explain the play situation (when and under what conditions it should be used), and to instruct your players that the player who is closest to the boards (opposite where the puck is recovered) is the man who should make the break. If a defenceman is in such a position, he can make the break. The play, of course, can be worked from either side of the rink. All your players should be told to watch for this situation whenever they are checking inside their own blue line.

Play No. 33

This is another type of post play that can be very effective. One player (X1) is assigned to take up the position as shown in the accompanying diagram. This position is a few feet in front of the attacking player who is on the point position on the centre of the blue line. He faces the play, ready to move defensively if possession is lost and a dangerous play develops. The moment one of his teammates gains possession as did

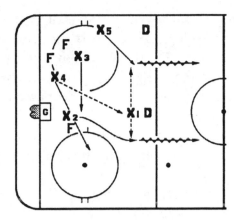

(X4) in the diagram, the puck is shot quickly to (X1). Then the two players in the best position to do so, (X5) and (X2) in the diagram, break fast to one side of (XI). The defenceman close to (X1) will probably move in to check him only to find himself well taken in by the lateral pass which (X1) makes to one of the breaking players, (X2) or (X5). After (X1) makes the pass, he turns and follows the play quickly. The two men deepest inside the zone, (X3) and (X4) in the diagram, take up defensive positions immediately after the play is made in case it goes wrong or a pass is intercepted. The diagram shows one situation but the same principles apply to similar situations.

General suggestions. If such break-out plays as listed, or any of the variations a coach can work out, are well practised, the team will develop greater skills at getting attacks started. There should always be a plan. The players should be well briefed on team responsibilities and their own particular responsibilities. Actually there are two phases of a break-out play – the actual break-out and the follow up. To take full advantage of the break-out, the two players who are closest to the breaking out player should be sure to follow up quickly, providing support so that the break-out will end up in a three-man play or more, if the coach wishes a four- or five-man attack to follow a break-out. All too often, you see the players who should be following up skating slowly after the play, watching with interest. They may have the best seats in the house but they should not take time out to watch! Just as the players get lazy in their back-checking chores, so do they in their following up. Such players should be jumped on very hard until they react instantly. Any player who offends frequently should be seated on the bench from where he can watch with greater comfort and with less effect on the offensive play of the team. The same thing should apply to the players who merely stand around and watch a teammate trying to bring the puck out, a very common habit. Every single man on the team should be playing some part to help make the break-out play work. If the coach is on the cautious side, he can use a trailer who stays behind the puck carrier as long as he is inside the blue line. This is a good idea when using Play 28.

If the break-out plays are not working well, the second best plan is to flip the puck out into the neutral zone. This move at least eases the pressure and can often build up the start of a play. A flip out, backed up by fast breaking after the puck immediately after they see the flip out has been made, can produce many scoring situations. For some reason the average player likes to carry the puck out, often hanging on to it until he loses possession.

FACE-OFF TACTICS

It is important is to have a plan if possession of the puck is to be gained. The coach, can figure out many patterns and by trying them find out the most effective ones for the various circumstances that might arise. You do not have to be a mental wizard to figure out that the team that gains possession most frequently on the face-offs will have a big edge, especially when the face-offs are inside the opposing team's blue line. Following are some of the tricks that can be used to gain control on a face-off.

Face-off tricks.
- As the puck is dropped, quickly slap your stick against your opponent's to knock it away, and then sweep the puck back. Aim at a spot about six inches above the blade using your stick blade.
- As the puck is dropped, move the stick blade quickly forward and then turn the toe of the blade of your stick toward the side (to the left if left-handed) and pull the blade quickly backward.
- Another good trick is to block the opposing centre's stick by quickly placing your blade between his and the puck, holding your stick with a tight grip and leaning on it to make your stick hard to move. Then, when his stick is stopped, flip the puck back.

If your opponent is slapping at your stick, try lifting your stick quickly away and then go for the puck as he misses hitting your stick. The best results are gained when you play your opponent's stick and then go for the puck. This strategy is sound because, if you can control his stick movement, you will be able to control the puck. The face-off expert should also study the way each referee drops the puck, the methods of the opponent. He should always mix up his technique so his opponent will not be able to get set. The idea is to be one step ahead. Getting the puck at the face-off is a high level skill and therefore must be practised long and hard. It is something that too few players do today. (See face-off section in Defensive Strategies and Tactics.)

The coach should take this into consideration when organizing his practice sessions and so should the young player ambitious to become a hockey star. A good plan is to have regular face-off drills and contests between the players or with your friends if practising on your own. Every now and then have a contest between those players assigned to face-off responsibilities. Such a contest can be organized by having the players concerned compete against each other or by having each man face-off four or five times with the other members of the team.

The importance of getting the face-off cannot be over-emphasized. Therefore, the development of such skill by the players assigned to the job should get top priority.

Summary. When considering the subject of offence play patterns, remember that the better organized the attack, the more chance it has to succeed. It will beat an ad lib attack any time, all other things being equal. By working on play patterns, the players develop a play sense that will enable them to ad lib plays when a new situation arises. There is a great opportunity for the coach who has the necessary facilities to develop the organization of the attack by charting play situations and developing the play patterns for each. The players should practise dealing with the various play situations so that they will make the right moves when they recognize the situation in actual play. For example, all forward lines should practise the various three on two (wings covered, etc.) situations. Practise them merely rushing three on two. All the situations should be practised with priority being given to the three on two (wings covered) and two on two (wings uncovered) situations. Surveys show these occur more often than others.

Finally, remember that the greatest weapon a team can have is mass quick break skill. It will provide most offence opportunities. It will lessen the effect of the opposing team's offence because they will be timid about coming in too strong when you continually break-away on them. When their attack is broken up, it will enable your players to set up their own play situation because they will be able to break-away from cover. Then, as a clincher, it will mean your plays will explode just as your opponents make what they believe to be the last move.

Defensive Strategy
and Tactics

The young hockey player, with few exceptions, loves to carry the puck and to score goals. When he comes home after a session at the local rink, he tells his folks about how hard he can shoot or how shifty he is. He rarely says, "Boy, you should see my poke check," or "You should have seen me take my man out." His father or mother often builds up his pre-occupation with the offensive phase of the game by asking, "How many goals did you score?" This is very natural because it is the more glamorous side of hockey.

However, this is the main reason why good defensive players are so hard to find. This situation is even more serious because, with most people, defensive play in any game involves hard work. It is a duty or an obligation that like most duties or obligations is unconsciously resisted. Most players consider offensive play fun and defensive play a chore. Research has shown that players became tired more quickly while playing defensively than when on the attack. According to psychologists, mental attitude plays an important part in fatigue. Those who enjoy what they are doing are able to sustain effort much longer than those who get no joy out of their efforts, even though their basic conditioning and physique are equal.

It is assumed, then, that the defensive success of an individual or team as a whole depends upon the attitude toward the defensive obligation. Therefore, every effort should be made by the coach to mould in his players a desire to play good defensive hockey. The player should help out by accepting his defensive obligations cheerfully, telling himself that in hockey, just as in life, there are things he will like doing and things he will not. And the more cheerfully he accepts and does the things he does not like, the farther and faster he will progress and the more enjoyment he will get from his activities. The coach can help a great deal by making his defensive instruction and practice work as interesting as possible.

INDIVIDUAL (FORWARDS)

To do his job well, the individual player must learn the following skills.

Skating agility. The most valuable of all weapons, of course, is skating agility, especially such agility manoeuvres as the quick break, change of direction, and stop and start. This is fundamental because the player with the most agility will find it easy either to get free from or to stick with his opponent. Therefore, any attempts to develop defensive skill should emphasize practice designed to increase the agility skating skill.

Covering the man. In covering a man, the basic principle is to strive always to stay between him and the puck. Then the defensive player will be in a position to intercept passes and control the actions of the players being watched. If this is impossible, for example, when the offensive player has already gained the inside position, the defensive player should try to regain control by staying a little ahead of and very close to the offensive player, thus establishing a position that will prevent the offensive player from going more than one way or breaking out in front if a pass is received. It is wise to keep a stride ahead of your man. The defensive player will then have a chance to make his covering play if the offensive player suddenly breaks fast in an attempt to get free. If the defensive player stays even, the man making the jump will have a big advantage. He will open up at least a stride because he will start first. The defensive player should watch the puck at all times and depend upon his peripheral vision to keep track of his man. Continual practice of this method and frequent participation in split vision drills will develop the needed skill.

If the defensive player loses sight of the puck, he should, of course, play the man, watching him carefully. In skating with an offensive man, the defensive player should take as many short strides as possible because he will be able to manoeuvre more quickly. In watching a man during scrambled play inside his own blue line zone, the defensive man should stay in such a position as to see the puck, between the offensive man and the goal, and close enough to make a quick play to intercept a pass. He should never turn his back on the play. In taking out a player who is trying to move in for a pass, the defensive player should lean the shoulder nearest to his opponent toward him and ride him away from the puck, always keeping a little ahead. He should make sure he plays the man. If he plays the puck he may lose control over his man and, if he does not succeed in intercepting the puck, he could cause a scoring opportunity.

If the opponent is out of the play, the puck does not matter. If he is left a little behind by a quick break, the defensive man should try very hard to catch up, keeping an eye on the puck in case a long reach with his stick can intercept or deflect it. It is a very natural reaction for the defensive player to slow and let his man go if he gets a quick break. This should be avoided at all costs. Even if the offensive player does get away and pick up a pass, the defensive man may well catch him just in time to save a goal or another pass. Usually the offensive man slows a little when he gains possession, or he may have to break stride to take the pass. This will give the defensive man a chance to catch up. A good defensive man never lags, even if he thinks he is out of the play. Covering a man, without resorting to illegal holding, is a difficult skill to master and cannot be learned by practising it only in games. It should be given a lot of attention during practice. A good drill is playing without the stick. For example, one forward line can rush on the defensive pair with the opposing wings trying to cover the offensive wing men without carrying a stick. The same system can be used for practising covering play during pressure plays inside the blue line. Playing without a stick will teach the defensive man to stay with his check as he will know his only chance is to keep close.

If the defensive man finds that he is a slower skater than his check, he should not try to skate in an even rhythm with his man. Instead, he should keep up with a series of quick breaks, digging in hard every few yards. This involves extra effort but it is the only answer. If the defensive man is a less agile and slower skater, he should keep as close to his man as possible, giving him the least possible amount of room in which to manoeuvre. If the defensive man finds himself a little behind the man who is about to pick up a pass, and the puck cannot be reached, he can give his opponent's stick a sharp rap up high on the shaft just as the puck comes across. This will often cause the offensive man to miss the puck.

When a pass is intercepted inside his own blue line zone, the defensive player should either carry or clear the puck away from the goal as soon as possible. The safest place to clear or head for is the side of the rink. The puck should never be cleared or passed blindly. If the defence player has a chance, he should turn quickly and break up the ice or pass to a teammate breaking out. However he should never attempt such a play if he is in doubt about the position of the players behind him, for he may well give the puck right back to an offensive player. If in doubt, carry or clear the puck to the side, away from the goal and the centre lane.

Stick checking. Clever stick checking pays off in many ways. For example, if the players are all clever stick checkers, who can actually gain possession of the puck with their checks, and not just knock the puck away, they will be able to hem in the opponents more effectively while ganging or exerting pressure at their end of the ice. The forecheckers, for instance, will be gaining possession of the puck more frequently and will thus be able to set up more scoring plays. A slashing, sweeping type of check rarely, if ever, leaves the checker in possession of the puck, even though it may be successful in breaking up the puck carrier's rush. Usually the checker must chase the puck after the check, if it has not been knocked away to some other member of the opposing team. Accordingly, it is suggested that you start right now, especially if you are a forward, to learn the art of stick checking that will bring you posses-sion of the puck.

There are three types of checks that will give you possession if com-pleted successfully; the poke check, the sweeping poke check, and the hook check. The following instructions are for a player who shoots left. Reversing the instructions make them applicable for a player who shoots right.

The poke check. As the puck carrier approaches, position yourself squarely in front of him. The stick should be held out in front of you with the toe of the stick blade pointed in and your elbow bent by your side. By doing this, you will force the puck carrier to slow down. When he comes within reach of your stick, "poke" (jab) out with the blade to check the puck off his stick. Remember not to lunge as this may throw you off balance and allow the puck carrier to go around you.

The sweeping poke check. As the puck carrier approaches, manoeu-vre, and fake with your body so as to make him come around to your left side. That is your first objective and is a trap you must set for him. As soon as you are sure he's coming around your left side, bend your knees until you are as close to the ice as possible. Then take a long stride to your left side, slightly toward the puck carrier, and shoot out your stick as flat on the ice as you can get it. The puck will come to your stick and stay there, ready for you to pick it up. The puck carrier will have over-skated the play and you will be free, for a second or two at least, to take possession and make a play. The blade of the stick can be placed toe first toward the approaching player, thus forming a hook, or it can be turned back toward the checker. The hook style involves a shift of the stick in the hand in order to turn the toe toward the approaching player. If done too soon, it will warn the approaching player of what to expect.

The hook check. As in the poke check, you try to force the puck carrier to come around a certain side, in this case, your right side. As he is skating past you, your first move is to bend your knees suddenly, take a step after him with your right leg, and lay your stick flat on the ice in front of the puck. The blade of your stick should form a hook and the puck should be trapped inside that hook so that it will stay there, ready for you to take it as the puck carrier over-skates the play. This is an especially effective check if the puck carrier does not expect it.

In making either of these checks, it is important to get lots of knee bend, going down as close to the ice as possible. The player who is stiff in the knees, or who will not go down close to the ice, will often fail to get the puck because he will have too little of his stick on the ice. Just as a puck carrier learns to fake one way and to go the other, the checker should learn to fake with his checks, faking as if going one way, then suddenly switching.

A variation of the hook check can also be used when skating beside the puck carrier. The checker reaches the blade of his stick ahead of the puck, with the toe of the blade turned back and toward the far side of the checker, then bends his knees and hooks the puck back. For example, if the checker was on the left side of the puck carrier, he would use his left hand to make the check.

A good poke and hook check drill is to place the checker between two pylons about twenty feet apart. Then, have a line of puck carriers go down the ice toward him, trying to carry the puck through the pylons. The squad can be divided into three or four sections, each man taking turns as the checker. The competitive angle can be worked in by scoring the number of checks made, counting two points for the defensive player if he gains possession of the puck, one point when the puck is knocked too far away from the puck carrier for him to reach it quickly. Any team that has a large number of players who are adept at using these two checks will have a defensive strength that will be hard to beat. Then, too, it will mean more goals because there will be a longer possession of the puck, and many more opportunities for offensive plays. The forechecking attack will be especially hard to avoid. Players who possess poke and hook check skill will be very useful during scrambled play, because they will be able to get the puck more often.

The sweep check. This check is made by sweeping the stick in a half-circle toward the on-coming puck carrier, with as much of the stick flat on the ice as possible. Just as in the poke or hook check, the player should get down low with lots of knee bend. The main advantage of the sweep check is that it covers a lot of ice surface and, if the stick moves quickly, the puck carrier has difficulty in avoiding it. The main disadvantages are that, even when the puck is contacted, possession is not gained because the puck will be knocked some distance away. It must be also started earlier than other kinds of checks, thus giving the puck carrier warning. It is most effective when used from the side when the checker is skating with the puck carrier. At such a time, the stick is swept around in front of the puck carrier. For example, if the checker was on the left side of the puck carrier, he would sweep his stick with his left hand toward the puck. Such checks are often missed because the checker does not get enough of his stick flat on the ice.

The skate off check and stick lift. This is a good check to use when the checker has an edge in speed on the puck carrier, or is going faster at the moment, for example after the puck carrier has been overtaken during a back-checking burst. As the checker gets to his man, he suddenly skates in front of him, knocking his stick off the puck with a sharp slap on the shaft, and then picking up the puck. A variation is when the checker lifts the puck carrier's stick up off the ice with a quick flip of his stick, placed just under his opponent's stick, using the bend formed where the blade joins the shaft to make the lift. This is a good check because the puck is usually easy to recover. When the opponent's stick is slapped, the puck is often knocked out of reach. Every player should practise this play because opportunities to use it are always occurring during games.

Back-checking. The average hockey player may try to skip to the next section because back-checking means work. However, if you keep in mind that a two-way player is always a welcome sight for a scout's sore eyes, you may well be inspired to greater effort. A player can make no more important contribution to his team's success than by doing a good back-checking job. The late Ted Reeve once wrote a verse about his experience as a blocker of kicks during his years as a Canadian football star. I will paraphrase it in order to describe the attitude of a hockey player who just cannot get around to back-checking.

When I was young and in my prime
I used to back-check all the time.
But now that I am old and grey
I only back-check once per day.

The verse, that you should print in large block letters and hang in your room, would go as follows:

Even though it seems a crime
I keep on going all the time.
I'll dig in hard each time I play,
Though it will turn me old and grey.

As mentioned in the chapter on Skating, the most important ingredient in the technique of back-checking is the quick tight turn. Every player should work on this phase of his skating until he can skate back with the least possible loss of time. The sooner he gets turned, the easier his back-checking job will be.

Another important factor is the attitude of the player when he sees he is well behind. He is inclined to think that it will not do any good if he does hustle back, because he is too far out of the play. Any good hockey player knows that if he does hustle back, he may get there just in time to save a goal. His attitude should be: "As long as I'm physically capable, I'll go back as hard as I can." If he is too tired, he should immediately head for the bench, not trying to hide his fatigue, or to use the time during which he should be back-checking to gain a short rest so that he will be able to go hard on his next shift – a habit all too common with many players. Such lazy players should be taken off the ice at the slightest sign of such behaviour.

Often the momentary disappointment that a player feels at seeing a promising offensive play miss will cause him to lag behind. This should also be avoided.

Conditioning, of course, is another prime factor in back-checking. If a player is not in shape, he will not be inclined to make the effort. He will naturally tend to save his strength for offensive work. Stopping quickly and then accelerating again is one of the toughest assignments the body can be given as any poorly conditioned player who has to back-check will tell you. The well conditioned player will rarely be a lazy player. If a coach wants a team of good back-checkers, be sure to get them into good physical shape so that they can go both ways without fatigue. (See the chapter on Training for suggestions.)

When the back-checker comes back, he should try to get between the man he is to cover and the goal. If he can not see his man, he should analyze the situation and head for the danger spot. He shouldn't come back haphazardly flying down the ice with no idea of what his job will be when he gets there.

Clearing the puck. As previously stated, the defensive player must be cool and calm when clearing the puck away from the scoring zone. He should clear as quickly as possible with no hesitation, or carry the puck if being forechecked. While you want to keep possession of the puck, if a break-out play cannot be quickly set up, then flip the puck out into the neutral zone or freeze it. Do not hang on to it and get checked. Poor clearing will cause problems. Keep cool.

Analytical attitude (read and react). The defensive player should study his opponent to learn his favourite plays. A careful appraisal of how the opposing player reacts under certain circumstances often enables the defensive man to keep him covered. A lot of players just go ahead trying to do their job without any attempt to understand why or how their man is getting free. Don't leave it up to the coach to tell you. The game may depend on one man's ability to outsmart his opponent during a key play. Therefore, keep ahead of the opposing player by studying his actions and habits. Just as a ball-carrier in football may give away the fact that he is going to carry the ball by some habitual preparatory movement, so will a hockey player give away his intention to break in for a pass or make a move designed to get him free. Then too, he will often have favourite spots to which he always skates, and favourite plays if he gets the puck. Being aware of such things gives the defending player a great advantage.

Fundamentals of individual defensive play. Good defensive play depends on a thorough grasp of a basic list of "do's" and "don't's." Some of these basic rules are stated below.

- If fighting for the puck on the boards, concentrate on getting your body between your opponent and the puck.
- Pick up your man as early as possible when the opposition has the puck. If you wait for him, he may be travelling too fast for you to stay with him.
- When coming back with your man, always be alert to move in behind the defence to pick up an attempted flip-through play or a loose puck.
- Never relax your attention if the play seems to be being concentrated at another point. Stay with your man regardless. Anything can happen; the situation can shift in a moment.
- If an opposing player shoots on goal from a position well away from you, do not watch the play as a spectator, or hope the puck will be picked up by a teammate so you can go on the attack. Instead, see that your man does not shake you and go in for the rebound.
- Leave your man only if there is an opposing player who is uncovered and in a more dangerous position than your man.
- When a teammate is forechecking always stay between your man and the puck so that you can intercept any attempt to pass it to him on a fast breakout play.
- If a puck carrier comes into your territory when you are already watching a man, only try to check him if you are the last man between him and your goal. Otherwise your duty is to see that your man does not get free. If you go for the puck carrier, he may pass to your man and break past you to leave you completely out of the play.
- When a puck carrier is using a lot of placement moves, such as playing the boards, or placing the puck between your legs, play the man, try to keep your body in front of him or skate with him and try to check him as you go.

- If a puck carrier is beating you as you move in to check, switch to the strategy of skating with him as you try to check. This will prevent him from using his stick or whatever to beat you.
- When you are trying to go with a man who is attempting to move out and around you or heading across the ice, play him with your body and hold your stick in the hand farthest away from the direction you are heading. This will protect you if he cuts back quickly inside you, as you will have your stick ready to prevent such a move. Use your body to force him wide into the boards or to an impossible position and use your stick to cover a possible cut back.
- Avoid at all costs that inclination to tag behind if a checker breaks past you or passes to another man. Break fast and stay with the play. The defensive objective of all players never stops as long as the opposing team has possession.
- Learn to fake with your defensive moves to force the puck carrier or your cover into making his move first.
- Never turn your back on the puck.

INDIVIDUAL (DEFENCEMEN)

The basic fundamental. The most important skill that a defenceman should learn and develop is skating backward. The defenceman who can skate backwards with good balance and be able to manoeuvre laterally quickly will always be a tough man to beat. The development of such skill should be given top priority. The technique and drills tested in the section on backward skating in the first chapter should be studied and practised carefully.

Stance. When waiting for the play to come in, the defenceman should make sure his stance is correct. If his stance is not basically sound, he will not be able to make his move as quickly or as effectively since he will be easier to fake off balance. Just as a blocker in football or a fielder in baseball must assume the best possible stance, so should the hockey defenceman. By working on your stance in practice, it will become second nature in a game.

The ideal stance is with the feet comfortably apart and parallel, knees bent a little, shoulders loose and easy, arms relaxed and the stick held in front with the blade on the ice. The stick is best held in the inside hand (right hand if left defenceman) so that, if the play goes to his left, he can go with the puck carrier, his stick already in position to take care of any cut back attempt. The feet must be parallel because if one foot is in front of the other balance and ability to go to either side will be spoiled. The whole body should be kept relaxed because a tense defenceman is easier to fake out of position.

As the play comes in. When a puck carrier approaches, the defenceman should move his stick slightly out in front of him, with his elbow by his side for a possible poke check. However, as he is working with his stick, the defenceman should try to keep his body in front of the attacking player moving slowly backwards. He should not lunge into the attacker or commit himself until the puck carrier makes his move. It is a battle to see who can make the other man move first. Having the stick out in front of him will enable the defenceman to force the puck carrier into making a move. If a defenceman is playing the puck carrier, he should always stay with him, blocking him with his body and riding him out of any future participation in the play if the puck carrier shoots, makes a pass, or flips the puck past the defenceman. Many defencemen make the mistake of turning to chase the puck instead of blocking out the attacking player.

Stick checking. Though it is wise for defenceman to learn all types of stick checking, the most important type for him is when he has his stick held out in front of him, jabbing at the puck in short, well controlled attempts to knock it away as he moves back, keeping in front of the puck carrier. A sweep or side hook check is also very useful when the puck carrier is trying to go around the outside and is pulling away as he has the jump or has superior speed.

Body checking. Every defenceman, of course, should learn to body check hard and accurately. He must make sure he only attempts a body check when his opponent is set up and be sure that a serious situation won't develop from a missed check. (See Tactics for various play situations.) There are two types of body checks, the shoulder check and the hip check.

Shoulder check. This check is used in close play when the puck carrier comes straight in. A typical shoulder check situation occurs when the puck carrier tries to break through the centre of the defence pair. The check is made by the defensive player taking a step into the puck carrier, pushing hard off the back foot. It is the drive off the back leg that provides the power for the check. The point of the shoulder is aimed at the puck carrier's chest. Care should be taken to develop skill at checking with both shoulders. The eyes should be open and on the target at all times. The check must not be made too soon, or the puck carrier will have a chance to avoid it, and the defenceman will be left floundering around behind him. The time to make it is when the puck carrier has committed himself, and is in no position to change his direction.

Hip check. The hip check is used by a defenceman whenever the puck carrier tries to get around the side or if he misses a shoulder check. For example, if a defenceman tries a shoulder check and misses, he can stay in the play by quickly swinging his hips around and into the puck carrier as he tries to go by him. When making the check, the defenceman should bend quickly from his waist, bend his knees, and push off from the far leg so that he moves well across into the puck carrier. If using a hip check to stop a puck carrier, the defenceman should be sure to get as close as possible to the attacking player before he starts the hip check. If it is started from too far away, it will be easy to avoid, and will put the defenceman in a bad position because he will find it hard to recover. Skill at making the manoeuvre is best developed by practising the various backward turns and side thrusts listed in the first chapter.

One common fault is not keeping the eyes on the attacking player during the hip check. This is an easy mistake to make because when the hips are moved well out behind and the body is travelling backwards, it is natural to take the eyes off the target. The eyes can be kept at work if the checker turns his head toward the attacker as the hip check move is made. Another common mistake is merely swinging the hips around and at the attacker, while keeping the feet stationary. This kind of check covers a very small area and is easier to avoid. The checker must drive sideways into the attacker. The body should be well bent and leaning forward with the arms and stick out in front so that it will be hard for the puck carrier to cut inside the hip check.

An excellent way to develop body checking skill is to practise frequently without sticks.

Body blocking. This is body checking without hard contact. The defenceman tries to block the attacker's progress by blocking him with his body, but does not drive in as he does with a body check. For example, the defenceman, on a two against two rush, takes the puck carrier, drives him to the side, or blocks him from following in after making a shot or pass.

If the defenceman wished to drive the attacking player to the side, he uses his shoulder and keeps skating with short, hard driving strides, moving the attacking player before him. Such a play can also be made with the chest, making direct contact, driving the attacker back, keeping contact by driving with short strides. The idea is to get the attacker off balance and keep him moving with an aggressive, short skating action. If the intention is merely to hold up the player for a moment or two, the best bet is a combination hip and shoulder check, much the same as a cross body block in football. The body is bent well over from the waist, the buttocks moved well out behind, and the knees are well bent. Contact should be made with the side of the body between the shoulder and hips as they are moved into the attacker. If the attacker tries to go past, the checker moves forwards or backwards with a series of short strides to prevent him. Any type of body block should only be sustained until the play that started as the check was made has been completed. If contact is held longer the player is wide open for an interference penalty.

PLAY SITUATIONS

What action the defenceman should take is governed by the play situation. The tactics that each should follow for the basic play situations are given here.

One on one. When one defenceman has one checker to stop, he should keep his stick out in front of him, reaching for the puck, and trying to force the puck carrier into making a move. He should back slowly and concentrate on keeping his body between the goal and attacker. Above all, he must not move too soon, or lunge out, and thus let the puck carrier by. He should play the man at all times, letting the puck go where it may. The situation will be safe as long as he can keep in front of the attacker. He should be alert for a fake shot and not go down to stop it or stiffen in an unconscious, protective move. He should be careful not to back up too far so as to allow the attacker to use him for a screen shot. A good tactic is to fake a move to the inside in order to start the attacker around to the outside. Then go with him, forcing him to the side boards, keeping the stick behind on the inside to guard against a cut back. Above all, the defenceman should be careful not to be caught standing still. He should start moving backwards when the puck carrier is still a fair distance away. If the defenceman is beaten, he should turn, skate forward, and get back as fast as possible. He will then be able to clear any rebound from the goalie after he stops the first shot.

The attacker should always be met as soon as possible. The defenceman then will still have room to catch up if the puck carrier beats him on his first move. As soon as he sees the attacker break away and start to come in, the defenceman should move up to meet him, and then start to come back in front of him before he gets too close.

The checker should remember that a fake check can be just as effective as a fake move by the puck carrier.

One on two. If a puck carrier comes down against two defencemen, the closest man should go for the puck carrier, forcing him into a move, and then try to body check or body block him. The other man backs him up, watching for the loose puck, or moving in if the attacker slips by his partner. A good tactic is to leave the centre lane open a little and then, as the puck carrier tries to break through, close in with a shoulder or hip check. The main danger is when the defencemen fail to work as a unit and one man rushes out to check.

The defencemen should communicate as the opponent comes in, calling to each other the move to make. Over-anxiety to body check the puck carrier always helps the attacker get by. If the attacker attempts to skate around the defence, the man closest to him goes with him. He tries to force him to the side, protecting the cut back possibility carefully while his partner goes back covering the centre lane to cut off the attacker if he gets around the first man. The defence pair should always try to keep in front of the attacker as he approaches, moving together laterally to keep directly in front of him. There is a tendency with some defencemen to stand around and watch, leaving the player to his partner. This can be a costly mistake. The defence pair should not back up when up against a lone attacker. This will likely give him a chance to use a screen shot. He should be forced into making a play.

Two on one. Two attackers come in and there is only one defenceman in position to make the play.

A good general rule to follow, in playing the two on one, is that the goaltender plays the shooter and the defenceman plays the pass. The defenceman should stay in between the two attackers all the way back and, at the same time, try to force the puck carrier well to the outside.

Coaches of older players should have the defenceman stay in the middle all the way back and when the puck carrier is no longer a threat, pay more attention to the open man. The defenceman must be careful not to be drawn completely out of the play by the open man, or he will allow the puck carrier to cut across the front of the net for a scoring opportunity. If your defencemen play the two on one this way, you must teach them that if the puck carrier starts across toward the front of the net, instead of shooting, the defenceman will have to confront the puck carrier to stop the scoring opportunity.

For younger players and when the puck carrier is deep enough that he is no longer a threat to cut to the inside, the defenceman can turn, face him, and attack if the opportunity allows. He should try to position himself between the puck carrier and the potential receiver, in case the puck carrier tries a pass to the slot.

The coach must also remind his defence that their duties don't end with a shot on goal. If help has not arrived by way of a back checker or defence partner, the defenceman playing the two on one must control the man in front of the net and stop him from picking up any rebounds. He should also communicate with his goalie so there is no confusion about loose pucks or possible rebounds.

Two on two. When two attackers come in (no back-checkers), the situation calls for man on man checking. Each defenceman should take the attacker closest to him. Do not attempt body checking because, if it misses, it will set up a two on one against the other defenceman. When the attackers are approaching, the defence pair should move up a little, and then start to go backwards in front of the play while the attackers are still some distance away. This will enable them to get going backwards quickly enough to stay with the attackers. If the defence pair allow themselves to be caught standing still, they'll be a lot easier to beat. The defence pair should be careful not to back up too far. Once they are twenty-five to thirty feet from the goal, they should force a play, trying to block it, or force it to the side, where a shot won't be as dangerous.

If the puck carrier flips the puck between the defencemen, the defenceman closest to the man who made the pass should block (pick) him out of the play and the other defenceman should go after the loose puck. If the puck carrier tries to split the defence, the nearest defenceman should block him out of the play, either with a body block or body check (if he goes through the centre). The other defenceman picks up the loose puck. If the puck carrier tries to go around the defence, the on-side defenceman should block him off to the side of the rink with the other defenceman going back toward the goal ready to intercept a pass out. If the puck carrier takes a shot from outside, and then bursts in quickly for the rebound, the closest defenceman should block or body check the man making the shot. At the same time, the other defenceman goes back to pick up any rebound.

Three against two. This is a tough situation for the defence to handle and, if a goal is scored, it is hard to blame the defence. However, if certain principles are followed and the defence keep cool and well organized, the rush can often be broken up or slowed down long enough to give the back-checkers, who (we hope) are hustling back as hard as they can, a chance to get back and in on the play.

First of all, the defence pair must keep together and back up down the centre lane. They must start to back up soon enough to get up sufficient speed to stay with the play. If possible, they should move to a spot well in front of the blue line before they start to move back. As they come back, they should watch the play carefully, trying to catch any indication of what the attackers are going to try.

When a pass is made to the wing, the defenceman on that side must cover by moving over with the receiver, trying to force him into the corner or sideboards. When going over he must keep alert for a pass back to centre and guard the cut back angle in case the puck carrier cuts behind him in an attempt to move into the centre lane. In covering such a play, it is important for the defenceman to keep his body between the attacker and the goal. The other defenceman goes back down the centre lane, watching the other two men and the play at the side. If a pass is made into the centre lane, he tries to intercept it and clear. However, he must not attempt to intercept a pass unless he is sure he can reach it. If he misses, a scoring opportunity will be set up. His job is to keep in front of the two attackers he is guarding.

If the wing, who took the pass earlier, beats the other defenceman, the beaten defenceman's partner, going back down the centre, must try to check him. However, he can make the best of a bad situation by moving over to make his check, always keeping inside, between the puck carrier and the free attacker, and faking a check to draw a pass which he may be able to intercept. If a trailer play is used, the defenceman closest to the attacker who picks up the puck should move toward him, forcing a play. His partner should keep in the centre lane close to the goal, trying to keep between the goal and the attackers. He must watch the play carefully to see where the puck carrier is going to pass the puck when forced into a play by his partner. He should not commit himself by taking one of the two free men. In this case, he plays a zone defence, and waits for the attack to commit itself.

The basic principle to follow is to try to force the attacker into making a definite move as early as possible so that a defence pattern can be set up. When in doubt, the defenceman should always cover the man in the best scoring position.

Position during scrambles. When there is a scramble inside the blue line, for example, during a pressure play, one defenceman should always take up a position on the off-side (far side) of the goal post. The other man goes after the puck. Depending on the position of the defence when the play comes across the blue line determines which defenceman takes the far post and which one goes after the puck. If the defenceman who is in front of the net is drawn away from his position due to a quick change of play, the other defenceman should then take over the zone in front of the net. One of the defencemen should always be in this position. The team which has such a system and sticks to it will have fewer goals scored on it from scrambles.

Learn the offensive patterns. The smart defenceman will make a point of learning all the various play patterns so that he will be in a position to recognize them when the attackers start the play. Careful attention should be paid to keeping a book on the favourite moves and plays of the opposing players and the various line combinations. When such information is compiled and reviewed regularly, the defenceman will often find himself moving with the attacker because he anticipated the play or move. However, the defenceman should not guess the move or play; he must wait until it starts. If he guesses, he may commit too early. By being ready for a certain play, which he knows to be a favourite one, the percentage is on his side. But he must be alert for any play.

The coach should make sure his defence pairs have plenty of opportunity to practise breaking up or slowing down the various play patterns possible so they can use them in the different play situations. For example, the defence pair should be practised against all the play situations such as two on one and two on two, three on two, etc. Too often this type of practice is overlooked. The defence pair will only develop skill at handling the various situations if they get lots of work during practice, as they will not get enough experience in games or casual scrimmage.

Skate even. When a defenceman is skating with an attacker who has tried to go around him, or when he is trying to force an attacker who has taken a pass over to the side of the rink, he should stay even with him. If he goes ahead, even a little, he gives the attacker a chance to cut back into the centre of the ice.

Watching the man coming up. Often a defenceman fails to take a look when the attack heads down the ice. He lets himself forget everything but those players leading the attack. He should concentrate on them, of course, but, he should also check to see if there is another attacker or two coming up behind the first line. Perhaps it is a two-man break with another member of the line behind the play but coming up fast. Always look for any trailers. It will provide the defenceman with information that will help determine his action.

Rushing. The defenceman should only rush at such times as the opportunities present themselves. The coach should teach his defencemen to recognize such opportunities so they don't become rush crazy. Nevertheless, a coach must allow his defencemen some freedom to rush as it is through mistakes more than anything else that will help them recognize when and when not to rush the puck.

When Bobby Orr came to the NHL, he revolutionized the role of the defenceman from that of a "stay at home" defensive type player to one who became part of the offensive game. However, the defenceman must not get overly concerned with the offensive game or he will start neglecting his defensive duties. This is a tough temptation, especially if the defenceman is an excellent puck carrier. It has to be resisted. Usually, a defenceman shouldn't rush except when in a position to break into the clear. If a forward is in a better position, the defenceman should concentrate on passing the puck forward. The defenceman who performs his checking assignments in such a way as to try to turn the check into a quick break the other way, all the time, will be easy to beat because he is predictable. Think only of the defensive assignment until, and not before, the offensive situation develops.

Blocking shots. This refers to going down in front of a shot. There is no doubt that, when used properly, this play can be a goal saver. However, it should only be used during scrambles or when the puck carrier tries to break through the defence after it has backed in too far. It is a particularly effective way to stop screen shot attempts. During pressure plays, when the puck goes back to the point man who skates in quickly to make a shot on goal, the shot blocking play is also a good one.

To block a shot, drop quickly to both knees, which are kept close together, as the shot is made. The stick should be held flat on the ice on the inside of the attacker (left if the shooter is a left-handed shot). The other hand should be reversed and held beside the body, ready to take part in the blocking of the puck. By keeping the stick out to the inside of the shooter, the defenceman is in a position to check the shooter if he fakes a shot and tries to go by as the checker drops to his knees. The stick should be held to the left side if the shooter is left-handed, right side if right-handed, because most often the puck carrier making a fake shot, will bring the puck around to his backhand side.

The checker should wait until the shooter's stick starts through in the shooting action, and then take a stride forward, drop to his knees, and get as close to the take off spot of the shot as possible. The upper body should be held erect as the checker goes down and toward the puck. There should be a straight line from his knees to his shoulders. The eyes should be kept open at all times and on the puck.

However, this play does have its disadvantages. To be effective, the play must be made late. If the defender commits himself too early, the attacking player will find it easy to go around him. It can set the defenceman up for a fake shot. If the puck gets through, he is out of the play for some time as he must get to his feet again before he can take part in the play. Also it can be physically dangerous when not done at the right time. The puck, too, is often smothered in the equipment of the checker, causing a face-off. It seems wise to suggest that the best principle to follow is to use the play only when it might save a goal. For example, it is most useful when the shooter is within twenty-five feet of the net and in a good position.

Do not hog the check. Just as there are players who hog the puck, so are there defencemen who like to do all the checking. This can be a serious fault. It will not only annoy the other defenceman but it will mean the positional set up of the defence pair will be spoiled. For example, when a lone checker approaches the defence pair, or when the wings are covered on a three or two man break, if one of the defencemen rushes out or over in front of his partner, it will immobilize the other man, perhaps cause a collision, and give the puck carrier a break. If the lateral defensive position of the defence pair is spoiled by one man moving in front, a quick move or shift by the puck carrier could well carry him past both of them. The defence pair should always act as a team. This won't happen if one man always tries to make the check.

Approach coolly. Many a defenceman, especially during pressure situations, will let his enthusiasm and determination run away with him as he charges headlong at an opponent who has just gained possession of the puck. The defenceman should, of course, move in as quickly as possible, but he should take a quick look to see the play situation before he rushes in. If he approaches quickly but coolly, set and ready for any move by the puck carrier, he will not be easy to beat. If he rushes in headlong, he's setting himself up for a deke by the puck carrier who can then go in on goal or set up a good play.

A headlong rush at the puck carrier with the objective being a smashing body check is an incorrect play. Just watch the defenceman who plays this way. You will see him land a few hard body checks knocking the player off the puck, but, more often, you will see him miss and blunder out of the play for a good second or two, perhaps longer. Very often you will notice that, even when hard contact is made, the puck goes free, perhaps to another attacker. Just as a puck carrier should approach a checker coolly and in good balance so as to be in a position to make the best possible play, so should the defenceman approach the puck carrier. Many goals have been scored by attacking teams because a defenceman missed a puck carrier with a headlong, excited rush.

Short strides in close play. When the play is scrambled inside the blue line, the defenceman should always skate with short strides. He will then be in a position to change direction quickly. If long strides are taken, it takes longer to stop and turn or make any quick change of direction.

Check with either hand. Almost all defencemen can check well with the stick held in one particular hand. Most left-handed players check better when the stick is held in their right hand and most right-handers with the left. An effort should be made to develop skill at using each hand. If this is not accomplished, the defenceman will have a weak side that the opposing players will soon take advantage of (at least they should). This is a special handicap during scrambled play when the defenceman often does not have time to manoeuvre to use his favourite hand.

Develop balance. The well balanced defenceman is a very tough man to shift by or break through, and is practically impossible to move away during a tussle for the puck or when he is covering. The better the balance, the harder the defenceman will be to knock off his feet or off the puck, and the faster he will be able to move in any direction. Therefore, he should do everything possible to develop his balance and sustain it during play.

Good balance depends upon several things: the spread of the feet, the flexion of the knees, the position of the upper body, and the general relaxation of the muscles. The feet should be comfortably spread. If the feet are close together, it is easy to be pushed off balance. The knees should be well bent; the upper body should lean forward so that the shoulders are directly above the knee; and the whole body should be kept relaxed when the checker is manoeuvring an attacker into making a move.

When a defenceman approaches a puck carrier during scrambled play, or when he is covering, he should assume the balanced stance. Then he will be ready to move. When tussling for the puck, the main thing to remember is to keep the feet well spread and the knees bent. When fast movement is necessary, short strides should be taken so as to keep the feet firmly under the body at all times. Just one long stride can set the player up to be knocked down or away from the puck when he is in the play.

If the defenceman is trying to move the attacker away from the puck, he should go in low, get his shoulder into the attacker, and drive upward. The forward and upward drive will spoil the opponent's contact with the ice, thus destroying his power to stay in there. The leg on the same side as the shoulder being used should be as close to the attacker as possible, the other one back behind about eighteen inches to two feet and spread laterally from the other leg the same distance. This will give the checker a firm foundation. When a checker expects pressure from the front, or when trying to apply it forwards, he should never allow his feet to get into a parallel position or else he will be easily over-balanced. One leg should be in front of the other. With the great amount of scuffling around the boards today, the learning of balance is very important. During practice sessions, the coach should be checking balance continually. The greatest emphasis should be made on the defenceman, but all the players should be taught the rules of good balance. All of them will need it when trying to check an opposing player. Keep hammering away until each team player is balance conscious, and can stay in balance at all times.

TEAM TACTICS

There are many problems of defensive play that are primarily a coach's concern. However, each player should study them. The better understanding a player has of the fundamentals of defensive strategy, the better he'll be. The following are some basic factors which a coach must consider.

Criss-crossing attackers. Often, an opposing coach will instruct his forwards to criss-cross in the centre ice area, trying to confuse the defence and thus work a man free. This tactic is usually tried when the wings are being well covered. The move is made by the wings crossing over quickly to exchange lanes. Should the covering wings then go with their checks or should they stay in their lane and pick up the player crossing to their side? Some coaches advocate a zone defence principle with the wings waiting for the new man to come over and then covering him.

However, there are several weaknesses to this. First, if the covering wing allows his man to go as he starts to cut across, the player may not continue across, but might suddenly cut straight again alongside the puck carrier. Second, if he does go all the way across, there will be a considerable length of time during which he is free. He can then break behind the defence to get a flip pass by the puck carrier, or take a pass, and go around the defence. Third, the crossing player will be on the inside of his cover as he gets across, and thus in a better position to take a pass. Finally, the man waiting to pick up the crossing attacker will have to do considerable manoeuvring to get into good covering position.

The only danger of playing a man on man defence pattern, with the wings following their man no matter where they go, is that it leaves a wing free in case a trailer comes up. If this happens, the back-checker or the checker whose man is the puck carrier should cover the free wing.

Covering the dangerous two. When the defence pair is up against three or more free attackers, the coach should instruct them to cover the two most dangerous players who are in the best scoring position. This is the only way to make the best of a poor situation. This tactic will, at least, prevent the attackers from making their scoring attempt from the best possible position.

Blame the right man. One of the worst morale shakers a defenceman can get is when the coach blames him unjustly for a goal or scoring opportunity. This is easy for a coach to do during the heat of a game. However, it should be avoided as much as possible. One good way is to make each defence assignment a very explicit one. The coach should explain his wishes carefully and then stand by his strategy. Do not throw the defence to the wolves if it works out wrong. For example, if the defence is told to play the puck carrier on a three on two situation with two back-checkers, and an opposing wing breaks free of his check to pick up a flip pass behind the defence, or knocks in a rebound off a shot through the defence, blame the back-checker and not the defenceman. It is impossible to set a definite defence plan for a defence pair with a lot of ifs and buts to it. You must go on the premise that your back-checker will do his job. Make as many as possible defence assignments clear cut and understandable so that the defenceman will not get flustered and try to do two things at once. If he does his particular job properly, nothing more can be asked. Whenever a new situation arises causing trouble, outline a rule for future use.

A defensive trailer. A good practice, that will prevent many goals, is to instruct one of your defencemen, the one in best position, to always trail any players on your team trying to carry the puck out of your defensive zone. He should trail slightly behind so as not to interfere with the manoeuvrability of the puck carrier. This will prevent any opposing player who checks the puck carrier from breaking quickly in on goal or setting up a play. It also guards against the possibility of possession by the opposing team if the puck carrier over-skates the puck, a frequent occurrence when the ice is sticky. Such a precaution is very worthwhile. The trailer should keep at his job until the puck carrier is safely over the blue line.

Tying up the key man. The opposing team may have a key man who sets up most of the plays or who is an outstanding puck carrier. Often, opposing coaches will have a player with excellent checking skills try and neutralize this man.

Organized clearing. Many goals are scored due to sloppy, disorganized, or excited clearing. Each man should be taught the basic rules of clearing, and sold the principle of keeping cool. Many dangerous plays occur when the defenceman, getting possession of the puck inside the goal scoring area, stops to take a look around before he clears the puck, makes a wild pass to a teammate who is breaking out, or starts to carry it out himself.

When there is pressure, a defenceman's first thought should be to get the puck away from in front of the goal. The fastest way to do this is to move it to the side. If he gains possession, the defenceman should skate away from the danger zone as quickly as possible and try to set up the break-out play. Carrying the puck into the goal scoring area while trying to avoid a checker is another unforgivable sin. The defenceman assigned to trailing the puck carrier can help here by yelling at the puck carrier if he heads in this direction.

When attempting to clear the puck up the boards or across the ice to a teammate trying to break out, look first and then try to make the pass accurately. All too often, such a play is made without thought or attention to making sure the pass is accurate. Frequently, the pass is weak or badly directed and, as a result, is intercepted or goes directly to an opponent. When the puck is already at the side of the rink there is no great element of danger that demands a frantic rush. Therefore, clearing plays made from the side should be coolly and carefully made. This will avoid the play that makes so many coaches turn grey. One of his players makes a poor clearing play, and the puck, gained by so much hard work, is returned to the opposition.

The same thing applies when the play is to shoot the puck down the ice to relieve pressure. The defenceman concerned often shoots it right to an opponent. An open space should be chosen and the shot made carefully. It doesn't happen often that a defenceman has so little time that he cannot take a look. The clearing habits of all players should be checked and each man carefully briefed on the correct tactics to use in the various situations.

Body checking. Hard, skilful body checking greatly enhances the defensive strength of the team. If the defence does not body check, the opposing forwards will be able to come in with abandon, concentrating only on their play, free from worry about running into a hard check. If the puck carrier has, in the back of his mind, a vision of getting knocked into the stands, he'll very naturally be more timid at the defence and will tense up, thus spoiling the free action of his mind and muscles. Accordingly, if the coach has a group of defencemen who are all good body checkers, he should instruct them to use their bodies at every good opportunity.

However, no matter how clever the defencemen are in the use of the body check, they should not attempt a body check in a situation that does not require it, for example, when there is a three on two situation. There is nothing that will set up the opposing attack as easily as when the defencemen try to body check and have not got the skill to do so efficiently. Then, too, inefficient body checking creates penalties as well as missed checks. Body checking is a valuable weapon, but only when used carefully.

The spotter. The use of a coach in the stands who can get a better view of the play can provide valuable information. Poor positional play can be noted much easier from above than at ice level, as can the plays and tactics of the opposing team.

General defence tactics. The general defensive strategy should be based on sound positional play, with each player will briefed, and certain of his specific assignments in all the various situations that might develop. There must be hard, continued back-checking. Aggressive checking is important all the way down the ice from the opposing goal to your own goal so that the attacking players will be less able to get organized. Keep the defence pair well in front of the blue line. They will then be in a position to move up quickly if possession of the puck is regained inside the opposing blue line, and they will be in a position to intercept passes or stop flip out break-away plays before they are successful. By keeping well in front of the blue line, the defence pair cuts down on the free ice available to the attacking team. If they wait back behind or on the blue line, the attacking team will be able to use the middle ice area more effectively to get organized. The defensive strategy should be to pressure the attack, always keeping the opposition off balance. If the puck is regained in the defensive zone, it must be cleared coolly and as quickly as possible through well-organized break-out plays. It must be realized that defence play involves hard work with plenty of tiring, physical activity. Superior conditioning is the first fundamental of a good defence set up!

Guard against the psychological lapse of effort when a checker is beaten by a move used by the puck carrier or with a pass. All checkers must stay with the play. This will prevent many of the dangerous three on two or two on one situations that often end up in goals. When beaten, the checker must turn and come back. Another psychological let down comes right after a scoring opportunity has been missed. Often the players in the play droop for a moment or two in disappointment. They must be trained to control this. Research has shown that many of the goals scored in a game are by the team who has just avoided what looked like a sure goal. The lapse by the attackers who failed opened up the scoring play for the other team.

When protecting a lead, the best strategy is to check aggressively and to try to keep the attacking team off balance. Special attention should be paid to careful passing and clearing and to keep possession of the puck as long as possible. The puck must not be given away. A two-man rush with a trailer, as advocated in the chapter on offensive play, is also a good strategy. Dropping back and letting the opposition bring the play to you is asking for real trouble. It will give the opposition the time they need to get organized for an attack. The best plan is to fight hard, keep the puck out of your zone, and don't give them a free chance to bring it in. Make them earn anything they get!

SHORT-HANDED PLAY

When a man short. There are many ways to play one man short in today's game. Some forms are the passive box, the aggressive box, the collapsing box, the diamond, etc. There are also penalty killing systems which have been designed by hockey teams from different countries around the world. There is neither the time nor the space to try and discuss all of them here. However, there are some general principles that you must follow when playing one man short.

The best plan involves aggressive forechecking, back-checking, and checking in your own end. Many coaches prefer to play this way as it does not enable the opposition to set up in any formation for any length of time and it forces such quick passing that errors are commonly made and the puck is cleared down the ice. If you have a team of less talented skaters, then you might want to play a system where the two forwards simply turn and come back with their check from the offensive zone so as not to allow the forwards to get caught deep in the offensive zone and possibly trapped by a quick breakout play.

It is important to have your strongest skaters and best checkers on the ice and to keep trying to break up the attack before it gets started. It is also important to have players who are going to react coolly and effectively when under pressure.

Finally, the wise coach will give his players plenty of practice in the one man short situation so that they will develop a definite sense of their duties and learn by experience the best tactics to use.

Two men short. The most commonly used formation used when two men short is the triangle. There are three basic ways to play the triangle.

Static triangle: Most coaches use the "static" triangle where two defencemen play low and one forward plays high in the triangle to cover the point men.

While it is an advantage to have the positions of the penalty killers easily defined with a minimum of movement, there are disadvantages to this system. If the point men pass the puck back and forth to each other, your high man will become tired very quickly chasing the puck. This will lead to errors and open up the slot area to a defenceman coming in as a fourth attacker for a scoring opportunity.

Inverted triangle: The second system is the inverted triangle. In this situation, the two high men cover the point men with the remaining player of the trio covering the front of the net.

Again, the advantage of this system is defined with a minimum of movement. However, the disadvantage is that the player at the bottom must control the forwards in front of the net. This makes him subject to picks by opposing players.

Rotating triangle: The third system, and perhaps the best, is the rotating triangle. However, it is not without its problems either. Nevertheless, if your team can execute the system and follow the three cardinal rules, it may be the best way to handle two men short.

Rule 1. The triangle must be played tight enough that a puck can never pass through it. This means the three players should be no further apart than an outstretched arm and stick to each other. You must be disciplined and keep the distance.

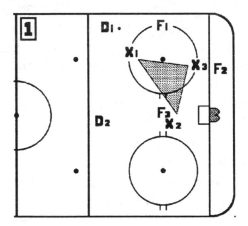

DIAGRAM 1: "D1" has the puck. "X1" challenges "D1" but doesn't go above the top of the circle. "X2" and "X3" form the bottom of the triangle.

Rule 2. If the defenceman passes the puck across the ice to his partner, then rotation must take place.

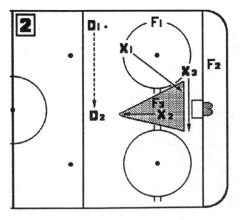

DIAGRAM 2: "D1" passes to "D2." Rotation takes place (Rule 2) with "X2" moving to challenge, "X3" goes to position of "X2" and "X1" rotates to position of "X3."

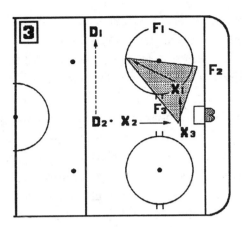

DIAGRAM 3: "D2" passes to "D1." Go back from where you came (Rule 3). "X2" goes to position of "X3," "X3" goes to position of "X1" and "X1" skates to challenge "D1."
The overload power play is shown here. Penalty killers must read the power play and react accordingly.

Rule 3. If his defence partner then returns the pass back across the ice to him, then all three players must go back from where they came (rotation.)

If the opposition passes the puck anywhere in the offensive zone other than from point to point, then the closest defender challenges the puck carrier with the two remaining players maintaining the triangle. Penalty killers should never try to take the opposition out with the body while playing the rotating triangle unless they are one hundred per cent sure of freezing the puck or gaining control of it.

The triangle formation should be kept on all parts of the ice. This includes forechecking in the opposition end, the neutral zone and, of course, your own end.

Your players must be disciplined and not panic if this is to be successful. Practise this system in the gym with a basketball or soccer ball. Once you feel your players have mastered it, then put it on the ice at practice in a five on three situation.

FACE-OFFS

Successful hockey teams take face-offs seriously. Unsuccessful ones look at face-offs as happenings before the real play gets started. Realizing face-offs are a vital part of the game is an important step for any good coach and team.

The modern game is a fast transition, read and react game, which doesn't allow a coach much time to implement specific strategy while it is going on. However, face-offs are opportunities where the coach can set up a specific strategy before the play begins. This is similar to what a football coach does on every play. This strategy does not simply involve telling the face-off man where to draw the puck. Every face-off must be planned with the three "A's": Attitude, Alignment, and Assignments. By following the three "A's," every player will understand what the coach expects from every face-off.

Attitude is the basic philosophy the coach has for each face-off. In the defensive zone, all teams should think defence first. Therefore, the players must have an attitude of preventing a scoring chance, rather than looking for a break-away pass. There may be times in the game when a coach will adjust his philosophy because of the situation in which he finds his team. For example, if his team is behind, the coach may want to take a risk and go for a fast break off a defensive zone draw. If ahead, he may simply have the centre tie up the opposition centre. The important thing is that everyone understand the attitude they must have going into the face-off. This may seem obvious but many players, if asked, would not be able to explain the philosophy behind each face-off. A coach could end up with centres going ahead without the draw in their own zone or wingers leaving the zone before a teammate has control of the puck. In the offensive zone, many defencemen stand like pylons rather than being ready and prepared to get a shot on goal. Often wingers don't realize how important it is to do a good job blocking out. You must have a team attitude on every face-off.

Alignments can be set up once attitude is understood by the players. A team gets into trouble after a face-off usually because of faulty alignment. Defensive face-off alignments are determined by the positioning the other team employs. Players must be taught to read what the opposition is trying to do with the face-off and then align themselves accordingly.

Offensive draws are different in that they give the coach an opportunity to be creative by setting his players to give them a good scoring opportunity. Having a variety of offensive alignments is important if you hope to catch the opposition off guard for a possible scoring chance.

Players must understand the importance of alignments. It's not okay to line up outside when you are supposed to be inside or to line up on the boards when you are supposed to be behind the centre. In order to be successful, the alignment must be exact. A final point about alignments is that the players should be in position before the puck is dropped. This should be controlled by the centre, who must know the alignments perfectly and know where he is going to draw the puck. The centre should first correct players who aren't in position, checking to make sure everyone is ready. When a player gets into position early, it gives him a chance to think about the final "A," his assignment.

Assignments are what each player's responsibility is once the puck is dropped. These assignments must be carried out to perfection. Many players appear tentative about their assignments and that split second of doubt may cost the team a goal. On every face-off, each player must have a primary assignment that he will carry out once the puck is dropped. After the puck has been dropped, his assignment may change depending upon whether the draw is won or lost. Therefore, each player should have a secondary assignment based on the result of the draw. For example, every player in the offensive zone should concentrate on getting a shot on goal if they win the draw. However, if they lose it, the secondary assignment involves getting into a forechecking position.

The following comment and diagrams are part of a face-off system based on the three "A's." Not all of the possibilities are given here but this does show you the need for attention to details on every face-off.

Defensive zone – attitude. The players assume the draw will be lost: therefore, go into the draw thinking defensively. Their attitude prior to the draw should be to prevent the opposition from getting a shot from the face-off. They must be ready to bust through to the shooter and

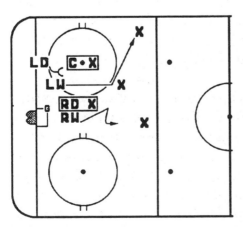

DIAGRAM 1: Defensive Zone – Loss
"C" doesn't allow a clear win. Tie up opposing centre on a loss. "LW" breaks through circle to shooter and stays with him until sure he won't get puck. Move to cover point if puck loose. "RW" breaks toward shooter in case "LW" can't get to him. Stay between high slot and middle point man. "LD" moves to close off lane to net but doesn't cross in front of goalie. "RD" locks up opposition winger off the draw to prevent deflections or rebounds.

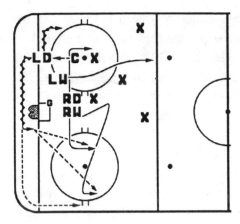

DIAGRAM 2: Defensive Zone – Win "LD" lines up to receive draw. Carry behind or up open side looking for open man. "RD" holds front of net ready to support partner if he can't find open man. "C" reads "LD" and loops across front of not or up ice to support. "RW" hustles to far boards for ring around or direct pass. "LW" breaks through two point men drawing them off the line.

block a shot. They may also have to tie up their man to prevent any easy shot off the draw.

Alignment and assignments. The alignment prior to the draw should put the players in good defensive position. The primary assignments are to prevent a shot. However, after the draw, if a teammate gains possession, then all the players should move quickly to offence. This is their secondary assignment.

Offensive zone – attitude. The players on your team must assume that the draw will be won by their own team. They go into the draw, therefore, thinking offensively. The attitude should be that they are going to work together to get a scoring opportunity off this draw. The players must be ready to block out, jump into a space quickly, and shoot under pressure to get a shot on goal.

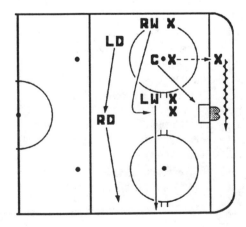

DIAGRAM 3: Offensive Zone – Loss "C" pressures the puck. "LW" moves across with the opposing winger. "RW" continues across into the high slot position. "RD" hustles to the far boards. "LD" moves to the middle to prevent a fast break.

Alignments and options. On offence, there are many options a coach can employ to get a shot off the face-off. Here, we will diagram two options off the same alignment depending on the set up of the defensive team. Keeping your offensive face-off alignment the same all the time is good for a conservative coach because there is less confusion should you lose the draw. However, offensive draws are a good opportunity for a coach to take a risk to set up a scoring opportunity.

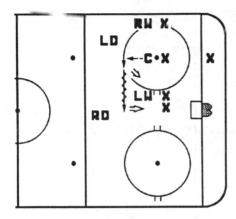

DIAGRAM 4: Offensive Zone – Win (Opposing winger on the boards)
"C" attempts to win the draw directly back "RW" lines up on the off wing. He jumps into the circle when the puck is dropped, picks up the draw back from "C" and takes a shot on goal. He can shoot quickly if the opportunity presents itself or skate across the high slot for a quick shot off a screen. "LW" blocks out the defenceman. "LD" holds his position. "RD" holds his position.

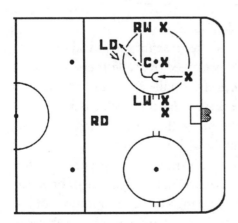

DIAGRAM 5: Offensive Zone – Win (Opposing defenceman is on boards)
"C" attempts to win draw directly back to "LD." "RW" jumps into circle when puck is dropped but instead of picking up the puck, he continues across and blocks opposition winger from getting to "LD." "LW" gets in front for a deflection. "LD" steps in and takes a low shot on goal. "RD" holds his position.

FORECHECKING

Properly organized and executed, forechecking can be one of the most effective tactics in hockey. It is not only an ideal defensive tactic, but also a great offensive one.

When you successfully forecheck an opponent, you are immediately set up to launch an offensive play because you have possession of the puck deep inside the opposing team's defensive zone. It is an ideal offensive-defensive system of play.

A lot of energy is wasted by the average forechecker because he just forechecks haphazardly without any definite plan. Hard, persistent forechecking is always effective, but it is much more so when there is a plan, a definite objective. The following diagram shows one theory of organizing the forechecking system.

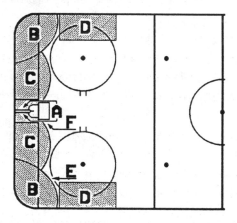

The area closest to the goal (A) represents the ideal area for forechecking. The reason this area is preferred over all others is that it is the place where the puck carrier has the smallest amount of room in which to manoeuvre. Then, too, in these areas the puck carrier cannot pass straight up the ice because the net will stop any such pass. Any passes up the sides can be intercepted by the forwards backing up the forechecker. In such areas, you have an advantage no matter how fast or shifty the puck carrier is as he can't use his skill through lack of open ice.

The (B) areas are the next best because the puck carrier is more or less hemmed in by the angle of the boards. The (C) areas are next because in these areas the puck carrier is blocked by the goal on one side and can only go one way if the forechecker blocks him properly. The (D) areas are included because the forechecker can manoeuvre along the boards in this area and force the puck carrier to go one way as the boards block him on one side.

When forechecking in the (B) areas, be sure you go after the puck carrier at an angle, trying to fake him into moving either to your left or right, so that you can then force him into the boards and check him without fear of his breaking out past you. Never go in as shown by arrow (E) because this leaves one side of the rink wide open for him to outskate you. In the (C) areas, you should try to force the puck carrier into either (A) or (B) areas by manoeuvring him there through the use of fake checks. Sometimes it is a good idea to leave a spot apparently free beside the goal (arrow F) in the hope that he will either try to get through and give you a chance to check him right in front of the goal, or make a wild, flustered pass.

The average forechecker makes an error by flying in at top speed to make his check, trying to make energy and effort take the place of controlled play and strategy. Remember, a good forechecker goes in under full skating control, at about three-quarter speed, not at full tilt. In this way he can fake checks to make the puck carrier commit himself, and he will be set and ready to change position quickly to combat any moves made by the puck carrier. The art of faking checks is one every potential forechecker should develop so that he can fake the puck carrier into moving the way the checker wants him to go. This kind of faking is just as important as faking with the puck. Above all, keep your forechecking cool and collected at all times while under full skating control.

Another thing to remember is to play the man by blocking his body. By playing the man, you have a better target, and even though you only get a piece of him, you will slow him up. If you play the puck, you can be beaten with one tricky stickhandling manoeuvre. Playing the man does not mean body checking, but merely body blocking, stopping him by getting your body in front of him, and then between him and the puck.

Another thing to remember when forechecking is to use short strides at all times so that you will always be ready to change direction quickly, and to make any other skating manoeuvres that may be necessary. Long strides commit you and spoil your manoeuvrability. It is also wise to study the puck carriers on the opposing team carefully, trying to detect their favourite moves when they try to beat a checker. If you do this, you will be prepared for their moves and able to handle them much easier.

Effective forechecking requires good conditioning. Very few forecheckers can keep up the pressure for very long. That is why, as the game progresses, you will see the would-be forecheckers hanging back, and letting the puck carrier get going, free from being checked in dangerous areas (those marked (A), (B), and (C)). A team of perfectly conditioned, well organized forecheckers is very tough to beat.

Here are a few general rules for forechecking. The forward closest to the puck carrier should go in to forecheck, with the other two forwards watching the offensive wings carefully in order to intercept any passes up ice (1-2-2). For example, if the right wing is the closest man to the puck, he should go in with the centre taking his place. By following this system, you can keep your men covered and prevent a lot of those breakout plays that often catch the forecheckers flat footed. When you send in two men (2-1-2), the first man goes after the puck carrier trying to tie him up while the second man goes after the loose puck. Skill at tight turns, pivoting, faking checks, stopping and starting quickly, poke and hook checking with the stick flat on the ice, should be developed by constant practice since these are the ammunition a forechecker has to use. A good hook check is an important asset but few bother to develop one. Agile, well-balanced skating will also be a great help.

Finally, remember that the most important fundamental of good forechecking is spirit and determination. You must keep driving in and driving in. Good coaches never forget that a team that makes hard, persistent, well-organized, and planned forechecking an important part of their system can disorganize and beat many teams that might otherwise be the winner. A well forechecked team will soon get irritable and upset and this will spoil their morale and cohesion and cause them to take penalties when tempers flare.

PENALTIES

In considering his general over-all defensive strategy, the coach should take a very careful look at the role that penalties play. Most penalties come when the player is attempting a defensive move. Actually, his attitude toward penalties will be coloured by the coaches' own particular philosophy of hockey. If the coach sees it as a game of skill, speed, and clever strategy, he will view penalties with a great deal of distaste and use every method open to him to avoid them. If he feels that hockey is a rugged game in which the physical contact element should dominate, he'll probably be inclined to accept penalties as a necessary part of hard play. He'll try to prove that, in the long run, the rugged play that produces them brings more benefits that the detrimental results of the penalty.

The coach must make up his own mind according to the personnel he has. If his player personnel runs to size and rugged temperament, he will probably want them to use the natural advantages, and will then have a penalty problem. If he has personnel featuring speed and cleverness, he will have less of a problem. The main objective will be to keep penalties to a minimum and never condone illegal play. In setting up a penalty control system, the coach should base his efforts on the fact that the majority of penalties are caused through a lack of technical skill on the part of the player concerned. When a player makes an illegal play, holding, or tripping for example, it is an admission that he lacks the skill to stop the player by fair means. An analysis of the penalties given to any particular player will usually result in the discovery that most of them were given when the player was forced into a defensive error due to a pet weakness – an inability to check to his left side for example. Therefore, the development of high level skill is a sure way to cut down on penalties. A quick analysis of the type of penalties a player is getting will often give the coach a clue to any technical faults he has.

Another cause of penalties is a lack of knowledge of the rules. Too many players have never read a rule book. This should be a must, with regular questionnaires presented by the coach to see that the players do know the rules. This is important because the player should determine his actions by what the rule book says and not by the experience he has had with different referees. For example, one referee may allow a lot of shoving in front of the goal, while another may call the same play interference. Then, too, a referee may suddenly change his view point during a game, pouncing on a player in the third period for something the player had been doing all during the game. This usually causes a surprised outburst by the player who thinks he is being hard done by. This sudden tightening up of attitude by the referee often comes when the play gets tense, with one goal becoming important. So a penalty assumes even more importance than usual. The only way to avoid this is to play according to the rules.

A further cause of penalties occurs when the coach allows illegal play at practice. This is all too common as the players, not under pressure of a game, often use illegal tricks to stop an opponent during practice. They view it as fun, and probably it is. However, it sets up a bad habit that may well carry over into a game. The players will spend their time more advantageously if they practise the correct method of checking. The rules should be strictly enforced at all practices.

The final cause of penalties is a loss of emotional control and discipline. This is the cause of penalties for slashing, fighting, charging, and similar infractions in which the player concerned makes some move not necessary to the play. It is hard to establish a full control of this fault, since it is only natural that in a rugged game such as hockey there will be moments a little too trying for any human being. Every attempt should be made by the coach to teach the player the strategic and moral value of self-control. A hot-headed slash or charge has lost many a game. One way to establish control is to make the getting of such penalties too unpleasant for the player concerned. This can be accomplished by developing a team attitude that such penalties are unnecessary and injure their chances of winning. Thus, the pressure of team opinion will create a desire for control among the players. It should be any coach's objective to cut temper penalties down to a minimum.

Another excellent way to cut down on penalties is to frown very severely on the habit of arguing with the referee. By blaming the referee, the player is only alibiing and, in doing so, he overlooks the real reason why he got the penalty and does not learn anything from the experience. The player should always be made to realize why he got the penalty. If the complainer cannot be convinced that he should keep quiet for reasons of sportsmanship, perhaps he will if he is made to realize that, through his complaining, he is using up valuable energy and upsetting his body so that its efficiency is affected. If a player is not tough enough in character to take a penalty no matter how unjust it seems, he is not tough enough to depend on when the pressure goes on. The player without discipline is always a poor bet when the chips are down. His lack of emotional control which he shows by complaining will likely cause him to blow up when the play gets tense. When you get the chance, watch a habitual complainer and see what happens. The complainer is the juvenile delinquent of hockey because he resists the rule of established authority.

One of the detrimental effects of a penalty that is often overlooked by the player and coach is its delayed effect on the conditioning of the team.

For example, when there is a penalty, the players, especially the goalie and the defencemen, must work extra hard to prevent a score. Therefore, the added effort, which is emotional as well as physical, will drain off an important amount of energy from the players concerned. This often causes a team to fade badly in the latter stages of a game. Analysis indicates that when there are a number of penalties in the first part of the game, the team getting them often fades later due to the extra work from penalties.

Another important point to remember is that special care should be taken to avoid a penalty when the other team is short a man. This often happens, if things haven't been going well. The team with the advantage gets irritated at their inability to score, gets chippy, and takes a penalty.

Finally, it is always wise for the coach to remember that his attitude and character are always painted in vivid colours by the actions of his players.

Goaltending

No position has been transformed more dramatically over the last twenty years than that of the goaltender. Once considered to be a club's least physically fit player and poorest skater, today's goaltender must now be the best conditioned player on the hockey team, as well as an efficient and powerful skater.

The ideal goaltender is physically strong and able to work at top speed when wearing in excess of 50 pounds of equipment and while holding off players who can be much heavier. He must have the muscular endurance to be able to maintain a workload over a 60 minute game in a highly efficient manner. He must have highly tuned motor responses (reflexes) so he can react quickly to high speed shots and pucks, which can unpredictably change direction through deflections and tip-ins. He must have excellent eyesight combining depth perception, peripheral vision, and the ability to focus quickly. He must be extremely agile so he can move quickly about the net. He must be flexible so he can stretch and contort himself in any way required to block or trap a puck.

Above all, the ideal goaltender requires mental toughness, excellent concentration, a good work ethic, an analytical predisposition, an ability to play while hurt (i.e., bruises from pucks), and an ability to work at high efficiency while under stress.

There are several aspects of today's game which make a goaltender's job more difficult. The development of a game programmed to reward results and not necessarily effort has taken place. Far too many coaches, especially at the minor hockey level, judge a goaltender's worth by how many goals he allows in a game without considering the number and quality of shots he must face.

Today's goaltender wears equipment which is lighter and more protective than that of his predecessor. This lightness, however, has been obtained through the use of plastic, nylon, and foam. This combination of materials hinders the skin's ability to breathe and therefore creates body heat buildup and water loss problems. To combat this, a goaltender is now allowed to keep a water bottle on the top of his net. This also cuts down on time wasted going to the bench for water. This loss of water in the system results in an easily fatigued goaltender.

Finally, a goaltender now has to face harder, faster, and more deceptive shots. He is also confronted by more opposing players who seem intent on eliminating him from competition through the administration of punishing bodychecks or blatant "cheap shots."

Although a goaltender requires certain pre-requisite abilities and skills, the day has passed when natural ability and learning via the hit and miss process could produce a competent goaltender. A sound basis in fundamental skills is the only way a goaltender can insure he will be prepared for the quick pace of modern hockey. All those abilities, once taken for granted, can now be improved upon. Visual acuity, response time, peripheral vision, depth perception, agility, balance, strength, stamina, mental toughness, and flexibility can all be enhanced through proper instruction. While we can't cover everything, we'll demonstrate how fundamental goaltending skills can be improved.

BALANCE AND STANCE

Balance. The secret to superior goaltending rests on having good balance. A goaltender may have quick reflexes and fast hands but if he has poor balance he will be defeated before he begins.

Balance starts with the goaltending stance. Several factors have transformed the goaltender's stance over the past twenty years. The overall speed of the game, the size of the rink, the speed and unpredictability of the shots, the finesse and play reading of the players, and the weight, size, and sophistication of the goaltending equipment have all contributed to the change in goaltending technique. Today the goaltender's stance must provide a solid base from which highly explosive reactive movements may originate.

The goaltending stance has three different conceptual approaches:

(1) The wall

(2) The wedge

(3) The shield

All three incorporate the same principles of the basic stance but there are distinct differences in their effectiveness.

The wall. This requires the goaltender to move to a particular spot where he stands as an immoveable barrier, a wall, which the puck hits. This traditional approach focuses on just stopping the puck and, if possible, trapping it. The goaltender is a rigid wall which cannot be penetrated. The flaw with this concept is that it is not as flexible as the modern game requires. As the shots become faster, harder and more unpredictable, it increases the chances that dangerous rebounds or deflected pucks will occur.

The wedge. This new approach exaggerates the goaltending stance so that the crouch is extremely low. The gloves are held well out in front of the body with the fingertips pointing toward the shooter. This creates a wedge shaped silhouette, which is angled back toward the net at a 45 degree angle. The goaltender's body acts as a ramp designed to direct the puck, not only to the side but, up and over and thus away from the net. The intention is for the goaltender to present an intimidating image to the shooter. However this conceptual approach has its flaws, as well. This stance is extended so far out in front that the body has to compensate. It does so by moving the weight over the heels. This weight distribution prevents the body from making quick lateral moves.

The catcher glove isn't open outwards to the shooter, ready to catch pucks. Instead, the palm of the glove is pointing down to the ice or in toward the mid-line of the body. It can't effectively stop or trap pucks properly. The blocker is extended in such a way as to place the stick blade too far out in front of the body and at a dangerous angle. The puck could quite feasibly hit the stick and go over the goaltender's shoulder. If a goaltender is short in stature, that could put the puck high into the net. The puck could also be improperly directed off to the corner since a stick at this angle can't control the puck. Instead, it just "chips" it off to the side.

The shield. This concept is much more effective. It sees the role of the stance as the ability to direct the puck away from the net. It can take the puck's initial velocity and use it to redirect the puck into the corner.

Therefore, it doesn't meet the puck's force with an equal amount of force. Instead, it uses part of the puck's own velocity to force itself to direct the puck away. This is done by positioning the goaltender's equipment in such a way as to present an angled surface and not a flat one. When viewed from above the angling of the pads resembles an inverted "V," or shield, which is pointed toward the shooter. This guarantees the puck will be directed off to a corner and not rebound back out to the opposition. Because of this passive ability to direct the puck away, the shield offers the most economical and most effective use of the goaltender's energy. This is the reason that this concept of the stance is the better approach.

Stance. To achieve an effective goaltender's stance, first position his feet slightly more than shoulder width apart. The leg pads should be angled away from the body's mid-line by pointing the toes out slightly. The ankles, knees, and waist should be flexed so that the body may be brought lower toward the base (feet). The most important aspect of the stance is the bend in the ankles. By lowering the goaltender's centre of gravity and placing the weight over the balls of his feet, the goaltender can greatly enhance his balance and his stability on his skates.

The upper body leans forward at the waist. This is the second most important portion of the stance. The upper body must not be too upright or too bent over. Your best guide is to view the stance from the side. Look to see that the ankles, knees, and shoulders are in a straight line at a 90 degree or right angle to the ice surface.

The chin should be up slightly to allow the goaltender to view the ice fully. The gloves should be positioned off to the side and ahead of the knees. The catcher glove should be open and ready to catch the puck at all times. A closed catcher glove or one resting on the knee will not be ready to catch or stop a puck emerging from the forest of legs standing in front of the net. The blocker glove should grasp the stick at the top of the shank or wide paddle portion of the stick. The blocker pad should be angled to deflect shots toward the corner of the rink.

The goaltender's stick blade should be completely on the ice. Sometimes only the heel or toe of the stick blade is in contact with the ice. This is not proper technique. The goaltender may have an incorrect stick lie or the heel of his stick may be worn down. Check the stick and if either problem exists, replace it.

The stick blade should be angled slightly toward the corner of the rink, thereby insuring that any puck which strikes the blade will deflect into the corner and not bounce back out dangerously in front of the net. The blade should also be positioned four to six inches in front of the skate toes. This will guarantee the puck strikes a flexible blade which can cup the puck and thus control it. A stick rigidly resting too closely against the toes of the skates will cause the puck to bounce off the blade uncontrollably, possibly right back out to the opposition.

MOVEMENT

Basic Moves. Moving about the crease requires quickness, agility, and the discipline to maintain all of this while continually remaining in the basic stance. Goaltending moves have to combine the efficiency of movement, while all the time maintaining a stance which is ready to block shots. Basic skating moves require lateral, forward, and backward movement.

Lateral moves. Moving across the crease following the play involves two types of movement:

- You are following the puck as it moves across the defensive zone either in close or in mid-defensive zone.
- You are following the puck as it moves across the zone from extreme point to other point or across the neutral zone.

The shuffle. The first situation requires the goaltender to move while maintaining the stance, ready to block shots at any time. The shuffle, has the skates parallel and at right angles to the goal-line. The lead foot is unweighted and the back or drive foot pushes off from the inside skate edge with the toe not quite fully extending. The goaltender stops by transferring body weight to the lead foot inside skate edge. With the feet parallel during this movement, the goaltender will be better able to change direction quickly should the puck's path be quickly altered (i.e., deflection or tip-in). This change of direction may be done by simply transferring the weight from the drive foot to the lead foot and then having the lead foot push off.

If the goaltender's lead foot is turned with the toe pointing into the intended direction, as in the T-push (described below), it would be difficult to switch body weight from the drive foot to the lead foot quickly. The lead foot would have to be first rotated back 90 degrees to bring it parallel to the drive foot before it could stop the initial lateral move and then move into the other direction. The split second it takes to alter this foot direction can be critical, especially if the puck is in close. That is why we recommend using the shuffle and not the T-push when the puck is dangerously in close to the net.

Lateral T-Push. The fastest and most efficient lateral move is the T-push. This requires the lead foot to be rotated out pointing in the goaltender's intended direction, parallel to the goal-line. The drive foot pushes off with the toe fully extending. The goal stick blade should be on the ice protecting the "five hole" (the open space between the legs) during the move. The catcher glove is open and facing out ready to catch any puck which may make its way to the net. To stop, the lead foot need only be rotated back until it is parallel with the drive foot. The weight is then placed over the lead foot inside skate edge. Some goaltenders stop incorrectly using only the drive foot outside skate edge. This move usually raises the upper body and leans it back in the opposite direction to the goaltender's intended direction. His centre of gravity is therefore outside his base and his balance is adversely affected.

When using either of these lateral moves, it is important to move efficiently and with an economy of motion. Any movement in any direction other than the one intended prevents the goaltender from moving as quickly as he should. To insure every ounce of energy is used to propel the goaltender across the crease, be sure the shoulders lean into the intended direction and not pop upwards. The drive foot must also be as fully extended before the body weight is transferred to the lead foot.

FORWARD SKATING

Nowhere has the speed of hockey today been more apparent than the goaltender's forward and backward skating. At one time, the goaltender moved in and out of the crease cautiously using the "telescoping" move. This involved moving out of the net by first spreading both feet wide apart with the weight extended through the heels and then drawing the feet back together, with the weight over the mid-foot, until the legs closed again. This allowed the goaltender to move out of the crease at a slow to medium speed. To move back into the crease, all the goaltender needed to do was spread both feet wide apart again but this time with the weight over the toes and then to draw the feet back together with the weight over the mid-foot until the leg pads closed.

Telescoping had three major flaws:
- It was too slow.
- It left the goaltender's weight over the heels too often and thus affected balance and the ability to move quickly.
- It left the goaltender vulnerable to shots fired at the "five hole" (the space between the legs)

To keep up with the quicker pace of the game, the goaltender should be able to move out faster and in control. When moving from extreme angle to extreme angle, as when the puck is at the point or in the neutral zone, the goaltender should use a forward T-push start. The short side foot, or the foot closest to the goal post, should be pointed toward the puck. The drive foot should be rotated quickly so it is at a right angle to the intended direction and is behind the lead foot. The length of extension of the drive foot toe is determined by the distance the goaltender wishes to cover. A short but explosive half extension will bring him out of the crease, to play the puck when it is in close. A longer explosive full toe extension will take him well out of the crease to play the extreme angle shots or to direct pucks away. The drive foot must quickly recover to its position along side the lead foot. By doing this, the goaltender presents both pads squarely to the puck for as long as possible during the move. Again, it is important to keep his body in the proper stance: stick on ice, catcher glove open and ready to catch any puck fired his way.

Forward stopping. The rules of physics dictate that for a body to come to rest, or stop, one has to apply an amount of force which will stop the body's momentum. All forwards and defence use the very efficient parallel two foot stop with the force applied at a right angle to the player's original direction. However, because the goaltender must keep his body in the proper stance, square to the puck at all times, it is not possible for him to use this traditional two foot stop.

To stop, and still maintain the proper stance, the goaltender has to employ a "snow-plow," or inverted foot, stop. For years it was thought a two foot "snow-plow" stop was the most effective. However, through the use of high speed film, it has been discovered this is no longer true. The use of a two foot "snow-plow" uses too wide a portion of the skate inside edge and the weight is applied through the arch of the feet and not through the toe. This makes for a slower, less controlled stop. It can also restrict the goalie's subsequent movements for a short but critical period of time.

To stop effectively, the goalie should use a one foot, "snow-plow" stop. The lead stopping foot is inverted or rotated in toward the body's mid-line. The other foot must point to the puck to keep that leg pad squarely to the play. The body's centre of gravity is lowered over the stopping foot by quickly deepening the crouch. This applies the weight down into the toe of the inside skate edge accentuating the stop and maintaining better control.

The goalie should be able to stop using either the left or right foot. The best stop is by using the long side skate, whenever possible. This will give the goalie the chance to react using the other foot and leg pad, if shots are directed to his short side.

BACKWARD SKATING

The average player's puckhandling and skating agility have vastly improved over the years. For this reason, a goaltender is required to be far more reactive and far more adept at keeping up with opposing players. The ability to skate backwards, quickly and efficiently, is a very important skill for any goaltender to be successful.

The goaltender with a confident backward skating technique can keep pace with attacking players. Effective backward skating insures a goaltender will not be left standing still by opposition forwards.

The key to backward skating is the start. To create the momentum needed to move backward, the drive foot must start in an inverted position (toe pointing in to the mid-line). The leg must fully extend quickly. This is another reason why it is recommended the goaltender use the one foot snow-plow stop. Not only does this stop him quickly but it also puts him in a strong position for the initial backward thrust. This thrust uses the inside edge of the skate blade. It leaves an ice marking which resembles a large inverted "C."

As the toe is extended, the body weight will transfer from the drive foot onto the other foot. The second foot then extends the toe in just as large a thrust as with the first foot. By the time the third or fourth thrust has been completed, the extensions can be shortened but are still powerful thrusts. With these shorter thrusts the body weight is centred more over the mid point of the foot. Remember, the inverted toe provides the power but only if the thrusts are made quickly. Also, these quick thrusts are done to insure the goaltender will be able to react rapidly, with either leg pad, to shots fired at the net while they are in motion. Again, as with all of the basic moves, the proper stance must be maintained through his entire skating move.

BASIC SAVES

The catcher. The catcher glove and the goaltending stick are the only pieces of a goaltender's equipment which are designed for use, rather than protection. The catching glove allows him to do what no other player can do: hold onto the puck. The catching glove also provides for the most spectacular saves a goalie can make.

The glove is held off to the side of the goaltender, approximately at the knee. The glove is always held open and slightly in front of the body. This insures the goaltender is ready at all times to catch the puck. In fact, there will even be the occasional time when the puck will strike the open glove, simply because it is open.

The catching or grasping action is perhaps the most instinctive of all goaltending moves. However, there are still several key points to keep in mind.

- Keep your eye on the puck as it moves toward your glove. Many goaltenders forget to follow the puck. The danger here is that the goaltender may misjudge the path of the puck or the puck might just simply change direction at the last moment. Following the puck with your eyes will insure you reduce either of these problems.
- The glove has to recoil or give with the puck. As with a skater holding his stick too tightly a glove too rigidly held can cause the puck to bounce out. It can also bruise your hand.
- Keep your glove open. A goaltender who lets his attention or concentration lapse often forgets to keep his glove open. A good way for your goaltender to remember this would be to use imaging. Imaging assists the learning process by providing the learner with an image which he can use to focus his movements and actions. It is recommended you

have the goaltender imagine his catcher glove has an "eye" in the palm. That "eye" must be open and able to see the puck at all times. A closed glove prevents the catcher glove's "eye" from seeing the puck. So have him keep the glove open so it can keep his "eye" on the puck.

The catching glove should be used to stop shots directed at the glove side of the body from the mid-line of the body out to the arm's full extension and above the waist. Those shots directed at the chest should be caught or trapped by the glove with the goaltender's body backing up the save. Often the goaltender will drop down into the butterfly on such shots and use his glove above his head to catch the puck. This waste of body movement does not help with the save. Quite often the puck can scoot through the glove and end up in the net. All of this is due to the goalie losing sight of the puck, because he is either afraid of having the puck hit him or he thinks the butterfly save looks better.

The goaltender should also make sure he doesn't try to stop every shot with his catcher glove. Reaching over onto the blocker side, or down to the feet, will compromise the goaltender's balance.

The catcher glove is also used to trap or smother the puck. The glove can trap the puck against any portion of his body. This usually occurs with medium to slow shots which strike the equipment but haven't sufficient force to create an immediate rebound. The goaltender allows the equipment to recoil or give with the shot. This controls the puck by lessening the chance of rebounds. The goaltender then brings the glove into play, to trap the puck firmly against the pad.

The catcher glove can also smother those loose pucks which may end up lying on the ice. Quick action to cover and immobilize the puck will often allow your team the break it needs to regroup or change when pressed by an opposing club.

To smother the puck effectively, the goaltender must lower his centre of gravity as he moves the catcher glove to the puck. This can be done by dropping to one or both knees or by diving onto the stomach. Once the catcher glove has firmly trapped the puck, the goaltender should insure it is not dislodged by an opponent. He can do this by gathering the puck into the body. He can also do it by putting his body weight into the glove and by protecting that glove with his stick. The goaltender can use the stick blade to cover the back of his glove, making sure he leaves a cushioning space between the blade and the glove. He can also use a raised stick, held at arm's length distance, parallel to the ice surface and at a right angle to the path of the attacking player. This raised stick shields the glove and the goalie and allows him to push off opposing players. This move requires the arm to be bent slightly so as to allow the arm to give a bit before it is extended, to ward off an attacking player.

When smothering the puck remember that if both leg pads are on the ice or if the goaltender is outstretched and lying on his stomach he can be very easily moved by opposing players. This is due to the reduced friction caused when nylon sweaters and pants and leather pads are in contact with the ice. It would be best for the goaltender to try and keep one knee up off the ice and one skate blade dug into the ice to help anchor himself and to prevent him from slipping about.

The Blocker. Originally a felt backed cricket glove, the blocker has become an excellent piece of equipment for the goaltender. The now rigidly backed blocker not only protects the hand holding the stick, but is also useful as a deflector. In this capacity, it can be used to direct high shots away from the net and into the corner. As with the catcher glove, the blocker is used most effectively when the goaltender follows the puck into the blocker with his eyes. The blocker should not be moved across the body to cover shots on the other side of the net or shots that are below the waist.

The blocker move is an acquired skill. If you recall how instinctive the clutching action is, you should realize that the same movement using the blocker will only serve to knock the puck back out as a rebound. The blocker move should involve a rotation of the wrist toward the corner. This angles the blocker and thereby directs the puck away from danger.

Because of the weight of the gloves along with the chest and shoulder pads, the goaltender should have well developed upper body strength, so he can make the required glove saves quickly.

LOWER BODY SAVES

Skates. The extremely durable goaltender skate blade provides the goaltender with yet another puck stopping tool. The inside edge of the goaltender's skates allow him an opportunity to deflect low shots away from the net and toward the corner of the rink. The skate blade is rotated anywhere from 90 to 130 degrees in an arcing motion. The upper body should be leaned into the move so as to help keep the entire surface of the blade on the ice. The goaltender can do the skate save while standing by simply rotating the ankle. The goaltender can also drop down to one knee and extend the skate blade further for those low shots which are harder to reach.

The stick can also support the skate save by being positioned in front and against the blade. The stick can also overlap the skate blade and extend the overall surface by either leading or following the skate blade. This deflection of either skate, or stick and skate, helps to propel the puck faster into the corner of the rink.

Leg pads – Standing pad. This save involves the goaltender using the leg pads to direct the puck away from the net while maintaining the basic stance. The stance allows the goaltender to angle or direct the puck down to the ice where it can be trapped. The pads can also be angled toward the corner of the rink, thereby allowing the puck to hit the pads and deflect away from the net toward the corner.

Butterfly pad. No other move has so dominated goaltending in the past twenty years than the butterfly save. It is no longer a passive or defensive move. The modern butterfly pad save is an aggressive move which can move the goaltender out or forward toward an opponent. The move can also allow the goaltender to move laterally quickly to stop deflections or block a deke.

The move requires flexibility at the hip, excellent leg strength, and a refined level of balance. It involves the goaltender dropping to his knees with both pads parallel to the ice and facing out square to the shooter. The upper body must be erect and the centre of gravity must be forward over the knees and not back behind the pads. The stick blade should be on the ice out in front of the pads protecting the "five hole." The gloves are open and out to the side and in front of the upper body.

The secret to success of the save is due to two specific factors: distance and timing. When the butterfly is timed to meet the ice, well before the puck is shot or deflected, then it will work. If it is done close to the opponent's stick blade then the chances of the puck going over the pads are minimized.

The butterfly save will fail whenever the goalie gambles. As with all saves, the goaltender must know what he has to do instinctively and refrain from playing on a "hunch." When moving to the butterfly the goaltender must keep the stick blade on the ice. The goaltender should resist the instinct to roll his weight back over his heels or to let his arms rest against his body as he drops to his knees. Both actions will cause the stick to rise off the ice exposing the "five hole" to the shooter.

When recovering from the move, be sure the goaltender is using both legs simultaneously to raise himself up. This will allow him to move either left or right in reaction to the direction of the next shot. This is done by having the goaltender moving or rocking his weight back over his heels very quickly and having both skate blade inside edges anchored rapidly to facilitate his standing up. He can also assist his recovery by moving his arms up and back quickly. This arm motion should be a small move since a large move will cause the stick blade to be lifted off the ice and will expose the "five hole." The goaltender should also keep his arms free of his body so he can move his arms quickly to stop high shots. Free arms will also insure the stick does not move up off the ice with every sudden move of the body.

Double leg pad. The double leg pad save can be used as a desperate move to stop the puck. It is most effective as a move designed to block the puck as it moves across a considerable distance and is redirected. This will occur with point shots which are deflected from the side of the crease, on quick shots from an extreme angle, or shots made from passes from behind the net and on breakaways.

Many feel that the double leg pad save is a severely flawed move. It can leave a goaltender flat on the ice vulnerable to high shots. It can be an unbalanced move in that it leaves the goaltender either face down or on his back unable to stop the puck and susceptible to injury. In actuality, when done correctly the double leg pad save can be an extremely successful and spectacular move. The save begins with an extended T-push. The lead leg drops first to the knee and then the drive leg follows. Both leg pads are extended and stacked, one on top of the other. This double leg wall is then able to block shots.

To achieve success when executing the double leg pad save, the goaltender has to remember a few important points. Just as with the butterfly, distance and timing play a vital role. The move is best done when it is timed to arrive close to the opponent's stick blade just before the puck is released. At one time, a goaltender was instructed to make the save to the near goal post. The implication was that the goaltender protected the net best by being in it. The opposing players did their best to oblige by carrying or deflecting the puck very close into the crease, thereby hitting the prostrate goaltender with the puck.

Today, the speed, strength, and skill level of the average player has vastly improved. Players are now able to shoot and direct the puck up into the top part of the net from virtually anywhere on the ice. A double leg pad save done to the post today will only leave the goaltender open to the high shot. The move is best done to the opponent's stick blade.

Remember the entire body. Each and every inch, provides the goaltender with a puck stopping surface. The double leg pad save utilizes the entire body, like a "wall." This "wall" has to be impenetrable. The goaltender has to insure that no holes are created in this "wall" through improper technique. There is a tendency of some goalies to allow their upper body to become raised off the ice by resting on the elbow closest to the ice. This produces an opening beneath the armpit. This hole is large enough to allow pucks to get through. Have the goaltender keep the armpit down on the ice. Also remember to have him fully extend his ice bound arm so it does not overlap any other piece of equipment. This will further extend the puck stopping surface. If the catcher glove is the ice bound arm, have the goaltender keep the glove open. If the blocker is the ice bound arm, have him rotate his blocker wrist so the stick is on its edge providing additional puck stopping surface.

When in the proper double leg pad save the upper arm should complement the save. If the upper arm is the catcher glove, the glove should be positioned just above the upper edge of the top pad with the glove open in order to be ready to catch any shots which may go over the sprawled goaltender. If the blocker is the upper arm, the wrist should be rotated so the stick blade is pointing up toward the ceiling. The stick should also be positioned just above the upper edge of the top pad in order to be ready to stop any shots directed over the goaltender.

Many coaches and goaltenders dislike the double leg pad save because it is quite often an unstable move. The move has too frequently been executed and the goaltender has ended up on his face or stomach. A slight alteration in the goaltender's final body alignment will correct this problem and make for a much more effective save. The goaltender should move into the double leg pad save being sure to keep the upper body bent slightly forward at the waist in a "pike" formation. The knees should remain slightly bent and the extended ice bound arm should be at a 30 to 45 degree angle from the upper body. This positioning makes the double leg pad save a much more stable move. A goaltender in this position is almost impossible to knock onto his back or stomach.

You will also find this positioning will speed up the goaltender's recovery to his feet and the proper stance. To assist with his full recovery, the knees have to be bent and drawn up quickly to plant the feet onto the ice. By performing the double leg pad save with bent knees the goaltender will actually accelerate his recovery.

The double leg pad save should be a calculated move. It should be done to an opponent's stick blade as it receives the puck or as it is about to redirect or release it. To properly execute the move for a deflection, the goaltender must first cut down the angle on the puck carrier. Have the goaltender keep the potential deflector in his field of vision by coming out to cut down the angle only as far as it takes without losing sight of the second player. The goaltender's developed peripheral vision will help him keep an eye on this deflector. As the puck moves off the first player's stick blade the goaltender will quickly be able to detect its intended path. If the puck is moving to the deflector the goaltender should execute the double leg pad save so the pads arrive close to the deflector's stick blade. If the goaltender cannot trap the puck, he must recover quickly to prepare for the next shot.

THE STICK

The goaltender's stick is a multi-purpose tool. It can:
- Block or stop shots with the blade and shank of the stick;
- Direct pucks into the corner;
- Shoot pucks away;
- Pass pucks;
- Scoop the puck into the goaltender's body or glove;
- Trap the puck;
- Be used as a barrier to protect the goaltender from attacking forwards;
- Point out options to teammates;
- Bat the puck out of the air and away from the net;

- Push off opposing players who may be screening the goaltender's vision;
- Check pucks away by poke, sweep or hook checks;
- Indicate if someone is beside or behind the goaltender through touch.

All of these skills have been developed and improved upon over the years. Needless to say there have been many other uses developed, but these fall outside the rules of the game.

STOPPING AND DEFLECTING SHOTS

The stick blade will provide the goaltender with the ability to cup or control most of the pucks fired at the net, along the ice. By cupping the puck the goaltender can stop it in front of him and thereby trap it with his catcher glove. In most cases the stick will serve as a deflector directing the puck wherever the goaltender wishes. The stick can best stop and deflect pucks off to the side by first insuring that it is kept slightly angled from the start. An angled stick will make for a better goaltender simply by insuring he doesn't direct the puck right back out toward the opposition. Remember too that the entire goaltender's stick – the blade, the shank, and the shaft – has the potential to serve as a puck stopping or deflecting surface.

The ability to direct the puck well, falls into two techniques:
- Passive deflections
- Active deflections

Passive deflections require only an angled stick blade. This is accomplished by rotating the stick or by simply keeping it stationary and angled. The puck strikes the stick and is directed away. Active deflections include the use of a back-up foot. The stick is angled and resting against a skate. The skate kicks the stick, either with a small or large kick, to direct the puck away. By adding the velocity of the kicking foot to that of the puck, the goaltender can actually redirect the puck off to the side at a greater speed than the puck had when it met the stick blade.

PASSING AND SHOOTING

Passing the puck requires the goaltender be a confident stickhandler. The goaltender should be able to control the puck with one or two hands. The blocker hand should be strong enough to backhand the puck away from the net. This is done by cupping the puck in mid-stick blade, well off to the blocker side. The stick is then drawn quickly across in front of the goaltender. The blocker wrist is quickly rotated. The puck is passed to the target with the stick blade following through in the open position. If the goaltender wants to shoot the puck away, the action is the same but the follow through involves a full rotation, which will have the toe of the stick blade pointing at the intended target.

With a two-handed forward pass or shot, the hand position is considerably different from that used by forwards or defence. The top glove holds the stick well out from the body so that the stick blade is fully on the ice. The upper hand is at the end of the stick shaft and the lower glove is positioned at the top of the stick shank.

Considerable time has been spent comparing the benefits and shortcomings of having the blocker slide up to assume the top glove position or in having the catcher glove grasping the top of the stick.

In the first case, the stick remains in contact with the ice and the blocker supplies a firm grip and wrist rotation to the top of the stick. The catcher is grasping the stick at the shank. The catcher is only able to provide a driving force to the stick's movement. The advantage to this move is that it allows the goaltender to regain the proper stance should the pass or shot be intercepted by the opposition.

In the second case, the catcher glove squeezes the butt end of the stick providing some wrist rotation. The blocker is positioned at the shaft just above the shank. It provides a secure bottom hand which can push the stick through and provide the wrist rotation needed for a strong follow through. In this latter case, it is important to keep the stick blade on the ice. Many times this second move will rotate the stick at the blocker so that the catcher glove may grasp the top of the stick. When this is done the blade leaves the ice for a dangerously long time. To correct this, have the blocker slide up the shaft as in a poke check. Then rotate the stick blade to the outside and use the catcher glove to grasp the top of the stick.

When passing, the goaltender positions the puck at mid stick blade. The entire blade is in constant contact with the ice. The stick cups the puck off to the side and then is drawn quickly across in front of the goaltender's body. The blade is opened and the puck moves off the blade toward the target. Again, when passing, the stick blade follows through in the open position. When shooting, the action is the same but this time the puck is positioned at the heel of the stick blade. Also when the stick follows through, the blade is rotated fully so that the toe of the blade is pointing at the intended target. In both passing and shooting, the upper glove acts as a pivot while the lower one provides the pushing action.

STICK CHECKS

Poke check. This check allows the goaltender to knock the puck off an opponent's stick blade or to intercept a pass. The action requires the goaltender to slide his blocker up the shaft of the stick by moving the stick out in front of them, as in a throwing action. The poke check must be quick and a surprise to the opponent. The check must not be executed when the puck is anywhere outside one stick length of the goaltender's reach.

Timing is very important. If the poke check is done too soon the attacking player will just draw the puck back out of the goaltender's reach and move around the committed goaltender. Often a goaltender will "telegraph" or forewarn the opponent of an impending poke check by moving his blocker up the shaft of the stick before the stick is extended on the ice toward the intended target. Opposing players will pick up on this signal and will leave the goaltender stranded as they move around him or they will simply shoot the puck low to the stick side where the goaltender will not be able to stop it.

Sweep check. The sweep check is used to clear the puck from a wide area. The goaltender will use this move when the puck is coming in toward the net from his catcher glove side. The goaltender extends his blocker glove up the shaft of the stick, as in a poke check, but the stick is first moved to the catcher glove side of the goaltender. The catcher glove grasps the stick just below the blocker and the entire length of the stick is pressed down onto the ice. The goaltender should drop down on his catcher glove side leg pad to assist the stick in meeting the ice. The stick is then swept across in front of the goaltender into the path of the oncoming puck and stick blade. This check can empty an area of the puck and any opposition players quite quickly.

Hook check. The hook check is used to knock pucks off the stick of opposing players moving from the goaltender's catcher side. This check requires the goaltender to rotate the stick so the crook or upper edge of the stick blade is moving toward the opponent's stick blade. The goaltender's stick should be pressed down onto the ice so that the entire length of the stick is in contact. The goaltender drops down onto his blocker side leg pad to get the stick this low. The stick is swept quickly across in front of the goaltender. This action will knock the puck off the opponent's stick.

ANGLE PLAY

Coaches often complain that their goaltender is letting in questionable goals. If he is allowing goals just inside either post, the problem lies mostly with angles.

A goaltender's angles are the most important fundamental skill he possesses, next to proper balance, of course. For too long coaches have used ropes or elastics to display a pie shaped area starting from the puck and connected to each post (Fig. 1).

This area or angle is what the goaltender must fill if he wants to play his angles properly. There are problems with this method of teaching. First of all, it focuses attention not on the puck but on the area that must be filled. Second, these ropes are improper cues since they are not found on

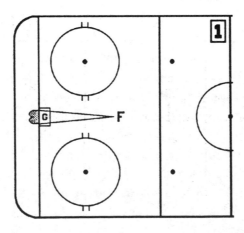

the ice in a game. What use do they have as a guide during competitions? Finally, the time it takes a coach to tie up the ropes can be better spent.

The centre line theory of angles does not require any ropes. It focuses the goalie on what really should be his centre of attention, the puck. It works as follows:

• Place a puck directly on the middle of the goal line.

• Have a forward or an assistant coach stickhandle a puck to a spot on the ice in the defensive zone and have him stop with the puck in full view.

• The goalie then skates out to cut down the angle without looking behind him. When he feels he has lined up the forward's puck properly, he takes a puck from his glove and places it on the ice between his feet, then moves away.

• Now if these three pucks (the forward's puck, the goal line puck and the goalie's puck) are in a straight line the goaltender has cut off the angle of the puck's flight by properly focusing on the centre line of the puck. (Fig. 2)

Quite often the goaltender is focusing incorrectly and is lined up either with the puck carrier or halfway between the puck and the man. (Fig. 3)

Once the goalie understands the centre line theory, he is ready to be taught his angles. Angles can be found by using those dots and lines that are already on the ice in front of the goalie in the defensive zone. If these cues are used properly then there is no need for the goalie to touch the posts with his stick or glove or to glance behind at the centre

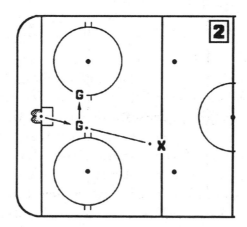

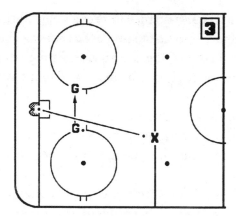

of the net. The game of hockey has sped up too much for any goal-tender to be back in his net groping or glancing for his angles while the opposition players are flying in on the attack. The goaltender can find his angles by using the following cues. (Fig. 4)

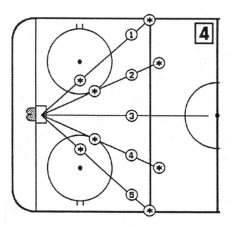

Position 3. Line up the centre ice face-off dot, the middle of the far net and the half-way point between the inside defensive zone hash marks.

Positions 1 & 5. Line up the intersecting point at which the defensive zone blue lines meet the boards with the half-way point between the defensive zone face-off dots and the inside hash marks.

Positions 2 & 4. Line up the neutral zone face-off dots above the nearest blue line with the intersecting point of the defensive zone face-off circles and the inside top or bottom hash-marks. (This may vary somewhat depending upon the arena). Once they know the five points, move the net away and have them align themselves to these points as you call them out. Make sure they do not look down at the crease or behind. The cues are out in front where the puck is and not behind.

Do your shooting drills using these points and, as a coach, refer to them as often as possible when describing shots on net or goals scored.

PUCK AROUND THE NET

Behind the net. When the puck is behind the net, the goaltender must keep in the proper stance with the body facing out to the slot. Turning to face the puck when it is behind the net will only leave the goaltender vulnerable to shots fired by any player in the slot who receives a quick pass out. Keeping the body in the proper stance, facing the slot, allows the goaltender to be ready to stop shots.

The head should be rotated over the shoulder so the goaltender can see the puck. The goaltender should not move to either post too soon. The head may have to be rotated back over the other shoulder *but only if the puck moves*. The goaltender should keep the puck in view and not assume the puck is somewhere without seeing it.

To the post. When the puck has moved out from behind the net or from the corner toward the side of the net, the goaltender must hold his ground and prevent the puck from being pushed into the goal between the post and his leg. The goaltender moves to the post and assumes the proper stance. The leg closest to the post should be tightly held against the post. The skate boot, outside portion of the lower leg, and the outside portion of the upper leg or thigh, should be tight against the post. This will prevent the puck from being squeezed into the goal between the goalie and the post.

The goaltender should use the nearest arm to hold to the post. If the blocker arm is the closest one, the elbow or upper arm should hold tightly to the post. The stick should be extended just back behind the goal line. The stick blade should be held so the puck can be stopped if it is passed out. The stick blade must also be able to pull the puck against the net to freeze it. If the catcher arm is the closest one to the post, the entire arm holds the post tightly and the stick blade is extended back over the goal line. The blade should be tilted ready to either poke check or deflect the puck as it is carried or passed by the post. If the puck comes free, the stick blade can sweep across and trap it on the net.

In either case, the stick blade should be ready to protect the space which occurs along the ice between the skate blade and the post. An important thing to remember is that the goaltender must stay on his feet in the proper stance. If the goaltender drops down to trap the puck, he could open up a space which could allow the puck to slip under a pad or in off the post.

Rebound off the boards. If the puck is shot wide and bounces back out over the goal line, the goaltender may be required to extend his reach and trap it. This will require him to block the puck with either the shank of the stick or to trap it under the catcher, depending upon which side of the net the rebound occurs. A goaltender should practise this move to improve his ability to quickly move out and to know how far he can reach. An improperly timed move could leave the goaltender out of position with the net open to the opposing player who retrieves the puck.

Stopping the puck behind the net. Quite often, the opposing team will dump the puck into your zone by ringing the boards with a shot. The experienced goaltender can use these opportunities to gain control of the puck and either drop it there for a teammate or pass it up and out of the zone. The goaltender must move out behind the net, gain control of the puck, and get back into the net quickly.

If the puck is shot around the boards off to the goaltender's blocker side, the goaltender must push off and move behind the net to stop the puck using his backhand, one hand on the stick as in the proper position. The stick blade is jammed into, and at right angles to, the boards. The blade should be cupped to help trap the puck. The leg must be ready to be pushed against the boards to block and trap those high shots which may ring the boards.

If the puck is shot around the boards off to the goaltender's catcher side, the goaltender must push off and move behind the net to stop the puck using his forehand, two hands on the stick in the shooting and passing position. The stick blade should be jammed into the boards and cupped.

The blade should be at a 45 degree angle to help trap the puck. Again, the leg pads must be ready to be pushed against the boards to block and trap high shots.

In both cases, if the puck is to be left for a teammate, the puck should be placed out from the boards about six inches. Too close to the boards and the players may have difficulty in picking up the puck.

Communicating with teammates. Perhaps the most improperly used asset any hockey player has is his mouth. It seems that players talk at the wrong times during a game. Instead of shouting and complaining to the referee or to opposing players and/or coaches, these players should be communicating more effectively with their teammates. The goaltender is no exception to this rule.

Defensively, the goaltender can communicate by calling out that: an opposing player is open in the slot, a potential deflector should be cleared from the line of fire, not to screen the goaltender, and look out for the checker coming up behind them. Offensively, the goaltender can assist the play by calling out: which teammates are open for passes, to take their time and set up behind the net, whether they have the time to carry the puck or if they should pass, and whether they have a checker on them. By speaking out, the goaltender can also help to motivate his teammates and inspire confidence.

Play reading. In previous sections, we have discussed some aspects of play reading, i.e., tip-ins and deflections. A few other situations are described here.

Two on one. In this situation, the goaltender and defence must be in agreement. The defence should be between the two opponents ready to intercept any pass across. The defence should be forcing the puck carrier wide to an extreme angle. The goaltender can then focus attention on the puck carrier and cut down the angle. Once the shot is made, the defence should immediately move to neutralize the open man since this player will be the one more inclined to pick up any rebounds.

One on one. The defence should force the opposing player wide to an extreme angle. The goaltender can then come out further to cut down the angle, knowing the defence will prevent the player from moving across the net.

Another situation is when the defence or forward is back-checking the opposing player. If the back-checker has taken away the mid-ice area and has contact with the opposing player, then the goaltender can move out aggressively to cover the angle on the shot. If the opposing player has not been contacted by the defender, or if the opposing player has room to move across the net, then the goaltender should play the angle conservatively and be ready to move across with the puck carrier.

GOALTENDER SELECTION

The following information is designed to help you select your goaltender.

- Limit yourself to four or six goalies per tryout. This makes it easier to evaluate them. Also, use an even number of goaltenders to allow for equal routine both in the drills and in the scrimmages.
- Don't judge a goaltender by his size. Too many great short goaltenders have been cut as the coach felt that they would be too susceptible to high shots and just as many tall goaltenders were presumed to be too awkward. Judge by how the goaltender plays and leave your preconceptions on size at home.
- When talking to any prospective goaltender find out what other sports they may have played. Gymnastics and wrestling are sports that build great stamina, strength, flexibility, and agility. Handball, racquet sports, and baseball are sports that improve hand-eye coordination. Soccer, lacrosse, and basketball are sports that develop team play concepts and conditioning.
- Once the goaltenders are in the dressing room getting ready, you should be looking for specific signals. Does he look overweight? In what shape is his goaltending equipment? A good goaltender takes care of his equipment. Has he modified his equipment? A goaltender who improvises is a good student of the game and will likely have an analytical mind, an important asset to possess.
- Have each goalie wear a different coloured sweater. That should make it easier for you and your evaluators to distinguish between the contenders.
- Have each goalie do his own warm-up stretches at centre ice and observe what each one does. Does he stand around or does he start stretching properly on his own? This is a good indication of previous expert goaltending instruction. If he can take the initiative on his own

to begin properly preparing himself, this could also indicate that he is an individual who can take a leadership role.

- Does he look confident before entering the net? A successful goaltender must have confidence when under pressure.

Start off the warm-up with wrist shots from in close and then progress to harder shots from the blue line. Try to have the players moving when they shoot. Game situations should be duplicated as much as possible so that you can better evaluate your goaltenders. A moving shooter gives fewer cues and therefore is harder to stop.

- Stance and style. Do his stance and movement appear aggressive and confident? A goaltender who appears never to be ready to stop a puck usually isn't.
- When does the goaltender set himself for the developing play? Does he get into the ready position or basic stance too soon. (i.e., when the puck is still in the opposing zone?) Or does he wait too long and pick up the cues only when the play is right on top of him?
- When does he move back into the net on passing plays or breakaways? Does he wait properly for the puck to reach the top of the face-off circles or does he move too soon and give away too much of the net. Or does he move too late letting the player deke?
- When the goaltender stops pucks does he pull up? Carefully place some fakes into the shooting drills to see if he does fear the puck.
- Does the goaltender make too many unnecessary moves? If he drops down too much or makes an outlandish move to stop a shot then he has a problem. He could also fatigue too quickly.
- Does he play the puck with his body or arms? A goalie who relies on his hands and doesn't back up shots with his body misjudges them and allows goals.
- Does he move his body into the shot to control rebounds?
- Does he demonstrate second effort? A goalie is constantly trying to keep the puck out of his goal. The world is full of goalies who can stop the first shot but it is the great goaltenders who try to stop the second, third, and even fourth shots on any specific play.
- What kind of rebounds does he give off? Does he constantly kick the puck right back to the opposing shooters or does he control the rebounds?

- Does he gamble too much? Good goalies read plays, they don't guess.
- Does the goalie keep his eyes on the puck when he stops the shot or does he just reach out without looking?
- Does he recover well and get himself back into the play as quickly as possible? Slow goaltenders can be a hazard to themselves and the team.
- Does he look over his shoulder to align himself in the net? If a goaltender has to look behind himself to find the net he hasn't learned his angles.
- How does the goaltender react when he is hit with a puck? Good goaltenders are oblivious to the pain or at least don't let it interfere with their concentration.
- Check his skating forward, backward, and one foot snow-plow stops. When he skates he should be balanced, quick, and allow for no unnecessary upper body movement. i.e., bobbing shoulders.
- Keep stats on where goals go in. Were they high, low, between the legs, etc.? Stats confirm weaknesses and strengths.
- What does the goalie do when he's not in net? Does he stand around or does he practise specific moves? Does he appear to be analyzing the shooters?

The last two actions show a goalie constantly trying to improve.

Scrimmage. In scrimmage, have the goalies rotate every five minutes. With at least five minutes, you will insure that they will get some shots. You'll also see how quickly they can get into the game.

- How does he relate to the defence? Does he communicate well? Does he handle the puck properly and safely? Does he pass properly in the right situations?
- How does the goalie react when a goal is scored against him? Does he sulk or go into a tantrum? Or does he forget about it and prepare for the next play sequence? A good goalie doesn't allow his concentration to lapse with a goal against. He approaches the next play ready to stop the puck without allowing previous misplays to cloud his mind.
- How does he react to opposing players in his crease? Does he ignore them? Does he let them push him back in the net and out of the play? Does he retaliate and distract himself from the play? Does he make sure that the players standing in front feel his presence and decide not

to stand there again? A well placed tap from a goalie's glove or stick shows a toughness good goalies need.

Schedule either three on three mini-scrimmages or five on four power plays so that you can see the goaltender under pressure. Does he hesitate or panic in such situations? Or does he appear confident and ready to challenge at all times?

These are a few pointers you can use to pick your goaltenders. But remember, goaltenders can be as different as coaches. How they do it doesn't mean a thing as long as they stop the puck!

When selecting your goaltenders, you should also put them through a series of basic backward skating and agility drills. Scrimmages will also let you see what your prospective goaltenders can stop in a game-like situation, which should be your first concern. However, if you really want to see what they can do under pressure, then try using the following drills shown in the accompanying diagrams. Remember, the drills should be introduced the first time by qualified on-ice instructors. You should then let your goalies go through the drills the first couple of times slowly. Once they have learned the drills at a slower speed and have some confidence, have them execute the drills at full speed.

Summary. In conclusion, goaltenders stop pucks! Some use the butterfly, some are floppers, some stand up, and so on. There are probably as many goaltending styles as there are goaltenders. The main thing is that they stop the puck.

There are two areas that should concern coaches. The first is practice time. Goaltenders are the most neglected players at practice. It is commonly believed that this is, in part, the reason for the late development of them, especially at the professional level. Include them in your practice plans. They need instruction like any other player on the team. The second concern is coaching. Unfortunately, there are never enough good goalie coaches to go around. Coaches should try to ensure their goalies have good quality coaching. Too often, we see incorrect instruction leading to bad habits. A cardinal rule of instructors is that you don't try to change a goaltender's style, you try to improve it. Let him use the style he's most comfortable with.

Finally, the forwards can look to the defencemen to help if they make a mistake. The defencemen can look to the goaltender to help if they make a mistake. The goaltender knows that the puck must stop with him. Hockey is a team game but in the end, the greatest pressure is on one position. The puck stops here . . . with the goaltender.

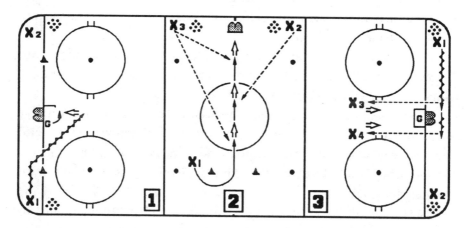

DRILL #1: Carry Out. "X1" skates from a corner (inside pylon) with a puck and moves across the front of the net. "X1" tries to stuff the puck into the net as he goes by the goaltender. The goalie must make sure he does not let the puck go into the net either through the "five hole" or in the short or long sides of the net. "X1" goes to opposite corner. "X2" now goes.

DRILL #2: Three Shot Drill "X1" skates around the pylon and skates toward the goal. "X3" passes a puck to "X1" who takes a shot on goal, then continues skating. "X2" then passes to "X1" who takes another shot on goal and continues skating in on goal. Finally, "X3" passes a final puck to "X1" for a final shot on goal. Players rotate positions with each shot.

DRILL #3: Pass Out "X1" skates behind goal line with puck. "X1" passes to "X3" or "X4" in front of net. Goalie must follow pass out and move to stop quick shot, being sure he doesn't let puck in either through "five hole" or in the short or long sides. See how quickly goalie moves across, out to stop the puck or if he pulls up. "X2" then goes, after which, players rotate.

Practice Organization
and Coaching Technique

It is the intention in this chapter to set forth at least some of the basic principles that should be followed in the hope that coaches will use more scientifically organized hockey practices. In the past few years, experts in the field of physical education and psychology have developed valuable information regarding how best to use practice time. Too much of this information has gone unused by coaches.

Organized hockey is still young in comparison with other "big money sports" such as football, baseball, and basketball. For example, when you compare hockey to football as played in the United States it is easy to see hundreds of football teams playing in important competitions, with each coach knowing that there are ten more waiting to take his place if he falters even a little, but there are only a few hockey teams in this category. If one man or one team would start scientific application of modern practice principles, others would soon follow.

Making the most of the practice time is one of the great fundamentals of success in hockey or in any other activity. This applies particularly to the coach of the young player. The coach who best utilizes his time cannot help but be a better coach. The following suggestions show how to get the most out of every practice minute.

The first step that must be taken in setting up a practice system, in order for maximum efficiency, is to know what you are trying to accomplish and then apply fundamental teaching skills to the task. Teaching hockey skills is not an easy matter; therefore the general principles of learning and skill development must be applied. Unfortunately, practices pose different problems for almost every coach. The professional coach, the junior amateur coach, the university and college coach, the coach of minor amateur teams, the high school coach, and the community or rep coach all have different setups. These range from the ideal (as far as time and facilities are concerned) in some of the higher levels of organized hockey down to no practice time or facilities at all (as is too often true for community, school, and rep league teams). The answer is to learn general principles and then adapt them to the situation and conditions at hand. This holds true for the coach and also the individual who is trying to develop skill by practising on his own or with a group of friends. In the following pages you will find a number of basic principles together with as many specific suggestions for each level of hockey as space and time will permit.

PRACTICE PRINCIPLES

Organization. If the practice session is to pay off, the coach must give first priority to its organization. Only by careful organization can the coach eliminate such time wasting factors as failure to utilize the full ice surface; having inactive players standing around; trying to decide which skills to emphasize; or using practice time for explanations that should have been done off-ice.

The average coach does give some thought to his practice sessions but is too casual in his approach. He often waits until he gets to the session before deciding how it will be conducted. Many coaches wait until the practice has actually started before they determine what skills they are going to emphasize or what drills they are going to use. Organize each practice on paper, before it begins, and then figure out exactly how it is going to be taught.

Every detail should be considered in this planning. The last practice should be analyzed and considerable thought given to how it can be improved. The coach should use some of his assistants or the team managerial staff to help him check each practice to figure out if time is being wasted and how. All the great coaches, like all the great athletes, are strong detail people whose attitude is that even the smallest detail is important.

After reviewing the previous practice, and the last game, the coach and his staff should then assess all the needs of the team and of the individual players, together with such points as what special preparation is needed for the next game, what weaknesses were uncovered during the last game, and so on. When all the objectives are listed, a priority system of selecting the various factors to be dealt with must be used. How much time should be spent on each should be decided.

YEARLY PLAN

An excellent system is to carefully evaluate, as early as possible, the job that must be done throughout the season. Then each individual practice should be worked into the master scheme. Various, unexpected situations will naturally come up from time to time and these must be given attention. To organize a practice properly the coach must have a lot of information at his finger tips regarding the needs of each player, the weak spots as demonstrated by past performances, the type of opposition the team is going to come up against, and so on. Like the organized player, every coach should be sure to keep a book on such matters. It is an invaluable aid.

In hockey today, a year round training program should be developed. The season can be divided into: preparation period; pre season; regular season; playoff preparation, and transition period. During these periods different percentages of time will be given to fundamentals, team play, specialty teams, and conditioning, depending on the skill level of the team involved.

Set an example. If the coach is not well organized, he can hardly expect his players to be well organized. A large number of coaches get angry when their players show disorganized attitudes or play, when they themselves are the epitome of disorganization. There is nothing that influences an athlete more than the degree of organization on the part of his coach. If the coach has everything planned, with the practice clear cut and well organized, the player will immediately develop a sense of respect and individual responsibility. Well organized practices that move smoothly from the moment the athletes arrive until the moment when they are all through will develop an atmosphere in which learning and skill development can flourish. A good attitude for the coach to take is that every wasted moment costs him money.

Dress them up. Every effort should be made by the coach to give his practice sessions colour and a true "big time" atmosphere. The equipment to be used should be laid out neatly. The training supplies should be set out so that they are readily available. The coaching staff should be dressed in a uniform that presents a good image to the players. These things really set the tone and any player walking into such a situation begins to feel that he is going to get somewhere, that he is a member of a successful organization.

Interest and variety. If the coach is not careful he can very easily develop an anti-practice attitude among his players. Athletes, being human, naturally resist hard work, especially when it is boring and uninteresting. When the practice sessions are uninspired and heavy with work, it is only natural that the player will not look forward to them and will find it an effort to turn out and give his best. If a practice is properly organized and planned, the player will look forward to it and enjoy it.

The secret of skill development is hard work. The greater the work capacity of the athlete or team as a whole, the higher level skill will be developed. Therefore, one of the basic principles the coach must encourage is the highest possible work ethic. Some coaches believe that the answer is to drive the players and get results by threatening penalties of some kind. This may work to a degree, but it will not work nearly as well as introducing variety into the practices themselves. The coach should introduce novelty contests, and should stress interesting drills. Everyone resents doing the same old thing in the same old way time after time no matter what activity is involved. Everyone also resents time wasted by standing around. The same is true of hockey players. The athlete with good character and attitude will try to keep working hard regardless of the conditions but he will find it very difficult and will always be having to drive himself if practices are dull or poorly organized. The main danger of hard, uninspired practice sessions is dealt with in the section on training in the discussion of staleness.

Hold the player's interest and keep his enthusiasm high. This can only be done by using lots of variety in the practice. All such practice ammunition as drills, tests, and so on, done on a competitive basis, questionnaires, frequent changes in the method of doing the same thing should be utilized. If the coach views each practice from the viewpoint of "How can I make today's session interesting and fun for the players?" he will be amazed at the level of work effort he will get from his players. This involves extra thought by the coach, but he should remember that, just as the level of skill is governed by the work capacity of the athlete, so is the level of coaching skill governed by the work capacity of the coach. Psychology teaches that when interest is high, the learning rate and capacity are greatly increased.

Tell them why. Psychologists maintain that when a person knows exactly why he is supposed to do certain things, he will be able to do them much better and with more drive than if he does not have a clear picture of the purpose behind the activity. The coach should not just say, "Do it." He should say, "I want you to do so and so because it will ... etc." A short talk before every practice explaining to the players what they are going to work on and the idea behind it will do a great deal to improve the results gained from the practice.

The pep talk before the big game or during periods of rest in the game has been discussed. Nevertheless, the coach should keep in mind that the best time to use pep talks and inspirational appeals is before practice, because they will then be used to develop the skill that will give the players the ammunition to respond to the coach's reminders during an actual game. Many coaches, before or during an important game, demand from their players levels of skill and endurance that are just not there. Using pep talks before practice is much more practical and effective. There are some who say that pep talks are wasted effort and will only work on young gullible athletes. This is simply an unscientific criticism because any normal human will respond to the right kind of inspirational suggestion, whether they want to or not.

HAVE DEFINITE OBJECTIVES

A study of the process of learning and skill development discloses the fact that people learn more, learn easier, and work harder when they have definite objectives. Things should not be just practised. There should be an objective of some kind.

Actually, there should be two objectives. There should be long term objectives, as represented for example by a level of skill hoped for at the end of a season, and an individual practice objective, which is aimed for at each and every practice session. At the start of the season, the coach should set a long list of objectives for the team and for the individual players. By doing this he will be doing the same thing as placing the proverbial carrot in front of the mule's nose. The individual player working on his own can set his own objectives. Objectives can be set for any phase of the hockey development plan. Shooting accuracy and power, speed and endurance, passing accuracy, positional play, and all the other skills can be tabbed with objectives.

A coach can tell a player to go out and practise shooting for ten minutes or he can tell the player to see if he can hit a target twenty-five out of fifty shots. The player will do much better when he has a definite objective. Research showed that those who practised with definite objectives in mind developed higher skill level much more quickly than did those working in a generalized way.

Keep it cheerful. Another very interesting psychological principle is that people learn faster and better, work harder, and for longer periods of time without becoming conscious of fatigue, when they are in a cheerful and optimistic state of mind. Therefore the wise coach will work very hard to develop this cheerful and optimistic attitude in all his practice sessions. The players should be inspired to talk it up during practice just as they are during a game. It should be made clear that there should not be a lack of serious application and hard work. Work hard, but with a background of cheerfulness. It is wise to keep in mind that the play instinct is one of the strongest instincts we have. This is true even in professional sport, where the athletes are combining business with pleasure in a very real way. The coach who keeps as much as possible of the fun and play element in his practice sessions will find that it pays off.

Presentation is important. If he is to get the most from his practice sessions, the coach should realize that the method in which the instructions are presented is very important. It is not enough for the coach to have a great knowledge of the game and to know what he is trying to do. The players must know too! No matter how much knowledge a coach has, it will not do much good unless he can get it across to the players. It is the same when coaching as it is when selling any product. It does not matter how good the product is if the salesman cannot make the customer realize it. This is one reason why many famous athletes who have turned to coaching have failed. They have the reputation, the prestige, and the knowledge, but they have not learned or organized or presented their material effectively. Therefore the coach should do everything he can to learn the technique of presentation. He can do this by making a study of the principles of salesmanship, of public speaking, and even of dramatics.

Every conceivable method of improving the effectiveness of presentation should be employed. Some people are naturally impressive in their presentation. Others must work hard to learn it, but it is something that every coach can learn. The athlete whose coach can give him his instructions in an easily understood, colourful, and impressive way, will learn more than the unfortunate athlete whose coach's instructions are presented in a manner predominated by rambling, disconnected sentences, oh's and um's, a dull monotone, and all the other irritating symptoms of poor presentation often heard at club meetings. If there is anybody that needs to develop the technique of presentation, it is the coach of a hockey team.

Learner's test. One of the most helpful things learned from psychology research is that different people learn in different ways. This knowledge can be used to good effect by the coach or individual trying to develop skill.

People are apparently divided into three types; those who learn best from what they see (visual); those who learn best from what they hear (audio); and those who learn best from actions and movements (motor). Every person is some combination of at least two of these. Most people are good visual learners. Tests have indicated that about seventy per cent of athletes learned best from what they saw. The breakdown of the average individual athlete showed him to learn as follows; sixty per cent visual, twenty-five per cent audio, and fifteen per cent motor. A greater percentage of instruction is given to an athlete by word of mouth. The athlete then is taking in most of his instruction through his second best channel. In visual-audio instruction the athlete is taught through a combination of demonstration and spoken explanation. Tests prove that this is by far the most effective method of teaching. This has been stressed by educators for some time. It is why video tape use has been found to be so effective in the coaching of athletes.

Nevertheless, the use of video tapes should be supplemented by the use of demonstrators to go through the various points to be emphasized. With this in mind, the coach should spend a lot of time on one or two players until they can demonstrate for him. If possible, the coach should learn to demonstrate each move himself. A very excellent plan is for the coach to have at least one assistant whose main job it is to demonstrate. Demonstrating is possible even in the lower levels of organized hockey. There are always plenty of people around who are only too glad to act as assistants without salary. Make sure any spoken instructions build up in the player's mind a mental picture of the action. This is why the use of careful similes and comparisons can be so effective.

The smart coach will test his players individually to find out what kind of learner each player is. He then will be in a position to organize his coaching technique accordingly. He may well find that he has a group of athletes who are strong audio and motor learners. If this is so, he should govern his methods accordingly, concentrating on verbal instructions and letting the players perform the motions slowly until they get the feel since this is the way a motor learner learns best.

Part of the technique of utilizing this information is to teach the visual learner to picture the various things he must learn in his mind in the form of action. He should be told to try to draw pictures of the points in question. In addition, he should be given as many illustrations, diagrams, and charts as possible. In using the written work, he should keep reading the instructions over and over again, closing his eyes at frequent intervals trying to see the action. The audio learner when reading, should read out loud so that he can hear what he is reading. He should also do a lot of discussion work so that the things he must learn can be heard. A motor learner should associate the things he hears and sees with some physical action. When learning a new skill, he should always start very slowly, trying to get the feel of what he is learning. To get a definite impression from what he reads, what he has been told, or what he has seen, he should write down the points he is trying to learn. For example, if the reader knows he is a motor learner and he wishes to get the most out of this book, he should copy out the things he wishes to remember. There have been many so-called dumb athletes who were dumb only because they weren't taught in the right way.

Research shows that a combination of physical practice and mental practice is the best and fastest method to learn and perfect a skill.

Don't overload. The more enthusiastic and better informed a coach, the more likely he is to commit one of the great teaching errors: trying to do too much at once. At an average practice you'll find a coach full of pep, enthusiasm, and desire to improve his team. Because of his attitude, he will give instructions too quickly, possibly telling the same man to remember to do nine different things within a period of two minutes. Though his enthusiasm is much to be admired, his system is not. Faster results are gained with a "one thing at a time" approach.

The coach should make every effort to make each particular point stand out clearly. This cannot be done when a large number of things are explained and emphasized at the same time. The coach who establishes priorities and then works on them one by one, segregating them from each other, will get better results. By trying to teach too much the coach can defeat his own purpose. If he is concerned with the feeling that there is so much to do, so much to teach, he should keep in mind the fact that his players will do a lot better if they know only two or three things well than if they know a little bit about a lot of things.

This is especially true when coaching young players who cannot stand a heavy learning load. A good example is found in the various play patterns listed in this book. A coach whose players are young should at first confine himself to teaching only a few plays. He can add to them little by little as each one is well learned. In this way he'll develop maximum skill, whereas if he tries to teach his team thirty or forty plays, his squad will not perform any of them at a high level of efficiency. The process of learning takes time and the more an attempt is made to hurry it the longer it takes. This is why it is so important for a coach (or individual player working by himself) to break down things into priorities, working on the important ones first, moving on only when the previous one has been well learned. Some of the priorities in the technique of playing hockey are listed later.

DRILLS VS. SCRIMMAGES

It is a natural instinct for a person to prefer the scrimmage in which he is actually playing under game conditions to instruction drills or other practice methods in which the various manoeuvres and techniques of the game are broken down into sections. However, this attitude must be controlled. It can slow the skill development process because, though scrimmages are very important, they can be over-emphasized to the disadvantage of everyone.

The ideal system is to make the various practice drills and instruction periods as interesting and competitive as possible so as to work in the "play" element. Suppose, for example, a player has to practise passing for a long period of time. He will become impatient with the activity and be always after the coach to have a scrimmage. But if the passing drill is conducted on a competitive level in the form of a contest, his interest will remain high. This is one reason why it is strongly recommended that the coach should use the competitive angle in as much of his practice work as he possibly can.

Start off with the instruction drills and then follow with scrimmage in which the players try to work into the practice actual game-like conditions, the things they have been learning in the drills. In other words, first they learn the part and then they try to work that part into its proper place in the whole. The main advantage of drills over scrimmage is that the player is concentrating on a specific skill, whereas in a scrimmage he has to do a number of things which may take away from the drill objective. The drills should always come first, and then be used under actual playing conditions before the skills are forgotten.

To be effective, scrimmages should always be organized with a purpose. Each player should be told before the scrimmage periods what he must concentrate on, and he should be given reminders whenever it seems necessary throughout the scrimmage. Haphazard scrimmage, without a definite plan behind it, during which the coach merely skates around hollering at the players to do this or that will not result in very good development. Through drills, each separate part of the game can be developed and polished to a high level. Then, through scrimmage, all these parts can be integrated into a smooth-working and efficient whole.

The Wonder Drill. This drill has both individual skills and team tactics. Actually, the correct name of the drill is "Five On Two." Used frequently and with careful organization it will develop a tremendous ganging attack; teach passing and pass receiving under pressure; develop positional awareness; improve agility and stickhandling skills; develop goalkeeping skill; improve shooting accuracy; develop defensive skill to a high level; and act as an excellent and interesting "conditioner." Here's how it works.

The drill is conducted inside the blue line. There are five offensive players and three defensive players (including the goaltender). The puck is dropped between a defensive player and an offensive player at the face-off dot to either side of the net; the position selected should be varied throughout the drill. If the offensive team gets the draw, the purpose is for them to pass the puck around until they can work the puck to a player with a clear chance to score. There must be no long or indiscriminate shooting. The offensive squad should have three players in and two out on the "points" at the blue line. The two defensive men separate with one man "chasing" the puck trying to get possession or forcing the play, the other should guard the slot area directly in front of the goal. They shift their position according to the way the play goes. If they get possession of the puck they must lob it out into the centre ice zone for a possible breakaway – they do not clear it with a hard shot. You'll be amazed at how well two hard working defencemen can stop an attack of five offensive players.

The team can be split up into two groups, one at each end of the ice. The two defencemen should be changed often as their job is very hard to sustain for more than one to two minutes at a time.

The offensive squad must really pass the puck around, utilizing the "point" men so that full use is made of the open men.

The goaltender will have to be constantly on the alert. This will give him game-like situation in practices.

A coach should stop the play frequently and correct any tendencies to get out of position, point out other mistakes, and appeal to the players to "pass it around."

This is an especially effective drill for teams with little practice time. It is fun, good conditioning, and provides an excellent learning situation.

Should they "do it again"? In teaching a particular movement many coaches use the repetition, forcing the player to repeat the action again and again and again. This will produce some results but is not the ideal method. After a person has done a certain thing for a certain length of time without rest, he becomes mentally and physically tired. When this happens, his body and mind throw up a barrier against what he is trying to do hoping to force him to stop it because of the way he feels.

Nature would not do this if it was not a wise precaution. Therefore, the coach or the individual player working on his own should remember that after a certain number of repetitions no value is gained; in fact, skill is being lost.

Teach a skill in short, hard periods of effort with frequent rest. For example, if a coach is trying to develop shooting accuracy and works his players for thirty minutes at a shooting drill without rest he will not get as good results as if he worked them for five minutes, rested them for a minute or two, and repeated the drill.

There are some coaches who figure that any rest period during a practice session is wasted time. This is not true. Production and psychology experts have clearly proved that more can be done and more can be learned when the effort is broken up frequently with short rest periods. Each person seems to have a different limit of effort. Therefore the coach should watch his players carefully and call a rest or change of assignment whenever there seems to be a sign of boredom, fatigue, irritation, or lack of attention. We learn by doing. This is why a lot of people think that if they do a certain thing a thousand times in a row they will be sure to learn it. However, what they should keep in mind is that they should take time off to have a brief rest at frequent intervals while they are doing it the thousand times.

Incentives. If an athlete runs out of incentives, he will not keep up a very high level of effort, especially at practice. This is particularly true of the star player who does not have to worry about working hard to stay on the team. It is natural that the player will find it very hard to make an effort if there is not some real incentive. Therefore, the coach should spend a lot of time developing incentives and studying his players to find out what type of incentives seem to work best for the team and each player.

An excellent idea is to have on-going team championships in the various drills and fundamentals. It is quite easy to have player compete against player, or line against line, and so on. If good records are kept, it is possible to keep the players informed about their progress. This is a good idea because if one player sees that another is pulling ahead of him in shooting accuracy, he will be inclined to start working a little harder. Charts showing the number of times each player lets his man get away from him during a week's practice or in the last game and other such points of play should be posted on the dressing room wall or handed out to each player. These provide incentives and sustain interest.

Catchy quotes posted in the dressing room, distributed, or used verbally by the coach can also be a help. For example, in the Montreal Canadiens' dressing room there is a quote from a poem on the wall which reads:

"To you from failing hands we throw
The torch; be yours to hold it high."

A never-ending variety of inspirational quotations can be used effectively. A list can be compiled by the coach of the appropriate messages that he wants most to sell the team.

Skill work first. The athlete will learn faster and better when he is fresh. The more tired he gets, the more his learning capacity decreases. Accordingly, the high level skill work should be done during the early parts of the practice when the player has the energy and enthusiasm he needs to give learning his full attention and effort. Stretching exercises should be done off-ice before the on-ice practices start. There should be a good on-ice warm-up to get the players physically ready for their effort, but any hard scrimmage or body contact work should be left to the later stages of the practice. Always start practices off by working on the most important and the most difficult things. When planning his practice beforehand, the coach or player working on his own should establish in his own mind what are the most important and the most difficult things on which there is going to be work done and then schedule them accordingly so the most difficult ones come first.

Conclusion. In general, the coach or the player interested in improving on his own should make a point of studying, in as much detail as time will allow, the actual technique of learning. The more you know about how to learn, the more you will be able to learn, or teach, as the case may be. This is the basis of great coaching. Learn more than anybody else and then pass on this knowledge more quickly and more completely than anyone else.

PRACTICE SCHEDULES

Such problems as just how a practice should be made up, how long it should be, how often practices should be held, what time of day is best, when the work should be hard and when it should be light, and many other problems of a similar nature must be satisfactorily solved by the coach. There are countless factors to take into account and it would take another book of this size to cover the whole picture in detail. However, it's possible to deal with principles and fundamentals that can be adapted to most situations and facilities.

Practice construction. The practice should be broken down into several categories: early season, before the first game; active season during the majority of games; and late season, when the team is nearing the play-offs or in them.

Early season. During the early season, ninety per cent of the time should be spent on fundamentals with the remaining ten per cent spent on scrimmage. Some coaches think that more time should be spent on scrimmage because this will give them a chance to select their players. However, if the coach uses well organized drills in teaching his fundamentals, he will get a good idea of player ability or at least enough to make it possible to judge. Many coaches are inclined to overlook fundamentals and instead concentrate on the development of play patterns and positional play. It is easy for the average coach to do this because there is a certain amount of pressure from his players to get started on such phases of the game. The stronger the fundamentals, however, the better any play patterns or strategy will work. An analysis of nearly any great team or individual demonstrates top level efficiency at performing the fundamentals. Emphasis on them through the career of the team or individual and especially during the early stages, will pay big dividends. The emphasis on fundamentals should be maintained throughout the season but especially stressed at the start of the season and at any time the players seem to be on a plateau of development.

In establishing a priority for working on fundamentals, they should be lined up in order of their importance as follows: skating, shooting, passing, puck-carrying; goal scoring plays, checking, and defensive play in general. These fundamentals should also be stressed in the scrimmage work. As the players improve, more emphasis should be given to organized play patterns, positional play, and systems in general. For example, after the final player selection is made, the practice breakdown can be as follows: seventy-five per cent fundamentals; fifteen per cent play patterns, positional drills, offensive, and defensive; ten per cent scrimmage.

As the season gets under way, the emphasis can be changed to fifty per cent fundamentals, twenty-five per cent special drills, and twenty-five per cent scrimmage.

As far as establishing priorities, the coach should remember that the success of his team will depend largely on the skill level of his players. At the start of the season and throughout it, this should be one of the important priorities.

Active season. During the actual season, the picture changes quite a bit and the coach must establish his practice priorities depending on what has been happening in the games. He should study the needs very carefully and organize his practice time accordingly. For example, if the team is going well on offence but showing defensive weaknesses, he should emphasize defensive work. Keeping a record and using spotters can be a great help in establishing these needs. However, the fundamentals must not be overlooked and close attention should be paid to sustaining the players' interest and working levels. This can be done by using variety and the competitive element in practice work. Care must be taken not to let a practice session assume the same old routine. The fundamental breakdown of a practice might then well be twenty five per cent fundamentals, fifty per cent special work, and twenty-five per cent scrimmage.

Late season. During the late season it is more important than ever to have an evaluation of the needs as demonstrated by the season's play and then go to work to strengthen these on a priority basis. During the late season, when the players have been working hard for some time, particular care must be taken to keep them interested through lots of variety, new incentives, and lots of innovations in ways of practising the more repetitive phases of the game. By doing this, the interest and enthusiasm of the players can be kept at a high level and staleness can be avoided. The fundamentals should be rechecked and given a good overhauling. A careful evaluation should be done of each player regarding his fundamentals because most players are inclined to develop bad habits and careless attitudes during the playing months. A good breakdown could then be twenty per cent fundamentals, sixty-five per cent special work, and fifteen per cent scrimmage.

Length of practice. At the start of the season the practices should be between one and a half and two hours long, if it is possible to get this amount of time. If not, they should be as long as time and facilities permit. The practice session should be longer during the early part of the season because there is a great deal to be done. If possible, you should try to have one or two practice sessions per day during the early part of the season, when the players are more receptive to learning. And remember that two or three half-hour or three-quarter-hour sessions will bring better results than one long one. The practice sessions should be scheduled every day if possible.

As the hockey season progresses, fewer practices are needed. In the early part of the active season, two or three 60 or 90 minute practices per week are plenty. During the middle of the active season two 60 or 90 minute sessions per week are enough. During the latter part of the season the practice schedule should be governed by the conditioning and play of the players. If they are going well, they should practise fairly lightly with just enough effort being made to keep them progressing. If they have fallen off in their skills and fundamentals or organization, the number and intensity of practices should be increased. If the team is playing a lot of games, or if the coach is only getting one practice per week, the best time is the day following a game. It is then that the various mistakes will still be fresh in the players' minds. The sooner such mistakes can be worked on, the better.

The poor facility problem. Due to lack of ice facilities and sometimes financial problems, many coaches are faced with the problem of not being able to schedule many practices. This is a very discouraging situation, but the coach trying to work under such circumstances is undoubtedly not alone. The other coaches in his league or conference are probably faced with the same problem.

The solution is to make the most of each practice session by working on priorities and organizing every little detail so that every minute is utilized. A few basic plays and the fundamentals of positional play and strategy can be emphasized but there should be no attempt to develop the fancy work. The coach trying to operate in such a situation can also help a great deal by holding frequent chalk talks and discussions that can be conducted in his home or in the club room or classroom. Many of his players will also be in a position to practise on their own on the corner or public park rink. If this is the case, he should assign homework to them, giving them a schedule of work to follow.

As far as strategy is concerned, the coach can do a great deal of good by drawing vivid verbal pictures of the various situations explaining what should be done in each. The players should be quizzed at great length on what they should do under certain circumstances.

THE "NO-PRACTICE" PROBLEM

Many coaches, in trying to do a job with a squad in a house league or school team, are faced with the situation that makes it impossible for them to practise at all. The only time the players can play together is during actual games. Usually there are a few practices possible at the start of the season to select the team, but from then on they are impossible. When such a situation exists the coach should use a lot of "mind" practices and discussion work together with the homework principle described in the previous section. However, he should confine himself to the most fundamental aspects of the game, working on a high priority basis. When the team plays, he should use the same method. Such fundamentals as backchecking, defensive position play, shooting every time a player gets within the goal scoring area, following in after a shot, and breaking fast should be emphasized.

The hour or two directly after the game should be used so that all the various lessons to be learned can be discussed while they are still fresh in the players' minds. This post game "mind" practice can be a great help to the coach who has a "no practice" problem. Another way of sneaking in the odd few minutes practice is to make sure the team is ready to go on the ice the moment the rink is available. There is often at least time to practise a few fundamentals or plays.

Another excellent device open to the coach with the "no practice" problem is to take his players in a group to see good teams in action, indicating the various important points as the game goes along.

The individual player trying to do a job on his own should study all the various practice principles and laws of learning and adapt them to his own activities. The player who does this instead of just going over to the public rink for a haphazard game of shinny will surprise himself and his friends with his rate of improvement over those not using such a system. The young player can get his parents or a friend to help him organize and conduct his own private little practice.

The only conclusion possible to practice organization is that how much you practise is less important than how you practise. And the old saying "practice makes perfect" only applies if the correct principles of practice are observed all the time.

Editor's note: Not all practices have to be on-ice. In addition to "mind" practices conducted in dressing room and/or classroom, a coach can also accomplish a major amount of work by running practice sessions in a gymnasium. Often, good coaches will practise fundamentals and systems in a gym and then go straight to an on-ice practice to reinforce what they have learned. It is an excellent way to save on valuable ice time if they know the skill and/or system prior to going on the ice.

Coaching suggestions. Here are a few suggestions that the coach will find helpful when conducting practices and when handling the team during games.

PLAYER CORRECTION

One of the greatest problems of the coach is trying to control his nerves and emotions when instructing players during practices or games. It is difficult to handle many kinds of players without showing annoyance, consciously or otherwise. However, this is something the coach must learn to do. If it can be said that any coach has a virtue, it should be that it is patience and still more patience. Anyone who does not have an extra amount of this quality should never take up coaching. There are times, of course, when the coach should be severe and very blunt. But there are more times when he should be understanding and patient in his instructions or advice.

Whenever possible, a coach should be friendly and cheerful. Encourage, do not threaten. You must sell your ideas, not impose them. Always invite questions and opinions. It is better to build a player's ego than knock it down, and in every case be prepared to substitute analysis for criticism. A player's failure is almost always the failure of his coach. Criticizing in public is not only bad for the player but also gives the coach a bad reputation with the rest of the team.

To develop coolness and relaxation among your players, make real friends of them. Cliques will develop, but try to break them up for the sake of team harmony, and never play favourites. You should not discuss one player with another to his disadvantage, and above all, never let your boys down. Criticizing your players in public will break down their own courage and spirit and drastically weaken your own effectiveness as a coach.

SELECTING PLAYERS

Give consideration to such fundamentals as character and attitude as well as technical skill when picking your players. Often the athlete with the better character and attitude will become a much better player than a more talented athlete who lacks these qualities. The players with determination, desire, and a good attitude are best. Player personality defects will always come out when the pressure is on.

The slow learner. Some people are slow learners but often keep on learning for a longer period of time than those that seem to catch on quickly. Make sure you give the slow learner a chance. A little patience often pays off. Never forget that the record books are full of stories of athletes who at one time during their careers were discarded by an impatient coach.

Forcing the style. The coach who has very definite ideas about the kind of player he likes best is often inclined to force all his player into this particular mould. This is a serious mistake. The smart coach will do everything he can to nourish the natural style and instincts of the player. He will not try to change or rearrange them. For example, the coach may have a hard driving but awkward skater who has a high fund of natural power and aggressiveness. If an attempt was made to make him into a smooth-skating player, a good man would probably be spoiled. Just as the person talented in music might be a failure as an accountant, so will a player naturally equipped to play a smooth, smart game, be spoiled if he is made to play a rough, aggressive, headlong game. Utilize your players' talents; do not fight against them.

PREP TALKS

In prepping a team for the game or between periods, the best plan is to map out clearly your line of strategy, giving your inspiration, and your general instructions in a cool, calm, and well organized style. The job should be done as clearly and as interestingly as possible, but it should not involve appeals to the emotions, except those designed to create a controlled desire to win. It is possible to motivate the squad so that they are practically foaming at the mouth and, as a result, will go out on the ice and "skate the opposition into the ice." However, this physical drive, based only on emotional appeals, can become an actual handicap to the player.

What the player will gain in physical drive he will lose in skill and intelligent play. The thing to do is to set forth the objectives calmly and coolly, working in as many suitable incentives as possible of a type that the coach knows will work with his players. The theory that "you have to hate them to win," which is often backed up with strong emotional appeals to the players to "knock 'em dead" or "go out there and kill them" has no basis in fact. In fact, it only backfires. Inspire by all means but inspire by appeal to the finer feelings, such as loyalty, duty, and the thrill of doing a great job instead of hate, anger, or resentment against wrongdoings. This is not only civilized but also most effective.

WHEN TO INSTRUCT

The average player is told too many things when he is tired. He is often lectured by the coach right after a hard session of play when all he is thinking of is getting his breath back or getting a drink of water. He is in no condition to take in any instructions. Therefore the coach during practice and games should be sure that any player he is instructing is in condition to concentrate on what he is saying. Instructing players who have just flopped on the bench after a hard session of play is not very effective. They will probably go right out and forget everything they have been told. Give them a chance to rest up a little first. The same advice applies between periods. Let the players rest and get settled away, using every possible method to hasten their physical recovery, and then talk to them.

Are you a bench wizard? Many coaches have a rather unusual conception of their job. This is true in all sports but especially so in hockey. The main mistake is believing that coaching is a matter of masterminding. The intelligent handling of a team during the game is of course very important, but there is a lot more to the coaching job than knowing when to change the player, what strategy to use, and so on. The coach should think of himself mostly as a teacher, a developer of skills who is always at work trying to increase the level of efficiency of each player and of the team as a whole. The secret of good coaching lies to a great extent along the lines of hard work and skill development, especially in the fundamentals. The coach who considers his job as mainly sitting on the bench and masterminding frequently finds himself trying to mastermind with players who are not capable of putting into action the schemes and ideas he dreams up for them.

Strengthen the weak spot. It is very easy for a coach to give up on a player who seems to have a weak spot. You often hear a coach say he dropped a certain player because although he was a good goal getter he was a poor skater, or although he was a good skater he could not carry the puck. Possibly a professional coach can afford to cast off such a player because he may be able to trade for or buy a better player. However, a coach in amateur hockey cannot do this. Instead of saying the player cannot skate or stickhandle, the coach should work to teach him. After all, that is a coach's job.

Training

In recent years, many new discoveries have been made about ways to develop higher levels of physical conditioning and skill in all sports. These new techniques and philosophies are now being used in hockey, especially since the 1972 Canada-Soviet series and the entry of European players into the National Hockey League exposed the inadequacies of traditional conditioning programs in North America.

Most NHL players now stay in shape year-round. Their teams hire physiologists to prescribe training programs, some of them tailored to individual players. The game is played at higher intensity by bigger, stronger, better-conditioned athletes than it was even 10 years ago.

The potential for such improvements in what was billed as "the world's fastest game" was predicted by research as far back as 1950, which proved conclusively that a player who used modern training techniques could develop far better physical condition and greater physical efficiency than was previously believed possible. You don't hear much about "playing yourself into shape" any more, but it was the standard approach back then. Training camp was simply a period of suffering as players paid the price for a summer of idleness and easy living.

In the pages of this chapter, the basic factors that should be incorporated into any comprehensive hockey training system are set forth.

ATTITUDE

The success or failure of a training program depends in large part upon the attitude of the coach. If he is lackadaisical or is not too interested in the program, the players will have the same attitude. If he believes, as every coach should, that the training and conditioning phase of hockey is the most important, the players will reflect his attitude.

Analysis of hockey or any other game makes it very evident that physical condition and efficiency form the structure on which everything else is built. It does not matter how fast the player skates, how accurately he shoots, how cleverly he dekes, how artfully he checks, or how brilliantly the coach directs the team, if the opposing squad has an edge in conditioning, the other advantages may be lost. The best strategy a coach can stress is to get his team into a higher level of conditioning and physical efficiency than the opposition and then use this superior conditioning to his advantage by forcing the play until the gap between the two teams grows so large that the better conditioned team takes over.

Although training and conditioning are so important, they are still overlooked to a large extent by those directing the average age level hockey team, even at the major junior level. For example, an analysis of the attention paid to the training and conditioning of a team that won the World Hockey Championship many years ago brought to light the fact that no special or detailed attempt was made to utilize many of the modern techniques of developing condition, physical efficiency, and physique. To the query, "They won the championship, didn't they?" we might answer, "Yes, they did, but only because the opposition they had to overcome paid even less attention to this phase of the game."

Junior players coming to professional training camps no longer have an edge in physical condition over the established pros, according to physiologist Howie Wenger, training consultant to the Los Angeles Kings. There was a time when they could shine in camp and catch the coaches' attention while the veterans nursed their aches and pains. Now, the pros train year-round while many juniors do not, in part because practice time is limited and the coaches put their priorities on other aspects of development.

There is a great opportunity at every level of hockey for the coach and player to learn and then utilize the great mass of information available to them.

One of the reasons why so few hockey coaches emphasize the training and conditioning program is because they are faced with the problem of time. It is difficult to fit conditioning into a schedule that cuts into practice hours. The solution is to conduct "tempo" practices that condition as well as teach skills to players, and to sell players on off-ice and off-season conditioning. The coach who puts in such a system soon will be able to prove the efficiency of it through results.

In most cases, the average player likes to play; he does not want to spend time training and conditioning. He has this attitude mainly because any training or conditioning he has done has probably been strictly hard work with no fun or interest attached to it whatsoever. He associates it with fatigue and other unpleasant symptoms and thus resists the idea in every way he can. The result is that unless the coach is willing to start a conflict with his players he does not emphasize training and conditioning. He spoils them, just as a parent often does a child who doesn't want to be bothered eating the right foods or going to bed on time.

However, a scientifically planned, well organized, and expertly directed training and conditioning program can be interesting and fun. This also is something that the individual player should keep in mind when he is trying to organize a self-improvement plan. His first step should be the organization of a training and conditioning plan based on sound, up-to-date techniques, and knowledge.

GENERAL CONDITIONING

The term general conditioning refers to the training designed to condition the heart, lungs, and body for the task of playing hockey. This type of training consists primarily of different types of skating drills. The objective is to develop the player's stamina so he can go for an entire game at full effort without suffering fatigue. The level of conditioning most desirable is one that accounts for the possibility of unexpected physical demands on the player – if the game is played at an unusually fast pace, if the ice is slow, if there are injuries that make it necessary for certain players to do extra work, or if certain players, because of their particular skill, play more frequently than usual to combat pressure by the opposing team. With this in mind, the coach, when putting into effect his training and conditioning program, should make sure it will develop the player's condition so that he will have sufficient reserve to meet such demands with efficiency.

Though hockey is a fast and rugged game, it is quite possible to develop the player's condition to such a high degree that he can play his hardest without suffering fatigue even in the closing stages of the game. In organizing the training program the coach should also remember that the fewer players he has the higher the level of condition they must develop. For example, if he has only two forward lines they must have a higher level of conditioning than if he can use three.

These days, knowledgeable coaches try to play their lines in shifts lasting no longer than 40 to 45 seconds. This is a result of the discovery that longer periods of hard effort promote rapid formation of lactic acid, the by-product of hard muscular work. Even well-conditioned players will start to "tie-up" after long periods of intense effort, like a 400 metre runner at the end of a race. Prevention of fatigue acid build-up through short shifts is the best way to assure game-long effort and physical efficiency.

Another thing to consider is the general calibre of the team. The less skilful they are, the more important their condition. No matter how skilful the players are, the conditioning factor remains important, but an especially high level of condition, accompanied by enthusiasm and determination, can often compensate to a large degree for a low level of skill. The coach who finds his player strength is not quite up to the opposition can often even things up and more by emphasizing the development of conditioning so that his players can use it as a weapon, forcing the pace until their superior conditioning begins to pay off.

There is great opportunity in the training and conditioning phase of the game for both the coach and individual player. Tests made of some one hundred players of different age limits and skill levels, made during the middle of the hockey season, when the players were supposedly in peak condition, indicated that no one single player had developed more than seventy-five per cent of his possible potential. That just playing hockey will develop the needed condition is a popular fallacy. For one thing, the player will adjust the pace at which he plays according to his condition. Conversely, his condition will be governed by the pace at which he plays. This means that if at any time the pace is increased, his conditioning will not be up to the extra effort. Just as a boxer must do other training besides boxing, so must the hockey player do other things besides merely playing the game to develop top level condition sufficient to meet emergencies and sustain top level effort.

A good comparison is found in track and field. If the track and field coach is training an athlete to run a 4.20 mile he does not try to condition the man by having him run at a 4.20 pace. The overload principle, which is designed to develop the athlete's condition to the highest possible peak, is used. Because such methods have not been used very often in hockey training, the hockey player rarely plays a whole game at his peak physical effort. If the hockey coach conditioned the player so that he was at his condition peak and then, through the use of good coaching developed in the player the character and desire necessary to keep him working at full speed, he would soon have a team that would be the envy of the league in which it played.

According to a survey of games at all levels of hockey, the work level of the defending team took its biggest drop immediately following the scoring of a goal against them. Their work level also dropped sharply after the opposing team scored a goal that put it into a two goal lead. As more goals were scored, the work level dropped more and more. A special work let-down was noticed by the scored-on players on the ice at the time the first goal of the game was scored. These let-downs are probably due to the mental setback with its accompanying short drop in morale and hope. The opposite reaction was noticed in the players on the team who had just scored a goal. Their work level increased sharply right afterwards.

Though some players sustained a regular work level throughout the game, the average player was hot or cold. Some players, for example, would work very hard the first time they were on the ice during a period of play, and then their work level would drop as much as forty per cent the next time they were sent out. All the players show the falling of work levels during the last fifteen minutes of the last period, some of them dropping as much as fifty per cent from their previous best work record. This tendency was also noticed during the end of every period. However, this was not because of poor attitude but through fatigue.

Coaches of higher level hockey teams could probably use a regular system of measuring the work level of their players to good advantage. It would be one sure way of discovering which players are giving their best.

In order to test the usual work level of the average hockey player and then compare it to his potential, our researchers conducted a series of tests. In these tests the players participating had to skate fifty yards at full speed, stop quickly, and come back at full speed to the starting point. Then they skated slowly up and down the same course. Then they stopped and remained stationary for ten seconds, went twenty-five yards at full speed, stopped again, and stayed stationary for ten seconds. They then went to the end of the twenty-five yard course, stopped for ten seconds and came back down the course to the starting point, stopping and starting again. This was done in bursts of three minutes with a rest of six minutes between each burst. The players continued for a full hour, resting every eighteen minutes for ten minutes. Every effort was made to make the test as close to the actual playing situation as possible and still make it simple to measure. The distance each player covered in his test was noted, as well as the speed with which he made the various bursts. The degree to which he slowed down as the test continued was also carefully checked. The squad was then separated into two sections. One section continued playing hockey in the normal way, the other section took part in a special training program. At the end of three weeks, the test was repeated.

In every single case those who took part in the special training program showed improvement ranging anywhere from ten per cent to forty-five per cent. In the group which merely continued playing hockey as before, only three showed any improvement and this only slight. The majority stayed approximately the same, but twenty-five per cent showed a dropping off, some of them as much as twenty per cent. This test was augmented by other selected individual tests all of which showed the same general results. All players taking the special work reported a much greater ability to go hard in the games they played, and mentioned the disappearance of many problems such as feeling heavy-legged, feeling sick, getting stitches, headaches, and other symptoms of physical strain and fatigue. They all said their spirit and sense of enjoyment was increased a great deal. Quite a few claimed that they played more skilfully. The most popular expression reported was, "Boy, I can really fly now!"

Other tests were made over set distances from 440 yards to two miles. In these tests the players tried to keep up as high a level of continuous effort as possible. They were actually time trials. The times turned in during the first trials were compared to the times made after three weeks of special training with the group separated into two sections, those not doing any special training and those taking part in a special training program. In every case the results were the same. Those who had taken part in the special training improved their times remarkably. Those who merely continued to play hockey showed little improvement, or a decrease. Other methods of measurement were also used such as special tests for cardiovascular response. These results corresponded with the results of the other tests. It was interesting to note that a special group who stayed with the training and conditioning program showed a continuing improvement in endurance during the season. When the physical test was made at the end of the season those who had merely been playing hockey were not only below those who had continued to train, but were also well below those who had only taken part in the three week test.

These tests not only indicated that the average hockey player is playing far under his physical potential, but also that it is comparatively easy to increase it. The training and conditioning program used in these tests was based on exactly the same principles as suggested in this book. These principles do not represent anyone's theories but have been developed from the study of basic principles of training that have been tested and adopted in other fields.

Some of these tests will supply the coach an idea of the condition of his players at various times during the season. For example, he can use the mile distance as a measuring rod. He can test his players over this distance at the start of the season and then at set periods during the season. He will be able to tell how the conditioning work is going. Generally, the players whose endurance tests are highest should be able to sustain a faster pace during the game than those with lower ratings. These tests can also give the coach a system of comparing his players' potential physical state with their actual work habits in games. Such tests can also be very useful in measuring the attitude of the player. The lazy player who does not work at his peak level during games will be quickly exposed during such tests.

To increase the value of the training program and add interest, the coach or the individual player can set objectives. For example, his objective might be to have every player on the team able to skate a mile in three minutes, ten seconds by a certain date. Then he can renew the objectives by improving this standard. The objective set will, of course, be governed by the age of the players and the facilities available. By using such a test, which can be organized on a highly competitive basis, the training program can be made more interesting and enjoyable for the players. Club records can be established in all the various tests and these will give increased incentive to all concerned. If careful records are kept of the tests, it will be easy to detect when something physical or mental goes wrong with a player. Then the necessary procedure can be followed to find out the trouble and eliminate it. All such tests should be well organized and conducted carefully like any other phase of hockey development work.

Physiological implications: A number of technical terms are now used to describe types of training work and the body's responses to them. For the hockey player and coach, here are some of the most important.

Aerobic training: This is your basic long, slow distance work in which the body depends on oxygen for fuel. In general, aerobic conditioning can be said to take place at training at medium intensity. This develops the heart and lungs, the oxygen transport system, and the ability of the muscles to absorb oxygen. Good aerobic capacity enables the athlete to endure longer and recover quicker from anaerobic effort. A strong aerobic capacity is the foundation on which the ability to do hard, anaerobic work depends.

Anaerobic training: This refers to muscular work done in the absence of oxygen – the principal concern of the hockey player. Simply put, this means the athlete is working so hard the heart and lungs are unable to keep up with the muscles' demand for oxygen, and so the body switches over to its so-called alactic energy system, in which stored energy supplies are used. The most important source of such energy is glycogen, a sugar synthesized from carbohydrate foods and drinks. As glycogen is "burned" by working muscles, lactic acid (fatigue acid) is produced. Production rises dramatically after 40 seconds or so of hard effort and the muscles lose their capacity to contract quickly. The athlete then starts to "tie-up."

During rest periods, most of the lactic acid is flushed from the muscles. Some of it is resynthesized by the liver into more energy fuel.

This is why a strong aerobic base is important. First, it postpones the time at which the muscles must begin to draw on stored energy fuel. Second, it hastens recovery between shifts, between periods of play, and between games. All recovery in the anaerobic systems after being used is done by the aerobic system.

A player will be unable to develop his alactic system effectively without a good aerobic base. This is why aerobic training should be emphasized during the early portions of the off ice training period.

CONDITIONING TECHNIQUE

General conditioning technique. The following is the general technique that was used during the tests and which has been thoroughly tested over several years.

Pre-season. In preparing for the start of the hockey season, it is wise to work on certain fundamentals of conditioning so that the player will be in sound condition for the training plan once the season gets under way. Since hockey is definitely a lung, heart, and leg activity, the best possible pre-season conditioners are running and cycling. Skating is, of course, ideal, but ice is usually not available. In-line roller skates are an excellent alternative.

However, just going for a long, easy run is not sufficient. Certainly it will develop stamina of a kind, but not the kind near the level of conditioning desired. The ideal pre-season program should include a lot of sprint work as well as distance work. In the early part of the off-season, the emphasis should be on longer, slow runs to develop oxygen uptake – the ability to take oxygen in and utilize it efficiently – and cardiovascular efficiency. Since hockey is a game of short speed bursts and agility movements, this type of training should be included too. As the competitive season approaches, the emphasis shifts more and more to speed or "anaerobic" work – sprints, muscle endurance/strength work such as one-legged hopping, 30 to 40 second bursts of all-out running. Do not neglect the longer, "aerobic" training altogether, however.

First day. Free, relaxed jogging for two or three minutes, then ten to fifteen fast bursts of fifteen yards, slowing down gradually and jogging back to the starting point between each burst. These bursts should be taken from a standing start with the feet comfortably apart, knees slightly bent, body square to the direction the athlete will be running. One start should be made with the left leg moving first, the next with the right. This should be alternated throughout the sprints. The athlete should be helped by somebody else who can start him by a hard clap of the hands. It is important that the athlete start from some sort of command because this will give his reflexes a better training. This work not only develops wind and heart conditioning but also leg strength and a certain amount of agility and co-ordination, which will be carried over into hockey playing when the season starts. After the session of short sprints, the athlete should jog off his fatigue by doing two or three minutes of slow, relaxed jogging. He can then do a longer, slow run at a steady pace for cardiovascular endurance.

Second day. On the second day, the athlete should do some distance work but not at a steady pace. He should use the system known to track experts as Fartlek, which is a Swedish word meaning speed play or variation. This is a good way of developing endurance that can be utilized in any physical activity. It is especially good for the hockey player because in hockey he must do a lot of pace changing.

This system is based on the overload principle. Running at an even pace is the most economical way to run because continually accelerating or decelerating throws an added strain on the body. Fartlek involves many pace changes and thus makes the body work at peak level.

Here is a basic Fartlek suitable for a hockey player.
- Slow, easy running – 4 minutes.
- Sprint 20 yards, walk 50 yards – 4 minutes.
- Good pace running – 5 or 10 minutes.
- Jog slowly – 2 minutes.
- Running backwards at best speed 25 yards, turn and run forward best speed 25 yards – 1 minute.
- Walk – 4 minutes.
- Hop on left foot 25 yards, hop on right foot 25 yards – 1 minute.
- Jog easily – 2 minutes.
- Run – 30 seconds, fast as possible.

Doing this workout in the country where there are hills is a very good idea. It is more fun and more beneficial under such conditions. It should be done on grass or soft ground rather than on roads or a track. A cooldown period of easy jogging and walking for about five minutes should wind up each of these workouts.

Third day. Same as first day.

Fourth day. Same as second day.

Fifth day, and sixth day. Same as first and second days.

Seventh day. Rest.

Each day the athlete should try to increase the amount of work he does even if it is by only a little bit. Six weeks of such workouts should put the athlete into a wonderful basic condition. Three to four weeks would also do a good job. The coach can either have his players do this under his supervision or he can suggest they do it in groups or individually. Wherever possible, supervision should be used because of the human inclination to take things easy. Individual players, working on their own, should get a friend or two to work with them.

Special exercises. In preparing the player for the actual training program, special exercises designed to develop his all-round muscle flexibility, co-ordination, and relaxation control should be used. Particular attention should be paid to any known weak spots such as tight back thigh muscles, hips or knees, weak ankles or wrists, and so on. During this pre-season period much valuable work can be done to develop mechanical efficiency and physique. Such work, if scientifically planned and organized, will not only improve the player's general condition but will greatly improve the complete machine with which he plays hockey.

However, the exercises should be of the right type with the program carefully devised for the purpose, otherwise no particular value will come from them. A haphazard routine of ordinary physical jerks cannot be compared to a properly devised program. The coach who includes a half hour of specific exercises five or six times a week in his team's pre-season training program, or the individual working on his own who does the same thing, will obtain very definite and favourable results. This is not a theory but a fact that has been proven by the many tests made by our researchers. The exercise program should be based on special exercises listed under the heading Mechanical Efficiency and Physique and scheduled as suggested later in this section.

Summary. During the pre-season period the player should also start paying special attention to his diet and other factors that develop and sustain his basic health and fitness. The smart athlete will watch such factors year round and if he does not he should start to emphasize them when he begins his pre-season program. If the athlete is over or under-weight he should take all the necessary measures to eliminate the condition by the time the actual hockey training season starts. It is a bad habit to wait until it gets under way because this will make the program at that time a lot tougher and harder to take. Then, too, if such things are left until the actual start of the season it will not be possible for the player to concentrate on other features of the program. As a result, he will always be behind the others in condition and skill development.

Probably the worst habit an athlete can acquire is the on-and-off condition situation in which he is either training hard to get in condition or doing everything he can to get out of condition. This sort of living puts great strain on the body and is one reason why some athletes have a much shorter career than others. Examples of this type of living are found in the athlete who smokes or lets his appetite run rampant just because he is not training. The level of physical efficiency possible for the athlete who lives a sound training life all the time is much higher than that of an on and off player. This sound training life will keep him fit and happy after his competitive playing days are over.

Research shows that athletes who run into health problems after their competitive days are over are usually those who have been on-and-offers during their playing career. A typical example is the athlete who, after he finishes playing, puts on a lot of weight and thus does the worst possible thing he can to shorten his lifespan and ruin his health. The coach who sells his players the idea of observing good training rules all the time will be doing both them and himself a big favour. The athlete working on his own who follows this principle will be making the smartest play he could possible make. The ideal situation is to keep in good shape all the time and intensify the training effort when the season starts. This is the way truly top level condition is developed and sustained.

A player who doesn't bother to prepare himself for the hockey training season is usually the one who resists the training program. The wise coach will try to organize a pre-season program so that once the season gets under way he will have less trouble with the lead swinger who resists the idea of making himself tired and aching to get into shape.

In season. Once the season starts the following program should be used. The intensity with which it is started should be governed by the condition of the players when they report and the length of time available for training before the first game. It is important that the program start easily and build up gradually. It should therefore be begun as early as possible in the season. If the training program starts off with a bang with a lot of heavy work, it may well do more harm than good.

Heavy work done before the various muscles and vital organs of the body are ready for it can harm the player both mentally and physically. On the physical side it will make the players prone to injuries such as muscle pulls and strains. Various muscles can be over-stressed and strained so that they will not regain their efficiency throughout the whole season, thus interfering with the player's skill development level and condition, and protection from injury. Players who are conditioned too quickly are prone to develop a loggy, stiff muscle tone that will bother them throughout the season. The straining of the cardiovascular system when hard work is started too soon is also a risk. Conditioning takes time. When an attempt is made to rush it too fast, the end will not justify the means. This is a very important fact that every coach and player should keep utmost in their mind.

One reason why you often hear a coach say "I don't know what's the matter with the team. They seem to have everything but they just can't get going" is because the team is suffering from the bad effects of a poorly organized training program in which too much was attempted too soon.

When the training program starts off too hard it is also possible that it will have a detrimental effect on the player's mental attitude. For instance, if the player suffers many unpleasant fatigue symptoms in the early part of the training program, it will be only natural for him to resist hard work. Such experiences can seriously affect the player's ability to concentrate on other phases of the early season practice session. A program conducted in this way will develop a lot of unenthusiastic athletes; you cannot very well blame anybody for trying to duck this type of training. Many poor mental attitudes toward physical effort are also developed in this way.

It may seem strange to bring up the subject of conditioned reflexes and neuroses in a book on hockey, but they are present just as they are present in any activity of life. For example, the player may turn out for a training program and be forced to work far past his level of basic conditioning. If he is very keen and anxious to make the team or has a well developed sense of responsibility or is a "try guy" by nature, he will be much more likely to pick up conditioned reflexes or neuroses from unpleasant fatigue experiences. This means that the best types are most likely to be hurt.

A good example of what can happen is when a player training hard in conditioning work gets a severe cramp, or a siege of nausea, or a painful pressure headache. From then on, his mind will associate this unpleasant experience (a cramp, for example), which may have scared him half to death (especially if it was on the left side), with hard work, etc. The player will find it very difficult to continue to work hard during conditioning. The same thing will happen during games. He may want to drive himself hard but his mental attitude, which is actually a neurosis, will prevent him. This is very common and is perhaps the story behind why many players, some very prominent, who seem to take it easy for some unaccountable reason. Such experiences can often preclude the possibility of the person ever learning to drive himself to full physical effort.

Neuroses can be avoided to some degree by explaining thoroughly to each player what causes the various aches and pains and unpleasant feeling he suffers after hard physical effort. If he understands them and knows that they are not serious and are not an indication of some physical weakness, he will be less inclined to develop an automatic reflex against hard physical effort. In straightening out an effort neurosis the technique is first to explain what the original unpleasantness was, that it did not indicate anything serious, and then gradually build up the player's condition, seeing to it that he does not have any more bad experiences.

The first step in training technique during the season is to make a very thorough physical evaluation of the player's condition. He should be given a complete medical examination with special attention paid to the heart, nerves, and physical condition. No player should be allowed to play a game such as hockey without first being thoroughly checked.

The individual player, and the coach of poorly organized teams particularly, may need to be reminded to take this into consideration. The
coach who lets his players participate without such a check is not
worthy of the name.

The next step should be to check the player's physique in order to see
what weak points need strengthening. The items checked should be
strength, flexibility of muscles and joints, ability to relax at will, and
heart efficiency. By staging the tests listed in the section Mechanical
Efficiency and Physique, it is possible for the person in charge of the
training program to organize his training so that everyone gets the kind
of work he requires. The special exercise section of the training
program should be conducted either before or after the actual ice work.
It is most effective when done in an organized group but if this is not
possible, the coach should assign these exercises as homework after
making sure they have been well demonstrated. Frequent follow-up
tests should be made in order to measure the athlete's progress and
whether or not he is doing his homework. The individual player
working on his own can do this special work by himself or with a friend
or two to whom he has sold the idea.

The next step is to measure the playing condition of the players and
setting objectives. This can be done by staging time trials over distances
from the quarter mile to two miles. Each player should be tested over at
least two of these distances, for example, over the quarter mile and over
the mile, or over the half mile and two miles. This does not take very
much time because the players can be worked in groups. This is usually
a good idea because it brings in the competitive element, thus acting as
an incentive to the player. In the first week quite a few tests should be
made, so as to establish a good average level. In setting objectives, after
two weeks' training, the coach can use the best times turned in as the
standard for all those who are slower, giving the person making the best
time the same standard improved by five per cent.

The coach might also set a percentage improvement goal according to
the times each individual turns in as compared to the best performance.
For example, the man who skates a three minute and fifteen second time
for the mile in his early season test can be given a three per cent improvement standard for which to aim. The player turning in a four minute
and fifteen second time can be given a fifteen or twenty per cent

improvement standard. The main thing is to give each player a definite goal. The first objective should be two weeks away with others set at intervals of the same length during the season.

Measurements should also be taken of the player's ability to do certain exercises for which objectives have been set. These measurements should also be checked at frequent intervals. The objectives must be attainable. If they are too tough, they won't act as incentives but be a source of discouragement. The best performance can be the standard. A measurement that should be featured is a heart recovery test. The ability of the heart to recover after exercise offers a very good system of judging its efficiency and condition.

First take the athlete's pulse when lying down, then when standing, and then after three minutes of stationary jogging. Then the pulse rate should be taken at two minute intervals until it returns to normal. As the player's conditioning improves, his natural pulse rate will be slower, the difference between his lying and standing pulse rate will be less and his return to normal will be accomplished more quickly. Any unusual results of such tests should be checked by a medical expert. In doing this test, smokers respond to conditioning more slowly than non-smokers and generally have a poorer score. Well-conditioned athletes will show a resting pulse rate of around sixty, a difference of ten or less between the lying and standing rate, and a quick recovery after exercise.

Once the measurement and testing work is done, the actual program can start. This program can be divided into two parts. Conditioning can be developed at the same time as skill work is being done. For example, a good deal of conditioning can be done through the use of skating drills and the other phases of practice such as scrimmage. The drills listed in the first chapter for skating agility development are excellent because they will not only condition the wind and heart, but also the various muscles used in different skating manoeuvres.

Give the players frequent rest intervals so they can sustain a higher work capacity in each drill. The principle of hard bursts of effort for short periods of time separated by frequent rests will bring much better results than the all too popular system of driving the player until he drops. During the early part of training, no player should be pushed beyond normal fatigue. The principle should be to increase the work level a little bit each day so that the player gradually develops his stamina. He must, of course, work hard on the program but it should be graduated. He should be left with enough strength and energy to carry over to the next day, or he will be in poor condition for the following day's workout. Once the player has developed a high level of condition, he can be worked as hard as possible but for the build-up period great care should be taken.

Special methods should be used in the training program that will develop a level of condition far exceeding that needed to play an ordinary game of hockey without fatigue. This is the overload section of training where the idea is to develop the player's endurance and condition until he is performing at his absolute peak of physical efficiency. Every attempt should be made to increase this peak gradually throughout the season so that he is able to play every game a little harder, with plenty of reserve left for special situations. The average hockey coach can accomplish a great deal of improvement in this section of the training program. This type of work should always be done at the end of the practice or, if possible, during a special session a couple of hours after a practice session in which most of the emphasis has been on skill development. If sufficient practice time is not available to do a good job, the player should be given homework with frequent tests made to see that he is doing it. This is quite possible because the kind of work suggested can be done by any individual or small group on any suitable sheet of ice.

In developing a system of training the hockey coach can learn a great deal from the track and field expert because the track and field expert's main job is to develop top level endurance and physical efficiency. They are his main objectives. A tremendous amount of research and testing has been done in this sport and many of these principles can be adapted with good results to hockey training.

The hockey player can be compared, in the type of physical effort he must make, to the sprinter, as both, during competition, must drive themselves at peak speed for short periods of time with opportunities to rest between them. The sprinter may run four or five, or perhaps even more heats. The hockey player must drive himself over shorter distances and with more periods of rest but over a longer period of time. They need, therefore, similar endurance factors. They must be able to explode into action and achieve a high degree of physical effort that does not have to be sustained for very long. They must be able to recover quickly so as to be ready to repeat and keep on doing this over a fairly long period of time without losing any of the ability to explode quickly and travel fast. However, as the hockey player must continue his explosive efforts over a longer period of time he needs a higher level of endurance than does a sprinter. These facts are all taken into consideration in the suggested program.

The basic principle on which the training should be based is what the track coaches call the "over and under." The athlete must go at faster speeds than usual, over shorter distances than usual, repeating them more frequently than usual. This develops a great work capacity. A much higher amount of fatigue acid is developed than normally. Thus when the athlete develops the tolerance for such a high amount of fatigue acid, he can sustain a much greater work load. This is the under principle which also emphasizes speed, co-ordination, and reflex training.

The over principle is that the athlete should perform his activity for longer periods of time at a slower pace than is ordinarily used. For example, the hockey player who has to make a physical effort for a minute or more at a fairly fast pace should work in training for longer periods at a slower pace. As the athlete's ability to perform both his under and over distance objectives improves, so will his ability to perform his normal activity improve. As the season progresses, the amount of work done should be increased so that the condition is always improving. If the player shows a tendency to be weaker at one type of training than another, he should be given more of the type of work at which he makes the poorest showing. Careful time checks should be made during all conditioning work. A good starting schedule would be as follows:

Begin with a warm-up of slow, easy skating with the odd burst of speed for a couple of minutes. Then do ten to fifteen 25-yard all-out sprints, slowing down gradually and returning to the starting position at a slow but even pace. Each burst should be started with the players taking a definite stance, feet comfortably apart, knees bent, and body square to the direction in which the burst is to be taken. Each burst should be started with a different leg. Repeat this quickly and as soon as possible. The players can be worked in groups and should be started by a signal, usually with a whistle. Care should be taken that each effort is an all-out one with times taken of each 25 yard burst. An effort should be made to sustain the time until the last several bursts when an attempt should be made to make the best performances of the workout. If this work is to be effective there must be no loitering or resting between the bursts. They should come one after the other. At their completion the players should cool off with two or three minutes of skating, starting out at a good pace, and then gradually slowing right down. As the season progresses, the number of bursts should be increased and every effort should be made to sustain a better speed in each burst. The players should be worked until they have done at least three or four more bursts than they think they can handle. The value of such conditioning really starts when the players are tired. This system teaches the players that they can go hard even when apparently physically finished. It proves to them the difference between the mental and physical limits, a subject dealt with later.

Occasionally an all-out endurance test should be conducted with the players doing bursts as long as they can before they drop below a certain level. For example, a three second time limit might be set for each 25 yard burst. The player is beaten when he cannot sustain this speed. Done on a competitive basis, after the players have developed a good basic condition, this can add a lot of interest and incentive to the workouts.

When doing this training, it is best to group your fast, slow, and medium skaters with each other so as to keep up a good competitive background. To add variety, the distance should be varied. Occasionally the players should do this skating backwards or pushing a teammate ahead of them, or carrying the puck and then without a stick. As much variation as possible should be used as long as the basic principle is observed. This type of training is not only a wonderful conditioner but is a great way to develop quick break skill, especially if your game plan emphasizes quick breaks.

In other systems of distance work there should be a definite distance established which would take at least one and a half to twice the length of time of any session the player is on the ice. For example, if he is used to playing a 40 second shift, he should do over-distance training for 60 to 80 seconds. You can also use longer distances, a mile, a mile and a half, or more. These distances should be done keeping up a steady pace. The players should try to cover the distance as quickly and steadily as possible. The competitive angle should be used by either staging a workout in groups or on the time trial basis. If desired, the players can take the puck along with them or they can skate without it. Another easy warm-up should precede each workout and an easy cooling off period should finish it up.

As the season progresses, the time it takes to go this distance should gradually improve. Occasionally the distance of this workout can be varied by cutting it down or increasing it a little. It can also be done half backwards and half forwards, or with any variation of backward or forward skating. Every now and then this type of over-distance training should be changed to a Fartlek type workout in which the players should go twice the distance of their usual over distance workout, mixing up the pace and style of skating at frequent intervals. The variations used can be constantly changed by the coach. The coach should keep in mind that the more interest and variety there is in the training assignments, the more interest the players will take in them and the better the results will be.

The variations included should be from very slow skating to all-out short bursts. They should include backward skating, one leg skating, stopping and starting, and every variation the coach can work in. They should start with a fairly long period of easy skating. Each section of hard effort should be approached with either slow skating, or medium paced skating. There is no better way of developing condition than to use this type of workout. As the need for more condition develops, the Fartlek type workout should be used more frequently over longer distances.

The coach with little or no practice time at his disposal can only assign such work on a homework basis. However, he can give regular tests to see if the work is being done. He can also ask for reports of how the player is getting along from the player himself. If no ice is available on which the player can do this sort of ice conditioning, as is sometimes the case, he can accomplish much the same results through running, using the same general system, doing it in running shoes instead of on skates. If the player is keen enough to do this, he will be able to develop a condition that will make it easier to play hard when game time rolls around. This is one sure way to avoid that unpleasant experience which often comes to the player who cannot practise and whose only hockey comes once a week during a game, when he gets so tired playing the game that he can never enjoy it or do well.

The coach can adapt this training system to his own facilities. The main thing is to observe the general principles, especially the inclusion of variety and the competitive angle, with careful records kept of all time trials and so on. Such a system will keep the players increasing their level of interest. During the latter part of the season, in the drive for a playoff spot or to prepare for the playoffs, the coach should carefully evaluate the weak spots in the condition of his team and then organize his training program to do the jobs most needed. For example, if a player shows good endurance but does not break quickly enough and seems to lack explosiveness, he should be given extra speed work. If his speed is good but he lacks endurance, he should be given more over distance work.

It may be the team is simply over fatigued from too many games and too many physical demands. There may be a residual lactic acid build up that cannot be dispensed. In this case, rest, rather than added work may be the cure.

From three to five weeks of early season training should get the players into peak condition. From here, a careful check should be kept through tests. If the conditioning seems to fall off then more work should be given. There is no danger of over working the player once he is in good condition as long as he is getting plenty of rest, and is paying careful attention to his diet. See the section on Staleness for further information.

MECHANICAL EFFICIENCY AND PHYSIQUE

In this section of the training program the objective is to develop the player's muscle length, balance, flexibility, all-round strength, co-ordination, and so on, so that his mechanical efficiency will be developed to the highest possible level and thus have a beneficial effect on his physical condition and playing skill. The development of controlled relaxation by the player is also a subject that is included in this chapter. The following is a list of special exercises and drills that will do the job most efficiently. The coach or player should study them, giving priority to the ones that will do the job most needed.

All of them should be done on a regular basis with emphasis on those for which there seems a special need. It should be remembered that these exercises will not only develop mechanical efficiency and physique but will also serve a useful purpose in creating the kind of muscles and the physical efficiency that make injury less likely or less severe. The player who has done them regularly will have a sense of confidence and physical tone that will be unknown to one who overlooks them.

Flexibility and muscle length. Tests indicate that the higher the flexibility and the longer the muscles, the greater their endurance, efficiency, and power. Then, too, the flexible, long-muscled athlete is much less prone to injury. The athlete who has tight, short, bunchy muscles and inflexible joints should pay special attention to the exercises in this section. Many of these exercises can also act as tests that the coach or player can use to measure flexibility and muscle length. The degree of difficulty in performing them can be the measuring rule. The greater the difficulty, the more the exercises are needed.

(Editor's note: Today's research indicates that stretches held over a longer period of time, 30 to 50 seconds, have a greater effect on increasing flexibility.)

Feet, ankles, and lower legs. It is important that the player's feet and ankles be strong and flexible because they have to do the majority of the work. You may find the following exercises are very useful.

- Lie flat on the back on the floor with the legs straight out in front. Reach forward with the toes as far as possible pulling the heels back as far as possible at the same time. Stretch hard for ten seconds. Relax. Then move the toes back toward the shin bones as far as possible and stretch forward with the heels. Hold for ten seconds and relax.

- From the same position on the floor as given in the first exercise, proceed as follows. Lift the foot off the floor twelve inches and then rotate it in as wide circles as possible, first going to the left, then the right. As the foot circles, the toes should be stretched out to the side, to the front, and back toward the shin as far as possible. Do for ten seconds. This can also be done without lifting the legs off the floor if the feet are extended over the edge of a bench. Repeat the exercise with the other foot.

- Stand with feet comfortably apart, toes pointing straight ahead. Then move hips to the right as far as possible so that you are on the outside edge of the right foot, inside edge of the left. Move to the side as far as possible and then rock back to the other side, moving your hips well to the left so that you come up on the outside of the left foot, inside of the right foot. Rock back and forth in this way, going as far to the side as possible. Start slowly, and gradually increase the speed. This exercise can also be done on the ice with the skates on. In fact it is even more helpful when done this way.

- Lie flat on the floor, feet out in front. Clench the toes as tightly as possible and hold for ten seconds. Stretch the toes so they separate as much as possible. Hold for ten seconds, start over.

- Stand an arm's length away from the wall. Place the hands on the wall. Keeping the feet absolutely flat, especially the heels, gradually move the feet backwards in a series of shuffling steps until the feet are as far away from the wall as you can get them and still keep the hands flat on the wall. Now lower the body a bit by moving the hands down the wall a little and then hold this position for ten seconds. Spend from one to two minutes on this exercise. If it is done properly, the athlete will feel a real pull in the back of his ankles and lower leg muscles.

Knees. There is no more important part of the body to the hockey player than the knees because they play such an important part in the skating action.

- Stand with feet well apart. Then turn the knees in toward each other as far as possible. Keeping the position, gradually lower the knees as close to the floor as you can. Hold for five seconds and then return to the original position. Each day try to spread the feet farther apart, thus increasing the difficulty of the exercise. This exercise can be done on-ice.

- Stand with the feet comfortably apart. Then place the weight on the left foot and lift the right knee in front of you until the foot is about six to eight inches off the floor. Then keeping the knee still and the lower leg relaxed, move the foot in wide circles to the left and then to the right. Do this six times to either side, then swing the foot as far to the left and as far to the right as possible, still keeping the knee still. Then do it with your weight on the right foot. This can be done on the ice with the skates on.

- Sit on the floor, and cross your right leg over your left so that the outside of the right ankle is on your left leg just above the knee cap. Take hold of the instep with the left hand and place the heel of the right hand on the top of the right knee. Then, as you press down with the right hand on the knee, pull the foot upwards toward you as far as it will go. Hold for ten seconds, relax, and repeat with the other leg. Do five to six times with each leg.

- Stand with feet comfortably apart, about shoulder width, then move the knees outwards in a bow-legged action so that you are up on the outside edges of your feet. Then keeping up on the outside edges of the feet, gradually go down in a deep knee bend as far as possible. When down as far as possible, hold the stretch for five seconds and then move back up to the original position.

- Spread legs as far as possible and still keep feet flat on floor. Toes should be pointed slightly outwards. Bend knees and try to lower buttocks gradually straight down until they touch the floor. Keep feet flat on floor at all times, and try to keep knees directly over feet throughout the exercise. When the lowest possible position is reached, hold and maintain as long as possible. Then, return to standing position and repeat. Do ten times. This exercise is also an excellent stretcher for the hips and muscles around the crotch.

Back thighs. The muscles running from the knee up to the buttocks on the back of the thighs are in many respects the most important muscles to the hockey player. They are not only used a great deal but may be injured easily because the average player has very short muscles in the back thigh. The longer and more flexible the back thigh muscles, the harder and faster the hockey player will be able to skate, and the longer it will be before he tires. Stretching exercises for this part of the body should be emphasized. This is especially true for goalies as these are the muscles that play an important part in the "splits" move.

- Stand with the feet comfortably apart, toes pointing straight ahead. Bend knees and place hands flat on the floor about two feet in front of the toes. Keep the feet flat on the floor, especially the heels, at all times. From this position slowly straighten the legs until they are completely straight with the back of the knees as far back as they can be moved. Hold for five seconds, then repeat with the hand moved three or four inches closer to the feet. Keep repeating with the hands moved a few inches closer to the feet each time until the legs cannot be completely straightened. Make a good effort to get the knees straight in this position and then relax and start over. Straighten the legs from each hand position two or three times. The objective is to do the exercises first with the hands flat on the floor right in front of the feet, then to place the back of the hands on the floor in this position and straighten the legs. It is important that the hands and feet be kept completely flat on the floor at all times.

- Hamstring stretch. Sit on the floor with legs out in front. With one leg, make a figure "4" with the bottom of the foot contacting the straight leg on the inside of the knee of the straight leg. Bring the upper body forward, trying to touch the underneath part of the chin with the knee of the leg that is straight out in front. The foot of the leg in front should be pointing straight up and down. The knee of this leg will tend to come up. Resist this inclination by doing your utmost to keep the back of the knee flat on the ground. Get the chin as close as possible to the knee, then bring the upper body back upright. Repeat the exercise five times, trying to get the chin closer to the leg each time. Then repeat with the other leg out in front. At first, it will be difficult to reach the objective. However, as the exercise is continued the muscles will gradually gain in length and flexibility. It is permissible to have someone pushing downward on the back of the person doing the exercise. Such pressure should be slow and gradual.

Front thigh. It is essential that the front thighs (quadricep muscles) be given a good stretching because they do a great deal of work in the hockey skating action. They are inclined to get tight and bunchy if not exercised properly. These muscles should be flexible and have a good tone because this is the spot where the charley horse injury most often strikes.

- Kneel on the floor with knees together; the feet should be held close together, toes on the floor, heels directly above the toes. Then the upper body is bent backwards as far as possible with the objective of touching the back of the head to the floor back behind the feet. This back bend position is held for ten seconds and then the upper body is returned to the upright position. Repeat ten times. It is important that the knees be together and on the floor as the upper body goes back.
- Stand as close to the wall as possible, chest touching the wall. Then lift one foot up behind and grasp the instep with the hand. Keeping the upper body flat against the wall, pull the leg back and up behind as far as possible. Do not merely pull the foot toward the buttocks, but back and up behind. The leg should be bent at a right angle at the knee.

Think of moving the knee up toward the ceiling. When the leg is back and up as far as it can be, hold the position for five seconds and then relax and do the same with the other leg. Repeat ten times with each leg. If the exercise is done properly, a real pull will be felt up the front of the upper leg. (It should be done facing a wall so that the upper body does not lean forward, thus releasing the pressure on the front of the upper leg).

Hips. The looser and more flexible the hips, the easier it will be for the hockey player to skate and manoeuvre.

- Stand with feet comfortably apart, then gradually spread feet as far as possible. Lean down, grasp ankles with hands, keeping the knees stiff. Then hold ankles trying to get head down on the floor between legs. Hold in farthest down position for count of three, then return to upright position and repeat ten times.
- Sit on floor with legs spread as far as possible, back of knees flat on ground. Reach forward and grasp ankles. Then, holding onto the ankles, try to touch top of head to the ground between the knees. Hold for count of three, resume original position, and repeat ten times.
- Lie on floor, flat on back. Bring the feet up underneath the buttocks and spread them as wide apart as possible so that they are resting on the inside edge. Then bring knees inward as far as possible, trying to touch the inside of the knees to the floor. Hold best position for count of three, relax, and repeat ten times. This is a very difficult exercise but if it is persevered with, it can do a good job stretching the hips.
- Stand with feet comfortably apart. Then place all weight on left leg. Keeping opposite leg stiff at the knee, move it in as large circles as possible at the side. Do six circles from left to right and then six the other way. Repeat with other leg. Make sure circles are large as possible.
- Stand with one shoulder and hip sideways against the wall. Keeping the other leg stiff, raise it quickly out to the side as high as possible. When lifting the leg do not point the toe upwards. Keep the inside of the foot and ankle facing the floor. Do ten times, then repeat with the other leg. This is a strenuous exercise and the athlete accordingly must force himself to lift that leg high. Done with heavy boots or pads on, it is also an excellent exercise to develop hip strength in goalkeepers.
- Sit on the floor with one leg out in front, the other out behind. Rest on the front of the back knee. The upper body should be facing the front

and the hands on either side of the upper body should be on the floor. Then gradually try to move the back knee farther and farther back until the crotch touches the floor in a "full split." When down to lowest possible position, hold the position for as long as possible. Repeat after reversing position of legs. Do five times in each position. At first the athlete may feel very crotch-bound, but perseverance will develop surprising ability.

- Stand beside a chair or table or any suitable platform that is about waist high. Then place the inside of the knee closest to the platform on the top of it so that the upper leg is at right angles to the leg on which the athlete is standing. Keeping the knee of the standing leg straight, reach down and touch the floor by the toe with both hands. Hold for a count of three, let body resume upright position and then repeat. Do six times and repeat with other leg on platform.

- Stand beside same type of platform as suggested for previous exercise (a chair or the corner of a table). Then lift the leg closest to the platform back behind. Bend the knee well and lift it as high as possible. Then bring it forward over and past the platform so that the foot can return to the original position on the floor. The action is just the same as the action of the back leg of a hurdler going over a hurdle. The knee comes up, is brought forward over the object with the foot trailing behind the knee, and then is whipped forward and down. Do slowly at first and then gradually increase speed. The upper body should be kept straight at all times and should not be allowed to lean to the side away from the platform because this will take the strain off the hips. Do fifteen times with ever increasing speed, and then repeat with other leg. This is an especially good hip stretcher and loosener.

- Stand with feet comfortably apart. Then rotate the hips in as wide a complete circle as possible, moving from right to left. Do ten times then repeat the action from left to right. Keep knees loose and relaxed. Start slowly but gradually increase speed of hip rotation.

Back. The back is important to the hockey player because much strain is thrown on it in the skating action, which is performed with the back leaned forward. Moreover, the back is a key point in absorbing the shock of body contact.

- Lie flat on the floor on stomach, hands stretched out in front of the head, palms down. Raise the upper body and hands off the floor, trying to lift upper body up and back toward the heels. Hold for a count of three and then relax. Keeping the legs still as the knees, lift the lower body as high as possible off the floor, bending it up and toward the head. Hold for a count of three and relax. Lift the upper body and lower body off the floor at the same time, trying to bring the heels and hands and head together. This is impossible but it should be the objective. Hold for a count of three and relax and then repeat each of the three movements. Do the whole exercise ten times.
- Lie flat on stomach with weight on the forearms. Slowly arch your back until a gentle stretch is noted in the lower back. This is attempting to loosen the joints or facets in the lower back. Repeat.
  Mid-section.
- Stand with feet comfortably spread, stomach well in, and chest high. Stretch hands as far as possible over head and hook thumbs together. Head should be square to the front, eyes facing dead ahead. Then bring upper body over to the left as far as possible. This position should be held for a count of three and then the upper body should be moved back and over to the other side as far as possible. This is done fifteen times to either side. It is important that the arms be kept as high as possible over the head at all times and that the body be moved directly sideways and not allowed to bend forward at all.
- Spread feet comfortably and then lean body forward from the waist so that upper body is parallel to floor, straight out from the hips. From this position, lift arms out to the side in a swan-dive position. The eyes should, of course, be looking straight down to the floor. Then, keeping arms straight out from shoulders at all times, try to reverse their position, bringing one arm up toward the ceiling, the other on down toward the floor and around to the same side as the other arm. The upper body should twist from the hips. The head should follow the arms. The legs should be kept straight at the knees at all times. Any bending of the knees releases the pressure on the mid-section. This is a twisting exercise. The upper body should be turned so much that both hands will be facing the ceiling, palms up, and the athlete will be able to look up and see it. There is a tendency

to allow the upper body to come up a little as the twist is made. This should be avoided. The right angle position with the upper body parallel to the floor should be sustained. The farthest position possible should be held for a count of three. Then assume original position and do to the other side. Do ten times on each side.

- Lie flat on floor, back of hands on floor out behind head. Legs should be comfortably apart. Keeping legs stiff, form a jackknife by bringing the hands and upper body up at the same time as the lower body and feet are brought up. The objective is to touch the toes with the fingertips at a spot directly above the hips. Make the touch and then return to original position, keeping the legs stiff at all times and then repeat.

- Lie flat on floor. Pull the stomach in and up as far as possible and puff the chest out toward the ceiling. Hold for a count of three and then deflate the chest and try to make a big mound of the stomach, pushing it up toward the ceiling as far as possible. Hold for a count of three. Alternate in this way for one minute. The athlete must make sure either the chest or the stomach is puffed as hard as possible. Every effort should be made to pull the stomach right back to the backbone and then puffed out to the ceiling as far as possible.

Chest. The higher, deeper, and more flexible the hockey player's chest, the better his condition will be. As the chest grows deeper and is held higher and develops in flexibility, the endurance will improve because the heart and lungs have more room in which to work.

- Sit on floor with ankles crossed. Then grasp insteps with hands, holding upper body upright. Pull backwards with the hands against the insteps. At the same time, pull stomach well in and puff the chest up and out as far as possible and move the shoulders back and down in an attempt to touch the shoulder blades together. This motion should be made in co-ordination with the pull against the insteps. The shoulders must not be allowed to hunch around the ears but should be kept as low as possible. Hold this big chest position for the count of five, relax, and repeat. Do ten times.

- Stand with feet comfortably apart, hands flat on lower chest just above solar plexus with the tips of the two middle fingers touching. Pull the stomach in and try to force the chest up and out to see how far the fingers can be forced apart. Hold for a count of ten, relax, and repeat. Do fifteen times. Do not use an inhale action to puff the chest, merely muscular effort to force it up and out.

Shoulders.

- Stand with feet comfortably apart, arms hanging at the sides. Move the shoulders back as far as possible, then up as far as possible, then forward as far as possible so that the points of the shoulders are going in circles. Do from back to front ten times and then from front to back ten times. Alternate four times. This exercise will not only develop shoulder flexibility but will aid in developing and strengthening the shoulder muscles so that injury will be less likely.

- Stand with your feet comfortably apart. Lift one arm out to side, keeping it straight at the elbow. The fists should be lightly clenched. Then swing the arm at the side in wide circles, keeping the elbow stiff and the body upright. The body must not lean to the side in a direction away from the swinging arm. Start the swinging slowly and then gradually increase speed, making sure that the circle is kept wide. Do from front to back twenty times, then from back to front. Repeat with other arm. Then reach one arm up above the head, elbow stiff, hand clenched. Then, keeping the upper body straight, make big circles up above the head, twenty to one side, twenty to the other. Repeat with other arm.

- Stand with feet well apart, knees well bent. Then bring upper body well forward and place the backs of the hands against each other, reaching as far as possible. Try to force the elbows together. Force hard for ten seconds, relax and then repeat. Do ten times.

- Stand with feet comfortably apart. Then interlock fingers with the hands held behind the head. Turn the palms up and stretch up toward the ceiling as high as possible, keeping the fingers locked, and palms up. Really stretch. Hold in highest possible position for a count of five. Relax and repeat ten times.

- Stand with your feet comfortably apart, interlocking the hands in front of your chest. Then move your elbows out in front as far as possible at shoulder level. Then try to bring the inside of the elbows together so they touch. Hold in this position for a five count. Relax, and repeat ten times.

Neck. It is very important that the player have a flexible neck because flexibility allows the neck to absorb shock. Any athlete who plays a hard body contact game such as hockey without developing the strength of his neck to the highest possible level is very foolish.

The following exercises will help develop neck strength:

- Stand with feet comfortably apart, then rotate head from right to left in as wide a circle as possible, making sure the chin is close to the chest during the front part of the circle and that the chin is high during the back of the circle. The ears should scrape the top of the shoulders during the sideways part of the circle. Start slowly and then increase speed. Do twenty times to either side.

- Stand with feet comfortably spread. Move back of head as far back as possible, chin up as far as possible. In this position open and close the jaw vigorously. Repeat ten times, relax for a few moments, and then repeat again.

- Stand with feet comfortably apart and bring chin forward to chest. Clasp hands on the top and back of head. Then pull head forward and down as far as possible. Hold for ten seconds, relax, and repeat ten times. Then move back of head back as far as possible, chin up toward ceiling as far as possible. Then place right hand flat on forehead and try to force head even farther back. Hold for ten seconds. Relax and then do the same with the left hand flat on the forehead. Repeat four times. Then stand with feet comfortably apart, hands at the sides, chin up, eyes straight ahead.

- Move head sideways, trying to place ear flat on top of one shoulder. Hold in best possible position for count of five, relax, and repeat to other side. Do four times. Only the head moves; the upper body should remain erect and straight.

- Move the head sideways, again trying to get the ear flat on the shoulder with eyes looking straight ahead. Place heel of the hand just above the ear and bring the head back as far as possible to the other side, resisting the movement with hand pressure all during the movement. Then do the same thing in the other direction. Repeat six times to each side. Finish by doing a short period of head rotation as described in the head flexibility section of exercises.

It is important that just the head be moved during any of these movements. The upper body must not move backwards, forwards, or sideways as the head is moved, because this will take the strain off the neck muscles.

Elbows.

- Lie on back, points of elbows on floor, hands up directly above elbows. Clench fists loosely. Then, keeping elbows on floor, move forearms and hands in big circles. Repeat ten times from left to right and then ten times the other way. Repeat cycle until one hundred circles have been made.

Hands and wrists. The hands and wrists are particularly important to the hockey player because they are used so much in checking, stick-handling, and shooting. The looser and more flexible they are, the better.

- Stand with feet comfortably apart; lift arms to shoulder level, elbows straight; then rotate hands in as large a circle as possible. The hands should be open. Rotate twenty times from left to right, twenty from right to left. Start slowly, gradually increase speed. Make sure the circles are as large as possible each time and that just the hands are used. Keep the elbows straight. Rest a moment and then repeat with hands clenched.
- From same position as given above, stand with hands open, back of hands facing ceiling. Then flip hands up as far as possible and then down as far as possible. Start slowly and then do it faster and faster.
- From the same starting position, hold hands in front, then stretch them with force, trying to spread the fingers to make as large a hand as possible. Hold for ten seconds, relax, and repeat. Do ten times, really stretching each time.

Summary. These exercises will be valuable in developing flexibility, looseness, and muscle length, thus increasing the general mechanical efficiency of the player. They are a particularly desirable part of the goal-keeper's routine. The number of exercises done depends, of course, on the time available. If the player does not have a great deal of time, the best plan is to do one each of the exercises given for each different part of the body, changing the exercise selected each day.

By using these exercises in a warm-up, the player can loosen up and stretch every important muscle to the point that they are really ready for action. Such players will feel looser and more ready to go. The exercises can be done after the player undresses and before he puts on his uniform.

It is equally helpful to use a selection of these exercises after a workout or game so that the tightening and shortening of the muscles and the muscular tension created by hard work can be corrected. The athlete's muscles will thus be returned to perfect shape for hard use the next day. If they are not stretched and eased, they will remain tight and short, injuries will be more likely, and the player will be unable to move at peak level. This is the reason you so often see a team who did well one night fail to do as well in the game on the following day. Practically everyone has noticed that stiff and sore feeling on the day following a hard workout, even in mid-season. One reason is that the muscles are still tight and short. At least give the hip and leg muscles a good stretching.

Doing stretching exercises between periods of play, during a game, at least enough to stretch and ease those muscles under the greatest strain, will keep the player going at peak level. It will also help avoid fatigue and injury, because the shortening of the muscles that always takes place during hard, muscular work will be retarded. As the muscle loses its ability to relax, it pulls against its attachments and prevents the full play of the joints.

The use of stretching and loosening exercises before and after work-outs, games, and between periods of play is highly recommended. The same applies to their use on a regular basis. There are some athletes who look upon such practices as a chore, as too much work. However, any effort made will more than repay the player. The smart coach will give a high priority to this phase of the training program. Professional teams and others, playing a long schedule, will find the special routines sug-gested invaluable. Players who do a lot of travelling should be sure to give their back thighs a good stretching immediately on arrival as these muscles shorten considerably during any long continued sitting posture.

STRENGTHENING EXERCISES

Whenever a pre-season evaluation brings to light certain physical weak-nesses, or whenever the player becomes conscious of them, a program of strengthening exercises should be instituted immediately. Many of the exercises listed in the flexibility group will help but these should be aug-mented by the use of some of the following. The old saying, "A chain is as strong as its weakest link" is particularly true here, because it describes the situation when a hockey player has a weak spot in his physique. If he is not frequently suffering injury to this part of his body, it will still be a detriment as it will tire easily and place an added strain on the rest of his body.

Research has demonstrated that strength is an important factor in the acquisition and employment of any skill. The stronger the athlete, the higher skill potential he possesses. For example, suppose a player possessing a certain rating in strength were given skill tests. If he subsequently increased his strength rating, his skill rating would show a corresponding rise. Although skill is not a necessary side effect of strength, strength is an important partner of any fully developed skill.

Once a muscle reaches the point of development that enables it to handle its regular job easily, it stops developing because there is no further reason for it to develop in size or tone. This is why weight lifting is such an excellent muscle builder. The load can be continually increased. Playing hockey alone will not provide the necessary muscle challenges. Therefore, if the hockey player wants to develop extra strength in all the muscles he uses in playing hockey, he must start increasing the work load of the muscles concerned. This can best be done by performing special exercises that can increase the work load, or by practising hockey drills that will throw a heavier load on the muscles than will be experienced in normal play. There probably is not a hockey player playing today, in any class of hockey, who could not improve his skating, shooting power, and drive, if he gave attention to this fact. An athlete can never be too strong. Strength does not necessarily mean huge, bulgy muscles, but tightly packed, expertly trained muscles designed to generate power – strength plus speed.

Such strengthening work can be done under the coach's or trainer's supervision or by the player himself. Young players should get to work as soon as possible, realizing that nothing can be of more help to them than a strong, well developed all-round physique. It is interesting to note that of several hundred hockey players tested, only thirty per cent failed to show a serious weak spot in their physique! Many of the seemingly huskiest players had definite weak spots.

The exercises listed below will give the trainer or the individual athlete considerable variation of conditions on which to work. Other exercises for the special needs of the athlete can be had from any first class physical education expert. The exercises listed can be used to build up a weak spot during the season, in a pre-season build-up program, or the whole group can be combined with the flexibility exercises previously listed to make up a general body development course to follow the year round until the physical objective is reached. If this is the chosen route, the athlete should alternate the exercises, doing a different selection each day until all are used, then repeating.

Upper and lower leg, knees, ankles, and feet.

- Stand beside a chair or table or a suitable object that can be used for support. Then, keeping the knees stiff, rock forward up on the toes as high as possible. Then come down and rock back on the heels as far as possible, trying to bring the toes up toward the shin bones. Start slowly and increase the speed. When you are able to do this exercise for a good length of time without any fatigue, do it on one foot, lifting the other one up off the floor. Be sure to alternate feet.

- Lift one leg well off the floor and hop ten times forward, turn, and come back. Then repeat on the other leg. Hop as high as possible landing heel first and rocking forward on to the ball of your foot. Move back and forth, alternating the leg on which you are hopping.

- Stand with feet comfortably apart, toes pointing out at angles. Keeping the feet flat on the floor at all times, especially the heels, go down in a deep knee bend moving your buttocks down well behind your knees, keeping your upper body straight. If necessary, grasp a support at first to sustain balance. Go down as far as possible, touch the buttocks to the floor if you can, and then return to the standing position. Do ten times very slowly. Rest a moment, and repeat ten times as quickly as possible. Rest a short time and repeat with toes facing straight ahead. Keep knees as close together as possible during the exercise. Continue, alternating with feet turned out and feet straight ahead. As soon as possible, do this exercise without using anything to sustain balance. Remember that the feet must be flat on the floor at all times.

- Squat down on heels grasping a table or chair to help balance. Then move one leg out in front until it is straight with the heel touching the floor. Then quickly bring it back underneath the buttocks as you move the other leg out in a straight-out-in-front position. Do slowly at first and then increase speed. The sitting position should be sustained at all times. As soon as possible, do without holding anything to sustain balance. This is the Russian Dance exercise.

- All different types of running are excellent for leg development in general. When muscular development is desired, speed running is most effective.
- A good leg developer that can be done on the ice is the tandem push. The player skates as hard as he can, pushing another player in front of him. The competitive angle can be worked into this exercise through time trials over different distances and actual races between groups.

Hips, groin, and mid-section.

- An especially good exercise to develop high level mid-section strength is the hanging jackknife. The athlete hangs from any suitable bar or ledge, preferably something that is just out of the reach when the hands are held as high as possible over the head. It can also be done from a rope. The idea is to hang motionless for a moment and then lift the legs, keeping the knees stiff at all times, up and toward the head until a complete jackknife is formed with the feet at head level and the buttocks well down toward the point in the jackknife. This position should be held for the count of three, and then the original position resumed. It should be done slowly twice and then quickly twice, alternating in this way until first signs of real fatigue. The legs must be kept straight and there must be no pulling by the arms. The body must be allowed to hang while the legs are brought forward and upward. Some athletes will not have the mid-section strength to do this but if they persevere, they will develop it.
- Stand with feet about twelve inches apart, toes facing straight ahead. Bend knees a little, then turn the buttocks back and to one side as far as possible, then to the other side, and continue turning them back and forth as quickly as possible. Do not move any other part of the body except the buttocks. The knees, of course, must be kept flexible but the feet should remain flat on the floor. A real effort must be made to whip the buttocks from side to side. After a brief rest period, take up the same position as before, but bend the knees and lower the buttocks about half way to the floor. Repeat the exercise.

  This is a very good exercise for the hips. Hip strength and flexibility correlate very highly with running and skating speed and endurance.
- Kneel on floor, then move one leg out to the side as far as possible so that the inside edge of the foot is on the floor, and the outside edge faces the ceiling; the toes should be pointed straight ahead with the

heels directly behind. Clasp the hands behind the head and keep the elbows directly out to the side. Then bend laterally at the waist, bringing the elbow closest to the leg that is stretched out to the side, down until it touches the outside of the knee. Hold for a second or two and then bring the upper body back and over to the other side as far as possible, making sure to keep the foot that is straight out to the side on the floor as the upper body is moved to the other side. Start slowly at first and increase the speed. Make sure the head is kept erect and the elbows face directly out to the side at all times. Repeat six times, then reverse leg position and repeat. The stomach should be held in throughout the whole exercise.

Chest, shoulders, arms, and back. The chest and back should be well developed because they stand a lot of the shock in any body contact. The arms and shoulders should not be neglected because there is a great deal of warding off and pulling and pushing in hockey.

- Everyone knows the push-up exercise in which the body is moved up and down from the flat on the floor starting position. This is an ideal exercise for the shoulders, back of the arms, and chest when done properly. In fact, it is a good all-over developer. The ideal way to do this exercise is between two chairs so that the body can be lowered well down between them each time, thus throwing greater strain on the muscles. When doing the exercise, two should be done slowly and two quickly. Further good results are had if the width between the two chairs is varied now and then.

- The chin-up is a great developer of the arms and shoulders and also certain large areas of the back. It is done by holding on to some bar, ledge, or rope with the arms at full stretch over the head and thumbs facing up, using a grip that has the back of your hands facing you. Then the body is pulled upward by the arms until the chin is higher than the hands. The rest of the body is allowed to hang limp. The exercise should be done once slowly, once quickly, and repeated.

The flexibility exercise previously listed, in which the athlete lies flat on his face and then tries to lift either the upper or lower part of this body up off the floor, is also a wonderful back developer. It builds those all-important back muscles that run up and down on each side of the spine. These muscles are very important to the hockey player because they absorb a lot of shock during body contact.

Hands, wrists, and forearms. The hockey player should make every attempt to develop great strength in these parts of his body because of the important role they play in shooting, stickhandling, and checking.

- Get a heavy baseball bat, and hold it out in front of the body at shoulder level. Maintaining a tight grip of the handle, twist, turn, snap, and revolve it in all directions, moving the wrist to its fullest stretch each time. Start slowly and gradually increase the speed of the movement. Then repeat with the other hand. As strength is developed, increase the weight of the bat by wrapping layers of tape around the thick end. Wire or heavy foil placed in between the layers of tape will add weight. Keep the arm straight at the elbow at all times and just use the hand and wrist. The arm is still.

- Stand with feet comfortably apart, holding a heavy book in either hand, thumb underneath, fingers on top. Hold arm straight out in front as explained in the first exercise, and then twist and turn the hand and wrist in every possible direction, snapping them out and down, revolving them, moving them from side to side. Keep arm still and just use the hands and wrists.

- Grasp a tennis ball in either hand and try to squeeze it flat. Hold the best possible pressure for a count of three, relax, and repeat. Continue until first signs of real fatigue. Special hand squeezers, available at most sporting goods stores, can also be used if desired.

Summary. Such activities as wrestling and weight lifting are wonderful all-round body builders. Wrestling is perhaps the best because it involves co-ordination, balance, and agility as well as strength. Such activities are especially good for the hockey player anxious to put on weight. There are some who claim that such forms of exercise will slow down the athlete. If they are combined with plenty of speed work, this will definitely not occur. Exercises such as these offer excellent off-season activities for the hockey player.

AGILITY, BALANCE, AND CO-ORDINATION

Many of the exercises already listed do a good job of improving the player's agility, balance, and co-ordination. When these are augmented by the various skating agility drills, the player will get a good all-round training. He should also take part in other athletic activities involving fundamentals. Tumbling and gymnastics in general and such games as handball and badminton are excellent. Tumbling is an especially good secondary activity for the hockey player, particulary the goalkeeper. The agility, balance, and co-ordination the player will develop in such activities will soon be noticeable in his hockey playing.

The goalkeeper should pay special attention to all those exercises previously listed, especially those demanding high levels of flexibility, agility, balance, and co-ordination. He can help himself even further by working on some or all of the following drills.

Goalkeeper's dance. A wonderful drill for the goalkeeper is known as the Goalkeeper's Dance, which is a series of movements done continuously one after the other. It is a real challenge to anybody who fancies his mechanical skill. The drill is a series of different movements that must be performed in sequence. Each step is started by the player returning to the basic position, which is bouncing up and down with the feet comfortably apart, in a series of low bounces. To start, the goalie bounces up and down in this way and then he continues on as follows. After each step he returns to the original position.

Step 1. Jump as far sideways as possible. The landing must be made on the outside foot, i.e., the one on the side to which you have jumped. The player bounces up and down on this foot two or three times without letting the other foot, from which he has driven off on the sideways jump, touch the floor. Then a return jump is made to the original position. This is done four times in either direction. The toes and body should be kept facing directly in front at all times.

Step 2. Keeping feet together, jump forward about two feet, then quickly backwards about two feet, keeping the feet together at all times. The player should go back and forth without hesitating after a landing. This should be done six times forward, six times back.

Step 3. Keeping the feet close together, moving them at the same time, jump to the side about two feet. Then jump quickly back again, going back and forth from side to side six times one way, six times the other. Land on the balls of the feet.

Step 4. The player should jump up in the air about six inches and land with his left foot about a foot in front of his body, his right foot about a foot behind. Then, as the landing is made, there is another jump in which the position of the feet is reversed. This is done about twelve times reversing the feet each time. There should be no hesitation between jumps.

Step 5. The player should then spread his feet as wide as he can and continue to hop up and down. He takes six hops and then, on the seventh hop, brings his feet together and across in front of each other as far as he can. He then quickly hops again exchanging the position of his feet. For example, the first time the left foot is crossed in front of the right, the next time the right is crossed in front of the left. The feet should be crossed as far as possible each time and there should be no hesitation between hops. This should be continued until the feet have been crossed twelve times.

Step 6. This time the player jumps in the air as high as he can and turns his body completely around so that he lands in the same position from which he took off. The moment he lands, he goes up again and twists around completely in the opposite direction. The first time the turn should be made to the left, the second time to the right. This is repeated until four turns have been made in each direction.

Step 7. In this movement the player jumps in the air about six inches high, kicks both feet out behind him and drops to the ground so that he lands on the flat of his hands with his toes on the floor out behind him. He then quickly brings his feet up underneath him again, jumps up in the air, and then repeats. Do six times.

Step 8. In this step the player jumps a little in the air then drops to the ground with his left leg as far ahead and his right leg as far behind him as possible and his hands on either side. He lands as far down in the split position as he can. As he lands, he immediately changes the position of his feet, moving the right one out in front and the left one well behind. This should be done without any hesitation. The position of the feet are exchanged six times and then the exercise is repeated four times.

Step 9. Next, the player hops up and down on one foot while raising the other leg out to the side as high as possible, keeping the toes pointing straight ahead. The player goes up in the hop and raises his leg to the side at the same time, bringing his foot back down from the side as he comes down after the hop. Then, another hop is made with a lift to the left. One should be made to the left side, one to the right until six hops and six side kicks have been made to either side.

Step 10. Finally, the player hops in the air, makes a half turn sideways, and goes down to the split position with hands supporting him on either side. As he lands, he shoves himself up in the air again and reverses the position of his feet. For example, the first time he will make a half turn to the left and will go down with his left leg forward, right leg behind, upper body facing to the left. Then as he reverses positions, his right leg will be out to his right side and his upper body will be facing in that direction.

Every effort should be made to go through the whole dance without a mistake in a smooth rhythm, working one step into the next one without hesitation. When learning the dance, the player can go through it slowly a few times until he gets it down pat. Then he can try to do it faster and faster. It is a good idea to keep a check on the time it takes so that the player can keep on trying to beat the time it takes him to go through the whole dance. The drill can be done in a gym or at home. It can also be done on the ice with skates on, and if desired, with full equipment. All the players or coach need do to test out the efficiency of this dance is to try it for a week and watch for results.

Eyes. Because the goalkeeper's eyes are the most important part of his body, every effort should be made to develop the greatest efficiency possible. A lot can be done in this respect through the use of special drills. Some of the best are as follows.

Flexibility and strength. The eye is a muscle and, accordingly, is governed by many of the rules that apply to all muscles. They most certainly do react well to special exercises. Such drills can be used to develop their efficiency so that they will be less subject to fatigue and strain. They can also be used to relax the eyes after hard effort, such as a long practice or game. A good drill that stretches the eye muscles and develops their tone consists of a number of different movements that should be worked one into the other and done in a continuous sequence.

Move the eyes upward as far as possible. Hold for a count of three, then move them down as far as possible. Then move them to the right as far as possible, hold for a count of three, then to the left. Then rotate them in as wide a circle as possible around to the left. Then, after one circle, repeat around to the right. Then, move them up and to the right as far as possible, hold for a count of three and then down and to the left as far as possible. Then up and to the left in the same way and then down to the right.

After each movement has been made, start over again. All the movements should be made six times. Each movement should be made to the maximum stretch. At first this may make the player a little dizzy but as the exercise is done for a few days, this will cease. To wind up the drill, place the heels of the hands over the eyes so that nothing can be seen; hold for a count of six; take hands away, look at an object at least thirty or forty feet away for six seconds and then repeat. Do ten or twelve times. This is called palming and is very restful to the eyes. This drill should be done two or three times a day by the goaltender and is especially important before and after every goaltending session. If persevered with, the goaltender will certainly notice that these exercises will make his eyes feel rested and more efficient.

Focus and acuity. An excellent method of training the eyes to move quickly and focus sharply is called looking the square. Sit or stand about twenty or thirty feet away from the end of a room, preferably a square room. Look at a spot directly in the centre at the end of the room. Then quickly look to the top left hand corner. Look at this spot until you see it clearly and then move the eyes to the top right hand corner, then to the bottom right hand, then to the bottom left hand. Continue moving the eyes in this way around the square and in variations. For example, instead of going around the square from left to right, go around from right to left and then mix things up by looking from the low right-hand corner to the top left-hand corner, and so on. When done quickly, the player will notice that it takes a little while to focus the eyes on the new spot each time and that there is sort of a blind spot as he moves his eyes around. The more the drill is done, the faster he will be able to focus. This should be done for five or ten minutes several times a day.

Calling the fingers. In this drill the player gets someone to stand about twenty or thirty feet away with his arms held out to the sides. The person then starts a semaphore action, moving his arms in different directions and then stopping for a moment in each new direction. Each time a stop is made the person doing the semaphoring holds out a different number of fingers in either hand. The player doing the drill must call out as follows: left hand two fingers, right hand three fingers. As soon as he calls it out, the person doing the semaphoring should change the position. A third person should be watching to keep the score, counting each time the goalkeeper is wrong. The player will be surprised how often he is wrong and how his ability will improve as he continues to do the drill. The player doing the drill is allowed only one second for his guess.

This type of drill can be done throughout the day as the player is travelling about. For example, on street cars or buses he can practise moving his eyes from object to object as quickly as he can, trying to detect a different thing about each one before moving them again quickly. The advertisements on the sides of the street car or bus can be used. The timid person should be careful when doing this as he may very well give the wrong impression to anyone sitting opposite to him. It is easy to get a reputation of being a little whacky by doing such things. However, even this is a small price to pay for the added eye efficiency it will bring.

Other extra-curricular activities any goalkeeper can use are such games as table tennis and such activities as tumbling, that involve high level acuity and hand and eye dexterity. Tumbling is an especially good activity. It would make an ideal hobby for any goalkeeper.

SUSTAINING CONDITION

Once the athlete is in first class condition, the problem is then to sustain his physical efficiency. This involves a different technique. It is something that is not always very carefully observed. As a result an athlete runs into many problems that affect his conditioning, causing it to diminish. An athlete trying to sustain a high competitive season is a very sensitive piece of machinery and unless certain general principles are observed, he can get into a lot of trouble. The factors that have the most to do with his ability to sustain a high level of efficiency are as follows.

Avoiding staleness. Staleness, or as it is often mistakenly called, burning out, is one of the great problems of the athlete who has to play through a long, hard schedule. Often it is the ability of the coach and trainer to bring the athletes through a season without periods of staleness that determines the team's chances of final success or failure. If special care is not taken many athletes cannot help but run into bad periods of play. Actually, nearly every slump or off-form period of play is caused by staleness. Unfortunately, the players who most often suffer from this trouble are the best players, the hard working players, whose loss of form will most affect the team.

The player who doesn't have any difficulty and never shows the slightest sign of becoming stale should be investigated as he is probably not giving all he has.

Staleness is considered to be more mental than physical by experts, although it does have many physical aspects. A major cause is a boredom which is often unconscious. For example, when a person does the same thing over and over again in the same old way, his mind gets sick of it and throws out physical symptoms in order to force a change. This is why staleness is a problem in any activity, from house work to playing hockey. It is a big problem for the school teacher and also for the business executive, who has to do the same kind of exacting work over and over again. Thus, in avoiding it, variety in the activity is very important. The more variety at practice and in the training program, the less likelihood there is of the athlete becoming stale. This is perhaps the most important preventive measure.

Research shows that the type of person who is most frequently bothered by this condition is the high strung, emotional type, whose nervous system is not as healthy as it could be. Usually, the person who suffers most from staleness is the sensitive type who does a lot of worrying, who feels his responsibilities keenly, and who has a highly developed sense of duty. Therefore, another preventive measure is to make sure the player learns to relax, to get lots of balance in his life, learns how to live philosophically with his problems and eats a great abundance of the foods that build sound, healthy nerves. If these things are looked after, staleness will become less of a problem, with the player able to keep up a tremendous pressure over a long period of time without showing any symptoms. Relaxation, diet, and balance in life are dealt with in the following pages.

The symptoms of staleness are irritability, loss of appetite, loss of interest, a listless, loggy feeling that makes the player have to drive himself, loss of weight, a drawn, tense look about the face, oversensitivity to remarks and situations, a pessimistic outlook, an unusual concern with bodily feelings and state of health, and slow recovery after hard work. There often seems to be a loss of sparkle and personality about the player. He seems to have little life and is not so inclined to joke and have fun. Everything is deadly serious to him or he is too lethargic to bother. When any two or three or more of these symptoms are present, a careful

check-up should be made. Curative measures should be taken at once as
the longer the player remains stale, the harder it is to cure and the more
likely it will return.

Chronic physical fatigue may be mistaken for psychological staleness.
Over a long season with day after day of games and practices, the need
for rest periods is often overlooked. The body needs time to recover
from effort. Indeed, this is the basis of physical development: the breaking down of tissues and cells through overload, and their replacement
and improvement by the body's physiological repair processes.

If rest periods aren't provided, the body may not be able to keep up
with its restoration work. The result is a weakening of the entire system
and a gradual increase in residual lactic acid within the muscles.

The antidotes are proper nutrition and rest or, at least, a switch to a
different type of training such as long, slow (aerobic) distance work, for
example. This does not break down tissues nor create lactic acid. Off-ice
sports such as soccer or basketball, which provide a change of pace and
utilize some different muscles, may provide fun.

Remember, too, that hockey is basically an anaerobic sport and hence
is not an efficient aerobic conditioner. Over a long season, aerobic power
will decrease and with it the player's ability to recover from anaerobic
effort. A switch to some aerobic training in the later part of the season
may therefore have added benefits.

Consider, however, the possibility that a few days of "R and R" may
be the simplest, and best, antidote.

If the difficulty is deeper in nature and severe psychological fatigue is
at the root of the problem, drastic measures may be called for.

First of all, the player should have a complete rest from all physical
activity or talk of any kind connected with the game. This should be sustained until the athlete shows a reawakening of interest. During this
period he should take frequent hot baths and gentle massage; should get
lots of rest and have a complete change in activity, doings things he has
not done for a long time; he should eat wholesome carbohydrate rich
meals and consult with a sports nutritionist to rule out dietary causes of
staleness. When the athlete returns to action he should get lots of variety
in his practice and training work; he should be given frequent short rests;
and care should be taken to teach him how to relax, how to get more
balance in his life, and how to eat properly. If these things are taken care

of, the trouble should not recur in any serious way. At the slightest sign of any further staleness the athlete should be rested. A one or two day rest at the right time often saves a week or more rest later on or a loss of form for two or three weeks or even longer. The coach and trainer should, of course, keep a close watch for any signs of staleness but the player can help by checking on himself. Concentration on the relaxation drills listed in this chapter should be a must for the player inclined toward staleness.

Regularity of habits. If the athlete is to sustain a high level of physical efficiency, he must regulate his life as much as possible as far as his basic habits are concerned. Although the body does not like to do one thing in the same way for extended periods of time, it does like to be used in a steady groove in certain ways. It likes to get set in certain habit patterns. When it does, it operates more efficiently and with better tone. When it is moved from its basic routine, there is a period of adjustment during which it does not perform as efficiently. This is why when the meal schedule is mixed up, the digestion often suffers and the person concerned does not feel as well as he normally would. Therefore, if the athlete is to sustain a good body tone all the time and thus avoid that irritating "feel good one day, not so good the next" feeling, he should regulate his basic habits.

Basic habits mean sleeping, eating, elimination, and sexual relationships. There are times, of course, when it is very difficult to sustain regularity but every effort should be made to do so as much as possible. Some athletes have the mistaken opinion that sleeping late on the morning of a game will give them added pep during the game. Actually, this usually has just the opposite effect. By upsetting the regular body routine, the athlete is more likely to feel a little sluggish and will not be able to untrack himself as well. The procedure on the day of a game regarding sleeping, eating, and elimination should be kept as close to normal as possible. Elimination should be watched carefully with a definite attempt made to perform the duty at the same time each day. The best time is after breakfast. If the athlete has difficulty doing this, he might use a natural laxative, such as applesauce, figs, or prunes the night before so that he will get the habit of eliminating in the morning. A glass or two of hot water first thing on waking up can help.

Ability to relax. Modern medical and physical education research has brought to light no more valuable factor in the field of health and physical efficiency than the important role controlled relaxation plays. The person who can relax when he wishes will not only be able to develop greater skill in all his activities but will also have less tendency to become stale. He will be able to stand pressure better, will feel fit and ready when the time for action comes up, will be able to do his best during tense moments, will be able to continue under pressure, will be able to exert a hard effort longer, and will avoid many of the common ills that beset the human race. Every athlete anxious to make a name for himself and enjoy his activities should give the ability to relax a number one priority, as should the coach, who lives under the highest type of pressures. Tension, the absolute opposite of relaxation, is one of the greatest enemies of man. It spoils physical and mental efficiency and it creates mental, emotional, and physical ills.

Until recent years, there was no actual technique of relaxation taught. People were advised to relax but not told how to do it. The term relaxation was commonly used to describe recreational activities.

Our research department has studied all the material available on the subject and done much practical work in developing methods of application and testing their efficiency. The results have been remarkable. Perhaps the outstanding job has been done with the athlete who suffers from the all-too common problem of not being able to do as well in a game, especially in an important game, as he can do in practice when there is no actual pressure. Those troubled with this problem solved it only when they learned controlled relaxation techniques and applied them.

The first step is to learn the difference between the relaxed state and the tense state. After the athlete has become conscious of when he is tense, he will be able to take the necessary measures to relax. Most athletes do not realize how tense they are because they have no way of comparing their feelings. It is necessary to tense the various parts of the body purposely and then relax them one at a time and all together. After this has been done for a while, the person cannot help but recognize either state.

A fundamental drill is as follows. Tense the hands by clenching the fists, the shoulders by hunching them toward the ears, and the jaw by clenching the teeth. Hold this position for a few seconds and then let these muscles go as limp as possible. As the muscles are let go, the player should exhale with a sigh. In relaxing, the idea is to just go limp as if suddenly exhausted or hit on the head with hammer. No conscious movement should be made, merely a letting go. The drill is done five or six times with these parts of the body and then the legs and feet should be tensed by clenching the toes and stiffening the leg muscles. Then the chest and stomach should be tensed and relaxed in the same way. Then the whole body should be tensed at once and then relaxed as before. This can be done lying down, sitting, or standing up. Best results will be secured if the athlete does this for two fifteen or twenty minute periods per day, say morning and night. This should also be augmented by frequent tensing and relaxing through the day whenever possible.

When tensing, it is not necessary to tighten the muscles very hard, but just hard enough to bring on the feeling of tension. After about a week of this the athlete will be able to notice a difference between tension and relaxation and will have developed a good deal of skill at letting himself go whenever desired. He will also have developed a liking for the feeling of relaxation. At this time the athlete should start concentrating on special work on the different parts of his body, scheduling the work he does according to where he seems to have the most tension and the most difficulty in letting go. For example, he should work on his hands and arms until he has developed the ability to relax them. Then he should work on his shoulders, and so on. He should also start studying his state of relaxation and tension whenever he is doing anything, be it talking, walking, sitting, reading, watching games, dancing, playing cards, eating, drinking, and so on. He will be very surprised how often he will notice he is tense when doing these things. When he does notice this, he can relax.

The idea is to apply the relaxation principle to every single activity because once the athlete does this, he will become a relaxed personality and will be able to do anything under pressure without undue tension. This principle should be applied to all his practice and playing and the moments in between, such as resting on the bench before the game, when listening to instruction, and so on. It should be remembered that the relaxed person will have a finer sense of hearing, balance, agility, perception, and everything else associated with bodily motion and feeling. The person who has worked at the technique of relaxation will notice a wonderful feeling of alertness and feeling "right," which once he has experienced it, he will never want to miss. Fortunately, he will not have to worry about this if he works hard to acquire the art because once it is learned, it is never forgotten. This is one of the wonderful things about it.

The coach who learns controlled relaxation will find it the best thing that ever happened. He'll be able to think clearer and faster, have greater patience, and will be a much more happy and efficient person. The player or coach who suffers from butterflies and jitters before the game will find that relaxation techniques provide very effective relief.

In applying controlled relaxation to the actual playing or practising of hockey, the same general principle of the drills already suggested should be used. For example, the player should go through the various manoeuvres used in his game, such as shooting, stickhandling, checking, skating, and so on, purposely tensing his body. He should then do them trying to keep his body relaxed, working especially on the parts of the body most concerned, such as the wrists, arms, and shoulders in shooting and stickhandling. Goalkeepers should do the same thing, working to gain relaxation in all their movements. When this is done for a while the player will soon develop the ability to work in a relaxed state. The player should also get the habit of relaxing by drawing himself tense and then letting go during any brief rest periods, such as the time preceding face-offs. He should work especially hard at letting himself go when resting on the bench and between periods. The more work done on this technique, the greater the skill developed, and the greater the skill, the more the athlete will want to develop it.

Collapsing drills. There are other drills that will help develop the technique of relaxation at will and which are particularly effective when used before the game if the athlete is bothered by tension. These are known as collapsing drills.

- Stand with your feet comfortably apart, then raise the hands as far as possible over the head. Stretch upward as far as possible while holding your breath. Hold this position for a count of three, then collapse, letting the arms drop down, the head slump forward, and the knees bend a little. Just hang there like a dishrag on a nail. Hang as limply as possible for a few seconds, then repeat the action. As the collapse is made, let the breath out in a long sighing exhalation, as if falling into a chair after a long, hard day. Repeat the exercise six to ten times, trying to collapse more completely each time you do it.

- Stand with feet comfortably apart and arms up over the head, shoulder width apart. Then collapse by letting your upper body and arms fall forward, keeping the knees stiff and letting the arms go completely. Hang in this way with the upper body well forward, head loose, for a few seconds, then repeat. Do six or seven times.

- Stand with feet comfortably apart, knees well bent, heels of hands resting on front of knees. Head should be up with eyes looking straight ahead. Then, tighten the body all over, hold for a few seconds. Collapse the upper body, head and arms down between your knees, so that the backs of the hands are resting on the floor. Really let yourself go. Hold for a few seconds and repeat six times.

- Stand with feet comfortably apart and the upper body bent over from the waist as far as possible, the flat of the hands resting on the shins. Then, keeping the knees stiff, raise the upper body half way to the erect position. Bring your arms up as far as they can reach in front of you. Hold for a count of three in this half erect position and then collapse, letting the upper body and arms come down between the legs. As you collapse, let the knees bend a little. Repeat this action six times.

- Sit on a bench or chair with feet flat on floor and comfortably spread. Place heels of hands on top of knee and sit erect. Then, keeping arms straight at the elbows, head erect, suck the stomach in and up as high as possible. Hold for a count of three, then let the stomach collapse down into your hips. Keep the arms straight all through the drill. As the stomach collapses, exhale with a sigh. This is especially good for butterflies. Do ten or twelve times. Really let the stomach go in a downward collapse.

- Sit on the lowest possible bench or stool you can find or a very low chair, with the feet well spread in front of you, feet flat on the floor, knees directly above the feet. Place hands on knees, keep head erect. Tighten all the body, especially the neck, shoulders and arms, hold for a count of three then collapse the upper body so that the hands and head drop between the knees. Let the arms dangle loosely on the floor. In this position take a deep breath, hold it for a second or two, and then try to collapse and let yourself go even more. Do this three or four times, then stay in the collapsed position for six or seven seconds, and then repeat four or five times more.

Summary. The athlete who is trying to learn the art of relaxation should be working at it all the time. It is important that whenever he runs into a situation involving tension such as an argument, a period of worry, or any other emotional upset, he should consciously try to let himself go and to relax his muscles. The more he uses the technique, the greater his skill will become. Soon he will relax against pressure as a natural reflex instead of reacting with tension as is usually the case. Once the habit is established, he'll be off to the races.

Activity balance. This refers to the day by day living habits of the athlete. Medical research has proved that man functions at his best physically, mentally, and emotionally when he keeps a good balance between work, play, and rest. Many athletes make the mistake of putting too much of the work emphasis in their life. When not actually playing or practising they are talking about it or thinking about the game. This overemphasis is not good. They should make sure that they have other interesting activities and hobbies to which they can turn whenever they are not playing. This is especially true of the professional or semi-professional hockey player whose play is actually his work. A good system is to give the athletic activities everything possible in effort and concentration but then, when the practice or game is over, turn to other pursuits. The three-way breakdown of eight hours rest, eight hours play, and eight hours work is a good system for all to follow.

DIET

Every day the results of medical and physical education research are emphasizing the fact that diet plays a very important role in physical and mental efficiency. All indicators point toward the fact that how you feel, the state of your morale, your degree of energy and endurance, your attitude, and all the factors involved in your personality greatly depend on the food you eat. Test after test is proving this fact. In the Sports College testing groups many controlled and practical tests were made and each one has resulted in the conclusion that diet has a huge effect on the athlete's efficiency.

The whole body is nourished by the vital elements it takes in. It is very important that everyone should eat properly but it is especially so for the athlete because he must function at a higher physical level of efficiency than the average person. The athlete who eats properly will not only function better but will establish a habit of good nutrition that will have a lot to do with his continued good health and longevity when he is through with competitive activity.

Sports nutritionists tell us that a good diet will include at least two servings daily from each of the four food groups: dairy products; grains/cereals, vegetables/fruits and meats. As a general rule, they should be balanced to provide about ten to fifteen per cent of daily calories as protein, twenty-five to thirty per cent as fat (saturated fats from meat products as low as possible), and sixty to seventy per cent as carbohydrate.

The carbohydrate ratio should be on the higher side when loading up with energy for a tournament, and when recovering from a particularly hard workout, game, or series in which there were a number of consecutive games. Carbohydrates – especially so-called "complex" carbohydrates such as pasta, bread, and starchy vegetables (potatoes, lima beans) – are the source from which the body recreates the blood sugars and muscle glycogen burned up during effort. Muscles use these sugars for fuel when working hard. Even your brain won't work without them. The by-product created when they are broken down is lactic acid. Hence, the name "fatigue acids."

Quick carbohydrate replenishment is essential in the first half hour after a hard workout or game; this is the crucial period. At this time, liquids containing sugar, such as fruit juices and sweetened drinks are best because they are absorbed easily.

Those who persevere in the habit of eating correctly will find they begin to develop reserve energy and endurance, suffer less from common ills, feel really full of pep more often, and will less likely be bothered by cramps and nausea during hard activity. Research has shown that the athletes who have accomplished great feats of energy, endurance, and skill are very healthy and have efficient functioning gastrointestinal tracts. This vital part of the human machine is tremendously affected by what we consume.

Calorie intake. If the athlete is to do his best, he needs to take in the proper number of calories each day. Fortunately, the active athlete can easily determine the approximate number of calories he needs by using what is called the number system. In this system, the athlete multiplies his body weight by twenty to twenty-five and then adds four hundred calories for each hour of hard physical activity in which he takes part each day. For example, a hundred and fifty pound athlete who plays two hours at practice or in games per day should take in 4,550 calories. If the hockey playing is done outdoors, add five hundred calories for each hour of activity. When the athlete is not active, he should eliminate the four hundred for each hour of hard play and multiply his weight by sixteen to twenty depending upon how active he is generally. If the athlete seems to be getting fat on this number of calories, he should examine his diet carefully and eliminate most of the fat-forming foods until he reaches the point that seems to be ideal. If he is losing weight on the calorie intake suggested, he has an especially active metabolism. He should then increase his intake of carbohydrates and perhaps add a few hundred calories until he reaches the point where he is either sustaining his weight or adding a little. If, no matter what he does, he continues to gain or lose weight, he should consult a good medical expert. The young athlete should show a gradual weight increase. The number of calories taken each day should be gained from the proper selection of the proper foods, which are listed below.

Big breakfast. All nutrition experts agree that a big breakfast, high in carbohydrates (cereal, bread, pancakes, etc.) is very important. This is especially true for the athlete; if he is to function at peak physical level throughout the day and evening he must have the proper kind of breakfast. Eating a light breakfast is one of the worst habits an athlete can acquire.

If the athlete has trouble eating a good breakfast, he should avoid eating heavily at night and should perhaps get up a little earlier and take a walk to stimulate his appetite. The foods eaten at breakfast should include large quantities of foods and beverages rich in natural carbohydrates. Such foods include whole grain cereals and breads; muffins; lowfat milk; oranges and grapefruit; honey or corn syrup. Fried and greasy foods and foods high in animal fat (bacon, for example) should be avoided. This hearty breakfast will keep the athlete's blood sugar (energy) high for as long as four or five hours and help build up stored energy reserves.

Foods to avoid. Just as there are some foods that are to be eaten in quantity, there are others that should be avoided because of their detrimental effects on the body. Such foods are fried foods, unless expertly fast-fried, most cakes and pies, fatty meats and thick, fatty soups, and gravies. Fried foods and overly fat foods are poor energy sources, and lead to the formation of excess cholesterol deposits in the arteries. A certain amount of fat is necessary but just a little too much can greatly affect the athlete's efficiency. Special care should be taken to avoid fatty foods including whole milk and cream if taken before hard effort. Actually, skim milk is better for you and can be taken at any time. Athletes would be wise to form the skim milk habit. If the athlete has a special liking for sweet stuff and cakes and cookies, he should eat those made from whole grain wheat or which feature a lot of fruit; for example, oatmeal cookies containing raisins, dates, or figs, bran muffins containing fruit, and so on.

Good foods. The foods that are especially good for the athlete and of which he should eat large quantities are lean meats, wheat germ, whole grain cereals and breads, lowfat cheeses, milk, buttermilk and yogurt, fresh fruit, and fresh vegetables (especially the dark coloured vegetables such as dark green lettuce). Oranges, dried fruits such as figs, raisins, dates, beans (especially the lima and navy bean), and fresh nuts of all kinds are also very good.

Protein foods. While proteins are the foods that build tissue and rebuild tissue when it is broken down by hard activity, an excessively high protein diet is not a good idea. The body can utilize only so much protein. For an active athlete, it is usually recommended that protein form about ten to fifteen per cent of the total diet (1 to 1.5 grams/kg of body weight). Ideal sources of first class proteins are lean meat, fish, poultry, and lowfat milk products.

Before game meal. The athlete should pay particular attention to what he eats before a game because what he eats will affect the way he feels. The important thing is to eat foods that are very easily digested and which will give a supply of quick, efficient energy. If cooked vegetables or lean meat are eaten, they should be minced so that they are easily broken down and digested. Spicy foods and raw fibrous vegetables may cause stomach distress. There is a popular fallacy that what is needed before a game is a big, thick, rare steak. All nutrition experts who have studied the needs of the athlete are agreed that this is a serious mistake. What are most needed are the energy producing foods: starchy carbohydrates such as pasta, bread, potatoes, etc. It is also important to replace carbohydrates after the game with similar foods. Quickly absorbed high sugar drinks such as fruit juice should be taken as soon as possible after activity. The first 30 minutes after a game or workout is a crucial time for such replenishment. What is most important on the day of the game is a big breakfast of the right kind and then one or more light meals high in energy foods that are easily digested. The last meal, prior to competition, should be taken two and a half to three hours before activity.

Replenishing. Replenishing refers to the action of taking liquid or foods that will replenish the vital carbohydrates used during hard activity. Any of the pick-ups mentioned earlier are excellent. It is also important that the after-exercise meal include plenty of high carbohydrate foods.

The use of energy pick-ups during and after hard activity will help the athlete recover energy quickly so he will not remain fatigued for very long. This is one great way to avoid that after-practice or game let-down that makes it difficult to get the homework done or to enjoy any social activities that have been planned. It will also avoid that tired-following-day feeling that often results in a poor showing in the second of a two-game series. Exhausted tissues will be restored to their normal working level and you will be able to put your very best effort forward.

Supplementation. The best possible way in which the athlete can get all the vitamins and minerals he needs, if he is to function one hundred per cent, is in his daily food. Nutrition experts are not at all sure yet how important it is for the various vitamins and minerals to be taken in their natural state. They have discovered that elements seem to depend upon one another to function properly. It is quite possible that when one element is separated and taken in big doses, it will not do the job it is supposed to do and may even do harm. Therefore, it is best to take the vitamins and minerals in the most natural form possible. However, due to the fact that our cooking habits are such that some of the good of the food is destroyed and because many of the foods are refined so that many of the vital elements are lost, supplementation of the right type seems to be a good idea as a safeguard.

Supplementation whenever possible should be taken in such natural form as brewer's yeast and wheat germ. The family doctor or nutritionist can also recommend other natural vitamin supplements. Wheat germ is one of the great musts for an athlete because, besides having much B Complex, it is high in vitamin E, which is a very difficult vitamin to find in sufficient quantities. Tests indicate that anyone doing hard physical work, like an athlete, should make sure he gets plenty of vitamin E. Capsules, which contain the complete Vitamin E complex, have been used effectively by many.

Summary. The athlete who expects to find a tremendous difference the day after he starts eating properly will be disappointed. It takes time to tear down the body and it also takes time to build it up. After three or four weeks, however, a very definite difference will be felt. Any one food or combination of foods will not perform wonders by itself, but when they are all combined, important results will be developed. In diet, just as in other things, success does not depend upon one thing but rather on a lot of little things.

INJURY CONTROL AND CARE

Often the success of a team is dependent on the number and severity of the injuries it suffers. The hockey coach would, therefore, be well advised to make sure his training system includes as much information as possible on the subject of controlling and caring for injuries. This is the subject for a handbook in itself and cannot be covered in detail here. However, excellent information is available from many other sources, especially *Modern Principles of Athletic Training* by Daniel D. Arnheim (Times Mirror/Mosby College Publishing, a division of the C.V. Mosby Co., St. Louis).

Teams should have expert staff as well as good facilities. Cutting down on the training staff as far as quality or quantity is concerned is poor economy. The team should also have an excellent doctor who knows physiology and sports injuries, as well as a good dentist and chiropractor. The players should be carefully examined for dental problems because many hidden physical and mental troubles that slow up the player are caused by tooth trouble of some kind, especially infections. The objective of a training program should be to subject the athlete's body to the same care and examination that is given an airplane before it takes off for an Atlantic crossing. This should be done not only at the start of the season, but repeated at regular intervals so as to check up on any problem before it has a chance to become serious. The governing principle is that players must not be allowed to play before injuries have properly healed or with a slight injury that can very easily develop into a serious one. It is better to lose one game and give an injury a chance to heal than win the game by playing the injured player and then have him out for the rest of the season.

In amateur hockey, particularly, the coach should give top priority to the welfare of the player. The team that cannot afford the training and medical staff should at least develop friendly relations with experts who live in the district or city in which the team operates. Many experts take a friendly interest and can be very helpful from time to time in offering general advice. Another good plan is to get some young fellow who is interested in sport but cannot be an athlete for various reasons and give him the job of training. If he studies hard and seeks out information, he can do an excellent job taking care of the minor training problems. However, any injury that seems to be in the slightest degree serious should always be treated by an expert – never take a chance.

Injuries most frequently occur to the player when he is either tired or in the early stages of the game when he has not warmed up. Top level physical condition and a good system of warming up can aid injury control. Ill-fitting equipment may lead to injuries. Although it is not always possible for a low level team to have the best equipment, each player can make sure the equipment he does have fits him. It is easy to make alterations. The average athlete is inclined to be a little lazy about his equipment and often runs into unnecessary trouble because of this. Make sure you protect your protection!

The relaxed athlete is always less prone to injury, which is another important reason why every athlete should be taught the art of relaxation. Another important principle to observe is that any injury to a joint requires special and immediate attention. Don't fool around with a joint injury.

Warming-up. Warm-up sessions conducted before practices and games can make a big difference, not only in avoiding injuries but in enabling the players to start off at the highest possible peak of efficiency and sustain a high effort throughout the game or practice. The warm-up period should be considered as a period in which the body is prepared for all-out effort. If this preparation is haphazard or insufficient, the player's efficiency can be severely affected.

Many athletes are afraid to warm-up sufficiently because they think it will tire them out. This can be avoided by organizing a warm-up procedure to use before practices and games so that they will learn by experience that only good will come from it. For every athlete who warms up too much there are a thousand who do not warm-up enough.

In warming-up, the athlete prepares his body by doing stretching and flexibility exercises. Then he should start slowly in his skating and gradually work in the odd bursts of speed. He should also do as many of the skating, shooting, and puck-carrying manoeuvres as he has time for so that the muscles he has to use will be ready. A casual skate around is not enough.

The warm-up should be organized so that all the muscles that are going to be used in the various playing actions of the game are given a proper workout with the same intensity as will be used in the game. The warm-up period should be conducted so that every player is sweating heavily before the game starts. This is one good indication of readiness. A team using a scientifically organized warm-up session will be able to break out much harder and more efficiently when the game starts than a team that does not bother with it.

However, particularly in low level organized hockey, there is sometimes insufficient time for a good ice warm-up. If this is so, special warm-up exercises should be done in the dressing room before the skates are put on. Included should be enough stationary running or loose bouncing up and down to develop a good sweat and get the heart working strongly. A good warm-up is especially important to a hockey player because hockey is a game of high speed, stops and starts, and hard bursts of effort in which the heart, lungs, and muscles take quite a beating if they are not ready for the action. A player starting cold can tighten up his muscles and develop fatigue that will interfere with his efficiency all through the game. For example, an athlete who is in good condition often finds that when he starts to play without a warm-up, his effort in the game seems to fall off.

The warm-up principles should also be utilized after periods of rest such as between periods, although it is not necessary to spend the same amount of time as before the game. The coach who makes a regular warm-up procedure a routine before all practices and games will find it will really pay off. Every attempt should be made to keep the players warm when they are resting on the bench. This is especially true if playing in a cold arena or on an outdoor rink. Unfortunately, because it involves some amount of bother, the training staff and the players themselves often overlook this part of their athletic program. This is a serious mistake.

Cooling off. Cooling off refers to the process of bringing the body back to normal after hard work. It is just as important as the warm-up. In the first place, if the athlete gradually tapers off after a game with special exercises, he will ease the strain on his heart, lungs, and muscles which are affected adversely when they are worked hard, then suddenly given a complete rest.

By doing a certain amount of work in the cooling off period after the game, the athlete helps the heart and lungs get back some of the blood they have been driving out to all parts of the body. Then too, if good circulation is kept up after hard activity, the lactic acids that have accumulated during the hard work will be eliminated more quickly. If a cooling off period is not used, they will tend to stay in the body longer and congregate in the muscles. This is one reason why so many athletes feel sore, tired, and sluggish the day after a hard workout or game. Those who perform a cooling off session will find they will recover a lot faster and will avoid those "day after" blues. The cooling off period is especially important when they have two games in a row. If they cool off gradually after the first game they'll be in a much better condition for the second.

A good method of cooling off is to run through the various flexibility exercises listed and then to do a little slow, easy, stationary jogging. Another excellent idea is to go for a long, fast walk, swinging the arms briskly. The popular habit of working like mad and then flopping down in the dressing rooms is a bad one. It sometimes takes some convincing to get the player interested in cooling off exercises. However, if he tries a cooling off system, he will be surprised at how much faster he will recover. After a hard practice, a good idea is to let the players skate around easily for a while to work off the fatigue.

Don't forget the role of carbohydrate replenishment in helping to get rid of lactic acid and rebuild blood sugar levels. The first hour after hard work is crucial.

Day before game work. The coach or trainer must decide whether or not to have a hard workout or training session the day before an important game. As a general rule, this is not a good idea because some of the fatigue and muscle soreness developed during this last workout may well hold over and affect the player's efficiency during the game. The best plan is usually to give the players a complete twenty-four hour rest, keeping them away from any hard physical effort. A light, fast workout at game-speed is permissible as is mental practice during which such things as tactics and positional play are discussed. However, the last practice before the game, for example, on the Thursday if the game is to be on the Friday, or even on the Wednesday, should always be conducted at peak effort with the players practising with the intensity the coach wishes them to use in the game. It is important that the last practice should be conducted in this way and not in an easy fashion because, according to psychology experts (and tests prove this out) it is very easy to break a habit, especially when it involves effort or body contact. For example, if the coach works very hard on Monday and Tuesday, making the players skate hard, check closely, and use plenty of body contact, this will develop a pattern or "set" in the players. But if at the last practice before a game he tells them to take it easy, he will break the pattern. As a result the players will not be as inclined to go hard. The last practice impression is important.

The water problem. Is it wise to drink water during hard physical activity? It's not only wise, it's essential. The body does not function as well when it is deprived of water, especially during physical strain when the water content of the body is quickly depleted. For example, the hockey player who develops a thirst after tearing up and down the ice will keep his physical efficiency at a higher level for a longer period of time if he takes in water than if he deprives himself of it. The intake of water not only sustains his actual physical efficiency, but also helps to ease the mental attitude that develops when the athlete is thirsty but is not allowed to satisfy his thirst. The ideal system is to take water when thirsty but not in large amounts. The athlete should not drink quickly. Drink water that is cool; the body will absorb it quicker than warm water. Only an amount of water sufficient to actually satisfy the thirst should be taken. The athlete should not give in and flood himself.

Blood count. If an athlete is to play with explosive energy and great endurance, he must have a high blood count. When a player has frequent spells in which he lacks energy and his endurance is poor in spite of careful attention to training, he should have his blood count taken by a good doctor who can prescribe a suitable blood tonic that will bring the blood count up if it is low. All lethargic, anemic players should be checked as should anyone who does not seem to be able to force himself to work hard.

Rest periods. The team or player who utilizes any rest period to the full will have an edge over the opponents who do not. Therefore, every possible method should be used to organize the rest periods so that the fullest possible benefit is gained. An ideal procedure is as follows.

- Loosen any tight equipment, and take the skates-off.
- Do a few stretching exercises to avoid muscle tightening.
- Use relaxation drills to eliminate tension and promote recovery.
- Rest with the feet as high as possible over the head. An ideal position is to lie on the back with the feet propped up against the wall. This is a very effective way of getting rid of the venal blood in the legs and eliminating fatigue (lactic) acids. It is one sure way of making the legs feel peppy again.
- When a player regains his breath and is at ease, he can take a carbo-hydrate pickup, one previously suggested.
- The dressing room should be kept as quiet as possible, with only the staff allowed in the room. No smoking should be allowed. The air should be as fresh as possible (a rule frequently broken).
- The players should not be talked to or instructed until they have settled down. The keynote of the first five minutes should always be the establishment of the highest level of relaxation possible. Players shouldn't be allowed to shout or talk, but concentrate on relaxing in order to give their bodies a chance to recover.

Smoking. Anyone who claims that smoking does not have an effect on the athlete's general condition is either a tobacco salesman or a "button-head." Test after test has shown that smoking has a detrimental effect on the body. The smoker has a faster heart beat. Smoking shrinks the capillaries and generally makes it tough for the vital organs to do their job. Smoking also sometimes has a detrimental effect on eyes, and should therefore be avoided. The hockey player who smokes can be assured of one thing – he would play with greater energy, better endurance, and more skill if he did not. One very important indication of the harm smoking does is that when a smoker quits smoking, his pulse rate will drop ten to twenty beats in a matter of hours. Any coach who allows smoking by his players, especially during the active season, is asking for trouble and will certainly not get the fullest amount of efficiency and endurance from his players.

Overweight. Hockey players, the same as any athletes, must be lean to be at peak efficiency. The ideal body fat weight for hockey players is 8 to 12 per cent. Even four or five extra pounds can seriously affect efficiency. Usually the overweight hockey player is the one who loves his sweets and fried foods, fatty foods, and drinks large quantities of whole milk. The needed weight reduction should begin by cutting down sharply on the preceding, drinking skim instead of whole milk, and cutting out sweets and fried foods. The daily caloric intake should be carefully checked using the number system prescribed previously.

It is not difficult to get good information on reducing diets. However, no artificial means should be used. The only safe and efficient way is through proper diet. The club doctor should always be consulted. The athlete should make sure he watches his diet during the off season to avoid putting on superfluous weight that will be a handicap once the season starts.

Mental attitude and endurance. Research into the factors involved in endurance indicates that the mental attitude of the athlete plays a very important role in his ability to endure. For example, the player who worries about whether or not he is going to get tired, whether or not he is going to get a stitch or feel sick, will have a much lower endurance than the player who goes out in an aggressive, determined, and cheerful state of mind, feeling he can keep driving no matter what. This is true even if the athletes have the same basic conditioning levels. The aggressive "try guy" who refuses to be concerned about his physical fatigue symptoms will always have better endurance, and the coach should try to sell the players on this idea. The athlete should be taught to expect aches and pains from hard effort, but that they are not important and that he must not let himself be overly concerned with them. The athlete who keeps a good stance and not showing his fatigue no matter how he feels will often find not only that he feels better, but that it is disconcerting to his opponents.

Research also shows that there are two limits of effort. The first is the mental and the second is the physical. Very few athletes use their physical capacities to the full. They stop driving when they think they have done their best, but actually they could have kept going even harder for some time. The athlete who learns to drive through his mental limit will be much more valuable to the team and to himself. Fatigue is much the same as hunger or sleepiness. Just as you can go hungry or go without sleep for some time after you become conscious that you are hungry or sleepy, so can you go on working hard after you feel tired. Feeling tired does not mean that hard effort is not possible. Most feelings of fatigue are merely symptoms of an approaching state of real fatigue – they are not real fatigue itself. These things should be explained to the player so he can react aggressively when he feels fatigue symptoms. Nine out of ten athletes are much too easy on themselves.

The mental factor in endurance and skill development and in many other phases of the game is so important that, where feasible, a team should have an expert psychologist as an adviser to study the players constantly and show them how to put forth greater effort, and to clear up poor thinking habits. If this is not possible, the coach can certainly seek out such knowledge by talking to an expert psychologist or by carefully studying the many excellent books and articles on the subject. Any playing defect such as showing fear, refusal to pass the puck, excessive complaining, lack of continued effort, or lack of loyalty to the team are all personality defects. The answer to the problem player (one who should produce and does not) is in applied psychology.

Fatigue symptoms. The symptoms of fatigue that are of common concern to the average athlete are nausea, dizziness, severe headaches, cramps, and stitches. These often occur when the athlete drives himself hard, especially during the early part of the season. A lot of them can be avoided by training, proper warm-ups, and careful attention to diet.

The development of fatigue (lactic) acid is usually the cause. Nausea can often be fixed up quickly be giving fifteen drops of oil of peppermint or aromatic spirits of ammonia in half a glass of water. Stitches will often disappear if the athlete perseveres in the effort. Stretching, bending, and twisting the part of the body in which there is a stitch is also helpful. Light massage and the application of alternate hot and cold applications to the back of the head and neck will often hasten the recovery from an "effort" or fatigue headache, although they will usually clear up quite quickly on their own. Muscle cramps are sometimes caused when the athlete depletes the water supply of his body and his store of salts and minerals becomes unbalanced. Sufficient water and attention to diet will avoid this condition. If the athlete perspires a lot, he should be careful to replenish his supply of salts and minerals. This is easily done by adding a little extra salt at the next meal.

These symptoms are all normal and to be expected from time to time. The only real harm they do is to the player's mental attitude, often causing him to let down when he does not need to. Therefore, the athlete should have each symptom explained to him so he doesn't unconsciously fear them. He should also be taught to work through them. Many of these symptoms precede feelings of real fatigue but they are actually symptoms of a false fatigue. They often appear after a fairly short period of hard effort and accompany the adjustment being made by the body to the work load it has to carry. This adjustment is what is commonly called "second wind." A good warm-up will cut down on the intensity of such periods of transition.

Fatigue inquiries. It is often a very good plan to ask the player exactly where and how he feels fatigue when it appears. By doing this, it is possible to find out his weak spots and his particular personal reactions to hard effort. Then it will be easy to determine the special training work that is needed. Every athlete seems to be a little different and such a careful check-up can often do much good.

BODY TYPES

In the early parts of this book, some mention was made of various body types. Each body type has different capabilities and weaknesses both mental and physical. When realized, the player or coach can govern his approach with more intelligence and understanding. Six important body types are easily distinguished.

Medial. This body type is a happy medium. There is nothing unusual about the build. No part of the body is particularly long or short. The proportions are excellent. As a result, the medial type has great all-round capabilities. He is the jack-of-all-athletic-trades. In this group, the best all-round athletes are found. Such players make excellent goalkeepers or centres because these jobs demand all-round skill. Their main weakness is that because they have all-round capabilities, they are liable to take on too much. This is why you will find so many medials playing basketball, hockey, taking part in gymnastics, and even participating in the school choir. Because of their inclination to work hard and do a lot of things, medials are inclined to be hit by staleness. They should learn to relax and use their energy on a priority basis, not wasting it or spreading it too thin over a lot of activities. This body type can usually learn to do practically any athletic activity well.

Meso-medial. This is a variation of the medial type, the only difference being heavier and stronger muscles. The meso-medial is the ideal athlete, possessing all the qualities of the medial plus added strength. He can better handle the task of being very active. In this body type group are found the greatest all-round athletes, and many of the great hockey stars. The medial and meso-medial should pay special attention to flexibility and muscle lengthening work. They should also work hard at learning controlled relaxation.

Mesomorph. The mesomorph is the big husky boy with strong thick legs, big chest, and narrow waist. His muscles, though big and strong, are smooth. He does not have a sharply defined muscular outline of the medial and meso-medial. He usually loves body contact and is best in the heavy going. Such players have high all-round ability, but prefer activities in which power and strength are important. They make good defencemen and hard, rugged wingmen. On the other hand, they are inclined to be a little slow and not as agile as some of the other body types. The mesomorph's great problem is making himself continue to go hard. He likes to take things easy and go in spurts. He is also inclined to exercise only when necessary, and to be a little easy going. He is also likely to over-indulge at the table, and therefore to become overweight.

Ectomorph. The ectomorph is the thinner edition of the meso-morph. He is usually a slim, tall athlete with long, smooth muscles that are not sharply defined. Because of his lean build he must guard against injury. He should strengthen his muscles as much as possible. Like the mesomorph, he is inclined to take it a little easy and over-indulge at the table. He is usually a smooth skater who is fast and cool, but rarely a quick-breaking, agile, buzzing-around type.

Ecto-medial. This is the thin, muscular, wiry type. He is usually fast, quick, very active and agile, but highly nervous. He is often brilliant, but suffers from bad spells. The ecto-medial is usually moody and does too much worrying and fussing. As he has a lot of nervous energy, he is inclined to reach terrific peaks of effort after which he goes to pieces quickly. He is very good in high skill activities. In hockey, he is usually a clever stickhandler, a very clever checker, and a remarkably good quick breaker. He is the ideal type for forechecking and ragging the puck. He rarely takes to hard body contact, staying more in the open ice and using his agility and speed. This is nature's way of protecting him, because he is not physically rugged, and consequently prone to injury. He should work hard learning to relax and should pay attention to his diet, getting a lot of foods that are good for the nerves.

Endomorph. This body type has a round, feminine body, usually with narrow shoulders and big buttocks and hips. His muscles are very loose, fatty, and lacking in tone. This type is rarely good for athletics, especially hockey. If he watches his diet carefully and builds up gradually into a lot of hard physical work featuring speed work, he may make a fairly good defenceman. However, he'll have his troubles.

There are other combinations of these body types; i.e., endo-mesomorph who is the mesomorph who gives into his love of eating and ease. However, the above classifications sufficiently cover the picture.

Special needs. Study indicates that the average hockey player, because of his inattention to special training procedures, lacks flexibility, is inclined to be tense in action, is not as strong as he should be in the abdominal and back areas and is prone to shoulder injuries due to a lack of development in the shoulder girdle area. The best possible injury protection is a well developed and flexible body conditioned to the highest level. Take a good look at his physique, evaluate it carefully, and then set out to build up his weak spots.

Mental attitudes. "You have to hate them to win." This is nonsense. The best competitive attitude is a cheerful "happy warrior" who tries his best, plays with full abandon and with the knowledge that any emotionalism of hate or anger will take away from his skill and physical ability. The sudden energy burst he may feel from anger or hate doesn't last and ends up having a toxic effect. Any gain in physical energy is offset by losses in judgement, relaxation, calm, cool alertness, and skill.

Hockey not enough. Coaches and players must remember that just playing hockey will not develop the physical needs of the player. If he is to perform up to his potential, he must build and condition his body for the job it must do. Hockey is a fast game and once coaches and players begin to give more thought to the use of modern and effective methods of conditioning and body building it will become a game of maximum thrills, pace, and excitement.

Index